The

ecco

GUIDE *to the*

BEST

WINES

of **ITALY**

D1441512

The

ULTIMATE RESOURCE

FOR FINDING, BUYING,

DRINKING, AND ENJOYING

ITALY'S BEST WINES

ecco

An Imprint of HarperCollins Publishers

The

ecco

GUIDE *to the*

BEST

WINES

of ITALY

IAN D'AGATA

THE ECCO GUIDE TO THE BEST WINES OF ITALY. Copyright ©
2008 by Ian D'Agata. All rights reserved. Printed in the United
States of America. No part of this book may be used or
reproduced in any manner whatsoever without written
permission except in the case of brief quotations embodied in
critical articles and reviews. For information, address Harper-
Collins Publishers, 10 East 53rd Street, New York, NY 10022.

HarperCollins books may be purchased for educational,
business, or sales promotional use. For information, please
write: Special Markets Department, HarperCollins Publishers,
10 East 53rd Street, New York, NY 10022.

FIRST EDITION

Library of Congress Cataloging-in-Publication Data is available
upon request.

ISBN: 978-0-06-158341-4

08 09 10 11 12 WBG/CW 10 9 8 7 6 5 4 3 2 1

To my mother, Stana

ACKNOWLEDGMENTS

THIS BOOK WOULD NOT HAVE BEEN POSSIBLE without Dan Halpern's great love of food, wine, and Italy, and whose belief in me allowed it to happen.

I also wish to thank Chris North, who got it all started, and Emily Takoudes and Greg Mortimer for their editorial help.

Last but not least, special thanks to André Simon, Serena Sutcliffe, and Luigi Veronelli, three people without whose example I would not be in wine today.

CONTENTS

PREFACE

I HAVE BEEN DRINKING WINE FOR LONGER than my mother cares to remember. If you know anything about Italian families in general, and Italian mothers in particular, then you also know that their opinions carry considerable weight. I am still trying to convince my mother that writing about wine is a time-honored, respectable profession.

In the 1970s my family moved from Italy to Toronto, where my father, an Italian psychiatrist in love with the open spaces and wonderful outdoors of North America, had accepted a post at a local hospital. Italian patients are the best the medical profession can wish for, as they have a truly endearing habit of inundating their doctors with all sorts of gifts come Christmastime, bottles of wine being foremost among these. However, even though we had a treasure trove of wine in our cellar, we rarely drank any, because my father, who liked wine, had seen too many families ruined by alcoholism and didn't want us drinking wine regularly. Thus, I had never really tasted any wine memorable enough to make wines seem interesting to me.

Then it happened. On a sunny day in the summer of 1979 a few teenage friends sitting around a pool wanted to drink wine and asked me to open a bottle of the Italian stuff, and so off I went to the cellar. I didn't know what I was doing, but remembering that my father had always spoken well of Barolo and Gattinara, I reached for a Barolo 1971, which—although this was completely unknown to me—was an absolutely stellar vintage. One taste and I was blown away: it was a true case of love at first sight, a love affair from which I have never recovered. The very next day I met one of those friends at his house, where I tried a 1976 Mulheimer Helenkloster Riesling Eiswein, to this day still one of the most enjoyable Eisweins that have ever graced my lips. After those two encounters, my life has never been the same. I began studying wine, reading about it, attending wine lectures and tastings, spending every penny I had, as a student, to buy wines from all over the world, and of course tasting, tasting and more tasting. In short, by the time I was 22 years old I had already tasted through thousands of wines not just from Italy but around the world. I was fortunate to begin my wine training with fine teachers of English origin (Britain has always had the best wine schools) and the large selection of fine wines to choose from at the Liquor Control Board of Ontario (LCBO), a state-run monopoly that remains the single largest wine buyer in the world. So it was easy to taste the best wines, not just from Italy but from Australia, California, and elsewhere; still, when I moved back to Italy after high school, Italian wines became my passion. In fact, Italy's wines didn't seem inferior to the world's greatest. As great as French wines were, Italy's grape varieties and wines also held impressive potential: nebbiolo, aglianico, sangiovese . . . Although these wines may not (at least not then) have been technically perfect like the best from France, they had soul and a sense of place and tradition, traits I still look for in my wines today. In today's world of overly alcoholic, way too tannic behemoths, and of wine making by the numbers with wines all too similar no matter where they come from, it's good to know that most Italian wines still have a certain "somewhereness." They talk to you about specific people and century-old traditions, and they go marvelously well with food.

Like almost everyone else who writes professionally about wine today, I too started out on a different path: I hold a degree in medicine. My love of wine, something I had studied and written about prior to undertaking medical studies, led me to give up the operating room and incur the incredulity and wrath of my mother, who couldn't believe her son would give up a career because of wine. After more than 25 years of writing and talking about wine all over the world, I am proud to write this new guide to Italy's best wines, made possible by the visionaries at Ecco, a publishing house with a long history of the very best in everything gastronomic. Even my mother is happy about it. Oh, I almost forgot: I dedicate this guide to her, so that she may see it wasn't all a huge mistake after all.

—IAN D'AGATA

INTRODUCTION

ITALY IS *THE* PLACE FOR WINE. NOT BY CHANCE was its ancient name Oenotria, the "land of vines" or, according to some experts, the "land of vines trained to poles." Back then it was already apparent that the best wines were produced from vines supported by poles rather than from vines running wild around trees or other natural supports (the foliage creating shade and not allowing for proper ripening of the grapes). This tells you something about how seriously wine production has always been taken here. In fact, one of Italy's many native grape varieties is schiava, or "female slave"; the name refers to its being "enslaved" by being tied down to a pole or cane, and documents from ancient Roman times inform us that land *cum vitis sclavis*—"with enslaved vines"—was worth four times as much as land on which the grapes were allowed to grow without such help.

Wine permeates every aspect of Italian life and society. Children begin drinking early; old-timers get together in the main village square to play cards and have a glass of wine; and if you show any interest whatsoever in wine when dining at an Italian's house, the host will be sure to offer you a taste of his own "special" wine. The wine is special in that it's made by him or a relative or a farmer he swears by, and not because of any particularly redeeming feature, so you're left to imbibe at your own risk and peril. Once you've tasted the artisanally made potable, you may find yourself wishing you had kept your mouth shut, but that is another matter altogether. It's the enthusiasm about wine here that counts.

Italy is the single country where you'll find the largest number of varieties of wine grapes. At last count, there were roughly 2,500, depending on who was doing the counting. Italians cling ferociously to what they perceive as "their" grapes and don't care to hear about the latest DNA analysis that might prove their grape identical to a grape grown somewhere else. In fact, only half of Italy's 2,500 grapes have been genetically identified, and of these, only about 600 are being used to make wine in commercially important amounts. Still, if Italy is offering wine lovers everywhere wines made from 600 varieties, plus all the possible blends thereof (and you know how creative Italians can be), you realize that no other place in the world can offer a similar plethora of fragrances and flavors. If you stop to think that about 99% of all French wines are made from 15 grape varieties, and that about 99% of all California wines are made from perhaps seven varieties, you realize how varied Italy's wines can be. In Italy there is no need for ABC clubs—those groups of wine lovers who are so bored with chardonnay and cabernet that they'll drink Anything But Chardonnay or Anything But Cabernet! Of course, this seemingly never-ending litany of grapes and wines makes for a highly confusing situation, and the fact that Italian wine labels seem purposely designed to further confuse is only part of the problem. It's one thing to read Merlot or Chardonnay on a label, as you know, more or less, what you might be getting. It's quite another to read "Pallagrello Bianco," "Cannonau," or "Nero d'Avola." The following pages aim to help you make sense of the wonderful world of Italian wines.

The

ecco

GUIDE *to the*

BEST

WINES

of **ITALY**

HOW TO USE THIS GUIDE

AT THE DAWN OF THIS PROJECT, I SET OUT TO write the guide to Italy's wines that I had always longed for but had searched for in vain. The fact is that choices are few when it comes to books dealing with Italian wines. Most books currently available are not wine- or vintage-specific, are only sporadically updated, and focus only on the more important wine production areas—giving little advice on buying the wines of other regions, for which the content is limited to a few of the better-known producers. Further compounding the problem is Italy's inherently difficult wine scene, with byzantine laws, a plethora of often obscure grape varieties, and new producers emerging all the time. The very nature of Italian wine, with countless wine-producing areas and estates, makes writing a comprehensive book on the subject a daunting task; and the book itself runs the risk of being much too long, and neither useful nor interesting. Therefore, I have deliberately set out to write a guide that gives a complete overview of Italy's best wines, with enough wines included so that the picture you get is accurate and thorough, but without turning it into a telephone book or an encyclopedia. Furthermore, in an effort to avoid frustration on the part of both reader and wine buyer, I have devoted Section I to wines that cost $100 or less, are imported into the United States, and (with few exceptions) are made in large enough quantities so that you ought to be able to find them in wine shops.

There are three sections in this book. Preceding the first section is a chapter that tells you how to read the guide and how to interpret the scores. Section I is the section describing the 200 best wines of Italy. It is divided into chapters on the 100 best red wines, the 60 best white, the 15 best sparkling and rosé wines, and the 25 best sweet wines. These 200 top wines are, to the best of my knowledge, all imported into the United States (as I mentioned above). However, some may be easier to find than others, and a few may have changed, or lost, their importers by the time this book goes to print. Wines may be hard to find because some great and famous wines are made in small quantities (a fact that increases a good wine's desirability and causes it to be sold for higher prices) and are much sought after, so new vintages that go on sale may sell out quickly. The wines within each chapter are listed in order of merit. Keep in mind that only a small number of wines make it into the guide, so they should all prove excellent, and there's only a small difference, if any, between a wine ranked number 37 and one that follows as number 38. Both exemplify well an aspect or style of Italian wine. All the wines are scored with the classic 100-point system used by many wine publications all over the world. For the most part, I have limited the wines listed in Section I to one per estate, so that I can name and describe as many fine Italian wines as possible. Only in those rare cases where an estate unquestionably makes more than one of Italy's greatest wines will more than one be listed.

Section II contains more "best of" lists; here you'll find everything from the most experimental wines to the best estates, and more.

Section III is devoted to useful information concerning Italy and its wines, important grape varieties, and an overview of the country's many regions. As I feel it helps immeasurably to know a little Italian geography in order to grasp the intricacies of its wines, I have broached this subject briefly. In fact, many of Italy's wines are labeled with a place-name instead of a grape type: for example, nebbiolo versus Barolo (nebbiolo is the grape with which they make the wine and Barolo is the name of a village and wine production area in the region of Piedmont). That being said, knowing at least a little bit about single grape varieties is also very useful, as knowing what a grape is about will give you a better idea of what to expect from a bottle of wine you are going to buy. Hence I have also described the characteristics of Italy's main grape varieties.

At the end of the book are a glossary and a vintage table.

The guide, then, is devoted to the best in Italian wine, those wines that over recent years have always been at or close to the top of the heap in terms of quality. For this reason, the wines listed are those with a proven track record over at least three vintages, so that you can be comfortable in the knowledge that no wine I recommend here is a flash in the pan. Every recommended wine has years of fine vintages behind it, and—I hope—in front of it as well.

How I Taste and Rate Wines

I wish to underscore the fact that this guide is a compilation of those wines that I feel are the best produced in Italy today. I have been tasting Italian wines extensively since 1979 (roughly 6,500 Italian wines a year since 2001) and was one of the first Italians to guide professional wine tastings in Italy, starting in 1983 in Rome. I live in Italy full-time, and this allows me to visit the wine estates here and in the rest of Europe regularly. In fact, I am the wine expert who travels the most to Italian wine estates each year, averaging about 160 days of the year on the road—and that's just to see Italian wine producers. The rest of the time I am visiting producers all over Europe. In short, this is the most up-to-date guide to Italian wines available anywhere, and it is full of insider information not available elsewhere.

I taste wines blind, and divide them into flights of similar types (among whites, for example, Sauvignons are compared with one another, not against Pinot Grigio or Chardonnays; and reds are divided similarly). I prefer to do my tasting alone. Although at times I do attend large trade tastings all over the world, these are usually large, chaotic affairs with far too many people in one room, and thus I never use them to score wines. I prefer to look at them as an opportunity to gain insight into the vintage or the particular aspect of wine that the fair or meeting has set out to present (for example, the wines of a specific production zone). Of course, I also taste directly out of cellars in the company of the wine producers, but in these cases also I do not score the wines; I limit myself to writing tasting notes and listening to and learning from what the producer has to say.

The result of all this tasting is the guide you hold in your hands. It is, in a sense, the "best of the best" of Italian wine production of recent years, but it is clearly not exhaustive. There are undoubtedly other fine wines made in Italy, though not many, and I seize this opportunity to apologize to producers whose fine wines I may have omitted. This list represents my personal tastes and experiences, and though you may not find yourself agreeing with all my choices, you I hope you will agree with most all of them.

The figure of $100 in the box, though steep for many pockets, is an amount that still allows for the inclusion of the vast majority of the best Italy has to offer, and I want to stress that many of the wines listed in this book are far less expensive. Should you be interested in knowing more about the hard-to-find, superexpensive cult wines Italy is also famous for, you'll find them listed in the list "25 Don't Ask Cult Wines." However, as good as those superpremium wines may be, I find that Italy offers a treasure trove of fine wine at affordable prices, so it's not necessary to focus only on the very expensive efforts.

Wines that cost $25 or less a bottle are marked by an asterisk (*).

EACH WINE ENTRY IN SECTION I CONTAINS:

- Number indicating its position in the BEST 200 rankings
- Name of the wine
- Name of the producer
- Score of the wine (out of 100 points)
- Region in which the wine is made
- Brief description of the wine and the producer
- *Specific information on the wine:*
  - Grape varieties (with percentages of varieties for blends)

- Number of bottles made
- Alcohol content
- Price: a range of prices at retail stores across the United States
- Try it with: recommended dishes with which to try the wine
- Name of the importer (with Web site)
- Past great vintages. Since this is not an annual guide, you will not find a specific vintage attached to each wine. Instead, a list of the better vintages is included for each wine described, and a general vintage table is found at the end of the book.

  ❧ *Specific information on the producer:*

- Exact name of producer, address, telephone and fax numbers, e-mail, Web site
- Total number of bottles produced: that is, the total number of bottles of all the wines made by that producer
- Total ha: refers to the total number of hectares (ha) owned and rented by the estate (one hectare is roughly four acres)
- Tasting room visit: indicates whether visitors are allowed at the estate or not. Most of the wine estates listed welcome guests, but it is best to call for an appointment first, as in most cases these wineries are also the producers' homes.
- Other recommended wines under $100: these are the other great wines made by the producer that I specifically recommend. Hence not every wine made is listed. In parenthesis you will find the grape varieties used to make the wine and whether it is a white, red, sparkling, or sweet wine.

Grape and Wine Names

In Italy, as in all other countries where wine production has been taking place for millennia, wines can be labeled with the varietal name, a specific place, a fantasy name, or a combination thereof. For example, in Italy there are wines labeled sangiovese or nebbiolo, which are grape types; and there are also wines called Brunello di Montalcino and Barolo, which are made with 100% sangiovese and nebbiolo, respectively. This is because over time it became apparent that some areas in the country were particularly suited to specific grape varieties, such as the countryside surrounding the hamlet of Montalcino for sangiovese and that of Barolo for nebbiolo. The wines that are made with these grapes in those places tend to be better than those made elsewhere with the same grapes. Hence, producers lucky enough to own vines in these privileged areas would much rather call their wines by the name of place, since theirs isn't just nebbiolo or sangiovese, but something superior. This is typical of countries where the culture of wine has always been strong, and we are beginning to see the same thing occur in "new" wine making countries such as the United States and Australia. In fact, it is now commonplace to refer to U.S. Pinot Noirs as coming from Russian River or Santa Barbara, or to Syrah as hailing from Barossa or Hunter Valley in Australia. In Italy (and France and Germany), where wine making has been taking place for aeons, people have taken this site-specificity to an extreme, identifying not just large areas such as Russian River but also little towns such as Castagnole Monferrato or Montepulciano. I am sure that a few years from now, much the same will take place in other countries; and to some extent, it is already happening, as we are hearing and seeing some people refer to, for example, a Napa Cabernet as coming from Calistoga versus Saint Helena.

Nonetheless, for clarity, as some Italian wines are labeled with the grape name only, in this guide you will find the grape name written with the initial letter lowercase, whereas the actual name of a wine will be capitalized. Thus, in this guide malvasia refers to the grape, and Malvasia refers to the wine.

Within the text and the listings, you'll notice that some names of wines are in quotation marks (for example, "Percarlo" or "Passione"). I have done this for all wines with fantasy names, created by the producer to better identify the wine in the minds of consumers. ("Passione," for instance, means passion; "Pietracalda" means hot rock.) Some wines do not have a fantasy name but rather have the name of a single vineyard: these wines are made from grapes grown in the specific vineyards. The vineyard is usually an important aspect of such a wine, as single vineyards are believed to yield the best grapes, and hence the best wine, of certain estates. The names of these wines are written without quotation marks. The name of the category or wine production area to which a wine belongs is listed first. This is followed by the qualification of the wine, if applicable, and the single vineyard or fantasy name (if any), or both. Last but not least comes the name of the producer or estate. Thus Barbaresco Martinenga Marchese di Gresy is a specific Barbaresco, where Martinenga refers to the fact that the wine is made from grapes grown in the Martinenga vineyard and Marchese di Gresy is the producer.

EXAMPLES OF HOW THE WINE NAMES ARE WRITTEN

- ☙ Pinot Grigio Ermacora
- ☙ "Fontalloro" Felsina
- ☙ "Mille e Una Notte" Donnafugata

Notice from the examples given in the box that I have simplified the names of some producers and wines at the top of the entries of section I and elsewhere in the book. This should avoid confusion and allow you to readily identify the wines so that you can find and buy them. For instance, rather than list Fattoria di Felsina as such at the top of the Fontalloro entry, I have listed it just as Felsina. The full name is included at the bottom of the entry, where, for each wine, you will find the producer's address and contact information. I have chosen this format because it's likely that you and the store clerk will go by the shorter names. I have taken a similar approach with the wine names, again in order to simplify things. In the case of obscure wine production areas such as Montecucco or Contessa Entellina, when possible I have often not listed them as such—I just start with the wine's name, which is usually easier to remember and better known. For example, if you want to buy Donnafugata's "Mille e Una Notte," that is probably what you will call it, rather than Contessa Entellina "Mille e Una Notte." This is because being aware that the wine comes from Contessa Entellina, a little-known producing area of Sicily, is not very helpful; unlike historically famous or better-known production areas, such as Barolo or Frascati, many of these obscure appellations have a short track record and aren't yet identified with characteristic wines. Although the words Barolo or Amarone tell you a little something about the wine you are going to be drinking or buying, places such as Contea di Sclafani or Lago di Corbara (which have only recently been created by the legislators in an effort to tidy up Italian wine names) have as yet to convey that sort of information.

Finally, I have chosen to form plurals by adding "s" to the name of the wine. So, when mentioning more than one Amarone or Barolo, I will write Amarones and Barolos, respectively.

I have also used some abbreviations in the wine files. Their meanings are listed below.

ABBREVIATIONS

a.s.l. above sea level

agr. *agricola* (agricultural, or devoted to agriculture; in Italy wine-producing estates are classified as either *vinicoli* or *agricoli*—respectively, wine-producing or agricultural, though both can produce wine)

az. *azienda* (estate)

cl. *classico* (refers to the classic, or historically most famous, wine production zone)

fraz. *frazione* (a fraction or a small segment of a town, at its periphery or just on its outskirts)

ha hectare, hectares

km kilometer, kilometers (sometimes part of an address, in which case it refers to the distance in kilometers you need to cover on the road before you get to your destination; for instance, your destination may be at km 8, eight kilometers along the road)

loc. *località* (a locality or a specific place, usually near a specific town but separate from it)

n.v. nonvintage

prod. *produttori* (producers, as producers or social cooperative in which the many members bring their grapes to the co-op headquarters where the wines are made under one label)

The Scores

All wines included in this guide were tasted blind throughout the years and rated by means of the 100-point scale, the scale most commonly used throughout the world. Each wine can receive a maximum of 20 points for color; 30 for aromas; 40 for flavors, length, texture, and complexity; and 10 for availability and being true to type and grape variety. The last rating is an important difference between the Ecco guide and similar publications: I strongly believe that for wine to be truly great, it has to represent accurately what the label states it to be. Guides and magazines have no trouble marking down or even decrying rosy-hued Barolos or Cabernets, finding them atypical. But these same guides or magazines never seem to do the same in the opposite case; that is, they do not lower the scores of wines whose color is too dark. A black-hued Barolo or Brunello is just as atypical and faulty as a pink or blush one. It makes absolutely no sense to give a high score to a pitch-black Barolo or Brunello, no matter how good the wine may be. This is because nebbiolo and sangiovese, the grapes used to make Barolo and Brunello, do not have the pigments capable of producing black wines; therefore, a high score for such a wine is at best misinformed and misleading. Another example might be a Pinot Grigio that reminds you strongly of Sauvignon Blanc when you smell it: this simply should not be so, because Sauvignon and Pinot Grigio have few aromas in common. So my scores always reflect a wine's accountability. Though "atypical" wines may be perfectly acceptable and even very good, it makes little sense to talk or write about a great Pinot Grigio, if the thing tastes of Sauvignon. The same applies to, say, a Dolcetto that smells and tastes of Merlot or Cabernet—grapes that are not supposed to be, or are said not to be, present in the wine you bought. You, the reader and wine buyer, should also start evaluating writers and wine publications in these terms. Of course, minor variations in the final composition of a wine won't have much effect on the way the wine looks, smells, and tastes, and most people, including experts, wouldn't be able to tell if there really is 1% or 2% more or less than the declared amount of merlot or sangiovese in the blend. However, overly liberal additions of grape varieties will cause some wines to veer sharply away from what they are supposed to look and taste like. Italy's famous Brunello di Montalcino area was rocked early in 2008 with this kind of scandal: the 2003 vintage of a number of producers of Brunello was embargoed because the investigative authorities suspected that some of the legal requirements for making Brunello were not being followed, such as maximum allowed yields (maximum hectoliters of wine you can produce per hectare of vines) and grape variety used (Brunello can be made only with sangiovese; making it with anything else is illegal). The result was that the wine has been put on hold and cannot be sold while the investigation continues; and the area's image and reputation have suffered greatly.

Please note that since the wines are scored relative to each other, it is possible for a Chianti to score just as highly as a Barolo. Some people may not consider this correct in absolute terms, as Barolos are usually richer, bigger wines than Chiantis; but the best Chiantis are fantastic and, though different, can be just as good as the best of Barolo or Brunello. Put it this way: a strawberry shake made from fresh ripe fruit may be wonderfully rich and fruity, but an iced tea made using spring water and tea leaves of very good quality and brewed perfectly prior to refrigeration can be just as wonderful, though an altogether different drink. I also take into account the number of bottles made, because wonderful wines made in large quantities are especially worthy of being identified for consumers. Many wine lovers feel frustrated and upset when they read about a very high-scoring wine that sounds as if it might be great to taste, and then they cannot find it. When only small quantities are made and a wine is much sought after, the wine ends up being virtually unfindable. To some extent, with regard to fine wine, this is unavoidable, since, for example, some of the world's great wines are the product of small, single vineyards and so there is only so much of these wines to go around. That being said, a wine guide that focused only or for the most part on these wines would be of little use to most people. Therefore, when deciding on which 200 wines to include in Section I, I tried to include more of the wines that you are most likely to find on retailers' shelves, depending on how many bottles the importer has available for sale into the United States.

All this also explains why you will find here a Barolo at a lower point in the standings than a Chianti or a Dolcetto, even though all three may have received the same score out of 100 points. A very fine Dolcetto made in large quantities is just as recommendable as a very fine Barolo made in small quantities, which will be hard to find. Furthermore, the Dolcetto or the Chianti will go with more dishes and cost a great deal less. By taking all these different factors into account (and by being sure that all the wines are excellent examples of their respective types) I arrive at the standings in the wine rankings.

The final score assigned to each wine is, for the most part, the arithmetic mean of my scores given each wine over the last 10 years, with highest and lowest scores always thrown out. In this guide, a score of 93 takes into account years and years of tasting of different vintages and is intended to give a global evaluation of the wine over time. For this reason, you might find that some famous Italian wines have been placed lower in the overall standings than expected. This might be because a wine had a spell when it was less than it ought to have been—something that happens when, for example, ownership changes at a winery, or a winemaker leaves and a new one moves in, or an owner temporarily loses interest or, conversely, decides to work on and improve a wine.

One more comment: as I rarely give wines a perfect 100 points, the overall average scores may not be as high as you would expect.

ALL WINES INCLUDED IN THIS GUIDE:

- Have been tasted blind repeatedly over the past 10 years
- Are rated on the 100-point scale
- Have been assigned a possible 20 points for color; 30 for aromas; 40 for flavors, length, texture, and complexity; and 10 for being true to type and grape variety

Please note also that all the wines included in this guide have also been tasted from bottles bought directly at wineshops, to ensure that what you end up buying as the consumer is identical to what I have tasted as the wine writer. Unfortunately there are "journalist cuvées," bottlings that are made with particularly fine samples of a wine but that bear little resemblance to what ends up on retailers' shelves. This is done to achieve the highest possible scores when wines are released, thereby making it easier to sell the wines. I have eliminated from this wine guide at least two fairly famous Italian wines that regularly perform well in blind tastings set up for wine writers, only to prove very disappointing when bought from wineshops. Finally, to analyze the accuracy of my scores, each year I routinely retaste blind a series of 30 randomly chosen wines that I may have included in the year's roundup of Italy's best wines. I do this to confirm that at another moment in time, with different bottles and different tasting conditions, my scores would have been more or less the same (and they usually are).

THE SCORES INDICATE:

95–100: a wine of exceptional quality

90–94: an outstanding wine

85–89: an excellent wine

80–84: a very good wine

Prices

Giving readers an exact retail price for the wines listed is an almost impossible task, for there are far too many variables that affect the final price of a bottle of wine. Different wineshops apply different markups, and discounters or very large retail chains can buy in large enough quantities at lower prices and pass the savings on to you, the final customer. Don't hesitate to do your homework: prior to buying, take time and consult the Internet. You will be amazed by the almost illogical swings in price for exactly the same wine and vintage! For example, the price on the 2003 Barolo "Brunate" by Mario Marengo varied, on the same day, between $39.97 and $52.99 at three different wineshops. Even worse, the price for the 2004 Tignanello varied between $66.99 and $120 in different shops in different states. For simplicity's sake, I have included, when available, a range of retail prices in the United States based on importer and wineshop information, as well as prices advertised on the Web. Still, it would be best for you to shop around and check with different local wine stores. Remember, wine store clerks are often wine lovers just like us, and they are usually very eager to help find wines they haven't heard about, for they're interested, too. Should your wineshop not carry a wine listed in the guide you might like to try, do ask them about ordering it: each wine entry in the 200 Best section gives you the name of that wine's main importer, as well as a Web site, when available, for that importer.

Past Great Vintages

This section in each entry details the very best wines made by the estate, sometimes going back 20 or 30 years. These are not "general" lists of the best vintages for that category of wine, but rather the vintages in which that specific wine was particularly successful, according to my tastings. All the past vintages rated have been tasted by me in 2007 and 2008, so these are up-to-date tasting notes— though brief, owing to space limitations. For this reason, although 1985 is a great vintage for most Brunellos and 1993 was less interesting, some wines did excel in 1993 as well. So if that was the case with a wine I have included in the guide, I point it out by including, say, 1993 in the list along with 1985.

Italy's 200 Best Wines Under $100

THE 100 BEST RED WINES UNDER $100

1 | Brunello di Montalcino Riserva
TENUTA IL POGGIONE • 97/100 • TUSCANY

Victor Hugo once said that if a writer wrote only for his own time, he'd have to break his pen and throw it away. The same can be said for the great wines made here: the reserve Brunellos from this estate are some of the best wines in the world, and the basic Brunello, which costs much less than $100, is always very fine as well. Congratulations to the Franceschi family, owners and one of the original names in Brunello, and the father-and-son team of Fabrizio and Alessandro Bindocci, who manage this estate extremely well. Theirs is always a Brunello that speaks clearly of vintage differences (their '02, a rainy, cool year, is less good than the '01, and you would expect it to be just so), as opposed to other versions that, strangely enough, never seem to differ year after year. You'll be enchanted by its extreme depth of pure fruit (red currants, red cherries, raspberries, and plums), the hint of fine leather and tobacco, and the estate hallmark of silky-smooth tannins. It also happens to age splendidly, and is among the longest lived of all Brunellos. It almost always enters its best drinking phase about six to eight years after the harvest, but that depends on the vintage characteristics. Whenever you do decide to open a bottle, the first sip will tell you that all these wines will, just like Hugo's work, be talked about in future times as well.

THE WINE
Grape varieties: sangiovese grosso (100%); **Number of bottles:** 35,000; **Alcohol:** 14.5; **Retail price:** $65–99; **Try it with:** roast pork, porterhouse; **Imported by:** Paterno Wines International (www.terlatowines.com); **Past great vintages:** 1955, 1967, 1970, 1975, 1982, 1983, 1985, 1988, 1990, 1999, 2001

The '82 is holding up nicely and has pretty red cherry fruit in a midweight, high-acid frame (93/100). The '90 is just wonderful, with much deeper, richer red cherry, leather, and truffle aromas. It's even better on the palate with ripe red cherry flavors and raspberry liqueur on the long complex finish (96/100). The '99 and '01 are two of the best wines of those very fine vintages, with rich fruit and smooth tannins. The '99 is sweeter and rounder (95/100). The '01 is more austere and refined (94/100).

THE PRODUCER: TENUTA IL POGGIONE
Address: Piazza Castello 14—Sant'Angelo in Colle, 53020 Montalcino (Siena); **Tel/fax:** 0577 844029/0577 844165; **E-mail:** ilpoggione@tin.it; **Web:** www.tenutailpoggione.it; **Total bottles:** 500,000; **Total ha:** 115; **Visit:** by appointment; **Tasting room:** yes; **Highway exit:** Firenze Certosa (A1)

OTHER RECOMMENDED WINES UNDER $100 BY IL POGGIONE:
Rosso di Montalcino (small barrel oaked red), "Il Poggione" (sangiovese/merlot—large barrel oaked red), "San Leopoldo" (cabernet sauvignon/merlot—small barrel oaked red).

2 | Barbaresco Rabajà
BRUNO ROCCA • **97/100** • PIEDMONT

Bruno, helped out by his daughter Luisa and son Francesco, makes a Barbaresco Rabajà that is one of the greatest red wines not just of Italy but of the world. Once you have tasted it, you won't forget it. Rocca's other Barbaresco, from the cooler Coparossa vineyard, can also be very fine, especially in warmer years such as 2003, when the Rabajà vineyard becomes almost too hot. Truly one of the great *grands crus* (best vineyard sites) of Italy, the Rabajà is an utterly beautiful, postcard-perfect site facing southwest with a soil composition of roughly 25% sand, 35% limestone, and 40% clay, rich in iron and manganese. This complex mineral environment contributes greatly to the many nuances present in the best wines made from the Rabajà. On the nose and the palate, the Rabajà by Bruno Rocca always shows a very evident note of cocoa, typical of this vineyard, but you'll also find plenty of red cherry, musk, truffle, and tobacco aromas. Very powerful in the mouth with similar flavors, it has almost chunky yet noble tannins that need years to resolve fully. It is a wine of unbelievable power, great complexity, and length. Drink it now or, better still, cellar it for another six to seven years and then enjoy it. The other wines made by Bruno are just fine, too, though he can get carried away by his enthusiasm for the small French oak barrel, yielding wines that are somewhat excessively oaky in their youth.

THE WINE
Grape varieties: nebbiolo (100%); **Number of bottles:** 18,000; **Alcohol:** 14.5; **Retail price:** $90; **Try it with:** grilled steak au poivre; **Imported by:** Trilussa Wine Company (www.trilussawine.com); **Past great vintages:** 1989, 1990, 2001, 2004

The '89 may well be the Barbaresco of the vintage, with a multilayered personality and complex aromas and flavors of red and black cherry, cocoa, and coffee. Long and very finely tannic finish (99/100). The '01 is almost as good and, again, one of the top wines made in Italy in that great vintage. Deep dark chocolate, plum, and smoky red cherry aromas are nicely followed by similar flavors on a rich, very long palate (98/100).

THE PRODUCER: AZ. AGR. BRUNO ROCCA
Address: via Rabajà 29, 12050 Barbaresco (Cuneo); **Tel/fax:** 0173 635112/0173 635112; **Web:** www.brunorocca.it; **E-mail:** info@brunorocca.it; **Total bottles:** 60,000; **Total ha:** 12; **Tasting room:** yes; **Visit:** by appointment; **Highway exit:** Asti est (A21)

OTHER RECOMMENDED WINES UNDER $100 BY BRUNO ROCCA:
Barbaresco (small barrel oaked red), Barbaresco "Coparossa" (small barrel oaked red). The special "Maria Adelaide" bottling of Barbaresco is very fine but costs in excess of $100.

3 | Barolo Cascina Francia
GIACOMO CONTERNO • 97/100 • PIEDMONT

The Barolo Monfortino, now made by Roberto Conterno, who took over the reins of the estate a few years ago, is arguably Italy's single greatest wine, but the Cascina Francia Barolo is often almost as good (witness the amazing 1990). It speaks well of the nebbiolo grown in Serralunga d'Alba, the village on the eastern border of the Barolo production zone, which gives wines of unbelievable power and concentration, as well as amazing aging potential. The soils of Serralunga, often of an almost sparkling chalky white color, have a somewhat higher limestone content than those in other parts of Barolo, but also contain a high percentage of clay, and this helps explain both the amazing finesse and the great power of the better wines produced here. The Cascina Francia is made from a steep southwest-facing site exposed to the elements (so much so that in bad years the crop is easily lost: for example, this wine wasn't made in '81 or '84). The site is at the southern tip of the Serralunga zone, between Arione and Falletto, two other of the better vineyard sites in the area. The wine has a medium deep brilliant ruby hue; great depth of red cherry, raspberry liqueur, and strawberry jam aromas with hints of dark chocolate and licorice; on the palate, more of the telltale Serralunga licorice element and gobs of ripe fruit, chocolate, and spicy plum flavors with a long, tannic, high-acid finish. Its trump card is a truly rare ability to magically combine uncommon refinement, ripeness of fruit, and huge structure in a balanced whole.

THE WINE

Grape varieties: nebbiolo (100%); **Number of bottles:** 18,000; **Alcohol:** 14; **Retail price:** $75–129; **Try it with:** lamb shanks baked with thyme, duck confit; **Imported by:** Doug Polaner Selections (www.polanerselections.com); Rare Wine Company (www.rarewineco.com); **Past great vintages:** 1988, 1989, 1990, 1994, 1996

The 1990 is the best Cascina Francia ever and about as good as the Monfortino of the same year. Pure pretty red rose and violet aromas are matched on the palate by luscious ripe red cherry and raspberry syrup flavors, with hints of nicotine and tar. It has unbelievable richness and depth of fruit, and is about as great a Barolo as there can be (99/100). The 1988 is less massive and almost graceful, with lovely red rose and sour red cherry aromas and high acidities, giving the fruit flavors definition and length (96/100). The '89 is a very fine wine, with a richer, jammier personality in both its aromas and its flavors, and a long mineral finish that ends with a pretty note of kirsch (98/100). The '94 is an unbelievable success for the vintage, and is drinking beautifully (93/100).

THE PRODUCER: AZ. VITIVINICOLA GIACOMO CONTERNO

Address: Loc. Ornati 2, 12065 Monforte d'Alba (Cuneo); **Tel/fax:** 0173 78221/0173 787190; **Total bottles:** 50,000; **Total ha:** 14; **Visit:** by appointment; **Tasting room:** yes; **Highway exit:** Ast est (A21) or Marene (A6)

OTHER RECOMMENDED WINES UNDER $100 BY GIACOMO CONTERNO:

Barbera d'Alba Cascina Francia (large barrel oaked red).

4 | "Paleo"

LE MACCHIOLE • **97/100** • TUSCANY

Cinzia Merli Campolmi is a wonderful woman, stronger than adversity (her husband, Eugenio, cofounder of the estate, died unexpectedly years ago). She leads one of Italy's best estates, with all her wines at or near the top of their respective categories: "Messorio," one of Italy's best Merlots and a true cult wine; "Scrio," a Syrah whose quality is unmatched in Italy and another cult wine; and this "Paleo," fully 100% cabernet franc with the '01 vintage (prior vintages contained cabernet sauvignon or sangiovese or both), and a Franc like very few in the whole world. In fact, the '01 bottling is one of the best wines made in Italy in the past 20 years. You'll love "Paleo's" pretty, deep ruby hue, and its lovely smoky red cherry and ripe plum aromas—it is seemingly immune to overripe, cooked aromas and flavors even in hot years. The tannins are satiny; the fruit is voluptuous; the elegance is guaranteed. Drink it over the 15 years following the harvest. A wine Eugenio Campolmi believed in, and that holds special meaning for Cinzia.

THE WINE

Grape varieties: cabernet franc (100%); **Number of bottles:** 25,000; **Alcohol:** 13.5; **Retail price:** $65–100; **Try it with:** grilled veal liver, roast lamb; **Imported by:** Domaine Select (www .domaineselect.com); **Past great vintages:** 1997, 2000, 2001, 2004

The '01 has uncommon depth of fruit, layers and layers of extremely pure aromas and flavors, and silkier-than-silk tannins (100/100), though there is some variation from bottle to bottle. The '00 is the last that contains cabernet sauvignon (70% of the blend) and is soft and pleasant (93/100). The '04 is a very promising wine that needs time to tame some of its youthful tannins (95/100). The '97 is extremely successful: a concentrated, herbal-accented red red infused with berry and cherry (97/100).

THE PRODUCER: AZ. AGR. LE MACCHIOLE

Address: Via Bolgherese 189/A, 57020 Castagneto Carducci (Livorno); **Tel/fax:** 0565 766092/0565 763240; **Web:** www .lemacchiole.it; **E-mail:** lemacchiole@etruscan.li.it; **Total bottles:** 80,000; **Total ha:** 21; **Tasting room:** yes; **Visit:** by appointment

OTHER RECOMMENDED WINES UNDER $100 BY LE MACCHIOLE:

Bolgheri Rosso (merlot/cabernet sauvignon/cabernet franc/ syrah—small barrel oaked red). Every wine made by this estate ranks among Italy's best, but unfortunately they are so in demand most cost over $100 a bottle.

5 | Tignanello

ANTINORI • **96/100** • TUSCANY

The Antinoris have been making and selling wine for more than 600 years, so you know they must be doing something right. Tignanello is a historic Italian wine, one of the first three super-Tuscans made (along with "Sassicaia" and "Vigorello"). Many people do not know that the first Tignanello ever made, from the '71 vintage, was in reality nothing more than a Chianti made without using any white grapes (Chianti had to contain white grapes back then, by law) and aged in small oak barrels—a very rare practice at the time. It was only with the '75 vintage, the second Tignanello to be released, that the current blend of sangiovese and the two cabernets began. Between those first two Tignanellos, there was much experimentation and tinkering, with more than a few doubts plaguing Piero Antinori. In the end, Tignanello, which takes its name from Antinori's single best estate among the many he owns, is recognized as the first super-Tuscan to have ever combined cabernet sauvignon with sangiovese (even though Piero's father had already added cabernet to his Chianti in the 1930s), so its place in Italian wine history would be safe even if it weren't so remarkably great. Always of a high quality standard, the '04 is the best Antinori wine of the vintage, better even than the famous "Solaia." One sniff of Tignanello will always reveal pretty aromas of violet, smoky plums, and graphite. One taste will tell you that it's relatively full-bodied yet elegant, never jammy or low-acid—soft, with plenty of fruit, sweet tannins, and good length. "Tignanello" is getting even better of late, no small feat in light of the large numbers made.

THE WINE

Grape varieties: sangiovese (85%), cabernet sauvignon (10%), and cabernet franc (5%); **Number of bottles:** 320,000; **Alcohol:** 13.5; **Retail price:** $79–90; **Try it with:** duck in orange sauce; **Imported by:** Château Ste. Michelle Estate (www.stimson-lane .com); **Past great vintages:** 1971, 1982, 1985, 1988, 1990, 2001, 2004

The '82 was great right away and is still amazingly refined with plenty of ripe, deep fruit and tobacco scents (96/100). The '85 was at the time the finest Tignanello ever, with rich red cherry and cassis aromas and flavors. An unbelievable 23,000 cases were made (97/100). The '88 is very fine, with a solid acidic spine and lovely core of truffled black cherry and plums with tobacco hints (95/100). The '01 is one of the best in recent memory, with concentrated red and black fruit, graphite, and underbrush aromas and flavors (96/100). The '71, all sangiovese despite what you may have read elsewhere, is still fine if well kept: ruby- garnet, faded violets, truffles, and porcini on the nose and palate (94/100). The '04 promises to be one of the all-time greats (95/100).

THE PRODUCER: MARCHESE ANTINORI
Address: piazza degli Antinori 3, 50123 (Firenze); **Tel/fax:** 055 23595/055 2358972; **Web:** www.antinori.it; **E-mail:** antinori@ antinori.it; **Total bottles:** 18,000,000; **Total ha:** 1,400; **Tasting room:** professionals only; **Visit:** professionals only; **Highway exit:** Firenze sud, nord or Certosa (A1)

OTHER RECOMMENDED WINES UNDER $100 BY ANTINORI:
"Santa Cristina" (sangiovese/merlot—large barrel oaked red), Chianti Classico "Peppoli" (sangiovese/merlot—large barrel oaked red), Chianti Classico Riserva "Tenute Marchesi Antinori" (sangiovese—small barrel oaked red), "Guado al Tasso" Guado al Tasso (cabernet sauvignon/merlot/syrah—small barrel oaked red). The last of these is a Tuscan estate also owned by Antinori, in the prestigious, high-quality area of Castagneto Carducci.

6 | "Graticciaia"
AGRICOLE VALLONE • 95/100 • PUGLIA

Back in the 1970s, Cosimo Taurino and his winemaker Severino Garofano had the brilliant idea of harvesting negroamaro grapes late, then letting them air-dry as well. This process revolutionized Negroamaro wines. In brief, the exact potential of what had been long considered just a workhorse grape was unveiled. At Agricole Vallone, one of the estates where Garofano consults, he took this process to the next level with "Graticciaia." The grapes are left to dry on straw or cane mats, much as Amarone is, if for a shorter time, given the warm southern climate. Hence the name of the wine: *graticci* means straw mats in Italian. The grapes are so overripe and sweet that in some years the wine may carry a little too much residual sweetness (the '98 vintage does, for example), but usually this is a smooth, velvety, dry wine. The aromas can also speak of a little volatile acidity (a very subtle hint of vinegar that actually adds freshness to the nose), but the ripe cherry, fruit, and clove aromas will mesmerize you. In the mouth, you will find the wine unleashing gobs of red cherries macerated in alcohol, raspberry jam, leather, and licorice flavors. This voluptuous wine can be drunk now or over the next 15 years.

THE WINE
Grape varieties: negroamaro (100%); **Number of bottles:** 25,000; **Alcohol:** 14; **Retail price:** $68; **Try it with:** grilled sausages; braised oxtails with red wine and onions; **Imported by:** Banville and Jones (www.banvilleandjones.com); **Past great vintages:** 1997, 1998, 2003

The '97 may be the best ever, with velvety tannins and a heady nose of red cherry, raspberry jam, and strawberries macerated in alcohol and similar flavors (98/100). The '98 is even smoother and softer, but it finishes noticeably sweet, though it's absolutely delectable and long (94/100). The '03 is a highly successful wine with less sweetness and a more tannic backbone (92/100).

THE PRODUCER: AGRICOLE VALLONE
Address: via XXV Luglio 5, 73100 (Lecce); **Tel/fax:** 0832 308041/0832 243108; **Web:** www.agricolevallone.it; **E-mail:** info@agricolevallone.it; **Total bottles:** 620,000; **Total ha:** 170; **Tasting room:** yes; **Visit:** by appointment; **Highway exit:** Bari (A14)

OTHER RECOMMENDED WINES UNDER $100 BY AGRICOLE VALLONE:
Brindisi Rosato "Flaminio" (negro amaro/montepulciano/malvasia nera—unoaked red), Brindisi Rosso "Flaminio" (negroamaro/montepulciano/malvasia nera—large barrel oaked red), Salice Salentino "Vereto" (negro amaro/malvasia nera—large barrel oaked red).

7 | "Percarlo"
FATTORIA SAN GIUSTO A RENTENNANO •
96/100 • TUSCANY

It is said that the secret of fine writing is the ability to create a context in which other people can think. Much the same may be said of "Percarlo," a wine first made in 1983. One sip of it and you wonder: where can I get many bottles of this? It is a 100% sangiovese super-Tuscan, and some of its vintages have now attained almost mythical status (for example, the '85). Percarlo has always been known for a stupendous sense of refinement. The nose has plenty of small red berry and cherry aromas and some initial oaky notes that resolve with time. On the palate it shows fleshy, almost sweet, cherry and smoky blackberry fruit of great depth, and the texture of a real breed. It finishes with suave tannins and an elegant herbal note that add to its charms. Percarlo ages extremely well: though it can be enjoyed upon release, give it four or five years of cellaring and then drink it over the following 10 years. Remember that any of the wines made by the brothers Luca and Francesco Martini di Cigala are among the best of their respective categories. The truly beautiful estate is well worth a visit: it is located in the famous Monti subarea near the village of Gaiole. Along with the Panzano subarea next to the village of Greve, this is arguably the single best spot for sangiovese in all of Chianti.

THE WINE

Grape varieties: sangiovese (100%); **Number of bottles:** 18,400; **Alcohol:** 14,5; **Retail price:** $90–95; **Try it with:** roast peppered rack of venison with dried-cherry sauce; **Imported by:** Marc de Grazia Selection (www.marcdegrazia.com; numerous importers); **Past great vintages:** 1985, 1988, 1990, 1995, 1997, 2001

The '85 is as good as sangiovese can get: rich yet light, a complex wine offering tea leaf, red currants, red cherry, and truffle aromas and similar flavors. Unfortunately, only about 4,000 bottles were made (99/100). The '88 is almost as good, just a touch less fleshy but refined, and it has a very long aftertaste with more tobacco and truffle scents to go along with the red fruit (98/100). The '01 is spectacular, rich, concentrated, and long (94/100). The '04 is even better, more intense yet refined (96/100).

THE PRODUCER: FATTORIA SAN GIUSTO A RENTENNANO

Address: Loc. San Giusto 20, 53013 Gaiole in Chianti (Siena); **Tel/fax:** 0577 747121/0577 747109; **Web:** www.fattoriasangiusto.it; **E-mail:** info@fattoriasangiusto.it; **Total bottles:** 83,500; **Total ha:** 30.5; **Tasting room:** yes; **Visit:** by appointment; **Highway exit:** Valdarno or Val di Chiana (A1)

OTHER RECOMMENDED WINES UNDER $100 BY SAN GIUSTO:

Chianti Classico (sangiovese/canaiolo nero—large barrel oaked red), "La Ricolma" Merlot (small barrel oaked red), Vin "San Giusto" (malvasia bianca toscana/trebbiano toscano—dessert white).

8 | Montepulciano d'Abruzzo "San Clemente"

ZACCAGNINI • 95/100 • ABRUZZO

It's always great to write about a wine such as this one, if for no other reason than that I know everyone who tries it will end up loving it and will thank me for the insightful recommendation. If that weren't reason enough to sing this wine's praises, then let me affirm that it is a rich, creamy, ripe mouthful of fruit that's an absolute joy to drink. "San Clemente" keeps getting better every year, and has to be considered not just one of Italy's best Montepulcianos (by far), but also one of its best wines, period. "San Clemente" on the label refers to a medieval abbey situated next to the winery, but don't let that fool you: this wine is a modern endeavor, with beautifully ripe and sweet tannins that are uncommon in most all-too-rustic Montepulcianos. It is concentrated and silky, with a wonderful delivery of delicately spicy, balsamic, ripe red cherries and plums, and its velvety texture will enthrall you and all your guests. This is a wine made for immediate enjoyment, but it will easily last 10 years and more. Also remember that the people at Zaccagnini have many other interests as well: you'll find works of modern art everywhere in the vineyards, and cultural events are organized at the estate throughout the year.

THE WINE
Grape varieties: Montepulciano (100%); **Number of bottles:** 25,000; **Alcohol:** 14.5; **Retail price:** $38–49; **Try it with:** roast chicken stuffed with onions and sage, high-quality cheeseburgers; **Imported by:** Viva Vino Import (www.vivavino .com); **Past great vintages:** 2003, 2004, 2005

THE PRODUCER: AZ. AGR. CICCIO ZACCAGNINI
Address: Contrada Pozzo, 65020 Bolognano (Pescara); **Tel/fax:** 085 8880195 / 085 8880288; **Web:** www.zaccagninivini.it; **E-mail:** zaccagniniwines@tin.it; **Total bottles:** 800,000; **Total ha:** 50; **Tasting room:** yes; **Visit:** by appointment; **Highway exit:** Torre dei Passeri (A25)

OTHER RECOMMENDED WINES UNDER $100 BY ZACCAGNINI:
Trebbiano d'Abruzzo "Chronicon" (unoaked white), "Yamada" (pecorino—unoaked white), Cerasuolo d'Abruzzo "Chronicon" (montepulciano—unoaked rosé), Montepulciano d'Abruzzo "Il Vino del Tralcetto" (large barrel oaked red).

9 | "Fontalloro"

FELSINA • 95/100 • TUSCANY

I always find it extremely difficult to choose between the Chianti Classico Riserva "Rancia"—for my money one of italy's two or three best Chiantis—and the "Fontalloro," a pure 100% sangiovese super-Tuscan. I'll opt for the latter, because I've been won over by its history of velvety tannins and gorgeous red fruit that would inhebriate anyone even in the absence of alcohol. Brilliant medium ruby (no black or inky so-called 100% sangiovese here), perfumed with red cherry, orange peel, tea leaf, and tobacco, it is fullbodied, dry, and extremely lithe and refined. Far from a blockbuster, it enchants from the get-go with grace and lovely fruit brilliantly delineated by high, refreshing acids. Interestingly, this great wine is not produced from exaggeratedly tightly spaced vines (here the vines are only at 2,800–5,600 feet/ha), and that fact may help explain its amazing elegance. I think Fontalloro ages very well up to 15 years after the harvest, but I find it doesn't improve much after that, though it remains a splendid wine. Giuseppe Mazzocolin is one of the greatest experts on sangiovese, but he excels with other varieties as well, and makes an absolutely fine series of olive oils you'd do well to try. These are made from single varietals of olives such as leccino and moraiolo and are vastly superior to most extra-virgin olive oils made at other wine estates where olive oil plays second fiddle to the wines.

THE WINE

Grape varieties: sangiovese (100%); **Number of bottles:** 35,000; **Alcohol:** 13.5; **Retail price:** $47–50; **Try it with:** crostini with chicken livers (cooked with bay leaf, celery, carrots, and wine); **Imported by:** Doug Polaner Selection (www.polanerselections .com); **Past great vintages:** 1985, 1988, 1990, 1995, 1997, 2001

THE PRODUCER: FATTORIA DI FELSINA

Address: via del Chianti 101, 53019 Castelnuovo Berardenga (Siena); **Tel/fax:** 0577 355117/0577 355651; **Web:** www.felsina.it; **E-mail:** felsina@dada.it; **Total bottles:** 450,000–500,000; **Total ha:** 62; **Tasting room:** yes; **Visit:** by appointment; **Highway exit:** Val di Chiana or Firenze Certosa (A1)

OTHER RECOMMENDED WINES UNDER $100 BY FELSINA:

Chianti Classico "Berardenga" (sangiovese—small and large barrel oaked red), Chianti Classico Riserva "Rancia" (sangiovese—small barrel oaked red), "Maestro Raro" (cabernet sauvignon—small barrel oaked red), Vin Santo del Chianti Classico (malvasia toscana/trebbiano toscano/sangiovese—sweet white).

10 | Barolo "Ciabot Mentin Ginestra"

DOMENICO CLERICO • **95/100** • PIEDMONT

One of the great names in Barolo and Italy, Domenico Clerico, an immensely likable and fun-loving fellow, rarely misses a beat and all his Barolos are fine. Unlike his other wines, they do not seem to be overoaked. (The Dolcetto and Barbera often are overoaked, which is a shame: the good news is that, starting in 2008, Clerico has reduced oak use by 15% in all his wines, and the difference shows.) This Barolo's complex-sounding name derives from the Italian *ciabot,* a shed in the vineyards where tools are kept, and from Ginestra, a prized vineyard site along with Mosconi, Le Coste, and other vineyards dotting the hills south of the bucolic hamlet of Castelletto di Monforte. Though this particular subzone is located in the Monforte area of Barolo land, usually thought of as giving some of the biggest and most age-worthy Barolos, its soil has a much higher sandy content than the clay-rich soils more typical of Monforte. Thus, Ginestra Barolos are perfumed and finer than most Barolos from Monforte, though they remain more powerful than those from Monforte's Bussia section, another prized area. In fact, Clerico once made a delectable Freisa from this site, and Ginestra is recognized as one of the best sites for perfumed Barbera as well. The "Ciabot Mentin Ginestra" Barolo always has classic aromas and flavors of sour red cherry, truffle, mushroom, and almond, with a hint of red rose. It ages splendidly, coming into its own at about 15 years after the harvest and remaining in top form for many years thereafter. Enough bottles are made so that you you should be able to find it in wine stores.

THE WINE

Grape varieties: nebbiolo (100%); **Number of bottles:** 18,000; **Alcohol:** 14–14.5; **Retail price:** $90; **Try it with:** brasato al Barolo (beef braised for hours directly in Barolo: in the best of all possible worlds, a young bottle of the Ciabot Mentin Ginestra in the pot, and two older vintages of it on the table); **Imported by:** Marc de Grazia Selection (www.marcdegrazia.com; numerous importers); **Past great vintages:** 1982, 1989, 1990, 1996, 2001

THE PRODUCER: DOMENICO CLERICO

Address: Loc. Manzoni 67, 12065 Monforte d'Alba (Cuneo); **Tel/ fax:** 0173 78171 / 0173 789800; **E-mail:** domenicoclerico@libero.it; **Total bottles:** 95,000; **Total ha:** 21; **Visit:** by appointment; **Tasting room:** yes; **Highway exit:** Ast est (A21)

OTHER RECOMMENDED WINES UNDER $100 BY CLERICO:

"Arte" (nebbiolo/barbera—small barrel oaked red), Barolo Pajana (nebbiolo—small barrel oaked red). The Barolo "Percristina" is also wonderful but costs more than $100.

11 | Chianti Rufina "Montesodi"

FRESCOBALDI • **95/100** • TUSCANY

One of the very best Chiantis, and proof enough that Chianti doesn't have to be Classico to be great. A top-notch team at Frescobaldi captained by the winemaker Niccolò d'Afflitto has managed to maintain this wine at extremely high and consistent levels of quality over the years. It was first made unofficially (and called San Martino) as an experiment in 1970 by Rinaldelli, at the time in charge of the vineyards. Frescobaldi released the wine under its new name with the '74 vintage, officially its first vintage. Loaded with rich ripe black fruit, lots of prune and licorice, coffee powder, and quite a bit of black pepper and spices—a d'Afflitto trademark, one might venture to say—but still kept in fine balance with an easy-to-drink charm. The tannins are youthfully tough, chewy, and dense when the wine is still young (another d'Afflitto hallmark). The rather deep hue and pepperiness on the nose suggest a syrah-like quality, but keep in mind that d'Afflitto and Lamberto Frescobaldi have conducted extensive studies on oak barrels of different toasts, forest areas, and barrel makers for many years now, and through a careful mix of different barrels they attain wines of greater color and spiciness than other producers. Another feather in Montesodi's cap is that it is a remarkably consistent wine, with very good wines made even in poor years, though in rain-plagued, very poor vintages the wine is not made.

THE WINE

Grape varieties: sangiovese; **Number of bottles:** 40,000; **Alcohol:** 14.5; **Retail price:** $35–50; **Try it with:** barbecued beef, beef stroganoff; **Imported by:** Folio Fine Wine Partners (www.foliowine.com);

Past great vintages: 1974, 1978, 1982, 1985, 1990, 1995, 2000, 2001, 2003

In a recent vertical tasting that I guided in Rome with Niccolò d'Afflitto, the Frescobaldi winemaker, I had the 1974, and it was easy to see why the Frescobaldi family was so excited at the time. It is still a very fine wine today, with tobacco, leather, and licorice aromas and flavors but with plenty of soft plum and blackberry fruit left (92/100).

THE PRODUCER: MARCHESI DE' FRESCOBALDI; **Address:** via Santo Spirito 11, 50125 (Firenze); **Tel/fax:** 055 27141/055 211527; **Web:** www.frescobaldi.it; **E-mail:** info@frescobaldi.it; **Total bottles:** 3 million; **Total ha:** 1,000; **Tasting room:** yes; **Visit:** by appointment; **Highway exit:** Firenze nord or sud or Certosa (A1)

OTHER RECOMMENDED WINES UNDER $100 BY FRESCOBALDI:
Pomino Bianco (chardonnay/pinot bianco/riesling—unoaked white), Pomino "Il Benefizio" (chardonnay—small barrel oaked white), Pomino Rosso (sangiovese/pinot nero/others—small barrel oaked red), Chianti Rufina Castello di Nipozzano Riserva (sangiovese/others—small barrel oaked red).

Frescobaldi is the owner of Ornellaia, one of Italy's 10 most famous wine estates, where the two cult (and extremely great) wines called "Ornellaia" and "Masseto" are made, but both of these are well above $100 a bottle.

12 | "Flaccianello delle Pieve"
FONTODI • 95/100 • TUSCANY

Many wonderful Flaccianellos have been made since the first vintage back in 1981. A 100% sangiovese super-Tuscan that has long been considered one of Italy's best and most important wines, it shows the heights this variety can achieve when properly tended to, without the need to resort to merlot or cabernet. It helps that Fontodi owns some of the best vineyards in all of Chianti, situated in the heavenly "golden amphitheater" of Panzano, a *grand cru* if there ever was one for sangiovese. Luminous medium ruby in hue, it always has aromas of violets and smoky plums intermingling with touches of leather, truffle, and tobacco. Rich and supple on the palate, it is a wine of uncanny finesse and extra-long finish. Stash it away for five to six years before even thinking of opening it, so that you'll give its not-too-shy tannins a chance to resolve more or less fully before you taste. Fontodi is one of Chianti's prettier estates to visit, and the owner, Giovanni Manetti, is one of the nicest and most charming wine people you'll ever meet. The estate also makes olive oil and raises the snow white cows of the Chianina breed that many sybarites believe give Italy's tastiest steaks. Given all of Giovanni's talents, we're grateful his family decided to stray from terra-cotta production in Florence in the 1960s to wine making and more.

THE WINE

Grape varieties: sangiovese (100%); **Number of bottles:** 50,000; **Alcohol:** 14–14.5; **Retail price:** $90–100; **Try it with:** meat loaf Tuscan style; roast pork loin with roast tomatoes, mashed potatoes, and sautéed spinach; **Imported by:** Vinifera Imports (www.vinifera-il.com); **Past great vintages:** 1982, 1985, 1990, 1997, 2001

THE PRODUCER: AZ. AGR. FONTODI

Address: frazione Panzano, via San Leonino 89, 50020 Greve in Chianti (Siena); **Tel/fax:** 055 852005/055 852537; **Web:** www.fontodi.com; **E-mail:** fontodi@fontodi.com; **Total bottles:** 200,000; **Total ha:** 61; **Tasting room:** yes; **Visit:** by appointment; **Highway exit:** Valdarno or Firenze Certosa (A1)

OTHER RECOMMENDED WINES UNDER $100 BY FONTODI:

Chianti Classico (sangiovese—large barrel oaked red), Chianti Classico "Vigna del Sorbo" (sangiovese/cabernet sauvignon—small barrel oaked red), Syrah "Case Via" (small barrel oaked red).

13 | Barbaresco "Martinenga"

CISA ASINARI MARCHESE DI GRESY
• **95/100** • AS PIEDMONT

Alberto di Gresy is a nobleman of many talents, from organizing car rallies with old Porsches to playing billiards (his skill as a billiards player is wondrous), who also happens to produce a series of wines that are practically unmatched, for quality, by any other estate in Italy. I remain fascinated by his personality, the history of his estate, his passion. His Martinenga estate is one of the more beautiful in Italy and well worth a visit: the

Martinenga hill itself is a monopole (a vineyard that has a single owner), and one of the three best vineyard sites for Barbaresco—many people consider it the absolute best. Barbaresco "Martinenga" is the entry-level or *normale* bottling, though there is little normal about it. Often (unfortunately) overlooked in favor of the more expensive single vineyard "Gaiun" and "Camp Gros" bottlings, it is a real tribute to the truest of nebbiolos: it has a light, almost pinkish ruby hue (due to a large presence of the rosé subvariety of nebbiolo used); delicate but incisive perfumes typical of the variety (sour red cherries, almond flowers, orange peel, tar); and great freshness and elegance on the palate, where the fruit and fine tannins show great persistence. A wine of finesse and subtlety rather than power or brute force. Should you want to try the very fine single vineyard bottlings, remember that "Gaiun" is made from the portion of the Martinenga vineyard that abuts the very great Asili *cru*, and "Camp Gros" is produced from the portion of Martinenga that is virtually attached to the famous Rabajà vineyard. Accordingly, "Gaiun" is immensely perfumed, typical of the wines made from Asili, and already quite approachable when young, whereas "Camp Gros" is firmer and more structured, more in line with the wines made from Rabajà.

THE WINE

Grape varieties: nebbiolo (100%); **Number of bottles:** 15,000; **Alcohol:** 14; **Retail price:** $50; **Try it with:** tajarin (a local pasta) with white truffles from Alba; **Imported by:** Dalla Terra (www.dallaterra.com); Classic Wine Imports (www.classicwineimports.com); **Past great vintages:** 1978, 1979, 1982, 1985, 1989, 1990, 1999, 2001, 2003

THE PRODUCER: TENUTE CISA ASINARI DEI MARCHESE DI GRESY

Address: strada della Stazione 21, 12050 Barbaresco (Cuneo); **Tel/fax:** 0173 635222 / 0173 635187; **Web:** www.marchesidigresy.com; **E-mail:** wine@marchesidigresy.com; **Total bottles:** 180,000; **Total ha:** 50; **Tasting room:** yes; **Visit:** by appointment; **Highway exit:** Asti est (A21)

OTHER RECOMMENDED WINES UNDER $100 BY DE GRESY:

Sauvignon (unoaked white), Chardonnay (unoaked white) Barbera d'Asti "Monte Colombo" (small barrel oaked red), Dolcetto d'Alba "Monte Aribaldo" (unoaked red), Barbaresco "Camp Gros" (small and large barrel oaked red), Barbaresco "Gaiun" (small barrel oaked red), L'Altro Moscato (moscato bianco—sweet white).

14 | "Cepparello"

ISOLE E OLENA • **95/100** • TUSCANY

Paolo De Marchi is an enological genius, who excels with just about any grape variety he touches. Recently he has tried his hand at nebbiolo in Piedmont (see wine number 43, page 64) and has made a stellar wine there as well. In Tuscany, where he has been producing some of Italy's best wines for the past 20 years, the list of his successes is never-ending. He makes one of Italy's few interesting Chardonnays, a solid Syrah, and a Cabernet that my British wine mentors were applauding back in the 1980s. Native grapes fare even better: his is one of the better entry-level Chiantis, and the "Cepparello," an almost pure sangiovese super-Tuscan (in poorer years a little cabernet finds its way in), is one of Italy's absolutely best red wines. If you can find a well-stored bottle, try the '82 or the '85; both are still splendid. The Cepparello has deep, intense aromas of licorice, fern, red berry and cherry fruit, and similar flavors, with a rich, thick mouthfeel characterized by suave tannins and a very long finish. As it ages, it develops more gamy, underbrush, and truffle aromas. A wine of uncompromising character—sexy, pure, and aristocratic—it can be enjoyed on release or over 20 years from the harvest.

THE WINE
Grape varieties: sangiovese (100%); in poor vintages, roughly sangiovese (92%), cabernet sauvignon (8%); **Number of bottles:** 40,000; **Alcohol:** 13.5–14; **Try it with:** grilled lamb shanks with garlic and herbs; grilled T-bone steak; **Imported by:** Petit Pois (Sussex Wine Merchants), Carolina Wine Company (www.carolinawine.com); **Past great vintages:** 1982, 1985, 1988, 1990, 1997, 2001

THE PRODUCER: FATTORIA ISOLE E OLENA
Address: Loc. Isole 1, 50021 Barberino Val d'Elsa (Firenze); **Tel/fax:** 055 8072763/055 8072236; **Web:** www.isoleolena.it; **E-mail:** marketing@isoleolena.it; **Total bottles:** 220,000; **Total ha:** 48; **Tasting room:** yes; **Visit:** by appointment; **Highway exit:** Valdarno or Firenze Certosa (A1)

OTHER RECOMMENDED WINES UNDER $100 BY ISOLE E OLENA:
Chardonnay "Collezione De Marchi" (small barrel oaked white), Chianti Classico (sangiovese/canaiolo/syrah—large and small barrel oaked red), Syrah "Collezione De Marchi" (small barrel oaked red), Cabernet Sauvignon "Collezione De Marchi" (small

barrel oaked red), Vin Santo del Chianti Classico (malvasia toscana/trebbiano toscano—sweet).

15 | Brunello di Montalcino

LIVIO SASSETTI—PERTIMALI • **95/100** • TUSCANY

Unlike the names of many Italian wines and estates, this name actually means something: "Pertimali" is an ancient building found on Sassetti's property that has been renovated as a residential and wine-making complex. This estate also happens to be the source of one of the better, more refined Brunellos each year. Medium deep ruby hue, with wonderful notes of licorice, red cherry, red currant, black pepper, and a hint of balsamic smoke on the nose, with similar flavors, it's long and clean on the suavely tannic finish. It ages splendidly, though unlike many other Brunellos it is usually very enjoyable at a young age. This is one name in Montalcino you can bank on for serious and well-made Brunello, year in, year out.

THE WINE
Grape varieties: sangiovese (100%); **Number of bottles:** 22,000;
Alcohol: 14; **Retail price:** $53–80; **Try it with:** rosemary lamb chops;
Imported by: Marc de Grazia Selection (www.marcdegrazia.com;
numerous importers); **Past great vintages:** 1985, 1990, 1997, 1999

THE PRODUCE: AZ. AGR. LIVIO SASSETTI—
PERTIMALI
Address: loc. Pertimali, 53024 Montalcino (Siena); **Tel/fax:** 0577
848721/0577 848721; **Web:** www.sassettiliviopertimali.com;
E-mail: lsasset@tin.it; **Total bottles:** 50,000; **Total ha:** 16.5;
Tasting room: yes; **Visit:** by appointment; **Highway exit:** Chiusi or
Firenze Certosa (A1)

OTHER RECOMMENDED WINES UNDER $100
BY PERTIMALI:
Rosso di Montalcino (sangiovese—large barrel oaked red).

16 | Nero d'Avola Selezione Speciale "Vrucara"

FEUDO MONTONI • **95/100** • SICILY

Fabio Sireci is the young, enthusiastic owner of this estate. It makes only three estate-labeled wines, and the two Nero d'Avolas may well be the best wines made from the nero d'Avola grape in all of Sicily. That is right; you read correctly. The "Selezione Vrucara" is Sireci's top wine, made from a parcel of old vines that are a unique, high-quality subpopulation of nero d'Avola. We know today that probably 100 subvarieties of nero d'Avola exist on the island, but Sireci's is so superior to most that many other producers have been asking him for cuttings so they can plant their own. He is happy to do provide them, for, as he humorously points out, if you don't grant such requests, Sicilians take matters in their own hands. According to Sireci, before he decided to become a producer in his own right, he used to sell the grapes to Tasca d'Almerita, and that estate used them to make the famous "Rosso del Conte" wine. "Selezione Vrucara" is just dandy, with a discernible saline and herbal quality both on the nose and on the palate, along with strawberry and plum notes and a delicate smokiness and pepperiness. The latter two qualities will no doubt remind you of syrah, of which nero d'Avola is a distant relative. Spicy plum and blackberry flavors add a little more sweetness on the long mineral finish. The estate's base Nero d'Avola, though less concentrated and complex, is actually much more juicy- fruity in nature and absolutely wonderful to drink: try it lightly chilled.

THE WINE
Grape varieties: nero d'Avola (100%); **Number of bottles:** 30,000; **Alcohol:** 13.5; **Retail price:** $30; **Try it with:** seared rib eye with rosemary and arugula; **Imported by:** Selected Estates of Europe (www.selectedestates.com); **Past great vintages:** 2003, 2004, 2005

The '03 and '04 were products of two years with little rainfall, and both are fine, as the vines are roughly 60 years old. The '03 is rich and fat, with concentrated red and black cherry aromas and flavors with a definite salty twist (95/100). The '04 is slightly less opulent, with slightly tougher tannins (93/100). The '05 is a much finer wine, with fresher fruit aromas and silkier tannins (97/100).

THE PRODUCER: FEUDO MONTONI DEL PRINCIPATO DI VILLANOVA
Address: Contrada Montoni Vecchi 92022, Cammarata (Palermo); **Tel/fax:** 091 513106 / 091 6704406; **Web:** www.feudomontoni.it; **E-mail:** info@feudomontoni.it; **Total bottles:** 150,000; **Total ha:** 72; **Tasting room:** yes; **Visit:** by appointment; **Highway exit:** Palermo (A19)

Cataratto (unoaked white), Nero d'Avola (steel and small barrel
oaked red). The latter wine is also aged in larger 500-liter
tonneaux, but the oak is used so deftly that it is hardly noticeable.

17 | Aglianico del Vulture Titolo
ELENA FUCCI • 95/100 • BASILICATA

Basilicata is one of Italy's hot, up-and-coming wine regions. You haven't yet read much about it in major wine
publications, but that is bound to change—especially
when there are wines as fine as this one, made by Salvatore
Fucci and his daughter Elena. They can be proud of a
string of excellent Aglianicos made from grapes harvested
from what may well be the best vineyard of the whole Vulture area called Titolo, 1,900 feet above sea level. The
Vulture is a long-extinct volcano with seven different
peaks. It is said to resemble that bird of prey, with wings
outstretched, but I have visited the area about 25 times in
the last three years, and I am still trying to see any resemblance. This is always a great red wine: very fine with
plenty of plum, rose petal, tobacco, and black cherry aromas and flavors. The usual telltale fine tannins on the long
clean finish and refreshing acidity—a hallmark of
high-altitude Aglianico (and of the Titolo vineyard in
particular)—keep what is essentially a big blockbuster of a
wine unusually lithe and lively, dancing happily on your
taste buds.

THE WINE
Grape varieties: aglianico (100%); **Number of bottles:** 15,000;
Alcohol: 13.5; **Retail price:** $38–55; **Try it with:** *cutturidde*-style lamb
(a local lamb stew made with onions, potatoes, bay leaf, olive oil,
and water; it comes in its own broth); roast leg of veal with porcini
mushrooms; **Imported by:** Montecastelli (www.montecastelli.
com); North Berkeley Imports (www.northberkeleyimports.com);
Past great vintages: 2000, 2001, 2002, 2004. The '02 is a huge
success in light of the poor vintage, but Fucci excels even in so-so
years (witness the '05).

THE PRODUCER: ELENA FUCCI
Address: Contrada Titolo, 85022 Barile (Potenza); **Tel/fax:** 0972
770736; **E-mail:** elenafucci@tiscali.it; **Total bottles:** 16,000; **Total
ha:** 5.35; **Tasting room:** yes; **Visit:** by appointment; **Highway exit:**
Candela or Foggia (A16)

No other wines made.

18 | "Grattamacco Rosso"

GRATTAMACCO • **94/100** • TUSCANY

Roland Barthes, the great French critic, once said that only diversity counts in life. "Grattamacco," a super-Tuscan different from many, has in fact always been counted among Italy's best wines. Unlike many of the wines made in the Bolgheri area, it is not a blockbuster top-heavy with heady merlot or cabernet aromas and flavors, but rather allows the more delicate sangiovese to shine through. Cabernet sauvignon, cabernet franc, and merlot do very well in Bolgheri, and you need to look no farther than "Sassicaia" and "Ornellaia," two of Italy's best wines made in this area with those very grapes. Still, sangiovese can also grow well around Bolgheri, and "Grattamacco" is a case in point. In fact, "Grattamacco" is one of the original wines to have followed in the footsteps of Sassicaia, at a time in the early 1980s when Bolgheri wasn't thought much about and "Sassicaia" was considered a stroke of luck. Though Grattamacco also contains quite a bit of cabernet and merlot, the sangiovese shines through so well that the goal of the estate is to increase its percentage in the future. Always characterized by intense red cherry, black currant, smoky plum, herbal, tobacco, and quinine aromas, in the mouth it has considerable weight and tannins and plenty more of the smoky red and black fruit evident on the nose. It also ages well, and with time in the bottle tends to develop more aromas and flavors of underbrush and truffle.

THE WINE

Grape varieties: cabernet sauvignon (65%), merlot (20%), sangiovese (15%); **Number of bottles:** 30,000; **Alcohol:** 13.5; **Retail price:** $90; **Try it with:** beef stew with olives and a side of cannellini beans; **Imported by:** Bedford International (www.winesfrom bedford.com); **Past great vintages:** 1985, 1988, 1990, 2001

The '85 is starting to fade, but it still has lovely smoky red cherry and plum aromas, with a nice herbal-peppery twist (92/100). The '90 is still grand, with more truffle, mushroom, and tar aromas and flavors to go along with the red cherry and plum notes (95/100).

THE PRODUCER: GRATTAMACCO
Address: Loc. Lungagnano, 57022 Castagneto Carducci (Livorno);
Tel/fax: 0565 765069/0565 763217; **Web:** www.collemassari.it;
E-mail: info@collemassari.it; **Total bottles:** 50,000; **Total ha:** 11;
Tasting room: yes; **Visit:** by appointment; **Highway exit:**
Rosignano (A12)

OTHER RECOMMENDED WINES UNDER $100
BY GRATTAMACCO:
"Grattamacco Bianco" (vermentino—small barrel oaked white),
Bolgheri Rosso (cabernet sauvignon/sangiovese/merlot—small
barrel oaked red).

19 | "Turriga"
ARGIOLAS • 95/100 • SARDINIA

The winemaker Giacomo Tachis is well known for what
he accomplished with "Sassicaia" in Tuscany, and his
achievements with "Turriga" are just as remarkable. I had
never thought that cannonau, a local variant of grenache
(the world's second most planted grape, but rare in Italy
outside of Sardinia), could possibly achieve these dizzying
qualitative heights on the island of Sardinia. Well, I was
wrong; and besides Tachis and the skill of all at Argiolas,
the almost 100-year-old vines contribute a great deal to
this wine's uniqueness. I also feel carignan helps out
quite a bit, though I have been told I am wrong on that
count as well, as the percentage of this latter grape is mi-
nuscule. The deep ruby hue and the almost voluptuous
aromas of ripe red fruit, dark chocolate, and sandalwood
with hints of fern, thyme, and rosemary will captivate
you. So will the compact, silky mouthfeel, characterized
by extra-fine tannins and a wonderfully long finish. Memories are made of this.

THE WINE
Grape varieties: cannonau (mainly), carignano, bovale, malvasia
nera; **Number of bottles:** 50,000; **Alcohol:** 14; **Retail price:** $70;
Try it with: roast suckling pig; **Imported by:** Winebow (www
.winebow.com); **Past great vintages:** 1990, 1997, 2001

Nowhere will you find a better lesson on different vintages than here, in comparing the '01 and the '02 "Turri-
gas." The '01 is fantastic, with rich and deep smoky plum
and red cherry aroimas and flavors with herbal and leather
accents (95/100), but the '02 is dilute (and even a little

musty, in some bottles), a result of ill-timed rains that year. It's actually not a bad wine, even very successful for the vintage (87/100).

THE PRODUCER: ARGIOLAS

Address: Via Roma 56–58 Serdiana, 09040 (Cagliari); **Tel/fax:** 070 740606 / 070 743264; **Web:** www.cantine-argiolas.it; **E-mail:** info@cantine-argiolas.it; **Total bottles:** 2,000,000; **Total ha:** 230; **Tasting room:** yes; **Visit:** by appointment

OTHER RECOMMENDED WINES UNDER $100 BY ARGIOLAS:

"S'elegas" (nuragus—unoaked white), "Angialis" (nasco/malvasia di Sardegna—sweet white).

20 | Amarone della Valpolicella "Vigneto Roccolo Grassi"

ROCCOLO GRASSI • 94/100 • VENETO

The producer Roccolo Grassi is one of the up-and-coming stars of this area, and though the owner, Marco Sartori, is storming the palaces of the old Amarone guard, up until very recently he wasn't very well known in the United States. However, this situation has changed of late, and prices for his wines have increased accordingly. Still, his Amarone costs considerably less than cult wines from producers such as Quintarelli or Dal Forno, so you might want to try a bottle of this Amarone before it is priced right out of the market for most people. All the wines made by Sartori are of extremely fine quality, though they are not made in particularly large amounts and thus may be hard to find. They are all well worth a search, especially his Amarone and the sweet Recioto. More than other, overhyped Amarone, his is a perfect fusion of power and elegance, opulence and refinement. It is a wine with which one can easily eat a meal, something you cannot always say about Amarone: many of these wines look (and taste) good only in organized tastings for the press. Deep ruby, his greets your nose with a vortex of red berries, red cherries, peach, flowers, and sweet spices. In the mouth it's velvety and well balanced, and hides its roughly 16.5 degrees of alcohol well, delivering fine though not shy tannins and wonderfully suave fig, red cherry macerated in alcohol, and spicy flavors. Another blessing is that it manages to stay fresh on the extremely long finish.

THE WINE

Grape varieties: corvina (60%), rondinella (20%), corvinone (15%), molinara e croatina (5%).; **Number of bottles:** 6,400; **Alcohol:** 16–16.5; **Retail price:** $75–100; **Try it with:** barbecued beef; Gorgonzola or Roquefort; **Imported by:** Chambers and Chambers (www.chamberswines.com); **Past great vintages:** 2001

THE PRODUCER: ROCCOLO GRASSI

Address: via San Giovanni 19, 37030 Mezzane di Sotto (Verona); **Tel/fax:** 045 888089/045 888900; **E-mail:** roccolograssi@libero.it; **Total bottles:** 35,000; **Total ha:** 12; **Visit:** by appointment; **Tasting room:** yes; **Highway exit:** Verona Est (A4)

OTHER RECOMMENDED WINES UNDER $100 BY ROCCOLO GRASSI:

Soave Superiore Vigneto "La Broia" (garganega—small barrel oaked white), Valpolicella Superiore Vigneto "Roccolo Grassi" (corvina/corvinone/rondinella/molinara—small barrel oaked red), Recioto della Valpolicella (corvina/corvinone/rondinella—sweet red).

21 | Barolo

BARTOLO MASCARELLO • **94/100** • PIEDMONT

The "old man" of Barolo is no longer with us, but his legacy is kept alive by his daughter, the talented Maria Teresa. The first wine was made in 1921, and this fact tells you they've enjoyed success long enough to know not to mess with a winning formula. This is great Barolo that requires a little patience, though the wines have never been as brutally tannic as some other Barolos. This is due at least in part to vineyards located in sites known for fragrant wines: Rué, Torriglione (actually, a parcel of vines not in the Torriglione vineyard but rather in Rocche), San Lorenzo, and Cannubi. This wine always shows very pure sour red cherry and raspberry flavors and aromas, with a beautiful mineral edge and truffled nuances as the wines age. I will be forever grateful to this family, because their wonderful wines (the '70 and the '71) made me fall in love with wine at the end of the 1970s and spurred me to devote my life to writing about wine. Some of the older wines were among the best wines ever made in Italy. The new vintages almost always sell for more than $100, but with some careful searching in stores and on the Internet you can still find excellent recent vintages for less than that. Keep in mind that Mascarello is a good address for more than just fine Barolo: the Dolcetto and especially the Barbera are also top-quality, and while it was made, the Grignolino was to die for. (Unfortunately light red wines such as Grignolino sell poorly, and so this producer opted to remove the vines in favor of barbera.)

THE WINE
Grape varieties: nebbiolo (100%); **Number of bottles:** 13,000; **Alcohol:** 14; **Retail price:** $70–125; **Try it with:** roast breast of veal with spinach, mushroom, and apple stuffing; **Imported by:** Robert Chadderdon Selections (www.classicwineimports.com); **Past great vintages:** 1964, 1967,1970, 1971,1978, 1979, 1982, 1989, 1990, 2001

The '78 is one of the three best wines of the vintage, and still phenomenal today (96/100). The '71 has always been slightly disappointing in light of the fantastic vintage (90/100). The '70 was actually a better wine (93/100). Some truffle and mushroom notes begin to emerge from the '89, also soft and ripe in the mouth (95/100). The '01 is sterner, but ultimately deeper and more interesting (94/100).

THE PRODUCER: CANTINA BARTOLO MASCARELLO
Address: via Roma 15, 12060 Barolo (Cuneo); **Tel/fax:** 0173 56125/0173 56125; **Total bottles:** 25,000; **Total ha:** 5; **Visit:** by appointment; **Tasting room:** yes; **Highway exit:** Ast est (A21) or Marene (A6)

OTHER RECOMMENDED WINES UNDER $100
BY BARTOLO MASCARELLO:
Dolcetto d'Alba (large barrel oaked red), Barbera d'Alba (large barrel oaked red).

22 | Aglianico del Vulture "La Firma"
CANTINE DEL NOTAIO • **94/100** • BASILICATA

You'll hardly ever meet a nicer husband-and-wife wine making team than Gerardo Giuratrabocchetti and Marcella Libutti: for that matter, you'll hardly ever find a better lineup of wines, either. A visit to their home in the sleepy town of Rionero or to their brand-new, state-of-the-art cellar will convince you that this is one of Italy's best wine producers. You want rosé? You'll love their round and voluptuous "Rogito." You have a sweet tooth? There's not much better available in the dessert wine department in Italy than their "L'Autentica," potentially one of the country's best sweet wines, but at times limited by a lack of acidity. The Aglianico del Vulture in the dry red version remains the house specialty, and "La Firma" is one of Italy's greatest reds. You'll trip all over yourself scrambling for another glass of this suave nectar, with gobs of ripe, velvety black cherry and plum aromas with inhebriating touches of balsamic vinegar and spices, and lots of milk chocolate, tobacco, and more balsamic black cherry fruit on the palate. The very long finish leaves you wishing that the bottle were bottomless!

THE WINE

Grape varieties: aglianico (100%); **Number of bottles:** 35,000; **Alcohol:** 14.5; **Retail price:** $36–60; **Try it with:** roast guinea fowl and mashed beans with garlic and mint; **Imported by:** Marc de Grazia Selection (www.marcdegrazia.com); numerous importers; **Past great vintages:** 1999, 2000, 2004

THE PRODUCER: CANTINE DEL NOTAIO

Address: via Roma 159, 85028 Rionero in Vulture (Potenza); **Tel/fax:** 0972 723689/0972 723689; **E-mail:** info@cantinedelnotaio.it; **Web:** www.cantinedelnotaio.com; **Total bottles:** 120,000; **Total ha:** 27; **Visit:** by appointment; **Tasting room:** yes; **Highway exit:** Candela (A16)

OTHER RECOMMENDED WINES UNDER $100 BY CANTINE DEL NOTAIO:

Aglianico del Vulture "Il Rogito" (small barrel oaked rosé), Aglianico del Vulture "Il Sigillo" (small barrel oaked red), "L'Autentica" (moscato bianco/malvasia—sweet white).

23 | "Mille e Una Notte"

DONNAFUGATA • 94/100 • SICILY

The multitalented Rallo family of Donnafugata can be proud of a truly amazing lineup of high-quality wines with few rivals in Italy. It never ceases to amaze me just how good some of these wines are, especially some of the lower-priced ones, and I cannot help wondering why more wineries (not just in Italy) cannot turn out similar quality at similar prices. For example, the "Sedara" and the "Polena" are so good and fruit-juicy that you'll find yourself gulping them down. However, the zenith is reached with the sweet Passito "Ben Ryé" and the romantically named "Mille e Una Notte" ("thousand and one nights"). The latter succeeds as do few other Sicilian reds, managing to unveil the great potential of its main grape variety, nero d'Avola, which all too often gives rustic wines. All vintages of this wine show a blend of power, ripe black fruit, the right touch of spice, a pleasant minerality, and sweet, well-polymerized if at times chewy tannins, and older vintages are even better than recent ones, at times too strongly marked by black pepper and herbal notes. Nonetheless, assertive acids and fine-grained tannins confer great clarity and cut, and the sweet, complex finish goes on and on.

THE WINE

Grape varieties: nero d'Avola (90%), other native grapes; **Number of bottles:** 45,000; **Alcohol:** 14; **Retail price:** $60–70; **Try it with:** couscous with lamb and sun-dried tomatos; **Imported by:** Folio Fine Wine Partners (www.foliowine.com); **Past great vintages:** 1999, 2000

THE PRODUCER: DONNAFUGATA

Address: via Sebastiano Lipari 18, 91025 Marsala (Trapani); **Tel/fax:** 0923 724200/0923 722042; **Web:** www.donnafugata.it; **E-mail:** info@donnafugata.it; **Total bottles:** 2.4 million; **Total ha:** 302; **Tasting room:** yes; **Visit:** by appointment; **Highway exit:** Mazara del Vallo (A29) or Marsala (A29/dir)

OTHER GREAT WINES UNDER $100 BY DONNAFUGATA:

"Lighea" (zibibbo, inzolia, cataratto—unoaked white), "Polena" (viognier—white), "Sedara" (nero d'Avola—unoaked red), Moscato di Pantelleria "Kabir" (sweet white), Passito di Pantelleria "Ben Ryé" (sweet white).

24 | "Patriglione"

COSIMO TAURINO • **94/100** • PUGLIA

Italy's deep south was always associated with big, inexpensive, ultimately rustic and uncomplicated reds—that is, until "Patriglione" came along. A wine characterized by layered, opulent aromas and flavors with unctuously textured rich, pure fruit, it is the product of faultless wine making. This is another of the truly historic wines of Italy, and the first to show inequivocally the great potential of the negro amaro grape. Made from late-harvested grapes, this wine always has a lush, creamy mouthfeel, very suave tannins, and beautiful ripe red cherry fruit, tobacco, and delicate leather notes both on the nose and on the palate. It also gains immeasurably with age, as its refinement and silkiness are not always evident when it is still young and still dominated by the *surmaturité* of the late-harvested grapes. It's much like an Amarone in its power and velvet, but with less obvious tannins and more of the warmth of Italy's south. Above all, it is an amazingly elegant and refined wine, especially with about 10 to 12 years of bottle age. Try all the old vintages you can find; this really is one of the world's great wines. Hopefully, the recent ownership change at Taurino won't have any ill effects on wine quality.

THE WINE

Grape varieties: negro amaro (100%); **Number of bottles:** 36,000; **Alcohol:** 14.5; **Retail price:** $60; **Try it with:** grilled lamb chops with mushrooms; **Imported by:** Winebow (www.winebow.com); **Past great vintages:** 1985, 1988, 1990, 2000

The '88 is a masterpiece of refined elegance and power, truly an iron fist in a velvet glove. Fine tannins and a very long finish in which the red cherry and smoky plum fruit go on and on (99/100). The '90 is just as good, less refined but richer, with a creamier mouthfeel and fleshier red cherry and raspberry fruit complemented by bay leaf and oregano accents (99/100).

THE PRODUCER: EREDI AZ. AGR. COSIMO TAURINO

Address: s.s. 605, 73010 Guagnano (Lecce); **Tel/fax:** 0832 706490/0832 706242; **Web:** www.taurinovini.it; **E-mail:** info@ taurinovini.it; **Total bottles:** 1.2 million; **Total ha:** 180; **Tasting room:** yes; **Visit:** by appointment; **Highway exit:** Bari (A14)

OTHER RECOMMENDED WINES UNDER $100 BY TAURINO:

"Notarpanaro" (negro amaro—small barrel oaked red).

25 | Chianti Classico Riserva
BADIA A COLTIBUONO • **94/100** • TUSCANY

One of my favorite Chiantis has always been that of charming Emanuela Stucchi Prinetti, who is surrounded by talent everywhere on this fantastically beautiful estate, an eleventh-century monastery. The name means "abbey of the good harvest"—an auspicious term, and with the superstar winemaker Maurizio Castelli, an expert in sangiovese, at the helm, you know Chianti isn't going to get any better, or any more authentic, than this. There's a lot to be said for a sangiovese wine that actually smells and tastes of sangiovese, and the area of Gaiole, in the heart of the Chianti Classico district, is a true *grand cru* for this variety. Stucchi

Prinetti's Riserva wine is now made with a very long maceration, even nine months, on the skins, a technique Castelli copied after having seen it applied by old Piedmontese farmers. As he liked the extra fat and body the sangiovese gains by this technique, he decided to implement it at Badia. Clearly, it is not an easy technique to use, as prolonged lees contact can cause unpleasant odors to develop: thus, a great deal of care and work is required in the cellar. The resulting wine, though, is splendid, a paradigm of finesse that proves wine doesn't have to be jammy to be explosively concentrated. This Chianti also speaks clearly of its cool microclimate, with a more than passing resemblance to a lighter *premier cru* Burgundy: light ruby hue, red currant, sour red cherry and tea leaf aromas, lots of nervy acidity, and a juicy, lip-smacking red fruit flavor. Remember, Coltibuono's lineup of wines is memorable; and you owe it to yourself not to miss the Vin Santo, one of Italy's very best.

THE WINE

Grape varieties: sangiovese (90%), canaiolo nero (10%); **Number of bottles:** 50,000; **Alcohol:** 13.5; **Retail price:** $30; **Try it with:** veal with prosciutto, sage, and butter sauce; **Imported by:** Dalla Terra (www.dallaterra.com); Classic Wine Imports (www.classicwineimports.com); **Past great vintages:** 1964, 1971,1982, 1985, 1988, 1997, 2001

The '82 was probably the best Chianti of the vintage, having an amazingly pure nose with hints of smoke and black cherry mingling with sour red cherry and truffle aromas (96/100). Fine acids give wonderful lift and precision. The '85 is a little jammier and rich, but pleasantly rich and smooth (94/100). The '88 is successful mix of the previous two, elegant and rich and with a mineral high- acid, long finish (95/100).

THE PRODUCER: BADIA A COLTIBUONO

Address: Loc. Badia a Coltibuono, 53013 Gaiole in Chianti (Siena); **Tel/fax:** 0577 746110/0577 746165; **E-mail:** info@coltibuono.com; **Web:** www.coltibuono.com; **Total bottles:** 1 million; **Total ha:** 72; **Visit:** by appointment; **Tasting room:** yes; **Highway exit:** Firenze Certosa or Valdarno (A1)

OTHER RECOMMENDED WINES UNDER $100 BY BADIA A COLTIBUONO:

Chianti "Cetamura" (sangiovese/canaiolo nero—unoaked red), Chianti Classico "RS" (sangiovese—small and large barrel oaked red), Chianti Classico "Cultus Boni" (sangiovese/merlot—large barrel oaked red), Chianti Classico (sangiovese/canaiolo—large barrel oaked red), Sangioveto (sangiovese—small barrel oaked red), Vin Santo del Chianti Classico (trebbiano toscano/malvasia—sweet white). Castelli and Prinetti tell me that starting with the '08 vintage, the "Cultis Boni" will no longer be made with merlot.

26 | Cesanese di Olevano Romano "Cirsium"
CANTINE CIOLLI • **94/100** • LAZIO

The rebirth of the wines of Lazio is embodied in the very fine wines made by Damiano Ciolli, a young man who has turned what used to be a sleepy domain into a high-quality estate. Its wines are among the very best, and least known, of Italy. That cesanese, a difficult grape that ripens late and grows in a cool part of Lazio's mountainous southern section, could yield excellent results was already evident in Renaissance times, when wines made from it were much sought after; but this legacy was lost in the twentieth century, when many poor, faulty wines were made. The "Cirsium" is a unique Cesanese, harvested late and then air-dried, made much in the manner of Amarone: you'll find the same fragrances and flavors of almost sweet ripe red cherry fruit and the high alcohol levels. The tannins, however, are a lot less brutal than those of Amarone, and the wine is easier to drink, with a lovely ultra-velvety mouthfeel. Cesanese is not considered a long-lived wine, but the truth is that not enough high-quality wines have been made, so the jury is still out. "Cirsium" is so enjoyable right upon release that aging it might well be an academic issue—I doubt that many people would want to defer gratification by cellaring it for any length of time. It's a shame that few wine lovers know about, and even fewer have written about, what is without question one of Italy's greatest red wines.

THE WINE

Grape varieties: cesanese d'Affile (100%); **Number of bottles:** 15,000; **Alcohol:** 14–14.5; **Retail price:** $40; **Try it with:** Oxtail *vaccinara* style (a typical dish of Roman cuisine, consisting of slow-cooked oxtail with tomatoes, carrots, celery, onion, and a small dose of powdered chocolate) is ideal, but any beef or lamb stew will do nicely; **Imported by:** David Vincent Selection; **Past great vintages:** 2003, 2004, 2005

The '03 is ultra-ripe and soft, but not jammy, with an inebriating aroma of ultra-ripe red cherries and plums macerated in alcohol, with tannins that aren't shy but are not unpleasant (98/100). The '04 is slightly more austere and closed on the nose, with great depth of fruit and extremely suave tannins (97/100). The '05 is lighter and elegant (93/100).

THE PRODUCER: CANTINE CIOLLI
Address: via del Corso, 00035 Olevano Romano (RM); **Tel/fax:** 06
9564547; **E-mail:** cantineciolli@alice.it; **Total bottles:** 20,000;
Total ha: 4.5; **Visit:** by appointment; **Tasting room:** yes; **Highway
exit:** Tivoli (A24)

OTHER RECOMMENDED WINES UNDER $100
BY DAMIANO CIOLLI:
Cesanese di Olevano Romano "Silene" (large barrel oaked red).

27 | "Le Pergole Torte"

MONTEVERTINE • **94/100** • TUSCANY

A blind tasting I organized in Toronto in 1983 or 1984
featuring the Chiantis of the '77 vintage is one of the unforgettable experiences of my life. That evening, the Chianti of Sergio Manetti (it was still so labeled then) blew
all the others away. It was an amazingly fine wine, on a
par with, though obviously different from, a couple of famous '75 red Bordeaux we had with the dinner that followed. Today Sergio's son Martino is proudly continuing
the tradition, and his most recent wines are in the mold
of some of the best made by his father. If you haven't already tried it and if it isn't sold out at your favorite wineshop, the "Montevertine" '01 is absolutely delicious, a
wine of crystalline class. The "Pergole Torte," one of the
most famous of all super-Tuscans, was first made in '77
and is the estate's top wine. It is textbook, almost benchmark sangiovese. Medium deep ruby, brilliantly fruity on
the nose with intriguing mineral, underbrush, and tobacco elements adding interest and complexity, it is also
suavely tannic and persistent, though it always tastes best
with at least four to five years of bottle age. In short, it's
everything that great sangiovese ought to be but seldom
is in the hands of less serious or less gifted producers.

THE WINE
Grape varieties: sangiovese (100%); **Number of bottles:** 23,000;
Alcohol: 13.5; **Retail price:** $90; **Try it with:** braised calves' cheeks
and rosemary-mashed potatoes; **Imported by:** Rosenthal Wine
Merchants (www.madrose.com); **Past great vintages:** 1979, 1982,
1983, 1985, 1988, 1990, 2001, 2003, 2004

THE PRODUCER: AZ. AGR. MONTEVERTINE ·
Address: Loc. Montevertine, 53017 Radda in Chianti (Siena);
Tel/fax: 0577 738009/0577 738265; **Web:** www.montevertine.it;
E-mail: info@montevertine.it; **Total bottles:** 60,000; **Total ha:** 11;

Tasting room: yes; **Visit:** by appointment; **Highway exit:** Valdarno or Firenze Certosa (A1)

OTHER RECOMMENDED WINES UNDER $100 BY MONTEVERTINE:
"Pian del Ciampolo" (sangiovese/canaiolo/colorino—light large barrel oaked red), "Montevertine" (sangiovese/canaiolo/colorino—large barrel oaked red).

28 | Chianti Rufina Riserva "Bucerchiale"
SELVAPIANA • 94/100 • TUSCANY

People are often surprised to learn that one of Italy's very best wines is a Chianti Rufina. In fact, the Riserva Bucerchiale bottling of Selvapiana is to my mind one of the three best Chiantis of all, one that illustrates clearly the differences between the two Chianti *terroirs*. Rufina, located northeast of the Classico area, is the home of wines that have leaner but more elegant textures, have higher acidities, and stand the test of time better. Francesco Giuntini's wines at Selvapiana are proof of just how well Chianti can age; bottles from the 1950s are still in fabulous shape. His base Chianti, often overlooked in favor of his more famous Riserva, is absolutely delicious, and a steal for the price. Even better, and still vary fairly priced, is the "Bucerchiale," which epitomizes everything great Chianti should be (but unfortunately often isn't): it has a medium- light hue typical of sangiovese; aromas of violets, porcini, and strawberries; and loads of crispy juicy red currant, strawberry, and licorice flavors with mouth-cleansing fresh acidity and tannins. The consultant winemaker Franco Bernabei understands sangiovese as few others do, and it shows. *Buonissimo!*

THE WINE
Grape varieties: sangiovese, canaiolo; **Number of bottles:** 26,000; **Alcohol:** 13; **Retail price:** $35; **Try it with:** Arezzo-style pappardelle (a large, flat pasta with duck meat sauce), seared sweetbreads with artichoke-eggplant hash; **Imported by:** Winebow (www.winbow.com); Ideal Wine and Spirits (www.idealwine.us); **Past great vintages:** 1979, 1985, 1988, 1990, 1997, 2001, 2003, 2004.

The '03 is spectacular considering the vintage, but cooler Rufina benefited (94/100). The '85 is a masterpiece, with elegant red cherry and raspberry notes mingling with tobacco and fine leather. Suave tannins and a long finish make this an outstanding Chianti (97/100). The '90 is just as good if slightly less fruity, with a silky mouthfeel, high acids, and plenty of ripe fruit on the long finish (97/100). Note that the '75, '56, and '47 were labeled simply Riserva and are still fine wines.

THE PRODUCER: FATTORIA SELVAPIANA
Address: via Selvapiana 3, 50068 Rufina (Firenze); **Tel/fax:** 055 8369848 / 055 8319605; **Web:** www.selvapiana.it; **E-mail:** selvapiana@tin.it; **Total bottles:** 150,000; **Total ha:** 45; **Tasting room:** yes; **Visit:** by appointment; **Highway exit:** Firenze sud (A1)

OTHER RECOMMENDED WINES UNDER $100
BY SELVAPIANA:
Chianti Rufina (sangiovese/canaiolo—large barrel oaked red), Chianti Rufina Riserva (sangiovese/canaiolo—small barrel oaked red).

29 | Gattinara "Osso San Grato"
ANTONIOLO • **94/100** • PIEDMONT

I wonder sometimes what it must feel like to be an Antoniolo—a member of the family that is unquestionably the best at making a wine famous throughout history, but that rarely garners the praise it merits. Gattinara is a wine not nearly as popular as it ought to be, in part owing to the more rigid climate of the Novara Hills, where nebbiolo doesn't always ripen as fully as it does in nearby Barolo and Barbaresco. The splintering of ownership doesn't help, either. There are only 120 hectares in all, but these have 100 different owners; and of the 100 only about 15 bottle on their own, the others preferring to sell the grapes. True connoisseurs search far and wide for the better examples, nebbiolos of great breed, amazing refinement, and a seductive persistence that lingers on the palate. The volcanic soils have a certain percentage of sand that help develop wines of greater perfume and lighter frames. Of all the Gattinaras made by Antoniolo—and they're all great—I prefer the more traditional "Osso San Grato," the toughest to appreciate when young. Its unusual name (*osso* in Italian means bone) derives from the tough, steep, rocky terrain of the terraced vineyard. Sinewy, brooding, even shy at first, the wine opens slowly, but really comes into its own after about 10 years of bottle age. Make no mistake about it: at that time, it is a far better, more elegant, and more enjoyable wine than many famous Barolos and Barbarescos. The other Gattinaras by Antoniolo are fine, too. The "San Francesco" ages in large casks and tonneaux, whereas the "Caselle" ages in new and once-used *barriques*, or small oak barrels.

THE WINE

Grape varieties: nebbiolo (100%); **Number of bottles:** 4,000; **Alcohol:** 13.5–14; **Retail price:** $59; **Try it with:** leg of lamb with white beans and onions; creamy polenta with mascarpone and porcini mushrooms; **Imported by:** Marc de Grazia Selection (www.marcdegrazia.com; numerous importers); **Past great vintages:** 1978, 1979, 1982, 1989, 1990, 1996, 2001

THE PRODUCER: AZ. AGR. ANTONIOLO

Address: corso Valsesia 277, 13045 Gattinara (Vercelli); **Tel/fax:** 0163 833612/0163 826112; **E-mail:** antoniolovini@bmm.it; **Total bottles:** 55,000; **Total ha:** 15; **Visit:** by appointment; **Tasting room:** yes; **Highway exit:** Greggio (A4) or Romagnano-Ghemme (A26)

OTHER RECOMMENDED WINES UNDER $100 BY ANTONIOLO:

Rosato Coste della Sesia "Bricco Lorella" (nebbiolo/bonarda/vespolina—unoaked rosé), Gattinara San Francesco (large barrel and small barrel oaked red), Gattinara Castelle (small barrel oaked red).

The small barrels used for the San Francesco are in reality the 500-liter tonneaux.

30 | "Giusto di Notri"
TUA RITA • 94/100 • TUSCANY

The owners, Rita and Virgilio Tua, were blessed when young Stefano Frascolla became their son-in-law. His passion and talent for wine making helped turn an estate where the initial concept of wine making was "Let's try and see what happens," and was more or less a hobby, into one of Italy's most exciting and very best addresses. The Merlot "Redigaffi," a cult wine if ever there was one, would be reason enough to be happy, but the fact is that all the other wines here are also fantastic. The "Giusto di Notri" is almost as good as the "Redigaffi" but gets less attention from the press and fewer rave reviews. It is dark in color, almost brooding, with a litany of blackberry, roasted coffee bean, and bitter chocolate aromas, and there's an inky, herbal twist livening things up. Again, it is a touch inky and herbal on the palate, with a rich, suave mouthfeel and an extremely long finish showcasing a definite saline quality. Stefano also has a couple of small barrels of 50% cabernet franc–50% petit verdot that would be exceptional on their own as a new wine, but he blends them in here.

THE WINE

Grape varieties: cabernet sauvignon (50%), cabernet franc (15%), merlot (30%), petit verdot (5%); **Number of bottles:** 30,000; **Alcohol:** 14–14.5; **Retail price:** $60–90; **Try it with:** wild boar stew with baked eggplant, zucchini, and parmigiano tortino; **Imported by:** Winebow; **Past great vintages:** 2001, 2004, 2006. The latter is the best ever made.

THE PRODUCER: TUA RITA

Address: Loc. Notri 81, 57028 Suvereto (LI); **Tel/fax:** 0565 829237/0565 829237; **E-mail:** info@tuarita.it; **Web:** www.tuarita.it; **Total bottles:** 100,000; **Total ha:** 22; **Visit:** by appointment; **Tasting room:** yes; **Highway exit:** Rosignano (A12)

OTHER RECOMMENDED WINES UNDER $100 BY TUA RITA:

"Lodano" (chardonnay/gewürztraminer/riesling—small barrel oaked white), "Rosso di Notri" (sangiovese/others—unoaked red), "Perlato del Bosco" (sangiovese/ syrah—small barrel oaked red), Syrah (small barrel oaked red).

31 | Etna Rosso Feudo di Mezzo "Il Quadro delle Rose"

TENUTA DELLE TERRE NERE • **94/100** • SICILY

This is a relatively new estate owned by one of the best-known importers of Italian wines into the United States. After the energetic, bright Marc de Grazia had done so much for wines of others, and for Italian wine in general, it must have seemed logical to him to take part in his own winery operation. The Etna wine area is one of the undeniable up-and-coming stars of Italy, and de Grazia did well to to start up in this part of Italy. The estate has been turning heads, owing to the obviously high quality of its wines: a fantastic and exceptionally priced white, a great rosé, and four red wines, including this "Quadro delle Rose," which earns my top mark. Rich and ripe on the nose with plenty of red cherry, raspberry, and balsamic aromas, it is less minerally than many other wines made with the nerello mascalese variety, wines that often leave you thinking of drinking liquid stones. That being said, this also has a much less than common amount of enticingly plump, pure, and juicy red fruit (as opposed to many other nerello mascalese wines that are leaner) to greet you on the palate. The creamy, complex finish is so redolent of yellow flowers, sea breeze, raspberry, red currant, and blackberry notes it seems to last in your mouth well into the next year.

THE WINE
Grape varieties: nerello mascalese (100%); **Number of bottles:** 5,200; **Alcohol:** 13.5; **Retail price:** $40; **Try it with:** roast chicken with basil mashed potatoes; **Imported by:** Marc de Grazia Selection (www.marcdegrazia.com; numerous importers); **Past great vintages:** 2004, 2005

THE PRODUCER: TENUTA DELLE TERRE NERE
Address: Contrada Calderara, 95036 Randazzo (Catania); **Tel/fax:** 095 924002; **Web:** www.marcdegrazia.com; **E-mail:** marco@ marcdegrazia.com; **Total bottles:** about 74,000; **Total ha:** 15; **Tasting room:** yes; **Visit:** by appointment; **Highway exit:** Giardini Naxos or Fiumefreddo (A16)

OTHER RECOMMENDED WINES UNDER $100
BY TERRE NERE:
"Bianco delle Terre Nere" (carricante/catarratto/grecanico/ inzolia/chardonnay—unoaked white), Etna Rosato (nerello mascalese—small barrel oaked rosé) Etna Rosso Calderara Sottana (nerello mascalese/nerello cappuccino—small barrel oaked red), Etna Rosso vigneto Guardiola (nerello mascalese/ nerello cappuccino—small barrel oaked red), Etna Rosso Prephylloxera (small barrel oaked red).

32 | Barolo "Bricco Boschis"
FRATELLI CAVALLOTTO • 93/100 • PIEDMONT

More than five generations of Cavallottos have been making very fine traditionally styled wines. The estate owns vineyards in two sections of Castiglione Falletto, an area that can potentially give the most balanced Barolos: Vignolo and Bricco Boschis. The latter was subdivided in 1961 in the three vineyards (Vigna San Giuseppe, Vigna Colle Sud-Ovest, and Vigna Punta Marcello) whose names you'll still find on older bottlings from this estate. In an effort to simplify matters for the consumer, the Cavallottos have recently decided to use only three names for their Barolos: Bricco Boschis and the Riservas Vignolo and Bricco Boschis San Giuseppe. The Bricco Boschis is as close to a "base" wine as there is, but very little about these wines is ever basic. You'll love its ripe red cherry and strawberry aromas of great depth, the soft yet rich mouthfeel, and the lovely mineral hint on the long, very pure finish.

This estate also makes a small number of bottles of Grignolino and of Freisa, two of the absolutely most delicious examples of these varieties, and I urge you to try them.

THE WINE
Grape varieties: nebbiolo (100%); **Number of bottles:** 18,000; **Alcohol:** 14–14.5; **Retail price:** $40–65; **Try it with:** chateaubriand with creamed spinach; **Imported by:** Marc de Grazia Selection (www.marcdegrazia.com; numerous importers); **Past great vintages:** 1971, 1982, 1999, 2001

The '71 is much better in the Riserva Speciale version, though the *normale* is fine too, with chunkier red fruit and a smoother mouthfeel (94/100). The '82 is a lovely Barolo with raspberry and violet aromas, smooth tannins, and sneaky concentration (94/100). Both the '99 and the '01 are noticeably richer and bigger than the others, with a creamier mouthfeel. The '99 is softer and more forward (92/100) than the '01, which has greater flavor intensity and length (93/100).

THE PRODUCER: TENUTA VITIVINICOLA
CAVALLOTTO—BRICCO BOSCHIS
Address: via Alba-Monforte, Loc. Bricco Boschis, 12060 Castiglione Falletto (Cuneo); **Tel/fax:** 0173 62814 / 0173 62914; **E-mail:** info@cavallotto.com; **Web:** www.cavallotto.com; **Total bottles:** 110,000; **Total ha:** 23; **Visit:** by appointment; **Tasting room:** yes; **Highway exit:** Ast est (A21)

OTHER RECOMMENDED WINES UNDER $100
BY FRATELLI CAVALLOTTO:
Freisa Bricco Boschis (unoaked red), Grignolino (red) Dolcetto d'Alba Vigna Scot (unoaked red), Dolcetto d'Alba Vigna Melera (large barrel oaked red), Barbera d'Alba Vigna del Cuculo (large barrel oaked red).

The Barolos Bricco Boschis Riserva Vigna San Giuseppe and Riserva Vignolo are stellar, but both retail at over $100.

33[*] | Vino Nobile di Montepulciano
| DEI • **93/100** • TUSCANY

It's hard not to like Maria Caterina Dei, owner of an estate that was producing wine back in the 1930s but really took off only when she arrived in 1991, following a successful career in theater. With the help of the consultant winemaker

Niccolò d'Afflitto (the longtime winemaker of Frescobaldi) since 1993, there was a further surge in quality, and Dei's wines are now some of the best of Montepulciano. Vino Nobile di Montepulciano, made with the prugnolo gentile subvariety of sangiovese, is a great introduction to the finer wines of Tuscany, as it's usually enjoyable when young, though it will repay handsomely those who wish to cellar bottles for 10 to 12 years. Dei's base Nobile is deep ruby, appealing in its up-front fruity, spicy, and slightly balsamic aromas, and in its elegantly structured, sleek, high-acid yet flavorful, clean finish. This wine may lack the extra punch of intensity the estate's Riserva "Bossona" will give you, but you'll be charmed by the suave, refreshing red berry and black cherry aromas and flavors it exudes right from the first sip.

THE WINE

Grape varieties: prugnolo gentile (80%), canaiolo nero (15%), mammolo (5%); **Number of bottles:** 90,000; **Alcohol:** 13–13.5; **Retail price:** $20; **Try it with:** pan-roasted skirt steak with onion and peppercorn sauce; **Imported by:** Marc de Grazia Selection (www.marcdegrazia.com; numerous importers); **Past great vintages:** 1990, 1996, 1997, 1998, 1999, 2001. The 1996 is refined and delicate in its high acid red cherry aromas and flavors, and has tremendous length (92/100). The '98 is fruitier and richer on the palate with smooth tannins and a long finish (93/100).

THE PRODUCER: AZIENDA AGRICOLA MARIA CATERINA DEI

Address: via di Martiena 35, 53045 Montepulciano (Siena); **Tel/fax:** 0578 716878/0578 758680; **Web:** www.cantinedei.com; **E-mail:** info@cantinedei.com; **Total bottles:** 200,000; **Total ha:** 37; **Tasting room:** yes; **Visit:** by appointment; **Highway exit:** Chiusi or Val di Chiana (A1)

OTHER RECOMMENDED WINES UNDER $100 BY DEI:

Rosso di Montepulciano (prugnolo gentile/canaiolo nero—large barrel oaked red), Vino Nobile di Montepulciano Riserva Bossona (prugnolo gentile—large and small barrel oaked red). The small barrels referred to for the latter wine are tonneaux.

34 | Taurasi Riserva "Radici"
MASTROBERARDINO • 93/100 • CAMPANIA

After three centuries of wine making and counting, the Mastroberardino family truly has one of the great names in

Italian wine and deserves credit for saving native varieties such as fiano, almost extinct in the 1950s. Today its best wine is the Taurasi (especially the Riserva bottling), but the base wine, always well made, is a great buy considering price for quality. Fresh and easy to drink, this exhibits less of the now prevalent jammy red fruit characteristic of many modern-day Taurasis, preferring to play the more traditionally and varietally accurate cards: rose petal, sour red cherry, and delicate tobacco aromas. In the mouth it is crammed with fruit, and though the high acidity keeps it seemingly light and lively, it has plenty of structure. A wine that manages to be easygoing yet serious and with great aging potential: the 1968 Riserva bottling is one of Italy's best-ever reds (the special Montemarano and Piano d'Angelo bottlings from '68 are fine, too). There is also a beautiful country hotel where you can stay and soak up the many beautiful aspects of this part of Italy: sun, art, food, and wine.

THE WINE

Grape varieties: aglianico (100%); **Number of bottles:** 80,000; **Alcohol:** 13.5; **Retail price:** $60–95; **Try it with:** quail with peas; daube of beef with red lentil stew; **Imported by:** Winebow (www.winebow.com); **Past great vintages:** 1968, 1971, 1975, 1985, 1989, 1990, 1997, 2000, 2003

THE PRODUCER: AZIENDA VINICOLA MICHELE MASTROBERARDINO

Address: via Manfredi 75–81, 83042 Atripalda (Avellino); **Tel/fax:** 0825 614111/0825 614231; **Web:** www.mastroberardino.com; **E-mail:** mastro@mastroberardino.com; **Total bottles:** 2.4 million; **Total ha:** 300; **Tasting room:** yes; **Visit:** by appointment; **Highway exit:** Avellino Est (A16)

OTHER RECOMMENDED WINES UNDER $100 BY MASTROBERARDINO:

Greco di Tufo "Nova Serra" (unoaked white), Fiano di Avellino "Radici" (unoaked white), Bianco "Avalon" (coda di volpe/others—unoaked white), Taurasi "Radici" (aglianico—small and large barrel oaked red).

35 | Chianti Classico
CASTELLO DI AMA • **93/100** • TUSCANY

There is undoubtedly a gap in quality between Castello di Ama's base Chianti and the single vineyard bottlings "Sanlorenzo" and "La Casuccia," but there is also a gap in price. In any case, this is always one of the better Chiantis. Kudos to Lorenza Sebaste and Marco Pallanti, a husband-and-wife team; they have always believed in the potential of great Chianti and set out in the 1980s to prove it, succeeding admirably. Their wine is very faithful to the *terroir* of Gaiole in Chianti (though at times the merlot presence makes itself felt, something that dismays Marco to no end and that he tries to avoid having happen), a cool microclimate in which the vineyards are located higher up, at about 1,600 feet above sea level. It has a bracing acidity that nicely delineates the violet, red currant, tea leaf, licorice, and quinine aromas and flavors. No extra-plump fruit here, but what this wine lacks in juiciness it makes up for with some of the prettiest perfumes you'll ever get a sniff of in Chianti. In fact, in some vintages, its aromas are downright pinot noiresque. You'll love this effortless and delicious drink, and it will age surprisingly well. And if you want to splurge, besides the two *cru* bottlings mentioned above, keep in mind the Merlot "L'Apparita"—one of Italy's very best reds and a true cult wine.

THE WINE

Grape varieties: sangiovese (80%), canaiolo (8%), malvasia nera and merlot (12%); **Number of bottles:** 150,000; **Retail price:** $50; **Try it with:** crostini with spleen or chicken liver and innards; roast rabbit with mustard; **Imported by:** Sorting Table (www .thesortingtable.com), Martin Scott Wines (www .martinscottwines.com); **Past great vintages:** 1997, 1999, 2000, 2001, 2003, 2004

THE PRODUCER: CASTELLO DI AMA

Address: Fraz. Lecchi, Loc. Ama, 53013 Gaiole in Chianti (Siena); **Tel/fax:** 0577 746031/0577 746117; **Web:** www.castellodiama.com; **E-mail:** info@castellodiama.com; **Total bottles:** 270,000; **Total ha:** 80; **Tasting room:** yes; **Visit:** by appointment; **Highway exit:** Valdarno or Firenze Certosa (A1)

36 | Taurasi "Macchia dei Goti"
ANTONIO CAGGIANO • 93/100 • CAMPANIA

This may well be a very modern interpretation of Taurasi, with its silky tannins and deep, extremely rich fruit, but it also happens to be one of the best, a wine that makes it really hard for you to put the glass down. Antonio Caggiano is one of the true stars of the area, and this is all the more remarkable because the estate was founded as recently as

1990 and the first grapes were vinified in 1994. An amazing cellar, three levels deep and built entirely of stone, is a sight to behold and a sign of Caggiano's commitment to quality. Also, the consulting winemaker Luigi Moio is one of the best in Italy and who knows aglianico like no other. All of Caggiano's wines are at least very good, including a rich, excellent Fiano called Béchar. Of the many various Aglianico wines he makes, the "Macchia dei Goti" is in a class all its own, with an incredibly rich, smoky, and very ripe set of black cherry, plum, and blackberry aromas, and a creamy rich mouthfeel with loads of black cherry and plum flavors with vanilla and balsamic highlights.

THE WINE

Grape varieties: aglianico (100%); **Number of bottles:** 18,000; **Alcohol:** 14–14.5; **Retail price:** $48; **Try it with:** braised lamb shank with roasted bell pepper salad; **Imported by:** Marc de Grazia Selection (www.marcdegrazia.com; numerous importers); **Past great vintages:** 1994, 1995, 1996, 2001

THE PRODUCER: AZ. AGR. ANTONIO CAGGIANO

Address: Contrada Sala, 83030 Taurasi (Avellino); **Tel/fax:** 0827 74043/0827 74043; **E-mail:** info@cantinecaggiano.it; **Web:** www.cantinecaggiano.it; **Total bottles:** 150,000; **Total ha:** 20; **Visit:** by appointment; **Tasting room:** yes; **Highway exit:** Grottaminarda or Benevento (A16)

OTHER RECOMMENDED WINES UNDER $100
BY ANTONIO CAGGIANO:

"Béchar" (fiano—small barrel oaked white), "Devon" (greco—small barrel oaked white), "Taurì" (aglianico—small barrel oaked red), "Mel" (greco/fiano—sweet white).

37 | Sagrantino di Montefalco
ANTONELLI • 93/100 • UMBRIA

Some people believe the name of Sagrantino derives from its past use in religious services, thanks to a high tannin content that allowed it to keep well. This being Italy, there's disagreement. Grown only in Umbria, where high-quality viticulture (with few exceptions) lagged behind the rest of Italy for a long time, the sagrantino grape was in danger of extinction only 15 years ago. Since then, thanks to the efforts of star producers such as Marco Caprai and Antonelli, it has enjoyed great success and has become one of Italy's most amazing wine stories, with many high-quality producers appearing on the scene. Antonelli's version is a wonderfully drinkable one, and there's something to be said for not having your mouth locked in a tannic vise. Pretty medium ruby, it has intense aromas of lilies, red currants, and cherries, with a delicate spicy twist. Lovely raspberry, strawberry, and plum flavors are nicely delineated by bright acids. Finely textured on the palate with assertive but smooth and silky tannins, it has a long, suave finish and a mineral, herbal nuance. Filippo Antonelli has managed to civilize the grape and has made an eminently enjoyable wine that is wonderfully balanced—you won't even notice the 16 degrees alcohol!

THE WINE

Grape varieties: sagrantino (100%); **Number of bottles:** 60,000; **Alcohol:** 14.5; **Retail price:** $31–45; **Try it with:** pork tenderloin with juniper berries and pureed potatoes; **Imported by:** Vino Bravo (www.vinobravo.com); **Past great vintages:** 1990, 2000, 2001

THE PRODUCER: ANTONELLI SAN MARCO

Address: Loc. San Marco 59, 06036 Montefalco (Perugia); **Tel/fax:** 0742 379158/0742 371063; **Web:** www.antonellisanmarco.it; **E-mail:** info@antonellisanmarco.it; **Total bottles:** 250,000; **Total ha:** 30; **Tasting room:** yes; **Visit:** by appointment; **Highway exit:** Orte (A1)

OTHER RECOMMENDED WINES UNDER $100 BY ANTONELLI:

Montefalco Rosso (sangiovese/sagrantino/merlot/cabernet sauvignon—large barrel oaked red), Montefalco Rosso Riserva (sangiovese/sagrantino/cabernet sauvignon—large and small barrel oaked red), Montefalco Sagrantino Passito (sweet red).

38 | Aglianico "Terra d'Eclano"

QUINTODECIMO • **91/100** • CAMPANIA

You always know it's a good sign when you have trouble picking just one wine from an estate, when they're all so good that you're truly left in a quandary. Congratulations to Luigi Moio, a winemaker to many fine estates who has also finally set out to produce his own wines in the brand-new estate called Quintodecimo (construction of the winery is still not completely finished). Located in Mirabella d'Eclano, long considered a top spot for quality aglianico, Moio makes only three wines, with another, a Taurasi from the single vineyard Quintodecimo due out next year. In the meantime, wine lovers can choose from a very good Falanghina and an excellent Fiano (and barrel samples of the new vintage are even better than what is already in bottle), but the best current wine is the Aglianico "Terra d'Eclano," a rich, heady blockbuster with voluptuous structure and length. Brimming with ripe red cherry and leather flavors, enlivened by a hint of ink and black pepper, this is an impressive wine from the very first mouthful. It also has the power and strength to age rather effortlessly, and it will be much better than it already is about five years after the vintage, once the tannins have resolved a bit.

THE WINE

Grape varieties: aglianico (100%); **Number of bottles:** 5,500; **Alcohol:** 13.5; **Retail price:** $50–60; **Try it with:** rib eye with thyme- and oregano-accented tomato sauce; **Imported by:** Supreme Wines (www.supremewines.net); **Past great vintages:** 2005

THE PRODUCER: AZ. AGR. QUINTODECIMO

Address: via San Leonardo, 83036 Mirabella Eclano (Avellino); **Tel/fax:** 0825 449321/0825 449321; **E-mail:** info@quintodecimo.it; **Web:** www.quintodecimo.it; **Total bottles:** 20,000; **Total ha:** 6; **Visit:** by appointment; **Tasting room:** yes; **Highway exit:** Benevento or Grottaminarda (A16)

OTHER RECOMMENDED WINES UNDER $100 BY QUINTODECIMO:

Falanghina "Via del Campo" (unoaked white), Fiano "Exultet" (small barrel oaked white).

39* "Zinfandel"

SINFAROSA—ACCADEMIA DEI RACEMI •
93/100 • PUGLIA

The Accademia dei Racemi project took Italy by storm when it was announced in the 1980s, and the impressive wines made were only part of the picture. Small producers who had previously been unable to follow vineyards and cellar procedures properly, or to market their wines effectively, united under the Accademia umbrella and were given technical and logistical support. Of the many fine wines made by various affiliated estates, the Primitivo by Felline (the first truly modern, non-rustic Taurasi

Primitivo from Puglia), and Sinfarosa's version called Zinfandel (it prefers to use the American name for its top Primitivo) are always the best. Over time, the latter has shone for elegance and refinement while maintaining typical Zinfandel aromas and flavors. Remember that most Italian Zinfandels shy away from the overly jammy, alcoholic style of some American versions, and Sinfarosa is the best example of a more laid-back approach to the grape (vintage permitting). Pretty aromas of red cherries, tobacco, and leather; silky tannins; and an easy, polished delivery of red fruit and spicy flavors, with more tobacco and leather on the medium-long finish, will win you over.

THE WINE
Grape varieties: primitivo (100%); **Number of bottles:** 36,000; **Alcohol:** 14; **Retail price:** $16–32; **Try it with:** grilled sausages; spaghetti with tomato and meat sauce; **Imported by:** Martin Scott Wines (www.martinscottwines.com); **Past great vintages:** 1998, 2000, 2001, 2005. The '05 is the richest, jammiest wine ever made by Sinfarosa, almost resembling a Helen Turley wine.

THE PRODUCER: SINFAROSA—ACCADEMIA DEI RACEMI
Address: via Santo Stasi 1, zona industriale, 74024 Manduria (Taranto); **Tel/fax:** 099 9711660/099 9711530; **Web:** www.accademiadeiracemi.it; **E-mail:** accademia@accademiadeiracemi.it; **Total bottles:** 100,000; **Total ha:** 30; **Tasting room:** yes; **Visit:** by appointment; **Highway exit:** Taranto nord (A14)

OTHER RECOMMENDED WINES UNDER $100 BY ACCADEMIA DEI RACEMI:
Masseria Pepe Primitivo di Manduria "Dunico" (small barrel oaked red), Torre Guaceto "Dedalo" (ottavianello—unoaked red), Torre Guaceto "Sum" (susumaniello—small barrel oaked red), Felline "Vigna del Feudo" (primitivo/malvasia nera/ottavianello—small barrel oaked red), Felline Primitivo di Manduria (small barrel oaked red), Pervini Primitivo di Manduria "Archidamo" (small barrel oaked red).

40 | Aglianico del Vulture "Don Anselmo"
PATERNOSTER • **93/100** • BASILICATA

Founded in 1925, Paternoster is the oldest high-quality estate of Basilicata. It succeeds admirably with a slew of wines, and this is the least you'd expect from a producer situated in a town called Barile ("barrel"), whose coat of arms depicts a child holding a bunch of grapes! The "Don Anselmo" bottling is the more traditional Aglianico of the maker's two top bottlings (so if you like rich ripe fruit you'll be better off picking its "Rotondo" bottling). Though it has pretty red cherry and rose petal aromas, these take time to develop in the glass, where you'll also detect aromas of leather, tobacco, and mushrooms. Powerful and long on the palate, with fine acidity and smooth tannins, it has plenty of red plum, tobacco, leather, and truffle nuances. The recently finished state-of-the-art winery is a joy to visit. Get Vito Paternoster, a boyish-looking, super-nice man, to take you to the old family cellar in downtown Barile, for that will give you an idea of how wine used to be made in Italy.

THE WINE
Grape varieties: aglianico (100%); **Number of bottles:** 12,000; **Alcohol:** 13.5; **Retail price:** $54; **Try it with:** fried pork with bell peppers (a local dish); **Imported by:** Quintessential Wines (www.quintessentialwines.com); **Past great vintages:** 1990, 1997, 1998, 2004

The 1997 is one of the best red wines made in Italy in the past 20 years, with unusual depth and lovely smoky red cherry and raspberry aromas and flavors with a hint of leather (98/100). All these wines have aged splendidly and taste considerably better today than upon first release. The '90 is charming and supple, with underbrush and red cherry notes (95/100).

THE PRODUCER: PATERNOSTER
Address: via Nazionale 23, 85022 Barile (Potenza); **Tel/fax:** 0972 770736; **Web:** www.paternostervini.it; **E-mail:** info@paternoster vini.it; **Total bottles:** 140,000; **Total ha:** 20; **Tasting room:** yes; **Visit:** by appointment; **Highway exit:** Candela or Foggia (A16)

OTHER RECOMMENDED WINES UNDER $100
BY PATERNOSTER:
"Barigliott" (aglianico—unoaked sparkling red), Aglianico del Vulture "Rotondo" (small barrel oaked red), "Clivus" (white muscat—sparkling sweet white).

41 | Torgiano Rosso Riserva Vigna Monticchio
LUNGAROTTI • 93/100 • UMBRIA

Lungarotti was for the longest time the only name to consider when looking for a high-quality wine, white or red, from Umbria. Today there may be a few more Umbrian names to choose from, but Lungarotti is still your best bet for a good to great wine, depending on how much you want to spend. The Riserva Vigna Monticchio is the most famous name in their lineup, one of the truly great sangiovese-based wines Italy has made over the years. Older vintages are fantastic, and it is fascinating to see how Italian wine making has changed over the years: whereas the wines of the 1960s and 1970s rely on lovely balance and high acidities nicely chiseling the ripe red strawberry and red currant aromas and flavors present, recent efforts showcase riper, almost jammy red and black fruit. Still, modern-day Vigna Monticchio always avoids jamminess and maintains a measure of refinement even in the hottest years, a specific characteristic of this wine that is in no small measure due to the large presence of canaiolo nero, a native Italian grape that used to be considered the ideal complement to sangiovese (and rightly so), whereas merlot, syrah, and cabernet sauvignon used by many producers today as sangiovese's partner often turn the sangiovese-based wines into heavier, often charmless behemoths. The estate is run today with real charm and flair by the two daughters of the founder, the more laid-back Maria Teresa (please, call her Teresa!), the first woman ever to graduate from enology school in Umbria, and Chiara, who has seemingly boundless amounts of energy. Regardless of whom you meet at the estate, you'll greatly enjoy the company and will be fascinated by yet another example of the strong Italian women that have so fashioned Italy throughout the centuries. Don't forget to grab a meal at the estate's truly beautiful country restaurant, called Le Tre Vaselle, and to visit the Lungarotti wine museum, one of the best of its kind in Italy.

THE WINE

Grape variety: sangiovese (70%), canaiolo nero (30%); **Number of bottles:** 50,000; **Alcohol:** 13.5; **Retail price:** $60–75; **Try it with:** lamb chops with tarragon; **Imported by:** Bedford International (www.winesfrombedford.com) **Past great vintages:** 1968, 1975, 1977, 1982, 1988, 1990, 2004

The '68 is still great after all these years, with a delicate garnet hue and very fine tannins, a marvel of balance (95/100). The '90 is a bigger wine by the standards of this estate, where finesse usually predominates: rich and round, with plenty of ripe red cherry and tea leaf notes, it is drinking beautifully (91/100). The '04 is superb: balanced, luscious, and long, it is a little riper and jammier than most of its ancestors, but is balanced and elegant (93/100).

THE PRODUCER AZ. AGR. LUNGAROTTI
Address: Via Mario Angeloni 16, 06089 Torgiano (Perugia);
Tel/fax: 075 988661/075 9886650; **E-mail:** lungarotti@lungarotti
.it; **Web:** www.lungarotti.it; **Total bottles:** 2,900,000; **Total ha:**
roughly 310; **Visit:** by appointment; **Tasting room:** yes; **Highway
exit:** Valdichiana or Orte (A1)

OTHER RECOMMENDED WINES UNDER $100 BY
LUNGAROTTI:
Torgiano Bianco Torre di Giano Vigna Il Pino (trebbiano/
grechetto—small barrel oaked white), Torgiano Rosso "Rubesco"
(sangiovese/canaiolo nero—red).

42 | Barbera d'Asti "Bricco dell'Uccellone"

BRAIDA • **93/100** • PIEDMONT

A sip of this wine is a sip of history. Created in the late
1970s by Giacomo Bologna, it was the first Barbera to be
aged in small oak barrels, and the wine, rich and complex,
was an utter revelation to everybody in Italy. Until then,
barbera had always been thought of as a workhorse grape,
capable only of giving everyday, tavern-style potables:
cheery, fun, ideal with hearty foods, but nothing more. The
Bricco dell'Uccellone changed all that and takes its place
alongside other important names in Italy's wine history,
such as Sassicaia and Gaja's Barbaresco. Today the wine is
as good as ever: it has a purple-ruby color, smoky plum and
blackberry aromas nicely lifted by violet and balsamic
touches, and a rich suave mouthfeel loaded with ripe red
and black cherry flavors that will leave you wishing for another glass right away. Barbera's trademark high acidity is
still present, and though it is somewhat tamed—thanks to
the small barrel treatment—there's still plenty of it to keep
this medium-bodied, fruity red wine highly refreshing and
long on the palate. Keep in mind that you won't go wrong
with any of the wines made by Braida: its Grignolino is one
of Italy's best; the Brachetto is a lovely aromatic lightly
sweet dessert wine your frends will love; and all the different Barberas made are splendid.

THE WINE
Grape varieties: barbera (100%); **Number of bottles:** 55,000;
Alcohol: 13.5; **Retail price:** $60; **Try it with:** goulash; grilled
hamburgers; **Imported by:** Vinifera Imports (www.vinifera-il
.com); **Past great vintages:** 1979, 1982, 1985, 1988, 1989, 1990,
2001; note that this wine is very fine even in less highly regarded
years, such as '84 and '87.

THE PRODUCER: AZ. BRAIDA DI GIACOMO
BOLOGNA
Address: via Roma 94, 14030 Rocchetta Tanaro (Asti); **Tel/fax:**
0141 644113/0141 644584; **Web:** www.braida.it; **E-mail:** info@
braida.it; **Total bottles:** 500,000; **Total ha:** 43; **Tasting room:**
yes; **Visit:** by appointment; **Highway exit:** Felizzano or Asti est
(A21)

OTHER RECOMMENDED WINES UNDER $100
BY BRAIDA:

Grignolino d'Asti (unoaked red), Barbera d'Asti "La Monella"
(unoaked red), Barbera d'Asti "Montebruna" (large barrel oaked
red), Barbera d'Asti "Bricco della Bigotta" (small barrel oaked
red), Barbera d'Asti "Ai Suma" (small barrel oaked red),
Brachetto d'Acqui (sweet red).

43 | Lessona

PROPRIETÀ SPERINO • **93/100** • PIEDMONT

As mentioned in the entry on "Cepparello," red wine number 14, Paolo De Marchi has a remarkable ability to succeed
brilliantly with any grape variety he chooses to work with.
This Midas touch continues with nebbiolo at the Proprietà
Sperino estate in Piedmont—in a sense, a return to roots
for Paolo, since his family is Piedmontese in origin. Lessona
is a less famous nebbiolo-based DOC (see the Glossary for
this term), situated northeast of the better-known Langhe,
where Barolo and Barbaresco are made; and it is a cooler
microclimate, so nebbiolo doesn't always ripen well. However, this wine clearly shows that wine lovers everywhere
might want to pay more attention to this very pretty corner
of Italy. De Marchi's Lessona, rare in that it is made only
with nebbiolo, is perhaps the best Lessona made today, and
in fact may well be the best "new" wine to have come out of
Italy in recent memory. Absolutely beautiful pure red
cherry and rose petal aromas have an intriguing smoky-
balsamic note and are matched on the palate by silky tannins and refined ripe fruit. The delicately spicy balsamic
flavors last and last on the long finish.

THE WINE

Grape varieties: nebbiolo (100%); **Number of bottles:** 4,000;
Alcohol: 13–13.5; **Retail price:** $50–64; **Try it with:** grilled duck
breast with black currant sauce; **Imported by:** Petit Pois
Corporation, Sussex Wine Company; **Past great vintages:**
2003

Address: via Orolungo 387, 13853 Lessona (Biella); **Tel/fax:** 055 8072763/055 8072236; **Total bottles:** 30,000; **Total ha:** 9; **Tasting room:** yes; **Visit:** professionals only; **Highway exit:** Carisio (A4)

OTHER GREAT WINES UNDER $100
BY PROPRIETÀ SPERINO:
"Uvaggio" (nebbiolo/others—large and small barrel oaked red).

44 | Barbera d'Asti Superiore Nizza "La Court"

MICHELE CHIARLO • 93/100 • PIEDMONT

"Nizza" is a relatively new denomination of higher-quality Barbera d'Asti, and there are some beauties being made. These wines differ from basic Barbera d'Astis in being richer, more complex, and age-worthy. Michele Chiarlo has invested a great deal of time and money in acquiring vineyards at some of the very best sites in all of Piedmont (Brunate, Cerequio, Asili); and though his wines have always received a good press, the truth is that they have become increasingly better only recently. A good example is this "La Court," one of the two best Barbera Nizzas. A serious wine, concentrated but not excessively so, with plenty of violet and grapey aromas on the nose; rich chewy black cherry, plum, and coffee flavors on the palate; soft noble tannins; and a lingering creaminess. It will appeal to all those who appreciate a modernist bent, as its soft tannins and many, but not all, of its oak-derived aromas and flavors are easy to appreciate. And note that Chiarlo's Barbaresco Asili and the Barolo Brunate are also highly enjoyable.

THE WINE

Grape varieties: barbera (100%); **Number of bottles:** 20,000; **Alcohol:** 14; **Retail price:** $36–42; **Try it with:** chicken marengo (a local dish prepared for Napoléon after the battle of Marengo, consisting of pan-roasted chicken with plenty of broth, carrots, onions, and mushrooms, though recipes will vary); beef in Barbera sauce with bacon and sage; **Imported by:** Kobrand (www .kobrandwineandspirits.com); **Past great vintages:** 2003, 2004

THE PRODUCER: MICHELE CHIARLO

Address: SS. Nizza Canelli 99, 14042 Calamandrana (Asti); **Tel/fax:** 0141 769030/0141 769033; **Web:** www.chiarlo.com; **E-mail:** info@chiarlo.com; **Total bottles:** 950,000; **Total ha:** 110; **Tasting room:** yes; **Visit:** by appointment; **Highway exit:** Asti est or Alessandria sud (A26)

Barbaresco Asili (nebbilo—large barrel oaked red), Barolo
Brunate (nebbiolo—large barrel oaked red).

45 | Brunello di Montalcino
COSTANTI • 91/100 • TUSCANY

Andrea Costanti is undoubtedly one of Montalcino's better producers and his wines have a remarkable purity and
precision to them every vintage. These are textbook
Brunellos, redolent with bright, high-acid red cherry and
red currant aromas and flavors that pick up considerable
flesh over time, becoming very rich and velvety. Andrea's
skills as a great winemaker notwithstanding, his wines
also benefit from ideally situated vineyards, close to the
hilltop town of Montalcino, one of the very best sites for
the grape. In fact, the area has always been renowned for the
high quality of its grapes: documents exist showing that
vineyards were already being cultivated on Costanti's present land holdings in the 700s (not 1700s!). The estate itself was founded in 1555, and the wines have long been
held in esteem: one of Andrea's ancestors, Tito Costanti,
is famous for having produced much-admired Brunellos
in the 1865 and 1869 vintages.

THE WINE

Grape varieties: sangiovese grosso (100%); **Number of bottles:**
40,000; **Alcohol:** 14; **Retail price:** $70–75; **Try it with:** lamb chops
with tarragon; **Imported by:** Empson USA; **Past great vintages:**
1967, 1970, 1975, 1982, 1985, 1988, 1990, 1995, 1997, 1999, 2001

The '67 is still great after all these years, with a delicate
garnet hue and very fine tannins, a marvel of balance
(95/100). The '97 is a big wine by the standards of this
estate, where finesse usually predominates: rich and
round, with plenty of ripe red cherry and tea leaf notes, it
is drinking beautifully (92/100). The '99 is superb: balanced, luscious, and long, it is one of the best wines of
the vintage (97/100).

THE PRODUCER: AZIENDA AGRARIA CONTI
COSTANTI

Address: loc. Colle al Matrichese, 53024 Montalcino (Siena); **Tel/
fax:** 0577 848195 / 0577 849349; **E-mail:** info@costanti.it; **Total
bottles:** 80,000; **Total ha:** 12; **Visit:** by appointment; **Tasting
room:** yes; **Highway exit:** Firenze Certosa or Chiusi (A1)

Rosso di Montalcino (sangiovese—red).

46 | "Sanlorenzo"

SASSOTONDO • 93/100 • TUSCANY

"Sanlorenzo" is unique, and one of Italy's most interesting wines, made from 100% ciliegiolo grapes. This wine lets the variety show what it's all about without covering it up with excessive amounts of new oak, and without blending in other varieties with more prominent personalities. Sanlorenzo is never too dark in color, and its nose has the delicate white pepper aroma typical of ciliegiolo—which sets it apart from the black pepper of other varieties such as syrah or nero d'Avola—nicely complemented by sour red cherry, strawberry, and tobacco nuances. On the palate, strawberry-rhubarb and sour cherry flavors are complicated by balsamic-leather and mineral notes lifted by bright acids. The acidity prevents it from becoming heavy even in hot years and guarantees good aging capacity (the '97 is still beautifully drinkable today, though I preferred it a few years ago). The estate has been devoted to organic farming (see Glossary) since 1994, and that may be paying off dividends if the excellent '02 and '03 wines, both the product of disastrous years but much better than expected, are any indication. The owners, Carla Benini and Edoardo Ventimiglia, seem to have made the right decision years ago, when they left successful careers in Rome to find a better life in a peaceful countryside setting.

THE WINE

Grape varieties: ciliegiolo (100%); **Number of bottles:** 7,500; **Alcohol:** 13.5–14; **Retail price:** $50; **Try it with:** lamb soup, pici (a typical thick Tuscan spaghetti-type pasta) with meat sauce; **Imported by:** Villa Italia (www.villaitaliawines.com); **Past great vintages:** 1997, 2000, 2001, 2004

THE PRODUCER: SASSOTONDO

Address: Loc. Pian di Conati 52, Sovana, 58010 Sorano (Grosseto); **Tel/fax:** 0564 614218 / 0564 617714; **E-mail:** info@sassotondo.it; **Total bottles:** 40,000; **Total ha:** 10; **Tasting room:** yes; **Visit:** by appointment; **Highway exit:** Orte or Orvieto (A1) or Tarquinia (A12)

Bianco di Pitigliano (trebbiano toscano/sauvignon/greco—
unoaked white), Ciliegiolo (unoaked red), Sovana Rosso
Superiore "Franze" (sangiovese—small barrel oaked red).

47 | Barolo

PAOLO SCAVINO • **92/100** • PIEDMONT

Castiglione Falletto is a Barolo commune known for
wines that fall somewhere between the tannic clout of
Monforte and Serralunga and the lighter ones of Barolo
and La Morra. Enrico Scavino is one of the original
"Barolo boys" who preferred using shorter maceration
times (up to 12 days instead of the 30 days commonly
used by traditionalist winemakers) and new small oak
barrels. The result is one of Barolo's more balanced
wines, ready to drink when young but with an uncanny
ability to age. The estate owns land at some of the best
vineyard sites in all of Barolo. The top *crus* cost more than
$100; however, insiders know that Scavino's base Barolo is
an outstanding buy: his top Barolos (Cannubi, Bric del Fi-
asc, Rocche dell'Annunziata) notwithstanding, this is just
as good as some of the other Barolos he makes (Bricco Ambrogio and "Carobric," for example). You'll love this wine's
pretty red rose petal, licorice, and sour red cherry aromas,
and its creamy-soft fruitiness on the palate, where vanilla
wafer and balsamic flavors really come alive. Above-average
concentration and refinement are its trump cards. Hats off
to Enrico and his daughters, Silvia and Enrica, for a lineup
of wines that never disappoint.

THE WINE

Grape varieties: nebbiolo (100%); **Number of bottles:** 12,000;
Alcohol: 13.5; **Retail price:** $50–60; **Try it with:** Braised beef with
three bean salad; **Imported by:** Marc de Grazia selection (www
.marcdegrazia.com); **Past great vintages:** 1985, 1989, 1990, 1996,
1999, 2001

THE PRODUCER: AZ. AGR. PAOLO SCAVINO

Address: via Alba-Barolo 59, 12060 Castiglione Falletto (Cuneo);
Tel/fax: 0173 62850 / 0173 62850; **Web:** www.paoloscavino.com;
E-mail: e.scavino@libero.it; **Total bottles:** 100,000; **Total ha:** 22;
Tasting room: yes; **Visit:** by appointment; **Highway exit:** Marene
(A6) or Asti Est (A21)

Langhe Bianco "Sorriso" (chardonnay/sauvignon/viognier—
small barrel oaked white), Dolcetto d'Alba (unoaked red),
Barbera d'Alba (unoaked red).

The Barolo Riserva Rocche dell'Annunziata, made only in
the best years, is a masterpiece, but sells for more than
$100. I also love, and strongly recommend, the Barolo
Cannubi, but this is another wine that will cost more than
$100 a bottle.

48 | "I Sodi di S. Niccolò"

CASTELLARE • **92/100** • TUSCANY

The friendship between the owner Paolo Panerai and Eric
de Rothschild (of Lafite-Rothschild fame) led to an en-
counter with Émile Peynaud, one of the greatest winemakers of all time. Today Panerai still gives credit to this
meeting for part of the success and critical acclaim his
wines have received over the years. A dedication to Italy's
native grape varieties is also typical of this estate. (One of
Peynaud's many suggestions for improving quality was to
devote more time and studies to the local native grape varieties such as sangiovese and malvasia nera.) In fact the "I
Sodi di San Niccolò," one of the better super-Tuscans, is a
rare sangiovese–malvasia nera blend, atypical in that
many people in Tuscany have forgotten about the latter
complementary grape. Its presence makes this wine quite
different from super-Tuscans in which cabernet and merlot
play a heavy, recognizable role. The wine's name comes
from the soils (*sodi*) that are best but hardest to work, and
the church of San Niccolò a Sterzi, where one of Castellare's
best vineyards is located. You'll love the red cherry aromas
(a tip-off to the presence of the malvasia nera), the silky
noble tannins, the luscious mouthfeel, and the long finish.

THE WINE

Grape varieties: sangioveto (85%), malvasia nera (15%); **Number
of bottles:** 25,000; **Alcohol:** 13.5; **Retail price:** $60–70; **Try it with:**
lentil soup with pheasant; **Imported by:** Winebow (www.winebow
.com); **Past great vintages:** 1977 (a few experimental bottles were
made that I was privileged to try years ago), 1979, 1982, 1985,
1986, 1988, 1990, 1996, 2001, 2002. The once much praised, and
very fine, '82 is beginning to fade, but the much less highly
regarded '86 (a weaker vintage) is wonderful to drink at present,

with plenty of red currant and tobacco aromas and flavors and great length (94/100). The '90 is fine but the product of a warmer vintage, and the fruit flavors are soft and ripe, with an herbal touch: there's great volume and good balance (92/100). The '97 is even riper and finishes a little too warm, with tobacco and truffle scents (90/100). The '02 is amazing for the vintage, with less than a third of the normal number of bottles produced: very sweet ripe yet elegant fruit; lovely texture and length (93/100).

THE PRODUCER: PODERI CASTELLARE DI CASTELLINA

Address: Loc. Castellare, 53011 Castellina in Chianti (Siena); **Tel/fax:** 0577 742903/0577 742814; **Web:** www.castellare.it; **E-mail:** info@castellare.it; **Total bottles:** 200,000; **Total ha:** 25; **Tasting room:** yes; **Visit:** yes; **Highway exit:** Valdarno or Firenze Certosa (A1)

OTHER RECOMMENDED WINES UNDER $100 BY CASTELLARE:

Chianti Classico (sangiovese/canaiolo nero—small barrel oaked red), Chianti Classico Riserva (sangiovese/canaiolo nero—small barrel oaked red).

49 | Rosso di Montalcino

SALICUTTI • 92/100 • TUSCANY

Francesco Leanza has a magic touch with Brunello even in poor years: his '02 wine was one of the best of the year, and it's interesting to note how, with regard to quality, a number of the organically farmed Brunellos were at the top of the heap in that difficult vintage. As wonderful as his Brunello is, the Rosso is just as wonderful, if in a different way. Less immediately oaky and brimming with ripe, balsamic, fleshy red cherry fruit, it has plenty of bay leaf, violet, red cherry, tobacco, and leather aromas on the nose, and similar flavors. It's one of the richer yet more elegant Rosso di Montalcinos you're ever going to try, a baby Brunello in all but name. By the way, when you get out of the car and look around, you'll be greeted by one of the most beautiful views from any Montalcino estate.

THE WINE

Grape varieties: sangiovese grosso (100%); **Number of bottles:** 8,000; **Alcohol:** 13.5; **Retail price:** $40; **Imported by:** Winebow (www.winebow.com); **Try it with:** *quaglie rincartate* (a Tuscan dish of quails seasoned with juniper berries, sage, and bay leaf and then placed within bread dough and baked); chicken breasts with truffles and porcini; **Past great vintages:** 1997, 1999, 2001

Address: Loc. Podere Salicutti 174, 53024 Montalcino (Siena);
Tel/fax: 0577 847003/0577 847003; **Web:** www.poderesalicutti.it;
E-mail: leanza@poderesalicutti.it; **Total bottles:** 15,000 to
20,000; **Total ha:** 4; **Tasting room:** yes; **Visit:** by appointment;
Highway exit: Chiusi or Firenze Certosa (A1)

OTHER RECOMMENDED WINES UNDER $100
BY SALICUTTI:
Dopoteatro (small barrel oaked red). Small barrel refers to
tonneaux.

Salicutti makes one of the silkiest, most delicious Brunellos of all, though it is best after a year of cellaring to let it
digest the new oak presence.

50 | Nebbiolo d'Alba "Valmaggiore"
BRUNO GIACOSA • 92/100 • PIEDMONT

For my money, Bruno Giacosa is Italy's single best winemaker and his wines are the stuff of legends. Unfortunately, his Barbaresco and Barolo wines have now become
virtually unotuchable for most people: believe it or not,
the Barolos now routinely sell for anywhere between $150
and $400. However, Giacosa also makes other wonderful
wines, including a nice sparkler; a fairly rich, thick Barbera; and this lovely Nebbiolo, which is a good introduction to higher-level Barolos and Barbarescos and to what
the master achieves with this grape. The wine is made in
the time-honored tradition of big oak barrels and a fairly
long maceration time. You'll love its medium ruby hue,
the delicate hint of sour red cherries and rose petals on
the nose, and the sweet but not overripe cherry and plum
flavors. Not a wine of fearsome structure, and it would be
strange if it were otherwise, for Nebbiolo ought to be refined and medium-bodied, an ideal mid-weight wine,
much like Chianti or Valpolicella, that will go well with
most foods, including pasta and meat dishes. There's a
wondrous sense of overall balance to it, and its clean,
long, mineral finish adds to the enjoyment.

THE WINE
Grape varieties: nebbiolo (100%); **Number of bottles:** 14,500;
Alcohol: 14–14.5; **Retail price:** $25–40; **Try it with:** spit-roasted
quail; beef stew with bell peppers; **Imported by:** Winebow (www
.winebow.com); **Past great vintages:** 2001, 2004

THE PRODUCER: BRUNO GIACOSA
Address: via XX Settembre 52, 12057 Neive (Cuneo); **Tel/fax:** 0173
67027/0173 677477; **Web:** www.brunogiacosa.it; **E-mail:**
brunogiacosa@brunogiacosa.it; **Total bottles:** 500,000; **Total ha:**
20; **Tasting room:** no; **Visit:** mostly or only professionals;
Highway exit: Asti est (A21)

OTHER RECOMMENDED WINES UNDER $100
BY BRUNO GIACOSA:
Spumante Extra Brut (pinot nero—sparkling white), Barbera
d'Alba Superiore Falletto (large barrel oaked red), Dolcetto d'Alba
Basarin (unoaked red), Dolcetto d'Alba Falletto (large barrel
oaked red).

51 | Rosso di Montalcino
POGGIO DI SOTTO • 92/100 • TUSCANY

Piero Palmucci is the best producer of Brunello today,
along with Gianfranco Soldera of Case Basse, but his
Brunellos, true cult wines, are unfortunately very expensive. However, astute wine lovers know that Palmucci's
Rosso is itself nothing less than a baby Brunello, as Palmucci likes to give it extra care, and time in the barrel. In
fact, it goes on sale a year after the Rossos of other producers. Its vineyards are perfectly situated in the Castelnuovo
dell'Abate area of Montalcino, a blessed area for the sangiovese grape. Whatever the secret, something right must
be going on, as the wine is an absolute success, rich in the
exuberant fruitiness (lots of red cherry and red currants)
and easy-to-drink appeal of the Brunello, though presented on Rosso's smaller scale. A sumptuous wine, a
perfect companion for the dining table, and one that won't
have any trouble winning admirers everywhere. Don't forget to marvel at its light, almost pink ruby hue, light-years
removed from the absurdly dark tonality of some Brunellos on the market today. True, there are new clones that
induce a deeper color, and other techniques are used to try
to improve upon sangiovese's lightish color— or so they'll
tell you. But the truth is that some makers, like Palmucci,
have decided to take the road less traveled, and that has
made all the difference.

THE WINE
Grape varieties: sangiovese (100%); **Number of bottles:** 12,000;
Alcohol: 13.5; **Retail price:** $35–48; **Try it with:** spleen crostini;

grilled marinated chicken with eggplant and red bell pepper relish; **Imported by:** Robert Chadderdon Selections (www .classicwineimports.com); **Past great vintages:** 1988, 1990, 1995, 1999, 2001, 2004. All of Palmuccis wines benefit greatly from being decanted a couple of hours ahead.

THE PRODUCER: PIERO PALMUCCI AZ. AGR. POGGIO DI SOTTO
Address: Fraz. Castelnuovo dell'Abate, Loc. Poggio di Sopra 222, 5302 Montalcino (Siena); **Tel/fax:** 0577 835502/0577 835509; **Web:** www.poggiodisotto.com; **E-mail:** palmucci@poggiodisotto.com; **Total bottles:** 25,000; **Total ha:** 12; **Tasting room:** yes; **Visit:** by appointment; **Highway exit:** Firenze-Certosa or Chiusi (A1)

OTHER RECOMMENDED WINES UNDER $100 BY POGGIO DI SOTTO:
No others made under $100, but whatever you choose to drink from this estate, it will always be at the top, or close to the top, of its category. The Brunello Riserva is one of Italy's top dozen wines.

52 | Savuto Superiore "Vigna Mortilla"
ODOARDI • 92/100 • CALABRIA

Gianbattista Odoardi is certainly not the only doctor to have started making wine, but he is probably one of the most successful. Thus, between X-rays, and with help from the star winemaker Stefano Chioccioli, Odoardi is now making some of Calabria's best wines in the DOCs of Savuto and Scavigna, which are still little known and even less recognized. The Vigna Mortilla is always one of his best wines. It is a blend of native grape varieties, and one sip reveals it as a wine of the deep south, loaded with field herbs and spicy, overripe fruit aromas nicely complicated by smoke, tar, and coffee. The rich, ripe mouthfeel has a mineral and licorice quality, and even though there's also plenty of almost jammy, macerated-in-alcohol fruit flavors, the wine nonetheless comes across as having a good deal of grace. First and foremost, it is a wine that speaks of sunny Calabria, and this "somewhereness" in the glass is high praise indeed.

THE WINE
Grape varieties: gaglioppo (45%), greco nero (15%), magliocco canino (15%), nerello cappuccio and sangiovese (25%); **Number of bottles:** 30,000; **Alcohol:** 14; **Retail price:** $42; **Try it with:** roast

goat kid with beans, *frisulìmiti* (a traditional dish consisting of long-cooked fatty parts of the pig cooked with salt and chili pepper); **Imported by:** Jan D'Amore Wines; **Past great vintages:** 1999, 2002, 2003

THE PRODUCER: AZ. AGR. ODOARDI

Address: Contrada Campodorato, 88047 Nocera Tirinese (Catanzaro); **Tel/fax:** 0984 29961/0984 28503; **E-mail:** odoardi@tin.it; **Total bottles:** 300,000; **Total ha:** 95; **Tasting room:** yes; **Visit:** by appointment; **Highway exit:** Falerna (A3)

OTHER GREAT WINES UNDER $100 BY ODOARDI:
Vigna Garrone (gaglioppo/nerello cappuccio/cabernet franc/cabernet sauvignon/merlot—small barrel oaked red).

The "Polpicello" is another wonderful red made from extremely old vines (as much as 100 years old) of native grapes, but it will cost more than $100 a bottle.

53 | Merlot "Brenntal"
PRODUTTORI CORTACCIA • 92/100 • ALTO ADIGE

Many years ago I organized a blind tasting of Italian Merlots in Rome for Jean Claude Berrouet of Petrus fame. Though not all the top bottles were present, the Merlot he liked best was this one. There are Italian Merlots more famous than Brenntal, but the truth is that year in, year out, this is one of the most consistent. Always at least very good, and usually downright excellent, it comes at a small fraction of the price of other, more famous Merlots. The color is always dark blackish ruby. The nose reveals violets, milk chocolate, coffee, fresh blackberry, and blueberry jam aromas, and is much warmer than the northern vineyards would suggest. The first sip will win you over with its joyfully exuberant ripe sweet fruit flavors and ultrasoft tannins, making Brenntal a pleasure to drink when it is still young. The long, creamy finish has coffee, chocolate, and prune nuances. This wine is easygoing and such fun to drink that one tends not to realize immediately just how complex it is!

THE WINE

Grape varieties: merlot (100%); **Number of bottles:** 10,000; **Alcohol:** 14–14.5; **Retail price:** $40–50; **Try it with:** roast turkey with red currant sauce; venison stew with mashed potatoes; **Imported by:** Wine Warehouse (www.winewarehouse.com) Note:

Zigzagando (www.zigzagando.com) also carries some of this estate's other fine wines; **Past great vintages:** 1995, 1997, 2000, 2001, 2003

THE PRODUCER: CANTINA PRODUTTORI CORTACCIA

Address: strada del Vino 23, 39040 Cortaccia (Bolzano); **Tel/fax:** 0471 880115/0471 880099; **Web:** www.kellerei-kurtatsch.it; **E-mail:** info@kellerei-kurtatsch.it; **Total bottles:** 1,500,000; **Total ha:** 220; **Tasting room:** yes; **Visit:** by appointment; **Highway exit:** Egna-Ora (A22)

OTHER RECOMMENDED WINES UNDER $100 BY CORTACCIA:

Müller Thurgau "Hofstatt" (unoaked white), Gewürztraminer "Brenntal" (steel and small barrel oaked white), Merlot-Cabernet "Soma" (small and large barrel oaked red), "Freienfeld" Vedemmia tardiva (yellow muscat/gewürztraminer—sweet white).

54 | "Passopisciaro"

PASSOPISCIARO • **92/100** • SICILY

Better-known for his wines from the Trinoro estate in Tuscany, the idiosyncratic winemaker Andrea Franchetti has also been responsible for some of the more exciting wines to have come out of Sicily in recent memory. Passopisciaro, which is the name of both the wine and the area in which the grapes are grown, is a wonderful introduction to the mysteries and charms of the nerello mascalese grape. This grape variety yields wines reminiscent of lighter pinot noir; the better examples are an ode to minerality and pure red fruit. I love Passopisciaro's light ruby hue and its perfumed nose, redolent of orange peel, almond blossom, and sour red cherries, nicely lifted by a sharply saline quality. Initially almost lean on the palate, it slowly builds up sweet, smoky, red fruit fruit flavors. Wonderfully long and complex, with a lingering, irresistible sour red cherry and intensely mineral finish. Recent vintages have seen Passopisciaro become fresher and less jammy-sweet, gaining in drinkability and speaking more of the *terroir* of the Etna volcano. A very fine wine and a "must try" for all those bored with Cabernet and Merlot.

THE WINE

Grape varieties: nerello mascalese (100%); **Number of bottles:** 34,000; **Alcohol:** 14; **Retail price:** $45; **Try it with:** *farsumauru* (a local dish consisting of a veal chop that is stuffed with boiled eggs, soft cheese, prosciutto, sausage, garlic, and parsley and cooked in oil and then in tomato sauce); **Imported by:** T. Edwards Selection (www.tedwardwines.com); **Past great vintages:** 2003, 2005

THE PRODUCER: PASSOPISCIARO

Address: Fraz. Passopisciaro, Tenuta La Guardiola 95030 Castiglione di Sicilia (Catania); **Tel/fax:** 0578 267110/0578 267303; **Web:** www.passopisciaro.com; **E-mail:** info@trinoro.it; **Total bottles:** 41,000; **Total ha:** 8; **Tasting room:** yes; **Visit:** by appointment **Highway exit:** Fiumefreddo di Sicilia (A18)

OTHER RECOMMENDED WINES UNDER $100 BY PASSOPISCIARO:

"Franchetti" (petit verdot/cesanese d'Affile—small barrel oaked red) is excellent but will cost more than $100. Note that Franchetti also makes an excellent super-Tuscan called "Le Cupole" that goes for less than $100 at his famous Tenuta di Trinoro estate in Tuscany.

55 | Barbera d'Alba

SANDRONE • **92/100** • PIEDMONT

Much admired the world over for his magnificent Barolos, which now cost well over $100 a bottle, Sandrone also excels at the other typical wines of Piedmont. His Nebbiolo, Barbera, and Dolcetto are all first-rate, and the first two are among the best examples of the wines you'll find in Alba or the rest of Piedmont. His Barbera is fairly modern in style, but true to *terroir*—it's very typical of the larger-framed, riper, and usually more alcoholic versions that come from the Alba zone, in contrast to the higher-acid, leaner Asti versions. The nose reveals luscious black cherry and black currant aromas enriched by sweet spices, roasted coffee, and sweet balsamic oak. Very rich and round on the palate, with just a hint of jamminess in the warmer vintages, it always shows fine tannins and a wonderful balancing acidity. You'll love its obviously balsamic edge on the smooth, creamy, highly enjoyable finish.

THE WINE

Grape varieties: barbera (100%); **Number of bottles:** 22,800; **Alcohol:** 14–14.5; **Retail price:** $28–38; **Try it with:** pasta with hare or duck sauce; polenta and sausages; **Imported by:** Vintus Selection (www.vintuswines.com); **Past great vintages:** 1989, 1990, 1999, 2003

THE PRODUCER: AZ. AGR. SANDRONE LUCIANO

Address: via Pugnane 4, 12060 Barolo (Cuneo); **Tel/fax:** 0173 560023 / 0173 560907; **Web:** www.sandroneluciano.com; **E-mail:** info@sandroneluciano.com; **Total bottles:** 100,000; **Total ha:** 22; **Tasting room:** yes; **Visit:** by appointment; **Highway exit:** Asti est (A21)

OTHER GREAT WINES LESS THAN $100 MADE BY SANDRONE LUCIANO:

Nebbiolo d'Alba "Valmaggiore" (small barrel oaked red). The small barrel refers to tonneaux.

56 | Montecucco Rosso Riserva "Colle Massari"

COLLE MASSARI • **92/100** • TUSCANY

With only a few vintages behind it (the estate was bought by Claudio Tipa in 1999), this wine is remarkable and very affordable. Blessed with rare balance, concentrated yet refined, it seduces right from the first sip with a wonderfully sweet and ripe red cherry presence and powerful yet smooth tannins. Curiously, the very fine '03 and '04 vintages couldn't be any more different from each other. The wine from the heat wave of '03 is much lighter and higher in acid, with bright sangiovese and ciliegiolo aromas and flavors of red currants, sour red cherries, violets, and tea leaf. In contrast, the '04 is much bigger, almost too chunky; it will have greater appeal to those looking for a fuller, sweeter mouthfeel. All the wines at Colle Massari have fairly long finishes—remarkably, considering how young the vines are. This wine is worth following closely over the next vintages, and at present it represents one of Italy's best values among high-quality reds. The estate plans to release a 100% sangiovese super-Tuscan in 2008. Given the talent and passion of the owner, this wine is likely to meet expectations.

THE WINE

Grape varieties: sangiovese (80%), cilegiolo (10%), cabernet sauvignon (10%); **Number of bottles:** 54,000; **Alcohol:** 14–14.5; **Retail price:** $30–35; **Try it with:** Maremma-style hunter's lamb (essentially a lamb stew: pan-roasted chunks of meat, garlic, onion, olive oil, tomato, and white wine, poured over grilled warm bread); **Imported by:** Bedford International (www .winesfrombedford.com); **Past great vintages:** 2003, 2004

THE PRODUCER: AZ. COLLE MASSARI

Address: Loc. Poggi del Sasso, 58044 Cinigiano (Grosseto); **Tel/ fax:** 0564 990496/0564 990498; **Web:** www.collemassari.it; **E-mail:** info@collemassari.it; **Total bottles:** 250,000; **Total ha:** 64; **Tasting room:** yes; **Visit:** by appointment; **Highway exit:** Firenze Certosa or Sinalunga (A1)

57 | Brunello di Montalcino "Schiena d'Asino"

MASTROJANNI • **92/100** • TUSCANY

The Schiena d'Asino is a superbly situated vineyard in the southeast corner of Montalcino, in the Castelnuovo area—which is, to my mind, the source of the most complete Brunellos along with those of Sant'Angelo in Colle. These all share the elegance and refinement typical of wines coming from vineyards on the northern part of the hill yet also have the power and texture of wines produced in the more southern reaches. Mastrojanni's Brunellos are pillars of traditional Brunello that never disappoint, though be forewarned: you won't find the silky ripe fruit that characterizes many modern-style, new oak–infused Brunellos. Rather, all of Mastrojanni's wines are better with a few years of bottle age, as their chewy tannins need time to resolve. A little air also helps them show their best, so don't hesitate to decant a few hours ahead before trying them. Then you'll be bowled over by the rich red fruit, tobacco, and underbrush aromas as well as red cherry, quinine, mushroom, and tarry flavors of unusual depth. The long complex finish and huge concentration add to the wine's intrigue and appeal, and are only part of the magic that make the Schiena d'Asino one of the best and more traditional Brunellos of all.

THE WINE

Grape varieties: sangiovese (100%); **Number of bottles:** 8,500; **Alcohol:** 13.5; **Retail price:** $75–85; **Try it with:** wild boar stew with roasted potatoes with rosemary and garlic; **Imported by:** Selected Estates of Europe (www.selectedestates.com); **Past great vintages:** 1983, 1988, 1990, 1999, 2001. Also a lovely "Poggetto" from 1980, no longer made.

THE PRODUCER: MASTROJANNI
Address: Fraz. Castelnuovo dell'Abate, Podere Loreto 53020
Montalcino (Siena); **Tel/fax:** 0577 835681/0577 835505; **E-mail:**
info@mastrojanni.com; **Total bottles:** 60,000; **Total ha:** 23;
Tasting room: yes; **Visit:** by appointment; **Highway exit:**
Firenze-Certosa or Chiusi (A1)

OTHER RECOMMENDED WINES UNDER $100
BY MASTROJANNI:
Rosso di Montalcino (sangiovese—large barrel oaked red),
Brunello di Montalcino (sangiovese—large barrel oaked red).

58 | Barolo "Brunate"

MARIO MARENGO • **92/100** • PIEDMONT

Four generations and counting, and the wines are improving all the time. This pretty estate has some wonderful vineyard sites: Valmaggiore is an excellent spot for
nebbiolo; Bricco Viole and Brunate in La Morra are top-
notch sites for Barolo at its most elegant and refined. Also,
there is a sure hand in both the vineyard and the cellar. In
particular, the plot of vines in Brunate, all 1.5 hectares of
it, is a jewel and a beautiful sight to behold: 75-year-old
vines on a south-facing slope from which one of the prettiest of all Barolos is made. This Barolo clearly reflects its
origin at La Morra—no small feat in this day and age,
when it's difficult at times just to recognize Barolo, never
mind the subzone where it comes from. With an extremely perfumed nose with a whiplash of fresh violets
and blueberries, and amazingly fresh and suave on the
palate, this is one of the lightest yet most flavorful Barolos you're likely to come across. Remarkably well balanced
and very long on the pure, high-acid, clean finish, it leaves
you with a wonderful aftertaste of blackberries, blueberries, and a delicate hint of mint. This is an absolutely
captivating Barolo that is uniquely delicate and flavorful
at the same time. Mario died in 2001, but his legacy is
safe in the capable hands of his son Marco, as enthusiastic a vigneron as there is. Insiders know that Elio Altare's
Brunate Barolo is actually made from grapes that Marco
gives him.

THE WINE
Grape varieties: nebbiolo (100%); **Number of bottles:** 5,000;
Alcohol: 14–14.5; **Retail price:** $45–55; **Try it with:** grilled filet
mignon with mushrooms and garlic; **Imported by:** Marc de

Grazia Selection (www.marcdegrazia.com) and numerous importers; **Past great vintages:** 1999, 2001. Some truffle and mushroom notes begin to emerge from the '99, also soft and ripe in the mouth. The '01 is sterner, but ultimately deeper and more interesting.

THE PRODUCER: MARIO MARENGO
Address: via XX Settembre, 34 12064 La Morra (Cuneo); **Tel/fax:** 0173 50115/0173 50127; **E-mail:** marengo1964@libero.it; **Total bottles:** 20,000; **Total ha:** 4; **Visit:** by appointment; **Tasting room:** yes; **Highway exit:** Ast est (A21) or Marene (A6)

OTHER RECOMMENDED WINES UNDER $100 BY MARIO MARENGO:
Dolcetto d'Alba (unoaked red), Barolo Bricco Viole (nebbiolo—small barrel oaked red).

59[*] Ruché di Castagnole Monferrato "Bric Maioli"

DACAPO • 92/100 • PIEDMONT

Ruché is like no other wine in Italy, a small work of aromatic art that comes in a package of great class and easy-to-drink charm. Essentially made only in the vineyards surrounding the hamlets of Castagnole Monferrato and Scurzolengo, it is one of Italy's best-kept secrets but one you'd do well to discover. You'll be thrilled by the luminous, vibrant ruby-red hue, and its very complex nose of wild strawberry, cinnamon, nutmeg, red plum, red rose petals, lavander, and soy sauce, which are echoed on the palate. (Ruché is a rare, aromatic red grape, much like Gewürztraminer, which is a white grape.) A completely different taste experience for those who have never tasted a Ruché before, and one that is guaranteed to leave everyone happy and amazed. Dacapo manages to capture balance and elegance in every bottle of this wine, which has been consistently fine over the past few years—another merit. Ruché is still very much an enterprise of friends and family; for example, this wine is made from a vineyard rented out to Dacapo by a relative, who also makes wines but is too busy running his fine hotel and restaurant to take care of all his vineyards. Dacapo's Barbera is also quite fine, and a wine the owners are passionate about.

THE WINE
Grape varieties: ruché (100%); **Number of bottles:** 3,000; **Retail price:** $25; **Alcohol:** 13.5; **Try it with:** seared tuna with soy sauce;

sushi; **Imported by:** JAO Imports; Zigzagando (www.zigzagando
.com); **Past great vintages:** 2004, 2006

THE PRODUCER: AZ. AGR. DACAPO
Address: strada Asti Mare 4, 14041 Agliano Terme (Asti); **Tel/fax:**
0141 964921/0141 964126; **Web:** www.dacapo.it; **E-mail:** info@
dacapo.it; **Total bottles:** 50,000; **Total ha:** 6; **Tasting room:** yes;
Visit: by appointment; **Highway exit:** Asti est (A21)

OTHER GREAT WINES UNDER $100
BY DACAPO:
Nizza Superiore Vigna Dacapo (barbera—small barrel oaked
red), Monferrato Rosso "Tre" (barbera/nebbiolo/merlot—small
barrel oaked red).

60 | Sagrantino di Montefalco
COLPETRONE • 92/100 • UMBRIA

Saiagricola is a large Italian insurance firm that, a little
like the AXA group in France (owners of Château Sudu-
iraut and Château Pichon Longueville, among others),
also owns numerous wine estates. Colpetrone is the firm's
youngest estate, born in 1995 and with only four hectares
to start with, but it has grown by leaps and bounds and
now probably makes Saiagricola's best wines.

The Sagrantino Passito is a stellar sweet red wine, and
the dry Sagrantino is also one of the best wines of the area.
Deep dark ruby with blackish tinges, it has pleasant aromas
of violets, blackberries, and balsamic herbs. On the palate
it has very fine but assertive tannins that require a little
bottle age to soften, as well as copious amounts of chocolate, coffee, and spicy plum flavors. Very long, almost
chewy finish. This is an immensely satisfying, full-bodied
wine.

THE WINE
Grape varieties: sagrantino (100%); **Number of bottles:** 41,000;
Alcohol: 14.5; **Retail price:** $35–50; **Try it with:** roasted rack of
lamb with green fig and bell pepper chutney; **Imported by:** Vias
(www.viaswine.com); **Past great vintages:** 2000, 2001

THE PRODUCER: COLPETRONE
Address: Fraz. Marcellano—via Ponte la Mandria 8/1, 06035
(Perugia); **Tel/fax:** 0742 99827/0742 96262; **E-mail:** colpetrone@
saiagricola.it; **Web:** www.saiagricola.it; **Total bottles:** 170,000;

Total ha: 63; **Visit:** by appointment; **Tasting room:** yes; **Highway exit:** Orte or Val di Chiana (A1)

OTHER RECOMMENDED WINES UNDER $100
BY COLPETRONE:
Montefalco Sagrantino Passito (sweet red).

61 | Barolo "Bricco delle Viole"
G. D. VAJRA • **92/100** • PIEDMONT

Aldo and Milena Vajra are wonderful people making wonderful wines. Their "Bricco delle Viole" Barolo is a great wine (the Riserva is even better, but this is almost as good and costs less). It eschews high-vanillin oak barrels but is far from tough or tannic. Rather, it is a traditional Barolo on a par with the modernist, riper versions of Barolo much sought after today. Made from grapes grown in the cooler Veglie fraction of the Barolo commune reknowned for highly perfumed, elegant wines, the "Bricco delle Viole" translates its microclimate very faithfully into the glass, its innate refinement setting it apart from its peers. Besides the higher altitude and cooler microclimate, the high proportion of the rosé subvariety of nebbiolo used (roughly 20%) contributes immeasurably to its delicate fragrances. Although many producers avoid using this subvariety because of its lack of color (hence the name), you might say Vajra shows that, at times, less is more.

THE WINE
Grape varieties: nebbiolo (100%); **Number of bottles:** 10,500; **Alcohol:** 13.5; **Retail price:** $58–75; **Try it with:** pan-roasted calves' liver with rice pilaf; **Imported by:** Martin Scott Wines (www.martinscottwines.com); Vino Bravo (www.vinobravo.com); **Past great vintages:** 1989, 1990, 1999, 2001

The '99 has great clarity in the red cherry and rose petal aromas, fine acids, and a refined mouthfeel (94/100) and is much better than the '00, a vaunted vintage but not a success for Vajra: there is some up-front charm but slightly jammy fruit and a lack of complexity (88/100). The '01 is almost as good as the '99: still closed but there's lots of rich fruit lurking beneath the steely tannic-acid grip (93/100). The '89 is rich and creamy, brimming with pure fruit and very long (95/100). The '90 is slightly more acidic and more sinewy, but has amazing depth of red cherry and rose petal aromas, with smoky plum flavors (95/100). Few people are aware that there was also a very good '82 Fossati *cru*.

THE PRODUCER: G. D. VAJRA

Address: via delle Viole 25, 12060 Barolo (Cuneo); **Tel/fax:** 0173 56257/0173 56345; **E-mail:** gdvajra@tin.it; **Total bottles:** 120,000; **Total ha:** 27; **Tasting room:** yes; **Visit:** by appointment; **Highway exit:** Asti est (A21)

OTHER RECOMMENDED WINES UNDER $100 BY G. D. VAJRA:

Langhe Bianco (riesling—unoaked white), Langhe Rosso "Kyé" (freisa—large barrel oaked red), Dolcetto d'Alba "Coste e Fossati" (large barrel oaked red), Barolo "Albe" (large barrel oaked red).

62 | Barbaresco "Serraboella"
FRATELLI CIGLIUTI • **92/100** • PIEDMONT

The Serraboella hill, located to the southeast of the town of Neive, is one of the top sites in Barbaresco land and would be a true *grand cru* if Italy adopted such a system. It has risen to fame only in the past twenty years, mainly thanks to the work of Renato Cigliuti. Cigliuti represents the fourth generation working this vineyard; he started in 1964, in the footsteps of his father, Leone, and his uncle Romualdo, and he is gradually turning things over to the new generation: in fact, you'll meet his charming daughters Elena or Claudia at wine fairs everywhere. The Serraboella Barbaresco is, simply put, one of the world's greatest wines: extremely perfumed by intense, archetypal nebbiolo fragrances of red roses and sour red cherries, with a can't-help-falling-in-love luscious mouthfeel and loads of ripe sweet red cherry fruit, silky tannins, and a never-ending finish that has a lingering, delicate, smoky twist. Even though Neive is considered the source of the firmest Barbarescos, very close in style to Barolo, Cigliuti's Serraboella is as fine an example as any of the greatness of Barbaresco: wines of magical grace and refinement, with a velvety, voluptuous, yet light texture rare in Barolo. In fact, one sip of the Serraboella clarifies immediately why nebbiolo is considered one of the greatest grape varieties and Barbaresco a king among wines.

THE WINE

Grape varieties: nebbiolo (100%); **Number of bottles:** 18,000; **Alcohol:** 14–14.5; **Retail price:** $75; **Try it with:** roast pork loin with

Barolo-prune sauce; **Imported by:** David Vincent Selections; **Past great vintages:** 1989, 1990, 1996, 2001

The '89 is a textbook Barbaresco from a fantastic vintage: there have been few fleshier, more voluptuous Barbarescos made by anyone in recent years. It is remarkably ready to drink from the start, but it will have no problem lasting another 10 years (97/100). The '90 is a slightly more austere but more elegant version, with tighter- grained tannins and less obvious juicy-sweet fruit (96/ 100). It will outlast the '89 and is as good a Barbaresco as you're likely to find. The '96 is a leaner, higher-acid bottle but still showcases the telltale juicy fruitiness of the Serraboella site (94/100). The '01 is smokier and tougher than usual, but with all the qualities to be mind-blowingly good around 2010–2012, and thereafter (96/100).

THE PRODUCER: AZ.AGR.FRATELLI CIGLIUTI
Address: via Serraboella 17, 12057 Neive (CN); **Tel/fax:** 0173677185/017367142; **E-mail:** cigliutirenato@libero.it; **Total bottles:** 30,000; **Total ha:** 6.5; **Tasting room:** yes; **Visit:** by appointment; **Highway exit:** Asti est (A21) or Marene (A6)

OTHER RECOMMENDED WINES UNDER $100 BY CIGLIUTI:
Barbera d'Alba "Serraboella" (small barrel oaked red), Barbera d'Alba "Campass" (small barrel oaked red), Barbaresco Vigne Erte (nebbiolo—large barrel oaked red).

63 | Rosso di Montalcino
BIONDI SANTI • **91/100** • TUSCANY

It is hard to say much that isn't already known about this venerable estate and Franco Biondi Santi, whose ancestor Ferruccio created Brunello all on his own at the end of the 1800s. The family has always been blessed with genial, far-thinking individuals, and another ancestor, Clemente, was responsible for the selection of the original sangiovese grosso clone that has always been linked to Brunello's outstanding quality. Though we now know that sangiovese is really a family of grape subtypes, rather than just one grape with one or two subvarieties, experimentation and research have never stopped at Biondi Santi. This is one of the very few families in the world to have grape clones named after them (in this case the sangiovese

BBS4 and BBS11, BS standing for Biondi Santi). The fame of this estate has been built on Brunellos capable of aging forever, but don't forget about its Rosso, which is everything you'd expect a 100% sangiovese wine to be. Lightly hued, and extremely perfumed in its array of red currant, tea leaf, and allspice aromas, it is wonderfully refreshing and acidic on the palate; you'll love the fruit cocktail juiciness of its flavors. Lithe and long, this is an example of how wines of great finesse weave their magic.

THE WINE
Grape varieties: sangiovese grosso (100%); **Number of bottles:** 12,000; **Alcohol:** 13.5; **Retail price:** $56–68; **Try it with:** braised lamb with white bean salad; **Imported by:** Shaw-Ross International Imports (www.shaw-ross.com); **Past great vintages:** 1997, 1999, 2001

THE PRODUCER: TENUTA GREPPO—BIONDI SANTI FRANCO
Address: Loc. Greppo, 53024 Montalcino (Siena); **Tel/fax:** 0577 848087/0577 849396; **Web:** www.biondisanti.it; **E-mail:** biondisanti@biondisanti.it; **Total bottles:** 80,000; **Total ha:** 20; **Tasting room:** yes; **Visit:** by appointment; **Highway exit:** Chiusi or Firenze Certosa (A1)

OTHER RECOMMENDED WINES UNDER $100 BY BIONDI SANTI:
Rosato di Toscana (unoaked rosé).
    The Brunello Riserva is one of Italy's greatest wines but costs more than $100 a bottle.

64 | Sagrantino di Montefalco
FRATELLI PARDI • 91/100 • UMBRIA

It's unclear whether sagrantino, the pride and joy of the pretty medieval hill town of Montefalco, Bevagna, and other nearby villages, is the ancient *itriola* variety described by Pliny the Elder or if it is a variety brought back from the Middle East by Franciscan monks in the fourteenth or fifteenth century. No matter—sagrantino has adapted incredibly well here and will forever be linked to the Montefalco area. The Fratelli Pardi are owners of a textile mill and are famous for their insistence on weaving cotton and linen with the old, traditional mechanical looms, but they're not really "new" wine producers. True, prior to 2002 the grapes were sold off, but the ancestors of the present owners made and sold finished wine during the first half of the twentieth century. The wines are all impressive, highly enjoyable, and easy to drink. The best of the lot is the Sagrantino, which, though rich and concentrated, is less extreme than some big-name Sagrantinos made today, exhibiting an uncommon amount of charmingly ripe, creamy fruit. Though on the long finish the typically forceful tannins kick in (it wouldn't be Sagrantino otherwise!), they are silky and suave. Then again, you wouldn't expect anything else from textile men.

THE WINE
Grape varieties: sagrantino (100%); **Number of bottles:** 60,000; **Alcohol:** 14.5; **Retail price:** $46; **Try it with:** goulash with roasted potatoes; **Imported by:** Marc de Grazia Selection (www.marcdegrazia.com) and numerous importers **Past great vintages:** 2000, 2001

THE PRODUCER: CANTINA FRATELLI PARDI
Address: via G. Pascoli 7/9, 06036 Montefalco (Perugia); **Tel/fax:** 0742 379023/0742 379023; **Web:** www.cantinapardi.it; **E-mail:** info@cantinapardi.it; **Total bottles:** 16,000; **Total ha:** 10; **Tasting room:** yes; **Visit:** by appointment; **Highway exit:** Val di Chiana or Orte (A1)

OTHER RECOMMENDED WINES UNDER $100
BY FRATELLI PARDI:
Montefalco Rosso (sangiovese/sagrantino—large and small barrel red), Sagrantino di Montefalco Passito (sweet red).

65 | "Nambrot"
TENUTA DI GHIZZANO • 91/100 • TUSCANY

The Tenuta di Ghizzano has been the property of the Venerosi Pesciolini family since 1370 and is headed today by the charming and dedicated Ginevra. Her wines have improved over the years and are fairly international and modern in their appeal, sharing the dark colors, sweet aromas, and creamy, low-acid fruit flavors typical of many wines being made all over the world today, regardless of grape variety and place of origin. Nonetheless, her wines have enough individuality to keep them interesting, and you keep going back to the glass. The famous winemaker and consultant Carlo Ferrini achieves two of his least big-framed or structured wines here, but that is not to imply a lack of concentration in either. Though the "Veneroso" is the more elegant of the two wines, the "Nambrot" is a can't-fail effort, and everyone you serve it to will love its dark violet-ruby hue; the smoky fragrances of blueberry, blackberry and tobacco; and the lusciously soft, sweet roasted plum, espresso, and milk chocolate flavors. An absolutely seamless wine of uncommon balance and harmony, it provides more proof that there's more to the wines of the Tuscan coast (a name used to identify wines produced in the provinces of the cities of Pisa, Lucca, Livorno, and Grosseto) than the world-famous Bolgheri.

THE WINE

Grape varieties: merlot (70%), cabernet sauvignon (20%), petit verdot (10%); **Number of bottles:** 10,000; **Retail price:** $50–60; **Try it with:** truffled pheasant (with the truffles of Peccioli—where Ghizzano is located—that have been famous and much sought after throughout history); pan-roasted pork with apple chutney and pepper relish; **Imported by:** Henriot USA; Classic Wine Imports (www.classicwineimports.com); **Past great vintages:** 2000

THE PRODUCER: TENUTA DI GHIZZANO

Address: Fraz. Ghizzano,Via della Chiesa 13 56030 Peccioli (Pisa); **Tel/fax:** 0587 630096/0587 630162; **Web:** www.tenutadighizzano .com; **E-mail:** info@tenutadighizzano.com; **Total bottles:** 55,000; **Total ha:** 16; **Tasting room:** yes; **Visit:** by appointment; **Highway exit:** Pisa sud (A12)

OTHER RECOMMENDED WINES UNDER $100 BY GHIZZANO:

"Veneroso" (sangiovese/merlot—small barrel oaked red).

66 | "Solare"
CAPANNELLE • **91/100** • TUSCANY

The beautiful hills of Gaiole in the heart of the Chianti Classico zone are a treat for the eyes, and your other senses won't be complaining when you drink the fine wines from this estate. The founder, Raffaele Rossetti, has since sold off his majority interest in the estate to an American, James Sherwood, but retains an interest and has stayed on as a consultant. From the start, Rossetti was one of the more visionary Italian wine producers, and especially clever at marketing, during a time when nobody in Italy thought public relations were very important in the running of a successful winery. Capannelle was among the first producers in the country to design special bottles for its wines and to have gold-leaf labels for limited-edition wines, a state-of-the-art cellar, and even a joint venture with Avignonesi that led to the creation of the "50&50" wine, made up of equal parts of the latter's merlot and Capannelle's sangiovese. All the wines here are great, but I feel the best of the lot is "Solare," a super-Tuscan that defines its cool-climate *terroir* very precisely in its red currant, blueberry, tea leaf, rosemary, and spicy licorice aromas and flavors. It's a wine that is always remarkably fresh and crispy, and living proof that the incredible lightness of being can be more than just a book's title.

THE WINE
Grape varieties: sangiovese (80%), malvasia nera (20%); **Number of bottles:** 24,000; **Alcohol:** 13; **Retail price:** $90; **Try it with:** paprika chicken with egg dumplings; **Imported by:** Neil Empson USA (www.empson.com); **Past great vintages:** 2000, 2001

THE PRODUCER: CAPANNELLE
Address: Loc. Capannelle 14, 53013 Gaiole in Chianti (Siena); **Tel/ fax:** 0577 74511/0577 745233; **Web:** www.capannelle.com; **E-mail:** info@capannelle.com; **Total bottles:** 60,000; **Total ha:** 16; **Tasting room:** yes; **Visit:** by appointment; **Highway exit:** Val di Chiana o Valdarno (A1)

OTHER RECOMMENDED WINES UNDER $100 BY CAPANNELLE:
Chianti Classico (sangiovese/canaiolo nero—large barrel oaked red), Chianti Classico Riserva (sangiovese/canaiolo nero/ colorino—large barrel oaked red), "50&50" (merlot/ sangiovese—small barrel oaked red).

67 | **Chianti Classico Riserva "Ducale Oro"**
| RUFFINO • **93/100** • TUSCANY

Ruffino is a name known the world over (in Italy wine lovers at times confuse it with the Rufina area of Chianti). The Ruffino estate was founded in 1877 by two cousins, Ilario and Leopoldo Ruffino, and now belongs to Marco and Paolo Folonari. Few Italian labels are more instantly recognizable than Chianti Classico Riserva "Ducale Oro," a wine that was first made with the 1947 vintage, and became a top-of-the-line version of the wine labeled with the cream-colored "Riserva Ducale" label without the word "Oro." It is not just a matter of successful artwork, though: this wine is one people tend to remember because it has always been extremely well made and very fairly priced; it deserves its success. Also, keep in mind that you may often find older vintages of this wine for fair prices—even at restaurants, where wine lovers can therefore try something a little older, and hence more complex and smoother, with their meal. This is always a very pretty wine, already soft and approachable when young but capable of aging very well. Of late, this wine has shown more sweet tannins and creamy texture, but there's always significant depth and complexity to keep it interesting. Though this estate makes many other good wines (including the whites at its Borgo Conventi estate in Friuli), today I feel that some of the older vintages of the Riserva Ducale Oro ('88, '90) were better, and much truer to Chianti, than more recent, very fine versions that reveal an overbearing presence of Merlot and other international varieties. However, it is really a matter of individual tastes, and only fair to say that you'll never get a bad bottle of wine from Ruffino.

THE WINE

Grape varieties: sangiovese (85%) cabernet sauvignon and merlot (15%); **Number of bottles:** 350,000; **Alcohol:** 13.5; **Retail price:** $40; **Try it with:** fillet of beef with anchovy butter; **Imported by:** Icon Estates (www.iconestateswine.com); **Past great vintages:** 1975, 1977, 1979, 1982, 1985, 1988, 1990, 1997 (the "Oro" has been added to the Riserva Ducale with the 1988 vintage)

The '88 and the '90 are two of the best wines, for the price, to have come out of Italy in a long time (both 95/100). The 1975 was a very underrated wine (93/100) as was the 1977, a little richer but less refined in style (92/100); both are still wonderful if kept in a good cellar.

THE PRODUCER: TENIMENTI RUFFINO

Address: piazzale Ruffino 1, 50065 Pontassieve (Firenze); **Tel/fax:** 055 6499717/055 649700; **Web:** www.ruffino.it; **E-mail:** info@tenimentiruffino.it; **Total bottles:** 14.5 million; **Total ha:** 600; **Tasting room:** yes; **Visit:** by appointment; **Highway exit:** Firenze Incisa or Firenze sud (A1)

OTHER RECOMMENDED WINES UNDER $100
BY RUFFINO:
"Libaio" (chardonnay—unoaked white),"Torgaio" (sangiovese—unoaked red).

68 | Sangiovese di Romagna Sup. Riserva "Ombroso"

GIOVANNA MADONIA • **90/100** • EMILIA ROMAGNA

This beautiful estate is at the foot of the Montemaggio hill; its cellars are housed in the underground base- ments of the owners' eighteenth-century villa. Quality was always first and foremost in their minds, as can be gathered from the initial vine plantings, in 1992, at a very tight 7,000 feet per hectare. This is a big, rich, thick wine with uncommon elegance for its sheer force, a rather civi- lized wine and far removed from the brute it could well be. You'll greatly enjoy the smoky-sweet, spicy ripe plum and black cherry aromas with hints of tobacco, prune, and leather. Very suave and rich on the palate, this has a very long, creamy finish with noble tannins, and you won't even notice the 14 months it spent in small oak barrels. The hue, darker than usual, is consistent with some of the Romagna clones of sangiovese, which regularly give wines much darker than those made with most Tuscan clones. Giovanna Madonia is a talented and passionate woman who makes a number of very fine wines that are certainly worth looking for and trying.

THE WINE
Grape varieties: sangiovese (100%); **Number of bottles:** 10,000; **Alcohol:** 14.5; **Retail price:** $40; **Try it with:** venison filet with Gorgonzola butter; **Imported by:** Elliot Bay Distributing Company; **Past great vintages:** 2004

THE PRODUCER: AZ. AGR. GIOVANNA MADONIA
Address: via De'Cappuccini 130, 47032 Bertinoro (Forlì-Cesena); **Tel/fax:** 0543 444361/0543 444361; **Web:** www.giovannamadonia. it; **E-mail:** giovanna@giovannamadonia.it; **Total bottles:** 45.000; **Total ha:** 9; **Tasting room:** yes; **Visit:** by appointment; **Highway exit:** Forlì or Cesena Nord (A14)

OTHER RECOMMENDED WINES UNDER $100 BY GIOVANNA MADONIA:
Sangiovese di Romagna Sup. "Fermavento" (small barrel oaked red), "Chimera" Albana Passito (sweet white).

69 | "Avvoltore"

MORIS FARMS • **91/100** • TUSCANY

Adolfo Parentini and his son Giulio are making this great wine in the hot, dry southwestern corner of Tuscany called Maremma. Here (unlike cooler parts of Tuscany such as Chianti) sangiovese has no trouble ripening. The result is full-bodied, rich wines that are luscious to taste. The name "Moris Farms" is in honor of Adolfo's wife, Caterina Moris, and also indicates that there are really two estates, or farms. These two vineyards are located, respectively, at Poggio Mozza in the Scansano area, where very fine Morellinos are made, and near Massa Marittima, which yields the grapes used for this maker's top wine, "Avvoltore." The latter is one of the best of the recent super-Tuscans, with a deep, inky hue; an otherworldly silkiness of texture; and a wonderfully perfumed nose redolent of spices, ripe cherry, and plum—aromas that never lose their elegance, even in hot vintages such as '03. A very fine example of a modern Italian red that can duke it out with the world's best and at a much lower price than other famous super-Tuscans. In fact, very fair prices are typical of all the wines of this estate. Parentini believes strongly in the quality of the relatively new Monteregio di Massa Marittima DOC; he also makes wine from there, and his Monteregio bottling (90% sangiovese, 10% cabernet sauvignon) may well be the best of them all.

THE WINE

Grape varieties: sangiovese (75%), cabernet sauvignon (20%), syrah (5%); **Number of bottles:** 55,000; **Alcohol:** 14.5; **Retail price:** $60–80; **Try it with:** braised beef short ribs with potato purée; **Imported by:** Doug Polaner Selection (www.polanerselections.com); **Past great vintages:** 1999, 2000, 2001, 2003, 2006

The '99 has plenty of spicy, sweet ripe red and black fruit aromas, a soft mouthfeel, and a long finish (94/100). The '00 has a heady nose of ripe blueberries, black pepper, and ultra-ripe black cherries, and a suave texture you're not likely to forget (95/100). The '01 is the best Avvoltore ever, built for the long haul, with lovely raspberry, plum, and milk chocolate aromas and flavors (97/100). Given the heat, the '03 is a great success, avoiding the astringent tannins typical of the vintage and with plenty of ripe, not jammy, fruit (93/100). No Avvoltore was made in '05, owing to a sudden hailstorm that pelted the vineyards. The '06 holds the promise of greatness (94/100).

THE PRODUCER: MORIS FARMS
Address: Loc. Cura Nuova—Fattoria Poggetti 58024 Massa Marittima (GR); **Tel/fax:** 0566919135/0566919380; **E-mail:** morisfarms@morisfarms.it; **Web:** www.morisfarms.it; **Total bottles:** 450,000; **Total ha:** 70; **Visit:** by appointment; **Tasting room:** yes; **Highway exit:** Rosignano (A12)

OTHER RECOMMENDED WINES UNDER $100 BY MORIS FARMS:
Morellino di Scansano (sangiovese/syrah/merlot—unoaked red), Morellino di Scansano Riserva (small barrel oaked red), Monteregio di Massa Marittima (sangiovese/cabernet sauvignon—small barrel oaked red).

70 | "Ampeleia"
AMPELEIA • 91/100 • TUSCANY

Ampeleia is a new Tuscan wine project headed by, among others, the famous Trentino producer Elisabetta Foradori, a member of Italy's "wine aristocracy." This new project is particularly intriguing, as it was born on the ashes of the old Fattoria di Meleta, which wine lovers know was one of the few estates making fine wines in the 1980s and early 1990s in this corner of Maremma. That the *terroir* is a good one cannot be disputed, and the new owners have invested considerable time and energy in new plantings, with all sorts of micro-vinifications of sangiovese, merlot, cabernet sauvignon, syrah, and even tannat. The flagship red wine carries the name of the estate and it's already a winner. Early vintages showed a little too much wood, with the lavish coat of new oak making it difficult for the underlying fruit to shine through, but this no longer appears to be the case. Beautiful and balanced, this wine offers plenty of herbal, smoky blackberry, mineral, and espresso aromas and flavors. It is full-bodied, with a beautiful silky texture and an elegant long finish, where echoes of smoky ripe plum and black cherry jam linger on and on.

THE WINE
Grape varieties: cabernet franc, sangiovese, others; **Number of bottles:** 54,000; **Retail price:** $31–36; **Try it with:** roasted duck

with red currant sauce.; **Imported by:** Domaine Select (www
.domainselect.com); **Past great vintages:** 2004

THE PRODUCER: SOCIETÀ AGRICOLA AMPELEIA
Address: Fraz. Roccatederighi, loc. Meleta 58028 Roccastrada
(Grosseto); **Tel/fax:** 0564 579663/0564 567146; **Web:** www.
ampeleia.it; **E-mail:** info@ampeleia.it; **Total bottles:** 60,000;
Total ha: 50; **Tasting room:** yes; **Visit:** by appointment; **Highway
exit:** Rosignano A12

71 | "Ombrone"
CUPANO • **91/100** • TUSCANY

There is no question in my mind that Cupano is one of the
most exciting discoveries I have made in the past ten years.
I remember having noted the stellar quality of Cupano's
initial Brunello vintages, and when the 2002 (a horrible,
rain-plagued year in Montalcino) turned out to be head and
shoulders above nearly all other Brunellos made that year,
it was easy to realize I was on to something. Once I met
the husband-and-wife team of Lionel and Ornella Cousin,
I was sure that Cupano was not going to be a short-lived
success story, such is their drive to make the best, most
natural wines possible. Their organically farmed vineyards
are picture-perfect, the cellar is spotless, the wines are
great, and their desire to try new approaches has even led
them recently to buy a horse and plow, in order to work the
soil in the manner of times gone by. A result of this attention to detail is that the Brunello isn't the only great wine
made at Cupano: the Rosso di Montalcino and the super-
Tuscan "Ombrone" are just as fine, and more reasonably
priced, since only a limited amount of the Brunello is made,
and it goes for more than $100 a bottle. The "Ombrone,"
named after a river that flows in the area of Montalcino, is
especially fine. Medium deep, almost dark red, this wonderfully complex wine displays a creamy, almost sweet nose
with pretty mineral-spicy-accented violet and smoky plum
aromas. On the palate, this velvety-textured wine offers extremely intense, mouth-coating red cherry flavors inter-
mingled with vanilla and grilled meat nuances. The finish
is long and pure. Drink this smooth, powerful wine now or
hold it for four or five years.

THE WINE
Grape varieties: cabernet sauvignon (62%), merlot (38%);
Number of bottles: 5,000; **Alcohol:** 13.5; **Retail price:** $70; **Try it**

with: braised lamb shanks with garlic and herbs; **Imported by:** Fairest Cape Beverage Company (www.fairestcape.net); **Past great vintages:** 2004

THE PRODUCER: AZ. AGR. CUPANO
Address: Podere Centine, 31, Loc. Camigliano, 53024 Montalcino (Siena); **Tel/fax:** 0577 816055/0577 816057; **E-mail:** cupano@cupano.it; **Web:** www.cupano.com; **Total bottles:** 10,000; **Total ha:** 3; **Visit:** by appointment; **Tasting room:** yes; **Highway exit:** Firenze Certosa or Chiusi (A1)

OTHER RECOMMENDED WINES UNDER $100 BY CUPANO:
Rosso di Montalcino (small barrel oaked red).

The Brunello is a wine you should not miss, but it costs almost $150 a bottle.

72 | Lagrein Riserva "Abtei Muri"
CANTINA CONVENTO MURI
GRIES • **91/100** • ALTO ADIGE

Initially founded by the Regulars of St. Augustine in 1165, the abbey of Gries existed as such until 1897, when it was suppressed as part of the Napoleonic reforms. Thanks to Prince Metternich, in 1845 it was inhabited by Benedectine monks, who moved to the area from Muri (hence the name) in the canton of Aargau in Switzerland. The good monks, recognizing a fine wine making spot when they saw one, quickly established successful commerce in wines of the Santa Maddalena area, ancestors of the Lagrein reviewed here. Characterized by a very deep, almost black color and not-too-shy tannins, all Lagreins had a bothersome, lingering, bitter aftertaste as recently as 10 years ago. The monastery has managed to tame this personality trait without resorting, as others in the area have done, to loads of new oak or to the addition of softer, international, grape varieties. This is about as enjoyable a Lagrein as you'll ever find, with pretty strawberry and raspberry aromas nicely complemented by cinnamon and fresh herbs. A touch of quinine and smoke on the palate add further interest. Lagrein can also be made in rosé or blush versions, and these wines are called "Lagrein Kretzer," as opposed to the red wines such as the one described here, which are called "Lagrein Dunkel" (*dunkel* means dark; *kretzer* means rosé or light). The Kretzer made at Muri Gries is one of the best around.

THE WINE
Grape varieties: lagrein (100%); **Number of bottles:** 50,000; **Alcohol:** 13.5; **Retail price:** $35–45; **Try it with:** roasted turkey with orange-chipotle salsa; **Imported by:** Doug Polaner Selections (www.polanerselections.com); **Past great vintages:** 2002

The '02 is generally considered the worst Italian vintage in ages, but in Alto Adige and Sicily it was quite good. This '02 is a remarkably well balanced mid-weight, with red fruit and spices galore on the nose, and a fresh vein enlivening the red cherry, licorice, and almond flavors on the long, mineral finish (95/100). This is considerably better than the disappointing '03, too ready and soft almost to excess (87/100).

THE PRODUCER: CANTINA CONVENTO MURI GRIES
Address: piazza Gries 21 39100 Bolzano; **Tel/fax:** 0471 282287/0471 273448; **E-mail:** muri-gries-kg@muri-gries.com; **Web:** www.murigries.com; **Total bottles:** 320,000; **Total ha:** 30; **Visit:** by appointment; **Tasting room:** yes; **Highway exit:** Bolzano sud or nord (22)

OTHER RECOMMENDED WINES UNDER $100 BY CANTINA CONVENTO MURI GRIES:
Lagrein Kretzer (rosé), Moscato Rosa "Abtei Muri" (sweet red).

73 * | Dogliani Vigna dei Prey
FRANCESCO BOSCHIS • 91/100 • PIEDMONT

You won't ever find a single bad wine from this estate—the highest possible praise indeed. Just try the Freisa or the Grignolino: excellent, even though this estate is one of the most sought-after names for Dolcetto di Dogliani. One reason is the location of the vines, the subzones of Pianezzo and Martina in the eastern, more internal part of the *denominazione*; the cooler climate allows for wines with higher natural acidity and crunchier, livelier fruit, which is what good Dolcettos always ought to be about. Few wines made in Italy, or anywhere else for that matter, can match Dolcetto's exuberant fruitiness and vinous aromas, and the ones made by Boschis embody these traits particularly well. You'll love all the Dolcettos from this producer, especially this one, which has a gorgeously vinous nose redolent of violets, blackberries, and bing cherries, and explodes on the palate with nervy acidity and lots of wild berry fruit cocktail flavors finishing clean and long with a welcome mineral edge. Try it with friends who may know only Chianti or Valpolicella and dazzle them with something completely different. In fact, if a wine could ever be described as fun, this would be it.

THE WINE
Grape varieties: dolcetto (100%); **Number of bottles:** 7,000; **Alcohol:** 14.5; **Retail price:** $22–26; **Try it with:** fettuccine with porcini; escargots (easy on the garlic!); **Imported by:** Marc de Grazia Selection (www.marcdegrazia.com) and numerous importers; **Past great vintages:** 2006

THE PRODUCER: AZ. AGR. FRANCESCO BOSCHIS
Address: Fraz. Pianezzo 57, 12063 Dogliani (Cuneo); **Tel/fax:** 0173 70574/0173 70106; **E-mail:** m.boschis@tiscalinet.it; **Web:** www.marcdegrazia.com; **Total bottles:** 40,000; **Total ha:** 11; **Visit:** by appointment; **Tasting room:** yes; **Highway exit:** Ast est (A21) or Marene or Carrù (A6)

OTHER RECOMMENDED WINES UNDER $100
BY FRANCESCO BOSCHIS:
Grignolino Piemonte (unoaked red), Freisa "Bosco delle Cicale" (unoaked red), Dolcetto di Dogliani Pianezzo (unoaked red), Dolcetto di Dogliani Vigna del Ciliegio (large barrel oaked red), Dogliani Sorì San Martino (unoaked red).

74 | Vino Nobile di Montepulciano
BOSCARELLI • 91/100 • TUSCANY

Vino Nobile di Montepulciano doesn't get any more elegant than the one made by Boscarelli—as beautiful an example of a traditionally made Nobile as there is. The hue is always medium-light ruby, while the fragrances speak of typical sangiovese aromas of tea leaf, sour red cherries, red currants, and licorice, with a pretty hint of violet. On the palate there is trailblazing acidity and obvious but silky tannins to go along with the lovely red cherry, strawberry, and tobacco and cedar flavors. The finish is long and has distinct mineral and orange-peel notes.

Boscarelli's vines are located in the central section of the Vino Nobile production area, where the most refined and best Nobiles are made, and Boscarelli, a relatively small family-run estate (Paola de Ferrari Corradi and her sons, Luca and Niccolò, are some of the nicest people you'll ever meet at a wine estate), stands head and shoulders above most of them, due to a sneaky concentration of lovely, pure fruit and wonderful complexity. The top two wines made here are the Vino Nobile Riserva wines and the "Nocio dei Boscarelli" cru, but as good as those are, the normal or base bottling of Nobile is almost as good, and is a great introduction to the wines of this famous area. And remember not to confuse Vino Nobile di Montepulciano with Montepulciano d'Abruzzo, another red wine that is made in the region of Abruzzo from a totally different grape called montepulciano!

THE WINE

Grape variety: sangiovese "prugnolo gentile" (90%), colorino, mammolo, canaiolo nero, and malvasia nera (10%); **Number of bottles:** 50,000; **Alcohol:** 13.5; **Retail price:** $29–50; **Try it with:** rabbit stew with mushrooms; **Imported by:** Empson USA; **Past great vintages:** 1982, 1983, 1985, 1988, 1990, 1997, 1999, 2001, 2004

THE PRODUCER PODERI BOSCARELLI

Address: Loc. Cervognano, Via di Montenero 28, 53045 Montepulciano (Siena); **Tel/fax:** 0578 767277/0578 766882; **E-mail:** info@poderiboscarelli.com; **Web:** www.poderiboscarelli.com; **Total bottles:** 90,000; **Total ha:** 13.5; **Visit:** by appointment; **Tasting room:** yes; **Highway exit:** Val di Chiana or Chiusi (A1)

OTHER RECOMMENDED WINES UNDER $100 BY BOSCARELLII:

Rosso di Montepulciano (sangiovese/mammolo—large barrel oaked red), Vino Nobile di Montepulciano Riserva (sangiovese/merlot—small barrel oaked red), Vino Nobile di Montepulciano Nocio dei Boscarelli (sangiovese—small barrel oaked red)

75 | Raboso "Gelsaia"
CECCHETTO • **91/100** • VENETO

Giorgio and Cristina Cecchetto's modern cellar is *the* address in Italy for Raboso, made from the native grape variety of the same name. This grape was long thought to be incompatible with high-quality wines, but the two versions made by Cecchetto offer proof that Italy's long-forgotten natives are able, when cared for, to provide interesting, world-class reds. In fact, the Venetian doges greatly appreciated the famous *vino nero*, or black wine, made from this grape. True, the grape can be difficult to tame, with mouth-searing acidity and brutal tannins running amok in poorly vinified examples. Some people believe that these characteristics led a farmer, Jacopo Agostinetti, to give the grape its name, in 1679 (*raboso* being a dialectal deformation of the Italian *rabbioso*, which means angry, a reference to its harsh mouthfeel). Raboso must never have had a good press, since its name actually derives from a small tributary of the nearby Piave River. Cecchetto makes a fine classic version that sees oak but is balanced and refined. The lusher, richer "Gelsaia" is both new and a return to tradition. It is made by a light air-drying of the grapes, in the manner of Amarone, a process of wine making applied in Veneto in ancient Roman times and again in the Longobard-dominated Middle Ages. You won't want to turn a blind palate to this wine's many charms: the brilliant, deep ruby hue; the ultra-ripe red cherry and smoky-spicy aromas; and the velvety, creamy mouthfeel that goes on and on.

THE WINE

Grape varieties: raboso (100%); **Number of bottles:** 7,500; **Alcohol:** 14–14.5; **Retail price:** $50; **Imported by:** Franco Wine Imports; **Try it with:** roast loin of pork with dried apricot sauce; **Past great vintages:** 2002

The '02 is medium-deep ruby, with lovely red cherry and raspberry aromas with a touch of alcohol and almond, similar flavors, and a suave, smooth, long finish (93/100). The '03 is a little jammy and has some harsh green tannins on the finish that make it less successful (89/100).

THE PRODUCER: GIORGIO CECCHETTO

Address: Loc. Tezze di Piave 31020 Vazzola (TV); **Tel/fax:** 0438 28598/0438 489951; **E-mail:** info@rabosopiave.it; **Web:** www.rabosopiave.it; **Total bottles:** 220,000; **Total ha:** 39; **Visit:** by appointment; **Tasting room:** yes; **Highway exit:** Treviso nord (A29)

OTHER RECOMMENDED WINES UNDER $100 BY CECCHETTO:
Raboso (large barrel oaked red), Merlot "Sante Rosso" (small barrel oaked red).

76 | Brunello di Montalcino
LE MACIOCHE • 91/100 • TUSCANY

Achille Mazzocchi and Matilde Zecca have created one of the most interesting, up-and-coming estates in Montalcino, with wines of great refinement and purity. The sangiovese expression is textbook here, and it couldn't be otherwise with a master winemaker such as Maurizio Castelli, one of Italy's true experts of the variety, at the helm. In fact, Le Macioche is everything Brunello ought to be but often isn't: a rather proper medium-deep ruby red hue eschewing the violet-purple tones foreign to even young sangiovese, and deep, pure, and almost lithe aromas of ripe raspberries, red cherries, tea leaf, whiffs of smoke, and delicate spices. It gets better on the palate, with a clean acidic spine wonderfully chiseling the red fruit, and with balsamic touches framing a mineral nuance that will captivate you and everyone else around. The vineyards are situated on the road that leads from the main town of Montalcino to Castelnuovo dell'Abate, possibly my favorite of all the subzones of Brunello. No Brunello 2002 was made, as the owners felt the wine wasn't up to their standards—another sign of their commitment to quality.

THE WINE
Grape varieties: sangiovese grosso (100%); **Number of bottles:** 8,500; **Alcohol:** 14; **Retail price:** $60; **Try it with:** grilled lamb chops with oven-braised Belgian endive; **Imported by:** Marc de Grazia Selection (www.marcdegrazia.com) and numerous importers; **Past great vintages:** 1999, 2001

The '99 is probably the best Le Macioche to date, with pretty red fruit, smooth tannins, and length unmatched in other vintages (97/100). The '01 is a little more austere, and the tannins are perhaps a touch astringent on the finish (93/100). Both wines are remarkably pure and elegant.

THE PRODUCER: AZ. AGR. LE MACIOCHE-PALAZZINA
Address: s.p. 55 di Sant'Antimo—km 4.85, 53024 Camigliano (Siena); **Tel/fax:** 0577 849168/0577 849168; **E-mail:** lemacicoche@tiscali.it; **Total bottles:** 19,000; **Total ha:** 3; **Visit:** by appointment; **Tasting room:** yes; **Highway exit:** Firenze Certosa or Chiusi (A1)

The Brunello di Montalcino Riserva is a bigger, deeper wine but will cost more than $100 in most wineshops.

77* Grignolino del Monferrato Casalese "Bricco Mondalino"

BRICCO MONDALINO • 91/100 • PIEDMONT

This red wine is out of fashion because of its pinkish color, high tannins, and acidity, but Grignolino deserves better and ought to be a welcome respite from over-oaked, over-alcoholic wines. The delicious Grignolino "Bricco Mondalino," fashioned by Mauro Gaudio, from vines grown on calcareous, fossil-rich soils of marine origin, is proof enough that the world does not need another bottle of oaky merlot or cabernet. Gaudio also makes another, more important, version of Grignolino that takes his name, but I prefer this one, truer to the grape variety. It is bright salmon pink to light ruby in hue; the lovely nose opens with a burst of floral, wild strawberry, sour cherry, and lemon peel aromas. Similar flavors in the mouth are nicely complemented by juicy raspberry and sweeter almond paste nuances that benefit from zesty acidity. Fresh and lively, with noticeable but fine tannins, this finishes remarkably long and very dry. I realize that Grignolino may well be something of an acquired taste but, given its light, easy-drinking charm, one you might want to acquire.

THE WINE

Grape varieties: grignolino (100%); **Number of bottles:** 7,000; **Retail price:** $20–25; **Try it with:** meat loaf Moncalvo-style (a local dish consisting of thin roast veal, bacon, garlic, and rosemary); vitello tonnato (veal with a delicate tuna, lemon, and caper sauce); cheeseburgers; **Imported by:** Empson USA (www.empson.com); **Past great vintages:** 1985, 1994, 1998, 2001, 2004, 2006

THE PRODUCER: AZ. AGR. BRICCO MONDALINO

Address: Loc. Bricco Mondalino, 15049 Vignale Monferrato (Alessandria); **Tel/fax:** 0142 933204/0142 933421; **Web:** www.briccomondalino.it; **E-mail:** info@briccomondalino.it; **Total bottles:** 80,000; **Total ha:** 16; **Tasting room:** yes; **Visit:** by appointment; **Highway exit:** Alessandria ovest (A21)

Barbera d'Asti "Zerolegno" (unoaked red), Grignolino del
Monferrato Casalese "Gaudio" (unoaked red).

78 | "Tassinaia"

CASTELLO DEL TERRICCIO • 90/100 • TUSCANY

There can be little doubt that Gian Annibale Rossi di Me-
delana owns one of the most wildly beautiful wine estates
of Italy. The estate is also so vast that you could get lost in
it and wander for days before seeing anyone. And it is the
estate that first revealed the potential of the coastal areas
around Pisa, at a time when everyone believed the only
coastal area worth planting in was the one along the Castagneto Carducci–Bolgheri axis, made famous by the likes
of Sassicaia and Ornellaia. Curiously, the first vineyards
planted at the estate were chardonnay in 1988 and sauvignon blanc in 1989, followed thereafter by more logical
choices: cabernet sauvignon and merlot. It should be
noted that the latter were obtained not from nurseries but
rather from prestigious Bordeaux estates, in order to guarantee a population of vines that had already proved themselves at high levels over time. This is the estate's least
famous red wine, somewhat obscured by the superexpensive "Lupicaia" and "Castello del Terriccio," but it is very
fairly priced for the high quality you get in the bottle. The
accolades for "Lupicaia" (a Bordeaux-style blend, of which
the '01 is stellar) and "Castello del Terriccio" (almost as
expensive, a rarer combination of syrah and petit verdot)
are well deserved (though these wines really do risk being
almost too expensive); but "Tassinaia" delivers unexpectedly intense and refined fragrances and flavors—pretty
violet, black currant, and balsamic aromas and similar
flavors. Compared with Napa or Australian bottlings, this
is a less chunky, less ripe, less intense style of cabernet-
merlot, but I love its spicy compact texture, its silky tannins, and its smooth mouthfeel, and I think you will, too.

THE WINE

Grape varieties: sangiovese (40%), merlot (30%), cabernet
sauvignon (30%); **Number of bottles:** 95,000; **Alcohol:** 14; **Retail
price:** $36–45; **Try it with:** roast stuffed leg of lamb; roast
lemon-pepper duck with red wine vinegar sauce; **Imported by:**
Kobrand (www.kobrandwinesandspirits.com); **Past great
vintages:** 2001, 2004

The '01 is the best ever, with beautifully deep, spicy red and black fruit on the nose and a luscious, silky mouthfeel that goes on and on (93/100).

THE PRODUCER: CASTELLO DEL TERRICCIO
Address: Loc. Terriccio, 56040 Castellina Marittima (Pistoia); **Tel/fax:** 050 699709/050 699789; **E-mail:** carlo.poli@terriccio.it; **Total bottles:** 320,000; **Total ha:** 57; **Visit:** by appointment; **Tasting room:** yes; **Highway exit:** Rosignano (A21)

79 | "Deliella"
FEUDO PRINCIPI DI BUTERA • **91/100** • SICILY

The noble title of prince of Butera was first conferred on Ambrogio Branciforti in 1543 by King Philip II of Spain, and remained the most important title of feudal nobility in Sicily until 1800. At the end of the 1800s, the royal house of Savoia created the princedom of Deliella, which gives its name to this wine. Since 1997 the estate has belonged to the Zonin family, Italy's single largest wine producer (the Zonins make wine in Virginia as well!) and its best wines are made here on the island. The nero d'Avola vines are planted in a marly-clay whitish soil that benefit from lots of sunlight hours, giving wines that revel in their southern makeup. You'll find plenty of warm sunlight in each glass, with rich, ripe, but not jammy black fruit; the telltale black pepper note of the variety (nero d'Avola is a distant cousin of syrah); and just a hint of saline minerality that, at least in this wine, never falls into overt anchovy or tomato paste aromas and flavors more typical of the Nero d'Avolas made in the Pachino-Ragusa area of Sicily, which aren't always to everyone's liking.

THE WINE
Grape varieties: nero d'Avola (100%); **Number of bottles:** 20,000; **Alcohol:** 13.5; **Retail price:** $35–40; **Try it with:** duck confit potpie with escarole and tomato salad with shaved Ragusano cheese; **Imported by:** Zonin USA (www.zoninusa.com); **Past great vintages:** 2001, 2003

THE PRODUCER: FEUDO PRINCIPI DI BUTERA
Address: Contrada Deliella, 93011 Butera (Caltanissetta); **Tel/fax:** 0934 347726/0934 347851; **E-mail:** info@feudobutera.it; **Web:** www.feudobutera.it; **Total bottles:** 600,000; **Total ha:** 180; **Visit:** by appointment; **Tasting room:** yes; **Highway exit:** Caltanissetta (A19)

OTHER RECOMMENDED WINES UNDER $100
BY FEUDO PRINCIPI DI BUTERA:
Syrah (small barrel oaked red). Zonin also makes fine wines at its
Castello del Poggio estate in Piedmont and in its native
Gambellara in Veneto.

80 | Barolo

ELIO ALTARE • **91/100** • PIEDMONT

Would you believe that young Elio, who wanted to change
things in the family cellar but didn't feel he was being
listened to, one day walked into said cellar and with a
chain saw proceeded to destroy all the large old barrels
there? Not surprisingly, this rebelliousness didn't sit well
with Altare's father, who proceeded to disown him. But
Elio Altare was destined for greatness, a leader in innovation among the "Barolo boys" who took Piedmont by
storm in the 1980s, avoiding the traditional long macerations and large Slavonian oak barrels common to all the
producers of the time and turning to small French barrels (225 liters) and shorter maceration times. He is considered one of the best producers in Italy, and his Barolos
are an accurate example of the more fragrant, supple,
precocious style of La Morra. What I have personally always liked about Elio's Barolo is the unique level of rich
fruit in a wine of such lithe structure. The single vineyard Barolos Brunate and Arborina are outstanding and
deeper than the entry-level or base bottling, but they usually cost more than $100: astute wine buyers may want to
focus on the less expensive base wine. All the wines made
at this estate are very fine and deserve a try, especially the
Langhe "Arborina" (nebbiolo) and the Langhe "Larigi"
(barbera). Elio is helped out by his daughters, Elena and
Silvia.

THE WINE

Grape varieties: nebbiolo (100%); **Number of bottles:** 8,000;
Alcohol: 14–14.5; **Retail price:** $90; **Try it with:** filet mignon with
anchovy butter and mushrooms; **Imported by:** Marc de Grazia
Selection (www.marcdegrazia.com) and numerous importers;
Past great vintages: 1982, 1985, 1988, 1989, 1990

The older vintages made Altare's reputation, and though
new vintages are just fine, I personally feel they're not at
quite the same exalted level. The '82 is a thing of beauty,
rich and deep, with raspberry, red rose, and sour cherry

aromas and flavors that go on and on (95/100). The '88 is an extremely elegant wine and one of the best of the vintage, a touch austere on the palate but with lovely balance to the fruit, tannins, and acids (94/100). For a lesson in the importance of *terroir*, compare the Arborina with the Brunate Barolo, and you'll find the latter (Brunate is a true grand cru) certainly the better wine.

THE PRODUCER: AZ. AGR. ELIO ALTARE—CASCINA NUOVA

Address: Fraz. Annunziata 51, 12064 La Morra (Cuneo); **Tel/fax:** 0173 50835/0173 50835ù; **Web:** www.elioaltare.com; **Total bottles:** 55,000; **Total ha:** 10; **Visit:** by appointment; **Tasting room:** yes; **Highway exit:** Ast est (A21)

OTHER RECOMMENDED WINES UNDER $100 BY ALTARE:

Barbera d'Alba (unoaked red), Dolcetto d'Alba (small and large barrel oaked red).

Langhe "Arborina" (nebbiolo) and Langhe "Larigi" (barbera) are just slightly over $100.

81 | Dogliani "Vigna Tecc"
LUIGI EINAUDI • 91/100 • PIEDMONT

This is one of Piedmont's truly historic estates, founded in 1897 by twenty-three-year-old Luigi Einaudi, a future president of the Italian republic. He was a passionate winemaker who really couldn't help doing well, since his motto was "Innovation with respect for tradition." His granddaughters Paola and Roberta are now at the helm, and the wines are going from strength to strength, divided mainly between Barolo and Dogliani. The estate owns some of the best dolcetto vineyards in Dogliani, such as Giardina in the San Luigi subzone and San Giacomo in the Santa Lucia subzone. As good as the Barolos made here are, they are also, alas, over the $100 barrier. But the Dolcetto is really enjoyable, and the "Vigna Tecc"—chewy fat and a fun, vinous bomb—will accompany your meal with glee. This wine manages to be immensely flavorful, and is richer and longer than the otherwise very fine base Dolcetto di Dogliani made here. It also manages to avoid being overly alcoholic and heavy, something that far too many Doglianis and even Dolcetto di Doglianis are nowadays.

THE WINE
Grape varieties: dolcetto (100%); **Number of bottles:** 20,000; **Alcohol:** 14; **Retail price:** $25–30; **Try it with:** bean soup; roast pork with apple cinnamon or blueberry reduction; **Imported by:** Empson USA (www.empson.com); **Past great vintages:** 2006

THE PRODUCER: AZ. AGR. PODERI LUIGI EINAUDI
Address: borgata Gombe 31, Cascina Tecc, 12063 Dogliani (Cuneo); **Tel/fax:** 0173 70191/0173 742017; **E-mail:** einaudi@poderieinaudi.com; **Web:** www.poderieinaudi.com; **Total bottles:** 250,000; **Total ha:** 50; **Visit:** by appointment; **Tasting room:** yes; **Highway exit:** Ast est (A21) or Marene or Carrù (A6)

OTHER RECOMMENDED WINES UNDER $100 BY LUIGI EINAUDI:
Dolcetto di Dogliani (unoaked red), Langhe Nebbiolo (small and large barrel oaked red).

82 | Brunello di Montalcino
LISINI • 93/100 • TUSCANY

The soils of the Montalcino differ greatly within the DOCG area (see the Glossary for this abbreviation), but in general it is correct to say that they contain more limestone and sand than those more typical of Chianti, for example. The amount of limestone, the warmer microclimate, and the often better sangiovese subvarieties present all contribute to Brunello's being a much bigger, more tannic, longer-living wine than other Tuscan reds. Yet Brunello can also be a remarkably elegant, lithe wine, and certainly Lisini's is an example of just how refined Brunello can be. You'll love the red berry, almond, and tea leaf aromas, as well as the strong mineral tone and the beautiful purity of fruit flavors on the palate. This wine is a little closed when first poured, but with aeration it offers increasing sweetness, and more floral mineral elements emerge. The estate has recently parted company with its winemaker, Franco Bernabei, under whose expert guidance many of Lisini's great wines were made. I hope the wines will continue to be just as good in the future.

THE WINE
Grape varieties: sangiovese grosso (100%); **Number of bottles:** 33,000; **Alcohol:** 13.5; **Retail price:** $50–70; **Try it with:** pan-roasted calves' liver with sweet and sour onions; **Imported by:** Neil Empson USA (www.empson.com); **Past great vintages:** 1990, 1993, 1997, 1998, 1999, 2001

The 1990 is very good, though it suffers in comparison with the "Ugolaia," which is the top Brunello of the estate and one of the greatest Brunellos ever made. It has a lovely light ruby hue, sour cherry and woodsy aromas, and high acids on the long mineral finish (92/100). The '98 is a surprisingly fine wine, as good as if not better than the '97, with a luscious creamy mouthfeel that turns just a little dry on the finish (91/100). The '97 is rich and full-bodied, but has developed quickly, with strong under-brush, coffee, and spicy aromas to go along with the red cherry and raspberry flavors (90/100). The '93 is a stand-out, one of the wines of the vintage with copious rich round red cherry fruit and still very young (94/100).

THE PRODUCER: LISINI
Address: Fraz. Sant'Angelo in Colle, 53024 Montalcino (Siena);
Tel/fax: 0577 844040 / 0577 844219; **E-mail:** azienda@lisini.com;
Total bottles: 80,000; **Total ha:** 13–13.5; **Tasting room:** yes; **Visit:**
by appointment; **Highway exit:** Chiusi or Firenze Certosa (A1)

OTHER RECOMMENDED WINES UNDER $100
BY LISINI:
Rosso di Montalcino (large barrel oaked red).

83 | Barolo "Le Coste"
GIACOMO GRIMALDI • 91/100 • PIEDMONT

One of the things I love most about Italy and its wines is just how local a phenomenon wine can be—a part of the daily life of people in some small corner of the world with few outsiders ever getting a glimpse of it. The Barolo Le Coste comes from a wonderful *cru* that had never been bottled for consumption outside the immediate area until a wise American importer came along. Until then, this estate, founded in 1930, had sold its wine in large demi-johns and all the wine was drunk by the locals, who obviously knew a good thing when they saw it! So every time you sip the wine by Ferruccio Grimaldi, it's like stepping back in time. The experience causes you to pause, relax, and get away far from the madding crowd. Not that the wine is an old-style stalwart: on the contrary, it is a modern, juicy-soft style of Barolo that is ready to drink almost upon release, one of the most approachable Barolos you'll ever taste. Grimaldi's parcel of 40-year-old vines in Le Coste is only 0.80 hectare; the rest has many other owners, as at Clos de Vougeot. This is a wine of wonderful texture, full and deep, with an innate velvetiness that is not altogether typical of Barolo, but rather a characteristic of the Le Coste vineyard. And therein lies only part of the magical charms of this wine.

THE WINE
Grape varieties: nebbiolo (100%); **Number of bottles:** 4,500; **Alcohol:** 14–14.5; **Retail price:** $50–60; **Try it with:** grilled T-bone steak with a mixed green salad; **Imported by:** Marc de Grazia Selection (www.marcdegrazia.com) and numerous importers; **Past great vintages:** 1996, 1999, 2001

The '96 was the first vintage bottled and an outstanding Barolo (96/100), the '99 is a lovely wine of creamy texture (93/100), the '01 a step up in refinement and austerity (94/100).

THE PRODUCER: AZ. AGR. GIACOMO GRIMALDI
Address: Via Luigi Einaudi 8, 12060 Barolo (Cuneo); **Tel/fax:** 0173 560536/0173 560536; **E-mail:** ferruccio.grimaldi@libero.it; **Total bottles:** 40,000; **Total ha:** 8; **Visit:** by appointment; **Tasting room:** yes; **Highway exit:** Ast est (A21) or Marene (A6)

OTHER RECOMMENDED WINES UNDER $100 BY GIACOMO GRIMALDI:
Dolcetto d'Alba (unoaked red), Barbera d'Alba "Pistin" (small barrel oaked red), Barbera d'Alba "Fornaci" (small barrel oaked red). Note that the Dolcetto here is a truly remarkable one.

84 | Cortona Syrah "Il Bosco"
TENIMENTI LUIGI D'ALESSANDRO •
91/100 • TUSCANY

The owner, Massimo d'Alessandro, is a highly regarded architect in Italy, and he's designed quite a lovely set of wines, among which I want to mention the Vin Santo. It is different in its fragrance and flavor profile, thanks both to Cortona's unique terroir and to the particular subvariety of trebbiano toscano used, characterized by an uncommon reddish skin. In reality, this estate is most famous for its Syrah, and was the first in Italy to demonstrate that the area of Cortona is particularly suited to this Rhône variety. You might call Luigi Italy's original Rhône Ranger. Attentive tasters will be fascinated by "Il Bosco," a wine that is getting better with each vintage as the vines begin to age. A brooding, inky wine, it has textbook syrah aromas of violet, black pepper, grilled bacon, smoke, and tar, and is big and rich in the mouth, especially in hot years such as '04. There is a nice velvety texture and a creamy finish. Last but not least, d'Alessandro likes to surround himself with talent, and besides having Luca Currado of Vietti helping out, he has signed on the "first lady" of syrah, Christine Vernay of Domaine Georges Vernay, as a consultant. Should we get lucky, maybe Luigi can persuade her to work on a pure Cortona Viognier . . . Perhaps we have an Italian Coteau de Vernon to look forward to in the future.

THE WINE

Grape varieties: syrah (100%); **Number of bottles:** 36,000; **Alcohol:** 14; **Retail price:** $38–50; **Try it with:** grilled duck breast with a strawberry-rhubarb reduction; **Imported by:** Vintus Selections (www.vintuswines.com); **Past great vintages:** 2004

THE PRODUCER: TENIMENTI LUIGI D'ALESSANDRO

Address: Loc. Camucia, via Manzano 15, 52042 Cortona (Arezzo); **Tel/fax:** 0575 618667/0575 618411; **Web:** www.tenimentidalessandro.it; **E-mail:** info@tenimentidalessandro.it; **Total bottles:** 140,000; **Total ha:** 50; **Tasting room:** yes; **Visit:** by appointment; **Highway exit:** Val di Chiana (A1)

OTHER RECOMMENDED WINES UNDER $100 BY LUIGI D'ALESSANDRO:
Cortona Vin Santo (trebbiano—sweet white).

85 | "Santa Cecilia"
PLANETA • **91/100** • SICILY

While this estate's Chardonnay garners a lot of attention and praise, it's not a favorite of mine. It is too butterscotchy, too fruit cocktailish, and so forth, but I'll admit the style has countless admirers. Personally, I much prefer the estate's other whites, such as "Alastro," where the chardonnay presence is somewhat more discreet; and "Cometa," an over-the-top Fiano if there ever was one, but fantastic indeed to drink. This very famous, extremely well run Italian estate also makes a number of fine red wines and a great little sweet wine called Moscato di Noto that you'd do well to try. Though I love the Moscato di Noto, I cast my vote for the "Santa Cecilia," by far Planeta's most improved wine over the past five years, now richer and deeper than it has ever been. It had always been a mystery to me why an estate as talented as this one wasn't making better Nero d'Avolas: in fact, the red wine everyone clamored for from Planeta was, until recently, the Merlot. Today, "Santa Cecilia" is on a par with the best Nero d'Avolas from the island, a reflection of the time and energy that Alessio Planeta tells me have been devoted to studying the variety and learning more about the many subvarieties. You'll love "Santa Cecilia's" intense nose of red and black cherry aromas, with pretty herbal and smoky nuances. The bright fresh acidity gives this mid-weight's spicy black fruit and intensely soft red cherry flavors lift and focus. Its pleasant long mineral finish adds infinite charm. You'll tend to want to drink one glass right after another, so don't say I didn't warn you.

THE WINE

Grape varieties: nero d'Avola (100%); **Number of bottles:** 70,000; **Alcohol:** 13.5; **Retail price:** $39; **Try it with:** grilled chicken breast with peppery tomato relish; flank steak with shallots and red wine reduction; **Imported by:** Palm Bay Imports (www.palmbay imports.com); **Past great vintages:** 2001, 2004

THE PRODUCER: PLANETA

Address: Contrada Dispensa, 92013 Menfi (Agrigento); **Tel/fax:** 091 327965/091 6124335; **E-mail:** planeta@planeta.it; **Web:** www.planeta .it; **Total bottles:** 2.2 million; **Total ha:** 350; **Visit:** by appointment; **Tasting room:** yes; **Highway exit:** Castelvetrano (A29)

OTHER RECOMMENDED WINES UNDER $100 BY PLANETA:

"Alastro" (grecanico/chardonnay—unoaked white), "Cometa" (fiano—unoaked white), Cerasuolo di Vittoria (nero d'Avola/ frappato—unoaked red), Merlot (small barrel oaked red), Syrah (small barrel oaked red), Moscato di Noto (sweet white).

86 | Barbaresco "Pajoré"
SOTTIMANO • **91/100** • PIEDMONT

I have a couple of important points to make here. First, I feel Sottimano is one of the finer Barbaresco estates today, but also one that has greatly improved its wines in a very short time, taking them from over-oaky and hyper-modern to pure and complex. In fact, you'll have a hard time finding anyone with a similarly large lineup of high-quality wines. Second, the wine I've picked here is a breath of history, an ode to all things good and with a sense of place. All the single vineyard Barbarescos made by Sottimano are excellent—Cottà, Currà, and Fausoni in the area of Neive; and Pajoré in the area of Treiso—but it's the Pajoré that you need to know about. As much as I love the wines of Cottà (rich, racy, full), I prefer Pajoré, one of the top *crus* of the Langhe. From here, Giovannini-Moresco used to make the "Poderi del Pajoré," one of my all-time favorite Italian wines and also one of the best and most truly historic wines of Barbaresco. The vineyard therefore has a long association with great wines, some of the more flavorful Barbarescos made. The Sottimano Pajoré has a remarkably clean feel and a pure texture, derived from a manicured vineyard. The roughly 40-year-old vines and low yields all lead up to a very concentrated yet refined Barbaresco brimming with deep red cherry fruit, red rose, and violet aromas and flavors. Twenty months in both new and used *barriques* round this wine out nicely. It really comes into its own about five years after the vintage date, with the trademark Pajoré bigger tannic structure benefiting from the extra bottle age.

THE WINE
Grape varieties: nebbiolo (100%); **Number of bottles:** 4,500; **Alcohol:** 14–14.5; **Retail price:** $54–75; **Try it with:** roast goose with a caramelized onion and Gorgonzola tart; **Imported by:** Marc de Grazia Selection (www.marcdegrazia.com) and numerous importers; **Past great vintages:** 2001, 2004

THE PRODUCER: SOTTIMANO
Address: Loc. Cottà 21, 12057 Neive (Cuneo); **Tel/fax:** 0173 635186/0173 635186; **E-mail:** sottimano@libero.it; **Web:** www.sottimano.it; **Total bottles:** 65,000; **Total ha:** 14; **Visit:** by appointment; **Tasting room:** yes; **Highway exit:** Ast est (A21)

OTHER RECOMMENDED WINES UNDER $100 BY SOTTIMANO:
Barbaresco "Currà" (small barrel oaked red), Barbaresco "Cottà" (small barrel oaked red).

87* | Chianti Classico
LE CINCIOLE • 91/100 • TUSCANY

In only about 15 years, Valerio Viganò and Lorenza Orsini have managed to turn this estate into a reliable source of highly enjoyable, fruity Chianti. Their Chianti always exhibits the grace and balance of the Panzano area, one of the true *grand crus* of the *denominazione*. Four of the 11 hectares owned by the estate make up one vineyard, the Vigna Valle del Pozzo, facing south-southwest and located at the higher reaches of the absolutely best site in Chianti, the famous Conca d'Oro of Panzano. The other seven hectares are near the cellar building in an almost similarly blessed position. This wine, aged one year in 20-liter oak barrels, reveals plenty of lovely red fruit and a mouthwatering crunchy bite. The Riserva "Petresco," made from older vines as well as vines of the Conca d'Oro plot, is a wine of perhaps greater breed and refinement (it is aged 18–24 months in new small barrels). But the fact is that it's hard to beat the up-front sour red cherry, violet, and almond flower aromas and the juicy loveliness of the base Chianti, a wine everyone needs a glass of at the dining table. On the other hand, I'm not as impressed with the "Camalaione," a perfectly fine Bordeaux blend but similar to many other cabernet-merlot wines being made all over the world.

THE WINE
Grape varieties: sangiovese (100%); **Number of bottles:** 35,000; **Alcohol:** 13.5; **Retail price:** $25; **Try it with:** beef tenderloin steaks with tomato, caper, fresh basil, and bread salad; **Imported by:** Marc de Grazia Selection (www.marcdegrazia.com) and numerous importers; **Past great vintages:** 1995, 1997, 2001

THE PRODUCER: LE CINCIOLE
Address: Fraz. Panzano, via Case Sparse 83—Greve in Chianti, 53020 Montalcino (Siena); **Tel/fax:** 055 852636/055 8560307; **E-mail:** cinciole@chianticlassico.com; **Web:** www.lecinciole.it; **Total bottles:** 40,000; **Total ha:** 11; **Visit:** by appointment; **Tasting room:** yes; **Highway exit:** Firenze Certosa or Valdarno (A1)

OTHER RECOMMENDED WINES UNDER $100 BY LE CINCIOLE:
Chianti Classico Riserva "Petresco" (small barrel oaked red).

88 | Barbaresco "Bric Ronchi"
ALBINO ROCCA • 91/100 • PIEDMONT

Angelo Rocca, capably helped out by his wife and two daughters, is a soft-spoken, likable man who makes some of Barbaresco's most enjoyable wines. The Vigneto Bric

Ronchi is a superstar, usually showing much greater breed and depth than the wine made from the Loreto vineyard, which though good rarely reaches the heights of this one. One of the original modernist winemakers, Angelo is now experimenting with bigger 20-hectoliter oak barrels, in an effort to reduce the role of oak. It is only honest to recognize the fact that too much oak was never really a problem with Angelo's juicy, fruit-forward, truly delectable wines; nonetheless, these new efforts are just as good as the old ones. The Bric Ronchi has lovely smoky red cherry and strawberry aromas, a terrific creamy texture, and a delicate spicy quality on the long, pleasant, mineral finish. This wine has brighter acids than the Loreto, which tends to be a little fatter in most years. Note that Angelo now owns land in San Rocco Seno d'Elvio, where the grapes for the base Barbaresco come from: it's not just good but one of the better buys of the whole appellation.

THE WINE
Grape varieties nebbiolo (100%); **Number of bottles:** 24,000; **Alcohol:** 14–14.5; **Retail price:** $85; **Try it with:** grilled flank steak with caramelized onions; **Imported by:** Marc de Grazia Selection (www.marcdegrazia.com) and numerous importers; **Past great vintages:** 1990, 1996, 2001

THE PRODUCER: ALBINO ROCCA
Address: strada Ronchi 18, 12050 Barbaresco (Cuneo); **Tel/fax:** 0173 635145/0173 635921; **E-mail:** roccaalbino@roccaalbino.com; **Web:** www.albinorocca.com; **Total bottles:** 90,000; **Total ha:** 15; **Visit:** by appointment; **Tasting room:** yes; **Highway exit:** Ast est (A21)

OTHER RECOMMENDED WINES UNDER $100 BY ALBINO ROCCA:
Barbera d'Alba "Gepin" (large and small barrel oaked red), Barbaresco Loreto (large barrel oaked red).

89 | Schioppettino
LA VIARTE • **90/100** • FRIULI VENEZIA GIULIA

La Viarte, which means "springtime" in the Friulian dialect, is a truly gorgeous estate that is well worth a visit and where you'll find, besides bucolic countryside, a lineup of excellent wines at nearly unbeatable prices. It goes to the credit of owner Giulio Ceschin that just about any wine made here is absolutely a benchmark for the variety: a very fine Ribolla gialla, delicate and fresh as a wine made from this variety ought to be; Pinot Grigio far removed from the industrial, insipid junk you might have thought was the real thing; Italy's best Tazzelenghe, made from a native high-acid variety (the name itself means "cuts the tongue," in reference to its high acids), a very good Merlot, and an above-average sweet wine called "Sium." The best red wine, though, is the Schioppettino, of which Giulio is a real expert and a grape he truly believes is a diamond in the rough, one that is destinied for greatness (and I agree wholeheartedly). The Schioppettino is very fine, lovely in its bright ruby red hue, combining blackberry, white pepper, and floral scents with black cherry and blackberry flavors, structured around a solid core of high acids and mineral nuances. A perfectly sculpted wine, elegant and fine, sleek and endowed with a beautiful, long, clean finish, with more pretty hints of white pepper on the finish. Schioppettino—especially in Ceschin's version, in which the grapes are not air-dried—is a light, midweight wine that is about as far removed from a blockbuster as there is: but it fleshes out beautifully with food, and you'll leave the dining table feeling light and content.

THE WINE

Grape varieties: schioppettino (100%); **Number of Bottles:** 3,000; **Alcohol:** 13–13.5; **Retail price:** $25–35; **Try it with:** grilled lamb chops with rosemary-thyme-mushroom butter; **Imported by:** Kermit Lynch Wine Merchant; **Past great vintages:** 1999, 2000, 2003

THE PRODUCER: AZ. AGR. LA VIARTE

Address: via Novacuzzo 51, 33040 Prepotto (Udine); **Tel/fax:** 0432 759458/0432 759458; **Web:** www.laviarte.it; **E-mail:** laviarte@ laviarte.it; **Total bottles:** 100,000; **Total ha:** 27; **Tasting room:** yes; **Visit:** by appointment; **Highway exit:** Palmanova (A4) or Udine Sud (A23)

OTHER RECOMMENDED WINES UNDER $100 BY LA VIARTE:

"Incò" (tocai/others—unoaked white), Pinot Grigio (unoaked white), Tazzelenghe (oaked red), Ribolla gialla (unoaked white), Refosco del Peduncolo Rosso (oaked red), Sium (picolit/ verduzzo—sweet white).

90 | "Mater Matuta"

CASALE DEL GIGLIO • 90/100 • LAZIO

There is a lot to be said for Antonio Santarelli, whose prowess and dedication have turned his modern, state-of-the-art winery into one of Italy's best sources for fairly priced and very good wines. No small feat when you stop to consider that the Agropontino, where his estate is located, is an area of Lazio never previously known for fine wines; in fact, this area was a swamp in the early twentieth century. Yet I think it is almost unfair to reduce Casale del Giglio's wines to just "good buys"; of course, they are, but a tremendous amount of investment and research have been devoted to the search for success. The result is that some exciting wines are being made, such as an ultra-delicious sweet wine called "Aphrodisium"—a name aptly suggesting aphrodisiac qualities—that is made by a combination of late harvest and ice-wine techniques (in which the natural sugars and flavor molecules are concentrated by the removal of frozen water). The most important wine of the estate is, however, this "Mater Matuta," a very powerful, structured red wine that will remind you of blackberry syrup, graphite, tar, fine leather, and balsamic smoky plums. It is very rich and long on the finish, with a bit of a tarry note. Among the other wines made here, there is also a fine Tempranillo (the tempranillo is a very rare grape in Italy). This has not yet been released on the market, but I have tasted it and it is yet another product of research and innovation.

THE WINE
Grape varieties: cabernet sauvignon (85%), petit verdot (15%); **Number of bottles:** 22,000; **Alcohol:** 13.5; **Retail price:** $50; **Try it with:** roast quail with potato and bacon hash; **Imported by:** Soilair Selection (www.soilairselection.com); **Past great vintages:** 2000, 2001

THE PRODUCER: AZIENDA AGRICOLA CASALE DEL GIGLIO
Address: strada Cisterna-Nettuno Km 13, 04100 Le Ferriere (Latina); **Tel/fax:** 0692902530; **Web:** www.casaledelgiglio.it; **E-mail:** info@casaledelgiglio.it; **Total bottles:** 855,000; **Total ha:** 125; **Tasting room:** yes; **Visit:** by appointment; **Highway exit:** Valmontone (A2)

"Satrico" Bianco (trebbiano giallo/chardonnay/sauvignon—unoaked white), Petit Manseng (unoaked white), Merlot (small barrel oaked red), Petit Verdot small barrel oaked (red), Shiraz (small barrel oaked red), "Aphrodisium" (petit manseng/viognier/greco/fiano—sweet white).

91* | "Pian di Nova"

IL BORRO • 90/100 • TUSCANY

The world-famous fashion house of Ferragamo has quite a few family members who have been bitten by the wine bug. Ferruccio Ferragamo is the owner of this absolutely beautiful estate and has invested an impressive amount of energy and money in the upkeep of the vineyards and of the many small houses on the grounds (really, the estate is a small town in itself). A drive and a walk through the vineyards with the winemaker Niccolò d'Afflito will impress you: painstaking attention to detail has gone into studying all the various soils present and matching rootstocks and appropriate grape varieties to each. This producer's most famous wine takes its name from the estate, but the most enjoyable one, and an excellent example of what Italy does so well in wine, is the entry-level "Pian di Nova," an absolutely delicious wine characterized by smoky, peppery, red currant and wild raspberry fruit aromas with an inky twist. Its flavors will remind you of ripe balsamic plums, with a smoky medicinal herb and mineral edge accompanying slightly chunky tannins on the medium long finish. Overall, a very enjoyable glass of wine that makes you wish for summer days and barbecues.

THE WINE

Grape varieties: syrah (75%), sangiovese (25%); **Number of bottles:** 80,000; **Alcohol:** 13.5; **Retail price:** $20; **Try it with:** pork chops; smoked chicken breast; **Imported by:** USA Wine West (www.usawinewest.com); **Past great vintages:** 2005

THE PRODUCER: IL BORRO;

Address: Loc. Borro 1—Fraz. San Giustino Valdarno, 52020 Loro Ciuffenna (Arezzo); **Tel/fax:** 055 9772921 / 055 9772921; **Web:** www.ilborro.it; **E-mail:** vini@ilborro.it; **Total bottles:** 180,000; **Total ha:** 40; **Tasting room:** yes; **Visit:** by appointment; **Highway exit:** Arezzo (A1)

92* | Montepulciano d'Abruzzo
MASCIARELLI • 90/100 • ABRUZZO

The energetic, hardworking Gianni Masciarelli, one of Italy's most famous producers, did much to help the image of Montepulciano all over Italy and the world. The top wine, called "Villa Gemma," gets all the accolades and is certainly very enjoyable, but I find choosing wines here almost too easy. In fact, Masciarelli could lay claim to two true works of art: the Marina Cvetic Montepulciano d'Abruzzo (Marina Cvetic is the name of his wife's estate) and the wine I have picked here—his unbelievably inexpensive base bottling of Montepulciano. This is one of Italy's five or six best wine buys; it goes down without any effort whatsoever and brings utter joy, and it is made in huge amounts. The pretty strawberry aromas are enlivened by strokes of coffee and leather; the palate finishes bright and fresh with more pretty red fruit and a clear-cut mineral edge. Other wines from this estate that you should try are the Cerasuolo (or rosé), also very fine, and the Trebbiano d'Abruzzo Castello di Semivicoli. I find the whites in the Marina Cvetic lineup, as well made as they are, a little too oaky.

THE WINE
Grape varieties: montepulciano (100%); **Number of bottles:** 700,000; **Alcohol:** 13.5; **Retail price:** $18–20; **Try it with:** roast lamb and grilled vegetables; **Imported by:** Masciarelli Wine Company (www.masciarelliwine.com); **Past great vintages:** 1999, 2001

THE PRODUCER: AZ. AGR. MASCIARELLI
Address: via Gamberale 1, 66010 San Martino sulla Marruccina (Chieti); **Tel/fax:** 0871 85241/0871 85330; **E-mail:** info@masciarelli.it; **Web:** www.masciarelli.it; **Total bottles:** 1.2 million; **Total ha:** 302; **Visit:** by appointment; **Tasting room:** yes; **Highway exit:** Pescara sud (A14)

OTHER RECOMMENDED WINES UNDER $100 BY MASCIARELLI:
Trebbiano d'Abruzzo Castello di Semivicoli (unoaked white), Montepulciano d'Abruzzo Cerasuolo "Villa Gemma" (unoaked rosé), Marina Cvetic Montepulciano d'Abruzzo "San Martino Rosso" (small barrel oaked red).

93 | Cesanese del Piglio

CASALE DELLA IORIA • **90/100** • LAZIO

This is real mountain viticulture, that of the cesanese d'Affile variety. The vines cling to crooked crags described by Tennyson, and the steep slopes are impossible to work with farm machinery. To make matters worse for the local producers, cesanese ripens late in the year, when the weather often turns sour, so in many vintages there is a real risk of making poor wines. That being said, Cesanese had always been considered a first-rate wine and was sought by popes and princes. It fell by the wayside during the twentieth century, when too many lackluster wines were made; however, the fine wines made by Paolo Perinelli at Casale della Ioria have led a number of young producers to take over their family wineries and start bottling their own new wines, rather than selling their grapes to local cooperatives. The result is many very interesting and fine wines. The trailblazer and best producer in the area remains Perinelli. His best wine, the Cesanese del Piglio "Torre del Piano," is unfortunately not yet imported into the United States. I hope this will change, but meanwhile you can get an idea of what Cesanese is all about by tasting the entry-level version described here. This wine has pretty aromas of pure red cherry and raspberry, with hints of tobacco and licorice; is full-bodied; and has fine acids that help put it all into perspective. Although it lacks a little of the velvety refinement, the sweet fruit, and the luscious texture of "Torre del Piano," this is a wine, and a grape, that you soon ought to hear and read more about.

THE WINE

Grape varieties: cesanese d'Affile (100%); **Number of bottles:** 35,000; **Alcohol:** 14; **Retail price:** $30; **Try it with:** porcini gnocchi with prosciutto and parmigiano cream; **Imported by:** Domenico Valentino Selections (www.domenicovalentino.com), Vino Bravo (www.vinobravo.com); **Past great vintages:** 2001, 2003

The "Torre del Piano" '03 is an amazing wine, as the hot vintage helped cesanese ripen fully. It has pretty red cherry and plum aromas with hints of tobacco and delicate spices, with a luscious and atypical mouthfeel and considerable length (95/100). The "Torre del Piano" '01 is more austere, with somewhat less forthcoming aromas and a more tannic backbone, but with plenty of luscious red fruit and tobacco scents and flavors (91/100).

THE PRODUCER: AZ. AGR. PERINELLI CASALE
DELLA IORIA

Address: piazza Regina Margherita 1, 03010 Acuto (Frosinone);
Tel/fax: 0775 56031/06 6865913; **Web:** www.casaledellaioria.com;
E-mail: perinelli@tiscali.it; **Total bottles:** 45,000; **Total ha:** 35;
Tasting room: yes; **Visit:** by appointment; **Highway exit:**
Anagni-Fiuggi (A2)

OTHER RECOMMENDED WINES UNDER $100
BY CASALE DELLA IORIA:
Passerina del Frusinate "Colle Bianco" (unoaked white),
Cesanese del Piglio "Torre del Piano" (large barrel oaked red).

94 | Barbera d'Asti Sup. Nizza "La Crena"
VIETTI • **90/100** • PIEDMONT

Luca Currado is at the head of one of Piedmont's truly
venerable estates. I have had many outstanding wines
from it, and I'm still immensely fond of the old Barolo
"Briacca" 1971, a stellar wine made with the rarer "rosé"
subvariety of nebbiolo. Of all the many wonderful wines
made here—such as the fantastic Barolos (of which the
Villero is most famous but the Brunate and Rocche are
often as good), and the two wonderful Barberas—I have
selected the "La Crena" Barbera d'Asti Nizza, a wine that
offers an amazing bang for your buck. It spends six
months in *barrique* and eighteen in large oak casks, but
the oak is practically invisible: all you'll smell is lovely
blackberries, plums, and a hint of coffee, and you'll taste
more balsamic plums with hints of licorice, coffee, and
cocoa. This Barbera is somewhat richer and softer than its
stablemate from Alba, "Scarrone," but remains fun to
drink and not at all heavy.

THE WINE
Grape varieties: barbera (100%); **Number of bottles:** 8,000;
Alcohol: 14; **Retail price:** $32–40; **Try it with:** tortelli with cheese
filling; grilled steak and maître d'hôtel butter; goulash; **Imported
by:** Remy Amerique USA (www.remyusa.com); **Past great
vintages:** 2003, 2004

THE PRODUCER: CANTINA VIETTI
Address: piazza Vittorio Veneto 5, 12060 Castiglione Falletto
(Cuneo); **Tel/fax:** 0173 62941/0173 62941; **E-mail:** info@vietti.com;
Web: www.vietti.com; **Total bottles:** 220,000; **Total ha:** 37; **Visit:**
by appointment; **Tasting room:** yes; **Highway exit:** Ast est (A21) or
Marene (A6)

Barolo "Castiglione" (large and small barrel oaked red), Barbera d'Alba "Scarrone Vigne Vecchie" (small and large barrel oaked red).

The Barolos Lazzarito, Brunate, and Villero Riserva are fine but over our $100 price limit.

95* | Castel del Monte Rosso Riserva "Il Falcone"

RIVERA • **90/100** • PUGLIA

The "Falcone" has long been a fine and very fairly priced wine. It was also, for a long time, the only wine of note made (mainly) from the native uva di Troia variety, one that is now taking the south by storm—many new wines are made with it alone or in blends. So kudos to the De Corato family of Rivera, for uva di Troia does seem to be an above-average variety that was in danger of falling by the wayside. The "Falcone" Riserva is always at least very good the minute it hits the shelves, and it also ages tremendously well: I have had many fine bottles from the 1950s that attest to this. It is always a little tight and lean when young; its nose reveals initially only moderate red cherry and wild strawberry aromas, with faint echoes of marjoram, thyme, and stronger leather and tobacco notes. With age, these aromas veer noticeably toward underbrush, porcini mushrooms, and quinine highlights. In the mouth, it's a medium-bodied wine that has pretty, tarry, wild raspberry and strawberry fruit nicely complicated by nuances of leather and tobacco. Its medium-long and clean finish is softly tannic and refreshingly acidic, though unfortunately there is some bottle variation.

THE WINE

Grape varieties: nero di troia (70%), montepulciano (30%); **Number of bottles:** 155,000; **Alcohol:** 13.5; **Retail price:** $25; **Try it with:** braised veal chops with grilled eggplant; **Imported by:** Bedford International (www.winesfrombedford.com); **Past great vintages:** 1953, 1967, 1975, 1982, 1985, 2001

THE PRODUCER: AZ. VINICOLA RIVERA

Address: Contrada Rivera, strada provinciale 231, Km 60.6 Andria (Barletta); **Tel/fax:** 0883 569501/0883 569575; **Web:** www.rivera.it; **E-mail:** info@rivera.it; **Total bottles:** 1.45 million; **Total ha:** 85; **Tasting room:** yes; **Visit:** by appointment; **Highway exit:** Barletta (A14)

OTHER RECOMMENDED WINES UNDER $100
BY RIVERA:
"Marese" (bombino bianco—unoaked white), Rosé (bombino
nero—unoaked rosé), "Violante" (uva di Troia—unoaked red),
"Puer Apuliae" (uva di Troia—small barrel oaked red).

96 | Barbera d'Alba "Pian Romualdo"
PRUNOTTO • **90/100** • PIEDMONT

This venerable estate, owned by Antinori sice 1989, is one of the famous names of Piedmont and an excellent example of how large producers can be a source of wonderful, fairly priced wines even when large amounts are made. The estate's Barolo Bussia is absolutely fine, and very fairly priced for its quality: it has the distinction of having been the first single vineyard named Barolo back in the 1960s when Beppe Colla still owned the winery. However, as good as that wine is, my vote goes to this fresher, lighter Barbera d'Alba, a true standard-bearer for traditional, high-acid, lighter-styled Barbera that is a pure joy at a dinner table anywhere. It offers lovely strawberry and raspberry aromas and flavors, given admirable definition by bright acids that are a hallmark of the variety and this wine. A touch of licorice and violet on the yummy, juicy finish add to the overall pleasure of this wine.

THE WINE
Grape varieties: barbera (100%); **Number of bottles:** 15,000; **Alcohol:** 13.5; **Retail price:** $41; **Try it with:** roast chicken with sage and onion stuffing; **Imported by:** Winebow (www.winebow.com); **Past great vintages:** 1982, 1989, 1990, 1996, 2001

THE PRODUCER: PRUNOTTO
Address: Regione San Cassiano 4/G, 12051 Alba (Cuneo); **Tel/fax:** 0173 280017/0173 281167; **E-mail:** prunotto@prunotto.it; **Web:** www.prunotto.it; **Total bottles:** 600,000; **Total ha:** 54; **Visit:** by appointment; **Tasting room:** yes; **Highway exit:** Ast est (A21)

OTHER RECOMMENDED WINES UNDER $100
BY PRUNOTTO:
Nebbiolo d'Alba "Occhetti" (small and large barrel oaked red), Barolo Bussia (large and small barrel oaked red).

97 | "Sanleonardo"

SANLEONARDO • **91/100** • TRENTINO

One of the better examples of cool-climate Bordeaux-style blends made in Italy, this mainly cabernet blend varies greatly with the year's weather conditions, and so vintage characteristics might dictate whether you like it or not. In cooler years, there is an ever so slight herbal, green bell pepper note that speaks clearly of less-than-ripe cabernet. In hot years the wine is remarkably chunky and fat, especially in more recent vintages that have been tended to by the new winemaker, Carlo Ferrini (as opposed to earlier vintages taken care of by Giacomo Tachis). A glass of this wine always deploys youthfully rigid tannins and fine acidity, with crispy red and black small berry fruit, cedar, and coffee on the nose and the palate. In any case, it is usually one of Italy's more successful and elegant Bordeaux-style blends, and the marchese feels that elegance is a hallmark of the wine. If you're curious about a good Italian version of cab/merlot, this is one of a handful to pick. Beware the Merlot bottling made here, though: quite simply, it is not up to this estate's standards, as I think the marchese is aware.

THE WINE

Grape varieties: cabernet sauvignon (60%), cabernet franc (30%), merlot (10%); **Number of bottles:** 90,000; **Alcohol:** 13.5; **Retail price:** $50–75; **Try it with:** filet of beef with Cabernet wine sauce and sweet peas with onions and mint; **Imported by:** Vias (www.viaswines.com); **Past great vintages:** 1988, 1990, 1997, 1999, 2001, 2003

The 1990 is the best ever made, with cassis and cedar-box aromas, lots of bright acidity, and a fine texture (96/100). The '88 is almost as good, slightly more austere but with a deep core of rich fruit and fine tannins (94/100). The 1993 (86/100) and 1995 (88/100), though fine, are slightly vegetal and bell peppery, especially the '93.

THE PRODUCER: TENUTA SAN LEONARDO— MARCHESE CARLO GUERRIERI GONZAGA

Address: Loc. Borghetto, 38060 Avio (Trento); **Tel/fax:** 0464 689004/0464 682200; **Web:** www.sanleonardo.it; **E-mail:** info@sanleonardo.it; **Total bottles:** 145,000; **Total ha:** 20; **Tasting room:** yes; **Visit:** by appointment; **Highway exit:** AlaAvio (A22)

98 * | Rosso Piceno "Montesecco"

MONTECAPPONE • **90/100** • MARCHE

The Mirizzi family founded the estate toward the end of the 1960s, and it also runs a very nice and well-stocked wineshop in Rome. Hence, the work has been divided up among the various family members, and today the wines and wineshop are sure bets for all wine lovers. The wines of the estate are all fine and fairly priced, and the Verdicchio "Utopia," after years of going from strength to strength, is now among the best Verdicchios on the market. Nonetheless, as good as it is, my vote goes to this lovely Rosso Piceno, as good an everyday table wine as you'll find from anywhere in the world. First, I give the Mirizzis kudos for staying true to the Rosso Piceno formula, when most Rosso Picenos and Rosso Coneros are turning into almost pure Montepulciano wines. A little sangiovese was always used to make these wines easier to drink and ready sooner: few producers seem to remember that people actually have to drink wine with food! So here's to a great little wine, delectable in its up-front cheery frutiness of smoky red cherries and strawberries, hints of tobacco and herbs, and a bright refreshing mouthfeel where its lovely acids give it buoyancy and length.

THE WINE

Grape varieties: montepulciano (70%), sangiovese (30%); **Number of bottles:** 20,000; **Retail price:** $20; **Try it with:** rabbit porchetta style (oven-roasted stuffed with wild fennel and unsmoked bacon); pork chops with orange-tomato sauce; **Imported by:** Martin Scott (www.martinscottwines.com), Salvia Bianca (www.salviabianca.com); **Past great vintages:** 2001, 2004

THE PRODUCER: MONTECAPPONE

Address: via Colle Olivo 2, 60035 Jesi (Ancona); **Tel/fax:** 0731 205761/0731 204233; **E-mail:** info@montecappone.com; **Web:** www.montecappone.com; **Total bottles:** 120,000; **Total ha:** 70; **Tasting room:** yes; **Visit:** by appointment; **Highway exit:** Ancona Nord (A14)

OTHER RECOMMENDED WINES UNDER $100
BY MONTECAPPONE:

Verdicchio dei Castelli di Jesi Classico Superiore "Montesecco" (large barrel oaked white), Esino Bianco "Tabano" (verdicchio/sauvignon—unoaked white), Verdicchio dei Castelli di Jesi Classico Superiore "Utopia" (small barrel oaked white).

99 | Barolo
PIO CESARE • **90/100** • PIEDMONT

One of the best-known names in Italian wines both in Italy and abroad, this address is a sure bet for finding very good, dependable wines at often unbeatable prices. In fact, in a pinch, its red wines are the ones I always turn to in a restaurant with either crazy prices or a poorly chosen wine list. The Grignolino is lovely, if a little softer than most; the Barbera and Dolcetto are just fine; but the "Piodilei" Chardonnay is a little too oaky. By far best wine from this producer is the top Barolo, called "Ornato," though some people feel it's a little too modern, with its chocolatey, smoky aromas and flavors and lowish acidity (common to many of the world's wines regardless of the grape variety). The Barbaresco "Il Bricco" is underrated. The entry-level or base Barolo is also just delightful, and is usually very fairly priced, so it's a great find in restaurants: it allows you to drink well without going broke. I love its aromas of violets, smoky tar, and plums, with suggestions of raspberries and licorice. Full-bodied, with noticeably high acidity and tannins, it nonetheless remains civilized on the long, mineral finish. It's a wine with a remarkable track record for consistency over the years.

THE WINE
Grape varieties: nebbiolo (100%); **Number of bottles:** 80,000; **Alcohol:** 14–14.5; **Retail price:** $35–40; **Try it with:** lamb stew; Castelmagno cheese; high-quality hamburgers; **Imported by:** Maison Marques and Domaines USA (www.mmdusa.net); **Past great vintages:** 1999, 2001

The '99 is an underrated wine with plenty of soft creamy fruit and beautifully refined aromas of licorice and black cherry, with velvety smooth tannins (90/100). The '01 is a fuller-bodied wine, with more concentrated fruit, better acidity, and the trademark smooth tannins. This will keep for decades (91/100).

THE PRODUCER: CASA VINICOLA PIO CESARE
Address: via Cesare Balbo 6, 12051 Alba (Cuneo); **Tel/fax:** 0173 440386/0173 363680; **E-mail:** piocesare@piocesare.it; **Web:** www.piocesare.it; **Total bottles:** 370,000; **Total ha:** 45; **Visit:** by appointment; **Tasting room:** yes; **Highway exit:** Ast est (A21)

Grignolino (unoaked red), Dolcetto d'Alba (unoaked red), Barbera d'Alba (large and small barrel oaked red), Barbaresco "Il Bricco" (nebbiolo—large and small barrel oaked red). The Barolo "Ornato" currently retails at $100 or thereabouts but will soon be over our price limit.

100* Chianti Classico Riserva "Il Grigio"

SAN FELICE • 90/100 • TUSCANY

This wine has always been an "old reliable," a very competently made, true-to-type Chianti one could find easily, given the large production, and, even better, find at very affordable prices. I'm not so sure recent vintages are on the same quality level as wines from the 1970s and 1980s, as I feel that a stylistic change toward a softer, rounder mouthfeel undermines somewhat the high-acid, nervy personality of true Chianti. In any case, the wine remains an excellent value and a great pick at a restaurant, since some wine lists now carry prices that only the richest among us can afford. You'll enjoy the aromas of violets, red currants, and milk chocolate; the plum, coffee, and milk chocolate flavors; and the soft tannins. The people at San Felice have always been innovators. Almost 40 years ago they released "Vigorello," the first super-Tuscan; their latest wine, the promising "Pugnitello," is made from an ancient variety they have worked on intensely over the past 10 years, investing time and money in university field and lab research.

THE WINE

Grape varieties: sangiovese (100%); **Number of bottles:** 300,000; **Alcohol:** 13; **Retail price:** $17–27; **Try it with:** grilled rib eye with corn pudding and red peppers; **Imported by:** Opici Import Company (www.opici.com); **Past great vintages:** 1977, 1979, 1982, 2001

The '77 was one of the better wines of the vintage, and is still pleasurable and extremely aristocratic in its fine tannins and crunchy red fruit (90/100). The '79 is a real success; it is perhaps lacking a little intensity in keeping with the vintage, but it has a charming easygoing nature and its high acids nicely frame the red fruit (87/100). The '82 was richer than these two, with plenty of up-front ripe fruit of some depth, but finishes a little short (88/100).

THE PRODUCER: AGRICOLA SAN FELICE

Address: Località San Felice, 14—Sant'Angelo in Colle, 53020 Montalcino (Siena); **Tel/fax:** 0577 3991/0577 359223; **E-mail:** info@agricolasanfelie.it; **Web:** www.agricolasanfelice.it; **Total bottles:** 1.2 million; **Total ha:** 216; **Visit:** by appointment; **Tasting room:** yes; **Highway exit:** Firenze Certosa or Val di Chiana (A1)

OTHER RECOMMENDED WINES UNDER $100 BY SAN FELICE:

Chianti Classico Riserva "Poggio Rosso" (small barrel oaked red), Pugnitello (small barrel oaked red), "Vigorello" (sangiovese/cabernet sauvignon/merlot—small barrel oaked red).

THE 60 BEST WHITE WINES UNDER $100

1 | "Terre Alte"
LIVIO FELLUGA • 95/100 • FRIULI VENEZIA GIULIA

Along with Jermann's "Vintage Tunina," the "Terre Alte" has always been the best of the white grape blends that made Friuli's reputation in the 1970s and 1980s. Moreover, it has never fluctuated in quality: if anything, unlike other famous white blends, it's even better today. Its trump cards are intensity and concentration of fruit with a unique mineral, high-acid edge, allowing it to pack plenty of aromas and flavors while remaining lithe and fresh. That is no small feat for most wines in general, and it is even more difficult to achieve in the hot subzone of Rosazzo, where the grapes grow. The wine is straw yellow in color; the nose has chamomile, golden delicious apple, apricot, and herbal aromas. Vanilla wafer, almond, and tangerine flavors are enlivened by bracing acidity: the wine walks a fine line between steely and luscious personalities, and you'll love the long mineral finish. Don't miss this estate's bed-and-breakfast, "Terre e Vini," where the home-cooked food is nothing short of excellent.

THE WINE

Grape varieties: tocai friulano, pinot bianco, and sauvignon (roughly 33% each—in cooler vintages the estate lowers the percentage of sauvignon to prevent it from being too dominant); **Number of bottles:** 40,000; **Alcohol:** 13.5; **Retail price:** $45–50; **Try it with:** grilled salmon steak with citrus-balsamic vinaigrette; **Imported by:** Moët Hennessy USA (www.mhusa.com); **Past great vintages:** 1981, 1985, 1989, 1997, 1999, 2001, 2004

The '01 is rich, mineral, and fruity (95/100). The '04 has a riper fruit core, a richer mouthfeel, and a long finish, but is less refined (94/100). The 1997 is another excellent wine with pretty pear and apple scents, a honeyed mineral note on the palate, and a crisp finish (93/100). Since 10 years ago, the percentage of tocai used undergoes barrel fermentation, allowing the wine to age better.

THE PRODUCER: EREDI AZ. AGR. LIVIO FELLUGA

Address: Fraz. Brazzano, via Risorgimento 1, Cormons (Gorizia);
Tel/fax: 0481 60203/0481630126; **Web:** www.liviofelluga.it;
E-mail: info@liviofelluga.it; **Total bottles:** 800,000; **Total ha:** 215;
Tasting room: yes; **Visit:** by appointment; **Highway exit:**
Palmanova or Villesse (A4)

OTHER RECOMMENDED WINES UNDER $100
BY LIVIO FELLUGA:
"Sharjs" (ribolla/chardonnay—lightly oaked white), Pinot Grigio
(unoaked white), Tocai Friulano (unoaked white), "Sossò"
(refosco/pignolo—oaked red), Picolit Riserva (sweet white).

2 | Soave Calvarino
PIEROPAN • **95/100** • VENETO

If Soave can be taken seriously today, a lot of the credit has
to go to Leonildo (Nino) Pieropan, who persevered in bad
times when it was hard to sell a bottle of the stuff because
the wine's reputation had been tarnished by many watery,
neutral, industrially or poorly made versions. Pieropan
continued to make wonderful wines of amazing purity
and uncompromising quality, refusing to add sauvignon
or chardonnay as others did in an effort to make wines
that would sell better on world markets. Pieropan correctly believed that, in the long run, this would not be a
winning strategy, and time has proved him right; today,
it's almost funny to hear many of his colleagues extol the
virtues of the garganega grape and say that they never
added any other varieties, such as chardonnay, to their
wines. Pieropan's two different single vineyard bottlings—
"Calvarino" and "La Rocca" (barrel fermented and 100%
garganega)—are textbook examples of what great Soave is
all about; some readers may prefer La Rocca's sweet, oaky
veneer, but Calvarino best reveals the potential and aging
capacity of the native garganega grape, without any cosmetic oak to disguise it. Calvarino is pale straw-green in
color, with stone fruits, minerals, and a hint of licorice
aromas on the nose nicely complemented by lemon ice
and a flinty minerality; it is also very mineral in the
mouth, with flavors of green apple and grapefruit and a
delicate herbal twist. Unfortunately, hail badly damaged
vineyards (especially the La Rocca) in '07 and so there
may not be as much of these wines available for the next
couple of years.

Grape varieties: garganega (90%), trebbiano di soave (10%);
Number of bottles: 45,000; **Alcohol:** 13; **Retail price:** $30; **Try it
with:** pan-roasted sea bass and dill quiche; grilled calamari with
citrus-accented mayonnaise; **Imported by:** Empson USA (www.
empson.com); **Past great vintages:** 1979, 1982, 1986, 2003, 2004

The '79 was unbelievably fine: never before had I
tasted a Soave of similar power and concentration and aging ability.

THE PRODUCER: AZIENDA VITIVINICOLA
PIEROPAN

Address: via Camuzzoni 3, 37038 Soave (VR); **Tel/fax:** 0456
190171 / 0456 190040; **Web:** www.pieropan.it; **E-mail:** info@
pieropan.it; **Total bottles:** 350,000; **Total ha:** 45; **Tasting room:**
yes; **Visit:** by appointment; **Highway exit:** Soave (A4)

OTHER RECOMMENDED WINES UNDER $100 BY
PIEROPAN:

Soave Classico La Rocca (garganega—oaked white), Recioto di
Soave "Le Colombare" (garganega—sweet white), Passito La
Rocca (sauvignon/riesling italico/trebbiano—sweet white).

3 | Verdicchio dei Castelli di Jesi Balciana

SARTARELLI • **95/100** • MARCHE

Always one of Italy's best whites, this is also a fairly atypical one, a late-harvest wine with a clear-cut Alsatian bent.
Balciana is a particularly well exposed site that allows the
verdicchio grapes maximum ripening capacity, and so the
finished wine is often characterized by a touch of residual
sweetness. Produced in only the best years, the wine is
usually a luminous straw green-golden color. Citrus,
peach, almond, and vanilla custard aromas soar from the
glass, while the flavors veer more toward ripe peach, apricot, and pineapple. Zesty acidity adds an extra dimension
to the wine and keeps it long and pure on the honeyed,
slightly waxy mineral finish. Though it probably won't
seem totally dry to many consumers, the wine stays remarkably light and fresh on the palate, and its extra
inner-mouth volume will allow it to stand up perfectly even
to chicken and pork dishes. Congratulations to the owners, Donatella and Patrizio Sartarelli, who are dedicated to
making the highest-quality wines possible, and who have
created in Balciana an icon of modern Italian wine.

THE WINE

Grape varieties: verdicchio (100%); **Number of bottles:** 20,000; **Alcohol:** 14; **Retail price:** $40–45; **Try it with:** rabbit pochetta-style (oven-roasted with garlic, bacon, and white wine); scallops in orange-cream sauce; Oriental lemon chicken; **Imported by:** Young's Columbia Wine Company (NA); **Past great vintages:** 1999, 2001, 2003, 2006

THE PRODUCER: AZ. AGR. SARTARELLI

Address: Contrada Costa del Molino, Loc. Poggio—60030 San Marcello (AN); **Tel/fax:** 073189732/0731889902; **Web:** www.sartarelli.it; **E-mail:** info@sartarelli.it; **Total bottles:** 300,000; **Total ha:** 66; **Tasting room:** yes; **Visit:** by appointment; **Highway exit:** Senigallia (A14)

OTHER RECOMMENDED WINES UNDER $100 BY SARTARELLI:

Verdicchio dei Castelli di Jesi Classico Superiore "Tralivio" (unoaked white).

---

4 | Gewürztraminer "Nussbaumer"

CANTINA PRODUTTORI TERMENO
• **95/100** • ALTO ADIGE

If Alto Adige makes Italy's best white wines today, and the producers' cooperative of Termeno is the best of a very good lot of producers there, it follows that you can't go wrong with just about any label you choose from Termeno. Not one but two of Italy's best white wines are made by Termeno, and this Gewürztraminer is a work of art. Of the two main styles of Gewürztraminer, floral-refined versus tropical fruit–opulent, the "Nussbaumer" is the best possible example of the former. Considering all the fine vintages made, it is safe to say that this is Italy's best Gewürztraminer—not a backhanded compliment in view of the fact that this is a grape in which Italy excels. The color is a pretty light straw yellow with hints of green-gold. Very obvious rose petal and pink grapefruit aromas are complicated by Meyer lemon mousse and delicate spicy nuances. It's crisp and balanced on the palate, where tangerine, grapefruit, cinnamon, and nutmeg flavors abound, all nicely framed by bright lively acids. Finishes with a floral quality and excellent density and length. It's an absolutely thrilling wine, and a welcome change for anyone who wants a more elegant and truly dry Gewürztraminer. Be aware that some people refer to this producer by its German name, Tramin, though nobody in Italy outside Alto Adige would ever think of doing so.

THE WINE

Grape varieties: gewürztraminer (100%); **Number of bottles:** 55,000; **Alcohol:** 14; **Retail price:** $40; **Try it with:** onion tart with braised leeks; chicken curry and rice pilaf; **Imported by:** Winebow (www.winebow.com); **Past great vintages:** 1999, 2000, 2001, 2002, 2004

THE PRODUCER: CANTINA PRODUTTORI TERMENO—TRAMIN

Address: strada del Vino 144, 39040 Termeno (BZ); **Tel/fax:** 0471 860126/0471 860828; **Web:** www.tramin-wine.it; **E-mail:** info@tramin-wine.it; **Total bottles:** 1.4 million; **Total ha:** 230; **Tasting room:** yes; **Visit:** by appointment; **Highway exit:** Egna-Ora (A22)

OTHER RECOMMENDED WINES UNDER $100 BY TERMENO:

Pinot Grigio "Unterebner" (oaked white), Gewürztraminer Late Harvest "Terminum" (sweet white), Gewürztraminer Late Harvest "Roan" (sweet white), Moscato Rosa "Terminum" (sweet red).

5 | "Vintage Tunina"

JERMANN • 95/100 • FRIULI VENEZIA GIULIA

"Vintage Tunina" is one of the surest things to try, a highly perfumed yet luscious wine. It was one of the first truly great, world-class white wines made in Italy, and led the revolution in quality that took the country by storm in the 1980s. In fact, it had a primary role in setting an example of the greatness that was possible, and of what to strive for; it became the reference point for many young producers who were just starting out and who were beginning to take control of their family wineries. Named after one of Casanova's lovers, a young woman believed to have been the one true love of his life, this wine has an uncanny ability to seem light yet concentrated at the same time, and the bright acids always keep you coming back for just another sip. Though the wines made in the early 2000s seemed a little less exciting than the iconic, outstanding wines made in the 1980s and 1990s, "Vintage Tunina" seems to be back on track and is, simply, fantastic. Straw yellow with green-gold highlights, it opens with a burst of white stone fruit and floral aromas complicated by herbal and tropical fruit nuances, mango first and foremost. This exciting mid-weight wine has slightly more mature flavors that recall exotic fruits and pear but also citrus, nutmeg, coffee, and vanilla bean on the long, clean, mineral finish. And all this comes without the use of any camouflaging oak.

THE WINE
Grape varieties: mainly sauvignon and chardonnay (70%), malvasia, ribolla, and picolit (30%); **Number of bottles:** 65,000; **Alcohol:** 13.5; **Retail price:** $76; **Try it with:** linguine in lobster sauce; polenta-crusted sea bass with sweet corn and tomato salsa; **Imported by:** Empson USA (www.empson.com); **Past great vintages:** 1985, 1989, 1990, 1992, 1995, 2004

THE PRODUCER: VINNAIOLI JERMANN
Address: via Monte Fortino 21, 34070 Farra d'Isonzo (GO); **Tel/fax:** 0481 888080/0481 888512; **Web:** www.jermannvinnaioli.it; **E-mail:** info@jermann.it; **Total bottles:** 800,000; **Total ha:** 120; **Tasting room:** yes; **Visit:** by appointment; **Highway exit:** Villesse (A4)

OTHER RECOMMENDED WINES UNDER $100 BY SILVIO JERMANN:
"Capo Martino" (tocai/pinot bianco/malvaisa/ribolla/picolit—oaked white).

6* Fiano di Avellino
COLLI DI LAPIO—CLELIO ROMANO •
95/100 • CAMPANIA

Fiano is an unfolding success story, attracting the attention of producers from all over the world, and is likely to become an "international" variety. There are essentially two possible styles of Fiano: one is mineral, lean, and high in acid; the other is more opulent, softer, and rich in ripe tropical fruit, not unlike a smoky Chardonnay. Clelio Romano's Fiano is in the mineral–high acid group but is so good that in the mind of many experts, it is the best Fiano made in Italy today, regardless of these stylistic differences. Clelio's vineyards are situated at more than 1,600 feet above sea level, and the cool climate shows in the highly perfumed nose of citrus fruits and green apple, with hints of unripe peach, lime, mint, and tequila. Amazingly mineral in the mouth, with a beautifully long, minty finish, it captivates because of its fresh fruit, lemon-lime, thyme, and delicate cilantro flavors. By the way, this wine ages extremely well, and that's not something you can say about many Italian white wines.

I'm currently drinking the '98s and '99s from my cellar and they're an absolute joy. It's a clean, pure wine that really shows off its cool-climate origins.

THE WINE
Grape varieties: fiano (100%); **Number of bottles:** 35,000; **Alcohol:** 13; **Retail price:** $25–30; **Try it with:** octopus salad; poached turbot in caper-cherry-tomato sauce; **Imported by:** Marc de Grazia Selection (www.marcdegrazia.com), and numerous importers; **Past great vintages:** 1998, 1999, 2001

THE PRODUCER: COLLI DI LAPIO—CLELIO ROMANO
Address: via Azianello 47, 83030 Lapio (AV); **Tel/fax:** 0925 982184/0825 982184; **E-mail:** collidilapio@libero.it; **Total bottles:** 50,000; **Total ha:** 6; **Tasting room:** yes; **Visit:** by appointment; **Highway exit:** Avellino est (A16)

OTHER RECOMMENDED WINES UNDER $100 BY COLLI DI LAPIO:
Aglianico "Donna Chiara" (large barrel oaked red), Taurasi Vigna Andrea (steel and small barrel oaked red).

7 | Pinot Grigio
MARCO MARTIN—LO TRIOLET •
94/100 • VALLE D'AOSTA

Marco Martin began making wine only a few years ago and chose Pinot Grigio (which in homage to the French roots of Valle d'Aosta is always called Pinot Gris) because he liked his neighbor's homemade wine. Today, Martin is one of Italy's very best wine producers, excelling with any grape variety he touches. His two, totally dry, Pinot Grigios are among Italy's 10 or 12 best whites, but his Pinot Noir and Gamay are also delicious, as is the bigger "Coteau Barrage." It is hard to choose betweeen the non-oaked or the small barrel fermented Pinot Grigios: I'll pick the non-oaked version, which has an intensity of flavor that many barrel-matured wines cannot match. It is beautifully green-golden in color; the nose is redolent of beeswax, ripe pear, and white peach, given further lift and complexity by an herbal quality (thyme, oregano, coriander). There are plenty of ripe fruit and herbal flavors as well, and their intensity and purity leave the mouth feeling rich and satisfied. This is what true high-quality Pinot Grigio ought to taste like, but seldom does. Don't miss out on these wines, on a par with those of Antinori, Conterno, and other great names in Italian wine.

THE WINE
Grape varieties: pinot grigio (100%); **Number of bottles:** 5,000; **Alcohol:** 13.5; **Retail price:** $40; **Try it with:** grilled trout with warm thyme vinaigrette; pan-roasted pompano and caramelized shallots; **Imported by:** Small Vineyards (www.svimports.com); **Past great vintages:** 2001, 2002, 2004, 2006

THE PRODUCER: LO TRIOLET
Address: Fraz. Junod 7, 11010 Introd (Aosta); **Tel/fax:** 0165 95437 / 0165 95437; **Web:** www.lotriolet.vievini.it; **E-mail:** lotriolet@vievini.it; **Total bottles:** 30,000; **Total ha:** 3; **Tasting room:** yes; **Visit:** by appointment; **Highway exit:** Aosta ovest (A5)

OTHER RECOMMENDED WINES UNDER $100 BY LO TRIOLET:
Pinot Gris-Elevée en barriques (oaked white), Gamay (unoaked light red), Pinot Noir (unoaked light red), "Coteau Barrage" (syrah/fumin—oaked red), Mistigri (pinot grigio—sweet white).

8 | Müller Thurgau "Feldmarschall"
TIEFENBRUNNER • **94/100** • ALTO ADIGE

Long considered Italy's best Müller Thurgau, and actually one of the best made anywhere, "Feldmarschall" has also impressed famous foreign winemakers, such as Domaine Weinbach's Laurence Faller and Ernie Loosen. If truth be told, the wine has only recently reached top form again: the splendidly situated vineyard, at about 3,400 feet above sea level (one of the highest in all of Europe), was replanted about 15 years ago and the young vines are only now starting to hit their stride. The wine is brilliant straw-green; the nose is always a little closed when young and needs time in the glass to open and reveal its brightly aromatic and floral personality, with mint, gin, tequila, green apple, and white peach aromas. The mouth shows delicate herbal flavors at the outset, then swings into stone fruits and tangerines. The finish is extra long, pure, and very mineral. Almost any vintage of "Feldmarschall" is a benchmark for the variety and a clear-cut example of what a much-maligned grape variety can offer when properly cared for. The lower-priced wines by this house are, given their quality, a steal; and for nearly any wine, the Tiefenbrunner name on the label is a virtual guarantee of high quality. That being aknowledged, beware the "Linticlarus" Chardonnay, which is often over-oaked.

THE WINE

Grape varieties: Müller Thurgau (100%); **Number of bottles:** 20,000; **Alcohol:** 12.5; **Retail price:** $35–40; **Try it with:** gingered shrimp; Trentino-style trout (with sautéed onions, vinegar, parsley, mint, orange and lemon peel, and raisins); **Imported by:** Winebow (www.winebow.com); **Past great vintages:** 1979, 1985, 1988, 1989, 2003, 2004

The '79 is spectacular wine, still fresh and young, with lemon peel, thyme, and white peach aromas and flavors (95/100). The '85 is almost as good, with a pretty mineral edge and a green apple, apricot, and minty personality (94/100). Note that older vintages of pure Müller Thurgau very rarely have any hydrocarbon aromas typical of Riesling and some other more aromatic wines.

THE PRODUCER: TIEFENBRUNNER CASTEL TURMHOF

Address: Fraz. Niclara, Via Castello 4, 39040 Cortaccia (BZ); **Tel/fax:** 0471 880122 / 0471 880433; **Web:** www.tiefenbrunner.com; **E-mail:** info@tiefenbrunner.com; **Total bottles:** 750,000; **Total ha:** 20; **Tasting room:** yes; **Visit:** by appointment; **Highway exit:** Egna/Ora (A22)

OTHER RECOMMENDED WINES UNDER $100 BY TIEFENBRUNNER:

Castel Thurmhof Gewürztraminer (unoaked white), Goldenmuskateller (yellow muscat—unoaked white), Pinot Nero (unoaked light red), Castel Thurmhof Schiava Grigia (unoaked light red).

9 | "Fiorduva"

MARISA CUOMO • **94/100** • CAMPANIA

This is a fantastic white wine, and one that has never known a bad vintage. The consultant winemaker Luigi Moio helps make a number of great wines, and with these little-known native grapes of the beautiful Sorrento coast he has come up with something truly special. It is very rich yet comes across as light and refreshing, thanks to bright acids. You'll love the delicate citrus and mineral aromas with lovely oregano and bay leaf twists. There are more very delicate tangerine, pineapple, and orange flavors on the palate, with a noticeable touch of vanilla derived from the small oak barrels the wine ages in. Many white wines of the Amalfi coast are delectable in the light, breezy quality of their fresh fruit and floral aromas, but ultimately lack complexity; by contrast, "Fiorduva" is a wine of considerable depth and flavor with a seamless quality and very fine length. The husband-and-wife team of Andrea Ferrajoli and Marisa Cuomo always dreamed of making great wines in one of the world's most beautiful, if difficult, places for viticulture (the vineyards straddle and hug steep mountaintop slopes jutting out over the sea); and so in 1980 they bought the "Gran Furor Divina Costiera" brand, famous in the area since 1942, and called on Moio to help. Considering the quality of their wines, one has to say the two have succeeded in giving life to their dream.

THE WINE

Grape varieties: ripoli (40%), fenile (30%), ginestra (30%); **Number of bottles:** 16,000; **Alcohol:** 13.5; **Retail price:** $40; **Try it with:** spaghetti with shrimp, cherry tomato, and garlic sauce; grilled swordfish with lemon-caper butter; **Imported by:** Panebianco (www.panebiancowines.com); **Past great vintages:** 2001, 2004

THE PRODUCER: CANTINE MARISA CUOMO—GRAN FUROR DIVINA COSTIERA

Address: via Lama 14, 84010 Furore (Salerno); **Tel/fax:** 089 830348 / 089 8304014; **Web:** www.granfuror.it; **E-mail:** info@ granfuror.it; **Total bottles:** 96,000; **Total ha:** 3.5; **Tasting room:** yes; **Visit:** by appointment; **Highway exit:** Castellamare di Stabia (A3)

OTHER RECOMMENDED WINES UNDER $100 BY MARISA CUOMO:

Furore Bianco (falanghina/biancolella—white), Ravello Bianco (falanghina/biancolella—white).

10 | "Vespa Bianco"

BASTIANICH • **94/100** • FRIULI VENEZIA GIULIA

The Tocai "Plus" is without question this estate's best wine, but the "Vespa Bianco" blend is almost as good, and since it's available in much larger quantities, I'll give it my nod for this top-60 list. In any case, smart buyers ought to look for both these wines, as well as the entry-level Tocai Friulano, which is better than average. Joseph Bastianich, of the famous Bastianich family of restaurateurs in New York, bought the well-known Dal Fari estate and with help from the star winemakers Maurizio Castelli and Emilio Del Medico has turned it into a "can't miss" source for fine Italian wines. The "Vespa Bianco" is another in a long line of great Friuli Bianco blends, a wine in the mold of the famous "Vintage Tunina" or "Terre Alte," and is right up there with those two in terms of quality. It has pretty floral and herbal elements on the nose, with lots of honeysuckle, green apple, tangerine, vanilla, and pineapple twists. Clean acidity on the palate keeps it lively and fresh, but extended lees contact (the time the juice stays in contact with the pressed skins and yeasts) also gives it a pleasantly creamy texture. It develops pretty almond and hazelnut nuances with five to six years of bottle age, which also help resolve its oak component.

THE WINE
Grape varieties: chardonnay (45%), sauvignon (45%), and picolit (10%); **Number of bottles:** 26,000; **Alcohol:** 14; **Retail price:** $35; **Try it with:** grilled marinated filet of tuna; linguine in lobster sauce; **Imported by:** Dark Star Imports (www.bastianich.com); **Past great vintages:** 1998, 1999, 2001, 2004, 2006

The '98 may well be the best "Vespa" ever, with great depth of ripe, almost tropical fruit, and bright acids—a mind-blowingly good wine (95/100). The '99 is somewhat tighter-grained, with a less showy amount of fruit flavors (91/100). The '01 (still available at the winery) is aging wonderfully, with pleasantly pure, honeyed aromas of golden delicious apple, peach, and pineapple and similar flavors (93/100).

THE PRODUCER: AZ. AGR. BASTIANICH
Address: Loc. Gagliano, via Darnazzacco, 44/2—33043 Cividale del Friuli (Udine); **Tel/fax:** 0432 700943/ 0432 731219; **Web:** www .bastianich.com; **E-mail:** bastianich@ aol.com; **Total bottles:** 200,000; **Total ha:** 28; **Tasting room:** yes; **Visit:** by appointment; **Highway exit:** Udine Sud (A23)

OTHER RECOMMENDED WINES UNDER $100 BY BASTIANICH:
Tocai Friulano (unoaked white), Tocai Friulano "Plus" (oaked white), "Vespa Rosso" (merlot/refosco/cabernet sauvignon/ cabernet franc—oaked red).

Gavi di Gavi

11 [*]

ROVERETO "VIGNA VECCHIA" CASTELLARI
BERGAGLIO • **94/100** • PIEDMONT

Castellari Bergaglio produces nothing else but Gavi, and it makes the best expressions, bar none, of the cortese grape. You would think the wines would do much to revive Gavi's tarnished reputation, but that's not necessarily so. Ironically, the wines of Castellari Bergaglio are so much more intense and concentrated than the average lackluster, neutral Gavi product that at least one very famous importer (not American) turned them down years ago, saying that they were "atypical." Of the many different Gavis produced by Castellari Bergaglio, the best is usually the "Rovereto" bottling, from 80-year-old pre-phylloxera vines (see Glossary) in the Rovereto area: the name of the wine derives from the forest of *rovere*—oak—nearby, which creates a unique microclimate. This area is, for all intents and purposes, a *grand cru* for the cortese grape, which seems to thrive in the reddish clay and iron-rich soils of Rovereto. The wine has a brilliantly fresh nose, with herbal, mineral, pear, and spicy aromas; then it is mineral, herbal, and dry on the palate, with a honeyed note, and just a whiff of excess alcohol. There is a long, creamy, almost full-bodied finish. Nicely complex, made with 20 days of fermentation at 18–20°C that help the cortese grape juice or must develop complexity and show its best.

THE WINE

Grape varieties: cortese (100%); **Number of bottles:** 8,000; **Retail price:** $25; **Alcohol:** 13; **Try it with:** squid salad; grilled octopus with herbal-citrus vinaigrette; fried shrimp; **Imported by:** Panebianco (www.panebiancowines.com); **Past great vintages:** 2004, 2005

THE PRODUCER: AZ. AGR. CASTELLARI BERGAGLIO

Address: Fraz. Rovereto, 15066 Gavi (AL); **Tel/fax:** 0143 644000 / 0143 644900; **Web:** www.castellaribergaglio.it; **E-mail:** gavi@ castellaribergaglio.it; **Total bottles:** 60,000; **Total ha:** 12; **Tasting room:** yes; **Visit:** by appointment; **Highway exit:** Serravalle Scrivia (A7) or Novi Ligure (A26/7)

OTHER RECOMMENDED WINES UNDER $100 BY CASTELLARI BERGAGLIO:

Gavi del Comune di Tassarolo "Fornaci" (cortese—unoaked white), Gavi "Rolona" (cortese—unoaked white).

12 | Sauvignon "Sanct Valentin"

PRODUTTORI SAN MICHELE APPIANO •
94/100 • ALTO ADIGE

Hans Terzer, the *Kellermeister* (cellar master) of this high-quality cooperative, is one of Italy's most famous winemakers. His top wines, all called "Sanct Valentin," have long been the standard of reference for anyone wishing to make high-quality Italian whites. His Sauvignon "Sanct Valentin" and Gewürztraminer "Sanct Valentin" have had few rivals in Italy, and I love just how much flavor intensity and elegance he packs into them—especially into the former wine, which is made in relatively large amounts. It's one thing to make great wine in a limited number of bottles, but quite another to do it in the numbers he turns out. Given those production numbers, this may well be Italy's best Sauvignon Blanc: bright medium yellow, with pungent aromas of crystallized stone fruits, mirabelle, and lemon drop, it also has hints of exotic fruits and fresh flowers, with delicate grassy, green fig and yellow melon nuances. Beautifully mineral and pure on the palate, it has a long rich finish with more of the delicate grassy touch. This wine eschews the exaggerated, candied, overripe tropical fruit aromas that some New World Sauvignon Blancs exude, and goes far better with food. Bravo, Hans!

THE WINE

Grape varieties: sauvignon (100%); **Number of bottles:** 120,000; **Alcohol:** 13; **Retail price:** $28–38; **Try it with:** asparagus quiche and mixed green salad; goat cheese crepes with braised baby artichokes; **Imported by:** Martin Scott Wines (www.martinscott wines.com), Classic Wine Imports (www.classicwines.com); **Past great vintages:** 1990, 1995, 1998, 2004

THE PRODUCER: PRODUTTORI SAN MICHELE APPIANO

Address: via Circonvallazione 17–19, 39057 Appiano (Bolzano); **Tel/fax:** 0471 664466/0471 660764; **Web:** www.stmichael.it; **E-mail:** kellerei@stmichael.it; **Total bottles:** 2,000,000; **Total ha:** 355; **Tasting room:** yes; **Visit:** by appointment; **Highway exit:** Bolzano sud or Egna (A22)

OTHER RECOMMENDED WINES UNDER $100 BY SAN MICHELE APPIANO:

Pinot Bianco "Schulthauser" (unoaked white), Riesling "Montiggl" (unoaked white), Sauvignon "Lahn" (unoaked white), Pinot Grigio

"Sanct Valentin" (oaked white), Gewürztraminer "Sanct Valentin" (unoaked white), Passito "Comtess Sanct Valentin" (sweet white).

13 | Greco di Tufo "Vigna Cicogna"
BENITO FERRARA • 93/100 • CAMPANIA

Well led by Gabriella Ferrara, this estate produces some of Italy's best whites, with a fine Fiano and a very good base Greco. The "Vigna Cicogna" is by far the best wine of the estate, and one of the better white wines you'll ever taste from Italy. Usually more aggressive and structured than Fiano, Campania's other famous white, the greco variety is a finicky one that seems to show its best only in and around the town of Tufo. The nearby sulfur mines, now abandoned, may help explain the characteristic aromas of the wine, which has a unique citric, honeyed, floral, and gunpowder combination that you won't find in many others. The honeyed, almost resiny, and citrus twists are evident on the palate as well, with a strong mineral and herbal touch on the long creamy, powerful finish. The vines are 70 years old, are located in the *grand cru* area of San Paolo di Tufo, and have a full south exposure—yet another component of making great wines such as those by Gabriella. The "Vigna Cicogna" is also a wonderful example of how you can make a very fine white wine without using any oak whatsoever, allowing the pure floral and fruit aromas and flavors to shine through.

THE WINE

Grape varieties: greco (100%); **Number of bottles:** 18,000; **Alcohol:** 13.5; **Retail price:** $25–28; **Try it with:** calzone (oven-cooked focaccia stuffed with mozzarella, ricotta, salami, parsley, pepper, and basil); sautéed bluefish with toasted hazelnuts; **Imported by:** Marc de Grazia Selection (www.marcdegrazia.com), numerous importers; **Past great vintages:** 1999, 2001

The '01 is steely, yet rich and luscious, with a honeyed baked apple quality (93/100). The '99 is somewhat fatter, with ripe apple aromas and flavors with gunpowder tea and herbal nuances (93/100).

THE PRODUCER:AZ. AGR. BENITO FERRARA; **Address:** Fraz. San Paolo 14/a, 83010 Tufo (AV); **Tel/fax:** 0825 998194/0825 998194; **Web:** www.benitoferrara.it; **E-mail:** info@benitoferrara.it; **Total bottles:** 42,000; **Total ha:** 8; **Tasting room:** yes; **Visit:** by appointment; **Highway exit:** Avellino est (A16)

OTHER RECOMMENDED WINES UNDER $100
BY BENITO FERRARA:
Fiano di Avellino (unoaked white), Greco di Tufo (unoaked white).

14* | Kerner

MANNI NOSSING • 94/100 • ALTO ADIGE

Kerner is a cross between riesling and trollinger, a light red grape that in Italy is called schiava. The idea behind this crossing (and all other crossings where riesling is one of the players) is to obtain a new grape with riesling's positive traits (breed, aging capacity, elegance) without the defects (late ripener, small production). Kerner is often overlooked by experts who talk only about riesling and other aromatic varieties, but the truth is that Italy, or more precisely the cool Valle Isarco area of Alto Adige, makes great Kerners and this one by Nossing is the best. Production doubles with the '06 vintage, as Manni, who believes deeply in the grape's potential, has increased plantings in recent years. This wine's delicate aromatic character ought to appeal to those who feel that Riesling and Gewürztraminer are just too much of a good thing. The pretty straw-green color is followed by lovely mineraly white peach, nutmeg, bubble gum, and mango aromas. Fresh and mineral on the palate, it's concentrated, but the high acids and balance prevent it from seeming heavy or over the top. You won't notice the almost 14.5 count of alcohol, either. His Müller and Sylvaner are also fabulous, and top examples of these varietal wines.

THE WINE
Grape varieties: Kerner (100%); **Number of bottles:** 14,000; **Alcohol:** 14–14.5; **Retail price:** $25–30; **Try it with:** chilled crayfish and shrimp with spicy sauce; sea bass with cracked anise and mustard seeds; **Imported by:** Doug Polaner selection (www .polanerselections.com); **Past great vintages:** 2002, 2005, 2006

THE PRODUCER: HOANDLHOF MANNI NOSSING
Address: via dei Vigneti 66, 39042 Bressanone (BZ); **Tel/fax:** 0472 832672 / 0472 832672; **Total bottles:** 30,000; **Total ha:** 5.8; **Tasting room:** yes; **Visit:** by appointment; **Highway exit:** Bressanone sud (A22)

OTHER RECOMMENDED WINES UNDER $100
BY MANNI NOSSING:
Müller Thurgau (unoaked white), Sylvaner (unoaked white).

15* Müller Thurgau

KÖFERERHOF • 94/100 • ALTO ADIGE

Müller Thurgau is another cross, this time between riesling and perhaps chasselas, though confusion abounds on
the subject. Crossings rarely give high-quality wines (nature does know best), and it's the same with Müller, one of
the world's most maligned grapes. Part of this reputation
is deserved, as it's often planted in flatlands where it yields
oceans of lackluster syrupy sweet wines. Once again,
much as with Sylvaner and Kerner, Italy also makes some
of the world's great Müllers, depending on how seriously
the producer goes about it. The old vines (planted in the
1960s) at Köfererhof explain, at least in part, why this is,
pedigree and wine snobbery aside, one of Italy's great
wines. The rest of the explanation is the skill of the owner,
Günther Kerschbaumer, in the vineyard (he's greatly reduced yields recently) and in the cellar. Straw green in
hue, this wine has oodles of green apple, white peach, and
chamomile aromas. Lemon-lime and herbal flavors mark
this medium-bodied, crisp, clean wine; and if you haven't
been won over by all this, the mineral undercurrents on
the long, intense finish will convince you. Any white wine
made at this estate is an absolute benchmark for the variety in Italy, especially the Sylvaner, but the already very
good Riesling is undoubtedly the wine with the largest
potential.

THE WINE

Grape varieties: Müller Thurgau (100%); **Number of bottles:**
9,000; **Alcohol:** 13.5; **Retail price:** $22; **Try it with:** soft-shell crabs
with spicy carrot sauce; soufflé of smoked trout; **Imported by:**
Marc de Grazia Selection (www.marcdegrazia.com) and
numerous importers; **Past great vintages:** 2005, 2006

THE PRODUCER: KÖFERERHOF

Address: strada Val Pusteria—Novacella 3 39040 Varna (BZ);
Tel/fax: 0472 836649/0472 836248; **Web:** www.kofererhof.com;
E-mail: info@kofererhof.com **Total bottles:** 48,000; **Total ha:** 9;
Tasting room: yes; **Visit:** by appointment; **Highway exit:**
Bressanone (A22)

OTHER RECOMMENDED WINES UNDER $100
BY KÖFERERHOF:

Riesling (unoaked white), Sylvaner (steel and large oak barrel
white), Kerner (unoaked white), Pinot Grigio (steel and
large oak barrel white), Gewürztraminer (unoaked white).

16 | Trebbiano d'Abruzzo
VALENTINI • 94/100 • ABRUZZO

Trebbiano d'Abruzzo is a native grape that in other parts of Italy is known as bombino bianco, though after adapting over centuries to the Abruzzo microclimate it differs considerably from other bombinos, such as that of Puglia. Still, it's a versatile grape: although it is typically used to yield lakes of nondescript plonk, it can at times give something far more interesting. Valentini, one of Italy's cult producers, does use it interestingly. There was concern after the founder, Edoardo, died: his more than capable son Francesco has proved to be up to the task, if anything even improving one of the wines (the Cerasuolo). The Trebbiano remains without equals, with an incredibly mineraly and lemony nose accented beautifully by herbal-tangerine whiffs. Very refreshing with good minerality on the high acid finish, it will thrill you with its thyme, bay leaf, citrus, and almond flavors that go on and on. It also ages extremely well.

THE WINE
Grape varieties: trebbiano d'Abruzzo (100%); **Number of bottles:** 20,000; **Alcohol:** 12.5; **Retail price:** $65; **Try it with:** grilled calamari with lemon-thyme sauce; oven-roasted turbot with potatoes; **Imported by:** Domaine Select (www.domainselect .com); **Past great vintages:** 1988, 1992

THE PRODUCER: AZ. AGR. VALENTINI
Address: via del Baio 2, 65014 Loreto Aprutino (Pescara); **Tel/fax:** 085 8291138/085 8291138; **Total bottles:** 40.000; **Total ha:** 64; **Tasting room:** yes; **Visit:** no; **Highway exit:** Pescara nord (A14)

OTHER RECOMMENDED WINES UNDER $100
BY VALENTINI:
Montepulciano d'Abruzzo Cerasuolo (oaked rosé), Montepulciano d'Abruzzo (oaked red).

17 | Tocai "Ronco della Chiesa"
BORGO DEL TIGLIO ` •
93/100 • FRIULI VENEZIA GIULIA

Nicola Manferrari, a trained pharmacist, has, over the years, fashioned some of Italy's best white wines, including the wonderful "Ronco della Chiesa." This is Italy's best example of oaked Tocai; its name refers to the vineyard, atop a hill near a church. Manferrari owns perfectly situated vineyards in the prestigious Collio DOC; his simple Tocai is wonderful at any dinner table, and the "Ronco della Chiesa" bottling undoubtedly goes up one more notch. Straw-yellow color with hints of green, it has a fresh and clean nose with a sprinkling of citrusy–white pepper aromas and a welcome splash of field flowers and minerals; it goes on with hints of vanilla that are not as overpowering as they are in his otherwise fine Malvasia. Clean, rich, and mineral, it is a full-bodied wine that packs in so much intense flavor that it will surprise and impress you no end. Admittedly, many Tocais leave you wondering what all the fuss is about, but this luscious, elegant, flavor-packed wine draws everybody's attention. Be aware that although some people rave about Manferrari's Chardonnay "Selezione" bottling, which is competently made but similar to many others found anywhere else in the world, the real stars of his lineup are the wines made from native grapes, of which there are few equals in Friuli.

THE WINE
Grape varieties: tocai friulano (100%); **Number of bottles:** 2,600; **Alcohol:** 13.5; **Retail price:** $32; **Try it with:** sautéed red snapper with tomato-onion citrus compote; chicken casserole with mushrooms; **Imported by:** Petit Pois Corporation (Sussex Wine Merchants); **Past great vintages:** 1999, 2001

THE PRODUCER: AZ. AGR. BORGO DEL TIGLIO
Address: Fraz. Brazzano, via San Giorgio 71, 34071 Cormons (Gorizia); **Tel/fax:** 0481 62166/0481 630845; **Total bottles:** 35,000; **Total ha:** 9; **Tasting room:** yes; **Visit:** by appointment; **Highway exit:** Palmanova (A4)

OTHER RECOMMENDED WINES UNDER $100 BY BORGO DEL TIGLIO:
Tocai Friulano (oaked white), Malvasia "Selezione" (oaked white).

18 | Sauvignon "Voglar"
PETER DIPOLI • 93/100 • ALTO ADIGE

Peter is one of the most straight-talking Italian wine producers, so it's always a real treat to hear what he has to say on the world of wine in general. He is also one of the most knowledgeable, as he travels extensively to other wine-producing areas in Italy and abroad. The "Voglar" is one of the five best Sauvignons made in the country. Less gooseberryish than some examples from New Zealand, but less grassy and with more body than some Loire wines, this is a beauty that will strike the right chords with Sauvignon lovers everywhere. It is absolutely lovely in its minerally lemon ice, nectarine, and quince aromas with delicate hints of green fig and asparagus; the flavors veer more toward gooseberries, white pear, and chamomile. Suave yet with balanced bright acids, its very long finish will leave you with lasting memories. And it does last: older vintages have been shown to keep beautifully if properly cellared.

THE WINE

Grape varieties: sauvignon blanc (100%); **Number of bottles:** 20,000; **Alcohol:** 13.5; **Retail price:** $35; **Try it with:** smoked trout salad with rocket; steamed asparagus with citrus-Sauvignon vinaigrette; **Imported by:** Robert Chadderdon Selections (www .classicwineimports.com); **Past great vintages:** 1995, 1996, 2005

The '95 is splendid and still very young, with gooseberry, kiwi, and passion fruit aromas and flavors galore; bright and minerally, it's long and complex (95/100). The '96 seems warmer in its riper fresh fruit aromas and sweeter mouthfeel, but is just as complex and long as the '95 (94/100). The '05 is a fine Sauvignon with some hints of grassiness among the sage, lemon-lime, and green fig aromas and flavors (92/100).

THE PRODUCER: PETER DIPOLI

Address: via Villa 5 39044 Egna (BZ); **Tel/fax:** 0471 813400/0471 813444; **E-mail:** vino@finewines.it; **Total bottles:** 27,000; **Total ha:** 3.9; **Tasting room:** yes; **Visit:** by appointment; **Highway exit:** Egna-Ora (A22)

OTHER RECOMMENDED WINES UNDER $100 BY PETER DIPOLI:
"Iugum" (merlot-cabernet—oaked red).

19 | Pinot Grigio "Gris"
LIS NERIS • **93/100** • FRIULI VENEZIA GIULIA

Perhaps it's not surprising that Alvaro Pecorari, an architect by training and trade, was able to design an absolutely stellar Pinot Grigio. Simply put, this is one of the very best oak-aged Pinot Grigios made in Italy, if not the best, especially since recent vintages have shown that Alvaro has tuned down the oaky presence. Barrel fermenting or using new oak in the aging process of the wine is tricky with pinot grigio, because its delicate aromas and flavors can be easily overwhelmed by the oak, especially when it is new, but that's no longer the case here. In any event, the warm microclimate of the Isonzo area of Friuli, a riverbed basin strewn with rocks and gravel that capture heat and reflect it back to the grapes, allows for maximum ripening of pinot grigio, so this is the area of Italy where the most powerful examples of this wine are made. You'll love the pretty notes of pear, white peach, and apricot that "Gris" exudes. More pear, Golden Delicious apple, and apricot flavors emerge on the palate, which has a pleasant saline and herbal quality. Overall, the finish is long and complex, with a rich creamy, nutty mouthfeel, and with pleasantly rich caramel and vanilla tones that are civilized enough to be bearable and to let the fruit shine through. Don't forget to try Alvaro's excellent "Tal Luc" dessert wine, as good as anything in Italy.

THE WINE
Grape varieties: pinot grigio (100%); **Number of bottles:** 45,000; **Alcohol:** 14; **Retail price:** $30; **Try it with:** pan-roasted chicken breast wrapped with San Daniele prosciutto; grilled salmon with mango-papaya lemon pepper chutney; **Imported by:** Dancing Bear Cellars (www.dancingbearcellars.com); **Past great vintages:** 2004, 2005, 2006

THE PRODUCER: AZ. AGR. LIS NERIS ESTATE
Address: via Gavinana 5, 34070 San Lorenzo Isontino (Gorizia); **Tel/fax:** 0481 80105/0481 809592; **Web:** www.lisneris.it; **E-mail:** lisneris@lisneris.it; **Total bottles:** 350.000; **Total ha:** 54; **Tasting room:** yes; **Visit:** by appointment; **Highway exit:** Villesse (A4)

OTHER RECOMMENDED WINES UNDER $100 BY LIS IS NERIS:
"Tal Luc" (verduzzo/riesling—sweet white).

20 | Malvasia
VILLA RUSSIZ • 93/100 • FRIULI VENEZIA GIULIA

Villa Russiz is one of Italy's "noble" estates: the noble-woman Elvine Ritter continued her husband's work (he was the first to bring specific foreign grape varieties to Friuli); and she was followed later by another noble-woman, Adele Cerruti, who sponsored a project for indigent children leading to an institute bearing her name, situated on the grounds of the estate. The wines are noble as well, made by one of Italy's best winemakers, Gianni Menotti. Vintage charcteristics will determine which of his wines is the best in any given year: one year it's the Pinot Bianco, another year it's the Sauvignon, and so forth. But the truth is that you'll never go wrong with any of the wines made here, white or red. The wine I'm truly intrigued by is the Malvasia, the benchmark for the variety, an intellectual sort of grape and wine seemingly created to stir up more questions than answers in the minds of tasters. For one thing, it packs intense flavor into a frame that is apparently lean and thin. Pale straw-green, it has white flower, talcum powder, citrus, and Golden Delicious apple aromas with an intriguing mineral, white peach component. There is more minerality on the palate (a hallmark of the variety), with plenty of refreshing acidity to add life to the gin, tequila, minty white peach, and pear flavors. Menotti tells me he is intrigued by malvasia as well, and is planning to plant more of it in the next few years.

THE WINE

Grape varieties: malvasia (100%); **Number of bottles:** 4,000; **Alcohol:** 13.9; **Retail price:** $33; **Try it with:** steamed mussels with yellow peppers; pan-roasted trout with citrus butter; **Imported by:** Empson USA (www.empson.com); **Past great vintages:** 2004, 2006

THE PRODUCER: AZ. AGR. VILLA RUSSIZ

Address: via Russiz 6, 34070 Capriva del Friuli (Gorizia); **Tel/fax:** 0481 80047/0481 809657; **Web:** www.villarussiz.it; **E-mail:** villarussiz@villarussiz.it; **Total bottles:** 180,000; **Total ha:** 35; **tasting room:** yes; **Visit:** by appointment; **Highway exit:** Villesse (A4)

OTHER RECOMMENDED WINES UNDER $100 BY VILLA RUSSIZ:

Ribolla gialla (unoaked white), Pinot Bianco (unoaked white), Pinot Grigio (unoaked white), Sauvignon de la Tour (unoaked white), Merlot Graf de la Tour (oaked red).

21 | Sauvignon "Quarz"
CANTINA PRODUTTORI TERLANO •
93/100 • ALTO ADIGE

This cooperative is one of the oldest in Alto Adige; it was founded in 1893. Today it has more than 100 members and a wealth of different soils and vineyards that allow for wines of a complexity rarely seen elsewhere. The increased slate, limestone, and compacted sand content of the soils is responsible for some highly saline wines that are remarkably drinkable when young but will keep for ages. In fact, the wines of Terlano are considered the longest-lived of all Italian white wines. Its Gewürztraminer "Lunare" and the Pinot Bianco "Vorberg" have always been among the top wines in their respective categories, though the latter has seemed to me to be declining in quality in recent years. This is not the case with the "Lunare" or the Sauvignon "Quarz," which remains one of Italy's greatest white wines, a masterpiece of purity and depth, and one of the world's really great Sauvignons. It has a splendid nose of ripe fruit (passion fruit, kiwi, lime) but also a saline quality and a touch of vanilla that are not at all unpleasant. There are plenty of minerally citrus flavors in the mouth, where the acidity energizes the palate, and the dry finish is long and satisfying. Aged in oak, it's a wine of really amazing freshness and intensity, an archetypal Sauvignon. This is one Sauvignon that will go well with food, unlike many over-the-top hyper-fruity examples that are a meal in themselves.

THE WINE

Grape varieties: sauvignon (100%); **Number of bottles:** 30,000; **Alcohol:** 13; **Retail price:** $55; **Try it with:** baked goat cheese and artichoke tart; ragout of scallops and red and yellow peppers; **Imported by:** Banville and Jones Wine Merchants (www .banvilleandjones.com); **Past great vintages:** 1999, 2001

THE PRODUCER: CANTINA PRODUTTORI TERLANO
Address: via Silberleiten 7 39018 Terlano (BZ); **Tel/fax:** 0471 257135/0471 25622; **Web:** www.cantina-terlano.com; **E-mail:** office@ cantina-terlano.com; **Total bottles:** 1 million; **Total ha:** 150; **Tasting room:** yes; **Visit:** by appointment; **Highway exit:** A22 Bolzano Sud

OTHER RECOMMENDED WINES UNDER $100 BY TERLANO:
Gewürztraminer "Lunare" (oaked white), Pinot Bianco (unoaked white), Pinot Bianco "Vorberg" (large barrel oaked white), Lagrein Riserva "Porphyr" (small barrel oaked red).

22 | Verdicchio dei Castelli di Jesi Classico Riserva "Villa Bucci"
BUCCI • 93/100 • MARCHE

The Bucci family has been involved in agriculture since the eighteenth century, and today the estate grows maize, sunflowers, and sugar beets besides organically grown grapes. With the latter it has enjoyed particular success, and its Verdicchio Riserva is generally considered one of Italy's best wines and one of the few whites that age well. It is a pretty yellow-green in color, and the nose immediately speaks of verdicchio, showcasing a certain minerally apple-greenness with hints of citrus, hazelnuts, and almonds. Older vintages exude a clear-cut honeyed almond character that is even more typical of the grape variety. In the mouth it is at once taut and multidimensional, with a whiplash of citrus, thyme, and hazelnut flavors, complicated by hints of apricot and grapefruit. Multilayered and very mineral, it has a balanced, concentrated mouthfeel that lingers. Last but not least, this is a wine for which a little shopping around can get you a much better deal: there seem to be some fairly large price swings in stores.

THE WINE
Grape varieties: verdicchio (100%); **Number of bottles:** 20,000; **Retail price:** $35–55; **Try it with:** shrimp and asparagus wrapped in sole; sardines Marche-style (with oil, pepper, and white wine, and cooked in the oven); **Imported by:** Empson USA (www.empson .com); **Past great vintages:** 1995, 1996, 2001

THE PRODUCER: AZ. AGR. FRATELLI BUCCI
Address: via Cona 30, 60010 Ostra Vetere (AN); **Tel/fax:** 071 964179/071964179; **E-mail:** bucciwines@villabucci.com; **Total bottles:** 120,000; **Total ha:** 26; **Tasting room:** yes; **Visit:** by appointment

OTHER RECOMMENDED WINES UNDER $100 BY BUCCI:
Verdicchio dei Castelli di Jesi Classico Superiore "Bucci" (large barrel oaked white).

23 | Pinot Grigio "Unterebner"
CANTINA PRODUTTORI TERMENO •
93/100 • ALTO ADIGE

For those who love Pinot Grigio, and have never tried this one, do yourselves a favor—run, don't walk, to the nearest wine store and grab a bottle of this beauty. "Unterebner" is the other great wine from this house (the Gewürztraminer "Nussbaumer" is the number 4 wine in this list of whites) and a true, textbook example of lightly oaked Pinot Grigio. Pale straw-green, it has an immensely pretty nose reminiscent of buttercups, beeswax, green apples, ripe pear, and white peach. In good years there's actually a faint hint of strawberry, which is not so strange if you consider that pinot grigio is essentially a red grape. In the mouth there is a flavorful burst of elegantly crisp and mineraly-fruity flavors, and though the wine seems initially lean and racy, the green apple, lemon-lime, tangerine, and pear flavors shine brightly. However, there's an underlying intensity and concentration that give the mouth a building, rich quality, which carries through on the long clean, mineraly, fruity finish. This wine defines elegance and shows all the qualities that send the sales of Pinot Grigio wines through the roof.

THE WINE

Grape varieties: pinot grigio (100%); **Number of bottles:** 25,000; **Retail price:** $30; **Try it with:** penne with broccoli and clams; grilled trout filet with yogurt-horseradish sauce; **Imported by:** Winebow (www.empson.com); **Past great vintages:** 1999, 2001, 2004, 2005

THE PRODUCER: CANTINA PRODUTTORI TERMENO—TRAMIN

Address: strada del Vino 144, 39040 Termeno (BZ); **Tel/fax:** 0471 860126/0471 860828; **Web:** www.tramin-wine.it; **E-mail:** info@ tramin-wine.it; **Total bottles:** 1.4 million; **Total ha:** 230; **Tasting room:** yes; **Visit:** by appointment; **Highway exit:** Egna-Ora (A22)

OTHER RECOMMENDED WINES UNDER $100 BY TERMENO:

Gewürztraminer "Nussbaumer" (unoaked white), Gewürztraminer Late Harvest "Terminum" (sweet white), Gewürztraminer Late Harvest "Roan" (sweet white), Moscato Rosa "Terminum" (sweet red).

24 | "Flor de Uis"
VIE DI ROMANS • **93/100** • FRIULI VENEZIA GIULIA

Vie di Romans used to be called Gallo, the family name of the owners, who mistakenly thought they might be allowed to use their name on the label in the United States. As Gallo is a name that has long been associated with one family's wines and has almost become a brand of sorts, at least in the United States, Gianfranco Gallo had to change his company's name. He chose Vie di Romans, meaning "way of the Romans," in reference to an ancient pathway on his grounds that was once used by Roman troops. That is all the antiquity you'll ever get from this producer, which is one of the more modern, better-equipped, forward-thinking operations in Italy. The wines are excellent. They are all made in a high-alcohol, very creamy, rich, and full-bodied style, but considering their overall high quality, I'm sure you'll agree there are worse things in life. The "Flor de Uis" is golden yellow, with delicious aromas of white flowers, pineapple, candied orange peel, dried apricot, guava, mango, and more than just a hint of cinnamon, white pepper, and nutmeg. This is an aromatic, rich, mouth-coating full-bodied blockbuster that will smother your taste buds in an exotic fruit bath and leave you longing for more of its pretty warm caramel, apple pie, mineral finish. By the way, all the wines from this estate have an uncanny ability to age well.

THE WINE

Grape varieties: malvasia (50%), riesling (35%), tocai (15%), but the exact proportions of each vary with the vintage; **Number of bottles:** 25,000; **Alcohol:** 14–14.5; **Retail price:** $35–48; **Try it with:** grilled salmon steak with orange-ginger sauce; chicken curry and rice pilaf; **Imported by:** Marc de Grazia Selection (www.marcdegrazia.com) and numerous importers; **Past great vintages:** 2003, 2005

THE PRODUCER: VIE DI ROMANS

Address: Loc. Vie di Romans 1, 34070 Mariano del Friuli (GO); **Tel/fax:** 0481 69600/0481 697950; **Web:** www.viediromans.it; **E-mail:** viediromans@viediromans.it; **Total bottles:** 220,000; **Total ha:** 44; **Tasting room:** yes; **Visit:** by appointment; **Highway exit:** Villesse (A4)

OTHER RECOMMENDED WINES UNDER $100 BY VIE DI ROMANS:

Chardonnay "Ciampagnis Vieris" (unoaked white), "Dis Cumieris" (malvasia—unoaked white), "Dolé" (tocai friulano—oaked white), "Pieré" (sauvignon—unoaked white), "Vieris" (sauvignon—small barrel oaked white), "Dessimis" (pinot grigio—steel and small barrel oaked white).

25 | "Beyond the Clouds"

ELENA WALCH • **92/100** • ALTO ADIGE

From the vineyards of Kastelaz and Castel Ringberg, Elena Walch, who has a degree in architecture, designs some great wines. Her Gewürztraminer "Kastelaz" is highly thought of, though I feel that the site is a little too hot for the variety, even if it's undeniably well made and will appeal to those who prefer their wines tropical and full-bodied. The real star among the white wines here is the "Beyond the Clouds," in which the chardonnay is admirably fused in with aromatic varieties; in fact, it will make you think of gewürztraminer. Golden yellow, floral, lychee, and ripe yellow fruit aromas are evident on the slightly alcoholic nose. Extended lees contact (roughly six to 10 months) has given this wine great creaminess in the mouth, an impression heightened by malolactic fermentation and aging in small oak barrels. Full-bodied and spicy, very creamy, and with pretty peach and vanilla nuances, its rich and ripe mouthfeel carries through on the long finish. Though it packs considerable alcohol, you won't notice it, such is the balance and layered complexity of this very opulent and spicy wine. Remember Elena makes one of Italy's best Rieslings.

THE WINE
Grape varieties: chardonnay (80%), other aromatic varieties (20%); **Number of bottles:** 10,000; **Alcohol:** 13.5; **Retail price:** $62; **Try it with:** sweet-and-sour chicken; lobster in tomato-ginger-cilantro sauce; **Imported by:** Chambers and Chambers (www.chamberswines.com); **Past great vintages:** 2003, 2004

THE PRODUCER: ELENA WALCH
Address: via A. Hofer 1, 39040 Termeno (Bolzano); **Tel/fax:** 0471 86072/0471 860172; **Web:** www.elenawalch.com; **E-mail:** info@walch.it; **Total bottles:** 350,000; **Total ha:** 30; **Tasting room:** yes; **Visit:** by appointment; **Highway exit:** Egna-Ora (A22)

OTHER RECOMMENDED WINES UNDER $100 BY ELENA WALCH:
Castel Ringberg Riesling (unoaked white), Castel Ringberg Riserva Cabernet Sauvignon (small barrel oaked red), Castel Ringberg Lagrein Riserva (small barrel oaked red), Passito "Cashmere" (gewürztraminer/sauvignon—sweet white).

26[*] | Friulano
TORRE ROSAZZA • **92/100** • FRIULI VENEZIA GIULIA

Torre Rosazza is one of the wine estates of Genagricola, the agricultural holding of Generali, one of Italy's largest insurance firms. In recent years the folks at headquarters have been busy upgrading quality at all the wine estates, which are located in five Italian regions. Of them all, Torre Rosazza is clearly the leader in quality, a first-rate operation that is blessed with a beautiful eighteenth-century villa as its visitor center and vineyards in well-situated natural amphitheaters that ought to guarantee high-quality results. In fact, "Turris Rosacea" ("tower of roses") was highly regarded for its vines and wines more than 2,000 years ago. Tocai Friulano is a textbook example of the variety. Straw-yellow in color, it has an elegant floral nose uplifted by delicately spicy citrus fruit and a definite almond touch. There is good length on a slightly aromatic finish that again calls almonds to mind, as well as field greens, hazelnuts, and aniseed flavors. It finishes rich and long, with a typical (for the variety) pleasant bitterness and a closing nuttiness. Besides the Tocai, the white wines here are excellent, especially the Pinot Grigio and the Ribolla. Their second label, called Poggobello, is a great source of inexpensive Ribolla, Pinot Grigio, and Picolit.

THE WINE
Grape varieties: tocai friulano (100%); **Number of bottles:** 18,000; **Alcohol:** 12.5–13; **Retail price:** $22; **Try it with:** San Daniele prosciutto; asparagus risotto; **Imported by:** Bedford International (www.winesfrombedford.com); **Past great vintages:** 2005, 2006

THE PRODUCER: TORRE ROSAZZA GENAGRICOLA
Address: Loc. Poggiobello 12, 33044 Fraz.Oleis di Manzano (UD); **Tel/fax:** 0432 750180/0432 750191; **Web:** www.borgomagredo.it/torrerosazza.htm; **E-mail:** letenute@genagricola.it; **Total bottles:** 350,000; **Total ha:** 110; **Tasting room:** yes; **Visit:** by appointment; **Highway exit:** Udine sud (A23) or Palmanova (A4)

OTHER RECOMMENDED WINES UNDER $100
BY TORRE ROSAZZA:
Ribolla Gialla (unoaked white), Pinot Grigio (unoaked white), "L'Altromerlot" (small barrel oaked red), Picolit (sweet white).

27 | Petite Arvine "Vigne Champorette"
LES CRÊTES • **92/100** • VALLE D'AOSTA

Les Crêtes continues to be one of the best sources of high-quality Italian whites, with Burgundy-like Chardonnays, an above-average Pinot Grigio, interesting reds, and this absolutely delightful Petite Arvine, from a variety native to the Swiss Valais and rarely seen in Italy. In fact, at one time this variety wasn't even allowed in Italy. The owner, Costantino Charrère, who had always believed in its qualities, once told me—many years ago and tongue in cheek—that the first plantings in the region were vine cuttings he brought back by accident, forgotten, in a truck traveling between Italy and Switzerland. Thus another fine Italian white wine was born. Bright straw yellow, white flowers, thyme, mint, chalk, white peach, and green apple aromas greet your nose; the flavors veer more toward ripe citrus, with delicate banana and other exotic fruit nuances. The bright acids keep it lively on your palate with a delicate citrusy, almond-rich finish, and keep you going for one refill after another. This is an interesting, medium-bodied, immensely pleasing wine that delivers everything many Chardonnays and Pinot Grigios only hint at.

THE WINE
Grape varieties: petite arvine (100%); **Number of bottles:** 25,000; **Retail price:** $30–40; **Alcohol:** 13; **Try it with:** grilled swordfish in apple-tarragon sauce; linguine primavera; **Imported by:** Domaine Select (www.domaineselect.com); **Past great vintages:** 2001, 2004, 2006

THE PRODUCER: LES CRÊTES
Address: Loc. Villetos 50, 11010 Aymavilles (AO); **Tel/fax:** 0165 902274/0165 902758; **Web:** www.lescretesvins.it; **E-mail:** info@lecretesvins.it; **Total bottles:** 220,000; **Total ha:** 25; **Tasting room:** yes; **Visit:** by appointment; **Highway exit:** Aosta Ovest (A5)

OTHER RECOMMENDED WINES UNDER $100 BY LES CRÊTES:
Chardonnay "Les Frissonnières" (unoaked white), Chardonnay "Cuvée Bois" (small barrel oaked white), Pinot Gris Vigne Brulant (unoaked white), Fumin Vigne La Tour (small barrel oaked red), Syrah "Coteau la Tour" (small barrel oaked red).

28 | Gewürztraminer Kolbenhof
HOFSTÄTTER • 92/100 • ALTO ADIGE

As I've stated elsewhere, Gewürztraminer does spectacularly well in Italy, and the Kolbenhof is always at or close to the the top of a very good heap indeed. Paolo and Martin Foradori, a father and son who are the owners of Hofstätter, benefit from having vines in some of Alto Adige's best *crus* for both Pinot Nero (the Mazzon vineyard) and

Gewürz (the Kolbenhof). This wine is a deep golden yellow color; it opens up stupendously in a lavish, concentrated mass of grapefruit and tropical fruit (lychees, bananas, mango, papaya) and elegant white pepper, cinnamon, and rose petal nuances. It is also quite complex on the palate, where one appreciates a certain ginger and vanilla spiciness and the varietal richness of peach, passion fruit, and acacia honey as well as more grapefruit and mango. It is always a touch alcoholic on the finish, but you won't notice this much, thanks to its wonderful mineral-acid balance. Excellent year in, year out, Kolbenhof never disappoints.

THE WINE
Grape varieties: gewürztraminer (100%); **Number of bottles:** 40,000; **Alcohol:** 14.5; **Retail price:** $45–50; **Try it with:** curried grouper and pumpkin risotto; gingered shrimp and black beans; **Imported by:** Domaine Select (www.domaineselect.com); **Past great vintages:** 2004, 2005, 2006

THE PRODUCER: CANTINA VINI JOSEF HOFSTÄTTER
Address: piazza Municipio 5, 39040 Termeno (BZ); **Tel/fax:** 0471 860161/0471 860789; **Web:** www.hofstatter.it; **E-mail:** info@ hofstatter.it; **Total bottles:** 750,000; **Total ha:** 55; **Tasting room:** yes; **Visit:** by appointment; **Highway exit:** Egna/Ora A22)

OTHER RECOMMENDED WINES UNDER $100 BY HOFSTÄTTER:
Müller Thurgau (unoaked white), Pinot Nero Barthenau Vigna Sant' Urbano (small barrel oaked red), Vendemmia Tardiva "Joseph" (gewürztraminer—sweet white).

29* | Trebbiano D'Abruzzo "Colle della Corte"

COLLE FUNARO—ORLANDI CONTUCCI PONNO
• **90/100** • ABRUZZO

Here's an example of a light, fresh white wine that will prove highly enjoyable at lunch or dinner without giving you a headache from excessive alcohol or an excessive price. This is truly a "food wine," with plenty of freshness and a light body that delivers loads of flavors and aromas that will marry very well with what you're eating. It will never win medals or extremely high scores, as it lacks an extra-rich mouthfeel, the softening touch of a high alcohol content, and the cosmetic touch of vanilla provided by new oak, yet it will appeal to everyone looking for a wine to drink with a meal, rather than something to brag about at parties. The nose delivers pretty white flower and delicate herbal touches with hints of lime and tangerine, with more lemon-lime echoes on the palate. It finishes bright and lean, with a load of minerality and a bright lemony-apple touch. The Orlandi Contuci Ponno family was one of the first to plant French varieties such as cabernet sauvignon and even malbec in the area, and its red wines are just as enjoyable as its white wines.

THE WINE
Grape varieties: trebbiano d'Abruzzo (100%); **Number of bottles:** 27,000; **Alcohol:** 12.5; **Retail price:** $20; **Try it with:** shrimp risotto with cucumber and jalapeño; warm scallop salad with cilantro sauce; **Imported by:** Majestic Wines; **Past great vintages:** 2004, 2005

THE PRODUCER: AZ. AGR. COLLE FUNARO
Address: Loc. Pian degli Ulivi 1, 64026 Roseto degli Abruzzi (Teramo); **Tel/fax:** 085 8944049/085 8931206; **E-mail:** info@orlandicontucci.com; **Web:** www.orlandicontucci.com; **Total bottles:** 180,000; **Total ha:** 31; **Tasting room:** yes; **Visit:** by appointment; **Highway exit:** Roseto degli Abruzzi (A14)

OTHER RECOMMENDED WINES UNDER $100 BY COLLE FUNARO:
"Ghiaiolo" (sauvignon—unoaked white), Montepulciano d'Abruzzo "La Regia Specula" (large and small barrel oaked red), "Colle Funaro" (cabernet sauvignon/cabernet franc—small barrel oaked red).

30* | Vermentino "Crabilis"
FRATELLI PALA • 92/100 • SARDINIA

This estate makes many very fine wines that are true to the grape variety on the label. My favorite among its wines is actually not imported (yet?) to the United States: it is the Nuragus "Salnico." Nuragus is a native grape that was long forgotten and little thought of but can succeed admirably when properly tended to. This was considered a low-quality varietal plagued by low acidity, and only recently has it been understood that excessive exposure to sunlight is not good—yet overexposure is exactly what happens with modern training and pruning techniques aimed at increasing quality. By going back to the ancient *tendone*, or canopy, system, makers shield the grapes from excessive sunlight, and the ensuing wine is just delightful. Fine as the "Salnico" is, there is no denying the immense charm of "Crabilis," as good a vermentino as any made anywhere in Italy. It's like a breath of fresh air, a hint of sea breeze, of thyme, of field flowers on the nose and with a wonderful mineral purity on the palate. It opens to reveal iodine and lemon drop flavors, with an intensely herbal yet citric twist on the long finish. Congratulations to the Fratelli Pala for all their fine wines, and my hope is that their belief in native grapes such as nuragus will ultimately bring them more and more rewards. For me, it's enough that they make this absolutely delightful Vermentino and have turned "Salnico" into one of Italy's most interesting whites, though their red wines are fine too. I may add that the "Salnico," especially, is an example of a wine made from a native grape that doesn't hint of anything else, such as chardonnay or sauvignon. That is not always the case in Italy, even though many people talk about their wines made with native grapes.

THE WINE
Grape varieties: vermentino (100%); **Number of bottles:** 120,000; **Alcohol:** 13; **Retail price:** $20–25; **Try it with:** seafood salad; summer squash sandwiches with cream cheese and pecorino mayonnaise; **Imported by:** Banville and Jones (www.banvilleand jones.com); **Past great vintages:** 2004, 2005

THE PRODUCER: AZIENDA VITIVINICOLA PALA
Address: via Verdi 7, 09040 Serdiana (CA); **Tel/fax:** 070 740284/070 745088; **Web:** www.pala.it; **E-mail:** info@pala.it; **Total bottles:** 400,000; **Total ha:** 58; **Tasting room:** yes; **Visit:** by appointment; **Highway exit:** Serdiana (SS387)

OTHER RECOMMENDED WINES UNDER $100
BY FRATELLI PALA:
Nuragus "Salnico" (unoaked white), Vermentino "Stellato" (unoaked white), "Essentija" (bovale—unoaked red), Monica di Sardegna "Elima" (unoaked red). "S'Arai" (bovale/cannonau/ others—oaked red).

31[*] | **Ribolla Gialla**
| BORGO CONVENTI • **90/100** •
| FRIULI VENEZIA GIULIA

Borgo Conventi is one of the famous names in Italian wine, as it was one of the quality leaders in the 1980s and one of the first estates to produce much-sought-after bottles by wine lovers who felt the wines were on a par with those of, for example, Jermann or Livio Felluga. After a slightly difficult spell, the estate was bought in 2001 by Ruffino (of Chianti Riserva Ducale fame), and after spending the first few years assessing the vineyards and wines made, the topnotch team of wine professionals at work here seems to be moving in the right direction. Certainly the 2007 wines here are the best in a long while, which is logical enough, as those from 2005 and 2006 were already promising. The really successful wine is the Ribolla Gialla (not altogether surprising, since the Collio subzone of Friuli is particularly suited to this variety), an absolutely lovely lemony fresh and saline white wine that goes down like gangbusters. There is an underlying core of citrus and white stone fruit flavors that is delectable, and the mineral finish has a sprinkling of white pepper nuances very typical of ribolla. Paolo Corso, with the consultant help of Gianni Menotti, one of Italy's truly gifted winemakers, has come up with something he can be proud of, as high-quality Ribolla isn't always easy to find, many being neutral, acidic, and lackluster. Borgo Conventi also produces wines in the Isonzo subzone of Friuli (clearly indicated on the label), and it's fascinating to see how differently the same grape varieties behave in two very different *terroirs* (try the Pinot Grigio for comparison purposes).

THE WINE

Grape varieties: ribolla gialla (100%); **Number of bottles:** 15,000; **Alcohol:** 13; **Retail price:** $25; **Try it with:** grilled calamari with herbed yogurt sauce, warm scallop salad with cilantro sauce; **Imported by:** Icon Estates (www.iconestateswine.com); **Past great vintages:** 2007

THE PRODUCER: BORGO CONVENTI

Address: strada della Colombara 13, 34070 Farra d'Isonzo (Gorizia); **Tel/fax:** 0481 888004 / 0481 888510; **Web:** www .borgoconventi.it; **E-mail:** info@borgoconventi.it; **Total bottles:** 250,000; **Total ha:** 50; **Tasting room:** yes; **Visit:** by appointment; **Highway exit:** Villesse (A4)

OTHER RECOMMENDED WINES UNDER $100 BY BORGO CONVENTI:

Collio Friulano (unoaked white), Collio Sauvignon Colle Blanchis (unoaked white), Collio Chardonnay (unoaked white), Isonzo del Friuli Pinot Grigio (unoaked white).

32 [*] | Coda di Volpe "Amineo"

32 | Coda di Volpe "Amineo"
CANTINA DEL TABURNO • 92/100 • CAMPANIA

If this isn't Italy's single best white wine, given its cost, then someone please tell me what is (keep in mind that it's a nine-dollar wine in Italy and can be found in supermarkets everywhere). The grape is one of the most ancient, known a few millennia ago as *caudas vulpium imitata* ("foxtail," as the grape cluster resembles the bushy tail of that clever animal). Coda di volpe does well on volcanic soil like that in the area of the Taburno (an extinct volcano) where the best Coda di Volpe wines seem to come from (the Lacryma Christi wines from another volcanic area, Vesuvius, are usually less interesting). From the volcanic-clay-limestone soils typical of the Taburno, this is a straw-yellow wine, serving up a blast of citrus, honeyed pineapple, banana, and herbal aromas that will thrill you. The nose is followed by a creamy mouthful of ripe, juicy herb-accented fruit with plenty of buffering acidity ensuring mouthwatering freshness. It is long, clean, and complex on the finish. This extremely well run social co-op benefits from the talent of the star winemaker Luigi Moio, and is one of Italy's best sources for inexpensive, well-made wines. There isn't a single bad one among them, and most are great.

THE WINE
Grape varieties: coda di volpe (100%); **Number of bottles:** 60,000; **Alcohol:** 13; **Retail price:** $20; **Try it with:** risotto with prawns; lobster with chanterelles and white wine reduction; **Imported by:** Marc de Grazia Selection (www.marcdegrazia.com) and numerous importers; **Past great vintages:** 2001, 2004, 2006

THE PRODUCER: AZ. AGR. CANTINA DEL TABURNO
Address: via Sala, 82030 Foglianise (Benevento); **Tel/fax:** 0824 871338 / 0824 878898; **Web:** www.cantinadeltaburno.it; **E-mail:** info@cantinadeltaburno.it; **Total bottles:** 1.5 million; **Total ha:** 700; **Tasting room:** yes; **Visit:** by appointment; **Highway exit:** Benevento (A16)

OTHER RECOMMENDED WINES UNDER $100
BY CANTINA DEL TABURNO:
Falanghina (unoaked white), Fiano (unoaked white), Greco (unoaked white), Aglianico del Taburno "Fidelis" (large barel oaked red), Aglianico del Taburno "Delius" (small barrel oaked red).

33 * | "Masianco"

MASI • **92/100** • VENETO

Masi is one of the better-known Italian wine estates all over the world, expanding well outside Italy. It has started up an estate in Argentina's Tupungato valley (called "La Arboleta") and also a collaboration with Don Ziraldo of Inniskillin and Canadian Icewine fame to bring fresh new ideas to its sweet Recioto. Also helping to make it a household name is a long lineup of fine wines that are right for just about every wallet and palate. Though Masi is most famous for its very rich, powerful, expensive single vineyard Amarones "Mazzano" and "Campolongo di Torbe," I have been blown away by the quality of this white wine, humorously described on the label as a "super-Venetian." This wine is also a very clear reminder, if any was needed, of the innovative and forward-thinking approach Masi takes to wine making, while remaining firmly anchored in tradition. The "Masianco" is a previously unheard-of blend of pinot grigio and verduzzo, the latter a grape most often associated with sweet wines from Friuli. Yet this blend succeeds splendidly, with the chewy tannic texture of Verduzzo (aided by three months spent in small oak barrels) mixing in remarkably well with the lighter, more mineral, and drier qualities of the Pinot Grigio. It has a pretty, pale golden-yellow hue, and you'll just love its aromas of Golden Delicious apple, pear, mango, and chamomile that soar out of the glass, as well as the tropical fruit–laced, creamy, almost resiny texture it exhibits in the mouth and the very fine, honeyed length. In conclusion, a simply excellent wine, and one that won't cost you an arm and a leg.

THE WINE

Grape varieties: pinot grigio (75%), verduzzo (25%); **Number of bottles:** 200,000; **Retail price:** $10–15; **Try it with:** oven-roasted turbot with potatoes; warm mussel and potato salad; **Alcohol:** 12.5; **Imported by:** Remy Amerique USA (www.remyusa.com); **Past great vintages:** 2004, 2005, 2006

THE PRODUCER: MASI AGRICOLA

Address: Fraz. Gargagnago—via Monteleone, 37020 Sant'Ambrogio della Valpolicella (Verona); **Tel/fax:** 0456832511/0456832535; **Web:** www.masi.it; **E-mail:** masi@masi.it; **Total bottles:** 4.3 million; **Total ha:** 520; **Tasting room:** yes; **Visit:** by appointment; **Highway exit:** Verona nord (A22)

"Brolo di Campofiorin" (corvina/rondinella—large barrel oaked red), Amarone della Valpolicella Classico "Costasera" (corvina/corvinone/molinara/rondinella—oaked red).

34 | "Donna Adriana"

CASTEL DE PAOLIS • 92/100 • LAZIO

Castel de Paolis is Lazio's best producer, and its lineup of wines is very strong indeed (try the lovely "Rosathea," a delicately sweet pink muscat), so congratulations are in order to the father-and-son team of Giulio and Fabrizio Santarelli. This is very much a family operation: Fabrizio's mother and wife are very much involved day to day, and in fact the wine I describe here is named in honor of Fabrizio's mother because the men in the family wanted to acknowledge her contributions to the winery and the success it has had over the years. The "Donna Adriana" was previously called "Vigna Adriana," but the name had to be changed because not all the grapes came from a single vineyard. The name may have changed, but the wine is still the best white of Lazio and one of the best in Italy. The addition of some sauvignon in recent vintages has added refinement of aromas, but the wine seems to have lost some of the appealing resiny fleshiness of other vintages, in which the native malvasia puntinata stood out more. Nonetheless, it's hard not to like the apricot, peach, Golden Delicious, and thyme aromas and the brightly acid, finely textured mouthfeel, with enough apple, pear, melon, and peach flavors to keep everyone happy. You will wow your guests at the dinner table with a wine they have probably never heard of, and one that actually tastes good, too. The white wines of Lazio were famous and much sought after throughout history, and this wine keeps that tradition alive and well. Do remember, this estate also makes the best of all Frascatis.

THE WINE

Grape varieties: viognier (50%), malvasia puntinata (40%), sauvignon (10%); **Number of bottles:** 12,000; **Retail price:** $30; **Try it with:** grilled vegetables; haddock with chicory and bacon; **Alcohol:** 13.5–14; **Imported by:** Domenico Valentino Selection (www.domenicovalentino.com), Salvia Bianca (www.salvia bianca.com) (but the latter imports only the Frascati, which is very fine); **Past great vintages:** 1995, 1999, 2000, 2001, 2006

THE PRODUCER: AZ. AGR. CASTEL DE PAOLIS

Address: via Val de Paolis 00046 Grottaferrata (RM); **Tel/fax:** 069413648/0694316025; **Web:** www.casteldepaolis.com; **E-mail:** info@casteldepaolis.it; **Total bottles:** 100,000; **Total ha:** 12; **Tasting room:** yes; **Visit:** by appointment; **Highway exit:** Monteporzio (A1)

OTHER RECOMMENDED WINES UNDER $100 BY CASTEL DE PAOLIS:

Frascati (malvasia puntinata/bombino/trebbiano toscano—white), "I Quattro Mori" (syrah/merlot/cabernet sauvignon/petit verdot—red), "Rosathea" (pink muscat—sweet red).

35 | Pinot Bianco

TOROS • **92/100** • FRIULI VENEZIA GIULIA

Franco Toros, a soft-spoken, pleasant man, has one of the most dependable names in Italian wine and his is a lineup of products that most wine producers the world over would be proud of. He is very lucky to have Giovanni Crosato, one of Italy's less well-known but better wine-makers, as his enologist: all these wines have the telltale Crosato signature of amazing refinement, perfectly balanced acidity, and crispy floral and fruit aromas and flavors. This Pinot Bianco is, to my mind, the best one of Italy: it is pale straw with lovely green tinges, and its aromas of white flowers, white peach, and tangerine soar out of the glass with great precision and a distinct mineral quality. It is similarly focused on the palate, where the highish but very well integrated acids lift to the crisp Golden Delicious apple, pear, and tangerine flavors. It finishes very long and pure, with an enticingly wonderful mix of stony minerality and creamy, English custard notes. No hint whatsoever of chardonnay in this wine, which is not a trivial point, as many of Italy's older Pinot Bianco vineyards harbor quite a bit of chardonnay, owing to planting mistakes made many years ago. Remember: this is as pure and beautiful a Pinot Bianco as you'll ever find.

THE WINE

Grape varieties: pinot bianco (100%); **Number of bottles:** 8,000; **Alcohol:** 13–13.5; **Retail price:** $25–36; **Try it with:** salmon tartare with a dollop of dilled crème fraîche; tuna carpaccio; **Imported by:** T. Edward Wines (www.tedwardwines.com), Siena Wine Imports (www.sienawines.com); **Past great vintages:** 2004

Address: Loc. Novali 12, 34071 Cormons (Gorizia); **Tel/fax:** 0481 61327/0481630931; **Web:** www.vinitoros.com; **E-mail:** info@ vinitoros.com; **Total bottles:** 70,000; **Total ha:** 10; **Tasting room:** yes; **Visit:** by appointment; **Highway exit:** Palmanova or Villesse (A4)

OTHER RECOMMENDED WINES UNDER $100
BY TOROS:
Pinot Grigio (unoaked white), Tocai Friulano (unoaked white), Chardonnay (lightly oaked white), Sauvignon (unoaked white), Merlot (small barrel oaked red).

36* | Sylvaner
GARLIDER • **92/100** • ALTO ADIGE

Born as recently as 2003, this estate can count on wonderful vineyards, some of which are actually fairly old—a rarity in the Valle Isarco area of Alto Adige, where the extremely cool temperatures and sand-rich soils rarely allow a vine to live longer than 25 to 30 years. Located high up at about 1,500 to 1,700 feet above sea level, with schistose, quartzite-rich soils that are ideal for aromatic grape varieties, Christian Kerschbaumer's vineyards yield excellent-quality veltliner and the Müller-Thurgau grapes to work with; but even better are his sylvaner grapes, which yield this estate's best wines. Fresh, mineral, and apple-citrus on the nose with intriguing herbal touches (bay leaf, rosemary, thyme, oregano, mint), this surprisingly medium- to full-bodied Sylvaner shows more green apple and mint flavors on the palate. The long, clean, and mineral finish is a delight. This may not be the easiest wine in the guide to find, but a search is well warranted. Truly archetypal of the variety, the wine is also the umpteenth example of just how well sylvaner does in the Valle Isarco area.

THE WINE
Grape varieties: sylvaner (100%); **Number of bottles:** 4,000; **Alcohol:** 13.7; **Retail price:** $18; **Try it with:** shrimp with pineapple, coriander, and lemongrass; sautéed mussels in orange-Sylvaner broth; **Imported by:** Selected Estates of Europe (www.selected estates.com); **Past great vintages:** 2005, 2006

THE PRODUCER: AZ. AGR. GARLIDER—
KERSCHBAUMER
Address: Untrum 70, 39040 Velturno—Feldthurns (Bolzano); **Tel/fax:** 0472 847296/0472 847296; **E-mail:** garlider@z-ec.com;

Total bottles: 12,000; **Total ha:** 2.3; **Tasting room:** yes; **Visit:** by appointment; **Highway exit:** Chiusa (A22)

OTHER RECOMMENDED WINES UNDER $100
BY GARLIDER:
Müller-Thurgau (unoaked white), Veltliner (unoaked white), Pinot Grigio (unoaked white), gewürztraminer (unoaked white), Pinot Nero (unoaked red).

Note that though all the wines from this estate are aged in large oak barrels, these are so old and large that you can't tell the oak is there at all—hence the term "unoaked" that I have used above to describe these wines, Christian Kerschbaumer agrees with me about this.

37 | Soave "Du Lot"
INAMA • **92/100** • VENETO

Giuseppe Inama bought many of his vineyards in the 1960s, when they were far less expensive than they would be today, and he also had the foresight to buy them on the Monte Foscarino, which is a *grand cru* for the garganega grape. Since then, many new clones and training systems have been introduced, in an effort to maximize the potential of each single vine, and so, over the years, Inama has become one of the best-known and most respected names in Soave. Whereas the Foscarino bottling is mineral and fresh, the Du Lot is thick and creamy, showing a remarkable ability to digest the healthy amount of oak present—something that naysayers don't feel the garganega grape is able to do without a little help from its friends, like chardonnay. However, proper work in the vineyards allows this to happen, and gives the garganega a chance to show everyone what it's really got. In fact, the Du Lot is an amazingly rich, creamy Soave, not unlike a serious Chardonnay. Bright golden yellow in color, it starts off with very concentrated scents of chamomile, ripe apricot, dried tangerine peel, bay leaf, and roasted sweet corn, then follows up with flavors of tangerine-orange and hazelnut to go with more chamomile and bay leaf. Thick and opulent, but with enough crispness to avoid seeming heavy or flat. A "must try" for all those who never thought Soave could be this interesting.

THE WINE
Grape varieties: garganega (100%); **Number of bottles:** 13,000; **Alcohol:** 13; **Retail price:** $25–30; **Try it with:** poached salmon in dill-mustard mayonnaise; halibut steak with sweet pepper jam;

Imported by: Dalla Terra (www.dallaterra.com); **Past great vintages:** 2004

THE PRODUCER: AZIENDA AGRICOLA INAMA
Address: Loc. Biacche 50, 37047 San Bonifacio (Verona); **Tel/fax:** 0456 190171/0456 190040; **Web:** www.inamaaziendaagricola.it; **E-mail:** info@inamaaziendaagricola.it; **Total bottles:** 240,000; **Total ha:** 33; **Tasting room:** yes; **Visit:** by appointment; **Highway exit:** Soave (A4)

OTHER RECOMMENDED WINES UNDER $100 BY INAMA:
Soave Classico "Vigneti di Foscarino" (small barrel oaked white), "Vulcaia Fumé" (sauvignon—small barrel oaked white).

38 * | Soave Classico
PRÀ • **91/100** • VENETO

Graziano and Sergio Prà guide their estate from one success to the next. While the former takes care of cellar matters, the latter prefers the field, where he has actually devised his own training system, called *pergoletta*. As good as the top *cru* bottlings Monte Grande and Colle Sant'Antonio are, the real work of art is the base Soave, made in very large amounts but of extraordinary quality. It's rare to find so much intense flavor and definition in a glass of base Soave, and it's an ideal introduction to the wine for all those who have drunk nothing but the industrial stuff. A wine of great delicacy and finesse, with a pale straw yellow color and golden highlights, it reflects the crisp, nutty-almondy and subtle apricot character of the grape. In the mouth it is surprisingly concentrated and long and has a nice medium-long mineral, waxy finish. The two *cru* bottlings are also very fine and of course increase the concentration, but as good as they are I think it's the base wine that is truly worthy of admiration, as there are few entry-level Soaves with this much intensity, charm, and sense of place.

THE WINE
Grape varieties: garganega (100%); **Number of bottles:** 180,000; **Alcohol:** 13; **Retail price:** $15; **Try it with:** red mullet with artichoke-potato ragout; striped sea bass with mushrooms and spinach; **Imported by:** Vinifera (www.vinifera-il.com); **Past great vintages:** 2001, 2004, 2006

Address: via della Fontana 31, 37032 Monteforte d'Alpone (VR); **Tel/fax:** 045 7612125/045 7612125; **E-mail:** grazianopra@libero.it; **Total bottles:** 220,000; **Total ha:** 30; **Tasting room:** yes; **Visit:** by appointment; **Highway exit:** Soave or Montebello (A4)

OTHER RECOMMENDED WINES UNDER $100 BY PRÀ: Soave Classico Vigneto Monte Grande (garganega/trebbiano di Soave—large barrel oaked white), Soave Classico Colle Sant'Antonio (garganega—large barrel oaked white).

39 | "Alteni di Brassica"
GAJA • **91/100** • PIEDMONT

Angelo Gaja is a legend in his own lifetime. He single-handedly put Barbaresco and the nebbiolo grape on the world's map of fine wines, and they have stayed there. Sure, other fine producers in the 1980s were making wonderful wines, but it is undisputable that Gaja, by the sheer quality of the wines, an aggressive pricing policy, and unparalleled marketing skills, allowed nebbiolo and its wines to sit alongside the great Bordeaux and Burgundies. Also, Gaja experimented, successfully, with international grape varieties such as cabernet sauvignon and sauvignon blanc. One of his two Chardonnays, the "Gaja e Rey" (Rey being the surname of his grandmother Clotilde), is world-class, and the same can now be said for his "Alteni di Brassica" Sauvignon, which always needs a little time in the glass to reveal its plump, juicy, and very sauvignonesque personality. Lemon yellow, with rich aromas of lemon, tangerine, lime, sage, and green fig, it coats your mouth with rich, ripe citrus and tropical fruit flavors. There is a very long, freshly acid, and mineral finish.

THE WINE

Grape varieties: sauvignon (100%); **Number of bottles:** 20,000; **Alcohol:** 13; **Retail price:** $80; **Try it with:** crisp baked tilapia with tomato and mint; asparagus and mussel risotto; **Imported by:** Terlato Wines International (www.terlatowines.com); **Past great vintages:** 2006

THE PRODUCER: GAJA

Address: via Torino 18, 12050 Barbaresco (CN); **Tel/fax:** 0173 635158/0173 635256; **Web:** www.gaja.com; **E-mail:** info@ gajawines.com; **Total bottles:** 300,000; **Total ha:** 90; **Tasting room:** yes; **Visit:** by appointment; **Highway exit:** Asti est (A21)

Chardonnay "Rossj-Bass" (small barrel oaked white), Nebbiolo "Conteisa" (nebbiolo/barbera—small barrel oaked red).

40* | Kerner

ABBAZIA DI NOVACELLA • 91/100 • ALTO ADIGE

After having tasted, ever since the 1970s, any number of syrupy-sweet, dishearteningly low-acid, poor-quality German dessert Kerners, I would have never believed that this grape might actually give interesting dry wines. Yet the grape seems to have taken happily to the cool Valle Isarco area of Alto Adige, and many a fine Kerner is made here today. In fact, acreage devoted to this variety is increasing all the time. The Abbazia di Novacella, along with another very high-quality cooperative in the area, that of the Produttori Valle Isarco, turns out one of the very best, if perhaps lighter-styled, Kerners around. The Abbazia, a large social co-op initially founded as a monastery in 1182 by the Augustinian order, has always demonstrated an uncanny ability to turn out one brilliant wine after another at lower-than-average prices, and is particularly adept at making Sylvaner and Kerner. With Sylvaner, it pioneered the use of acacia wood to obtain a smoother product, an effort so successful that at least one Alsatian wine producer has copied the co-op and called the new wine "Sylvacello" in its honor. Recently, though, the Sylvaner has seemed to me to be a little dilute, so I pick as the best wine the Kerner. Brilliant straw-green, it has an elegant, delicately aromatic nose (white pepper, yellow rose petals, wild fennel, anise, white fruits), with more of the white peach, pear, and citrus found on the palate. Let me add that this co-op's top wines are sold under the label "Praepositus," but regardless of what you might read elsewhere, I don't feel they are much better than the base wines—so penny-conscious consumers may want to stick with the little guy in the lineup.

THE WINE

Grape varieties: kerner (100%); **Number of bottles:** 80,000; **Alcohol:** 13.5; **Retail price:** $18–22; **Try it with:** salmon filet in citrus sauce; chicken in ginger-coriander sauce; it also makes a great start to any meal as an aperitif; **Imported by:** Vias (www .viaswine.com); **Past great vintages:** 2001, 2004

THE PRODUCER: ABBAZIA DI NOVACELLA
Address: via Abbazia 1, 39040 Varna (Bolzano); **Tel/fax:** 0472
836189/0472 837305; **Web:** www.abbazianovacella.it; **E-mail:**
info@abbazianovacella.it; **Total bottles:** 500,000; **Total ha:** 70;
Tasting room: yes; **Visit:** by appointment; **Highway exit:** Chiusa
(A22)

OTHER RECOMMENDED WINES UNDER $100
BY ABBAZIA DI NOVACELLA:
Sylvaner (unoaked white), Kerner "Praepositus" (unoaked white),
Sylvaner "Praepositus" (large acacia wood barrels—white),
Moscato Rosa "Praepositus" (sweet red).

41 | Fiano "Pietracalda"
FEUDI DI SAN GREGORIO • **91/100** • CAMPANIA

San Gregorio is a subarea of Sorbo Serpico, where this estate was born in 1986. In the short time since then, it has
become one of Italy's main winemakers. Its huge production of many different wines has had some ups and downs
in quality over recent years (especially regarding the
entry-level wines), but it seems to be back on track now,
with new people in charge. If truth be told, the quality of
the top wines never fluctuated. The Fiano "Pietracalda" is
still one of the best examples of the rich, creamy, smoky
style of Fiano. It is a luminous straw yellow with gold
highlights, and one whiff reveals many aromas (Golden
Delicious apple, apricot, peach, mango, butter, mushrooms, and smoke) exploding from the glass. Creamy and
soft-textured, but with a welcome and refreshing citric
twist on the medium-long finish, it is redolent of green
apple and exotic tropical fruit flavors. The wine seems to
be less fat and opulent in recent vintages, and this is a
welcome change. Although slightly off the beaten track,
this is an absolutely beautiful estate, with gorgeous
grounds and a good example of a wine-country restaurant
(Marannà).

THE WINE
Grape varieties: fiano (100%); **Number of bottles:** 30,000;
Alcohol: 13.5; **Retail price:** $30; **Try it with:** grilled chicken breast
in pineapple sauce; baked pollock with tomatoes, zucchini, and
provolone; **Imported by:** Palm Bay International (www.palmbay
imports.com); **Past great vintages:** 2005, 2006

THE PRODUCER:
Address: Loc. Cerza Grossa, Sorbo Serpico (AV); **Tel/fax:** 0825
986611/0825986230; **Web:** www.feudi.it; **E-mail:** feudi@feudi.it;
Total bottles: 1,700,000; **Total ha:** 230; **Tasting room:** yes; **Visit:**
by appointment; **Highway exit:** Avellino est (A16)

OTHER RECOMMENDED WINES UNDER $100 BY
FEUDI DI SAN GREGORIO:
Greco di Tufo "Cutizzi" (small barrel oaked white), Taurasi
Riserva "Piano di Montevergine" (small barrel oaked red),
"Serpico" (aglianico/merlot—small barrel oaked red).

42[*] | "Ferentano"
FALESCO • **91/100** • UMBRIA

Rossetto—also called trebbiano giallo—is a member of
the large trebbiano family, which has some members that
meet with more success than others. Rossetto is of far better quality than trebbiano toscano, for example. The trouble is that there's not much of it around: most producers
in Umbria, and especially in Lazio, where it was always
very important, now own at most only a few rows of rossetto vines. This is not an uncommon destiny, in fact, for
many of Italy's high-quality native grape varieties, which
have been long forgotten or overlooked in favor of more
productive, easier-to-grow varieties (though these often
produce far less interesting wines). Because of Falesco's
success with this variety, more Rossettos might come out
of Italy in the near future. True, this interpretation is
fairly modern and international, with aromas and flavors
somewhat reminiscent of chardonnay; nonetheless, its
juicy fruit quality and creamy texture win admirers everywhere. Medium golden-yellow, with a nose of citrus, pineapple, vanilla, and butter, it has a creamy texture not
unusual with extended lees contact and small barrel fermentation. You may find that it resembles some New
World wines more than it does higher-acid versions of
Italian natives, but it's a wine you'll enjoy. Every wine
lover hopes that the attention and hard work lavished on
rossetto by the Cotarella brothers will help it to convey the
grape's specific aroma and flavor profiles. The winery has
recently shifted its headquarters to nearby Umbria, but as
the vineyards are mainly associated with Lazio, this is
generally listed as a Lazio winery, even though that isn't
technically correct.

THE WINE

Grape varieties: rossetto (trebbiano giallo—100%); **Number of bottles:** 25,000; **Alcohol:** 13.5; **Retail price:** $22–26; **Try it with:** macaroni Sangiovannara-style (with butter, egg yolk, and parmesan); grilled salmon steak with habanero-peach salsa; **Imported by:** Winebow (www.winebow.com); **Past great vintages:** 2004

THE PRODUCER: AZ. VINICOLA FALESCO

Address: Loc. San Pietro, 05020 Montecchio (Terni); **Tel/fax:** 0744 95561/0744 951219; **Web:** www.falesco.it; **E-mail:** info@falesco.it; **Total bottles:** 1.3 million; **Total ha:** 370; **Tasting room:** yes; **Visit:** by appointment; **Highway exit:** Orvieto (A1)

OTHER RECOMMENDED WINES UNDER $100 BY FALESCO:

Montiano (merlot—small barrel oaked red), Marciliano (cabernet sauvignon/caberet franc—small barrel oaked red).

43 * | Moscato di Terracina Secco "Oppidum"

CANTINA SANT'ANDREA • 91/100 • LAZIO

Readers may want to pay special attention to the wonderful wines made here; this is one of the best estates in Italy for high-quality wines at exceptionally fair prices. It all started with Andrea Pandolfo, the great-grandfather of the current owner, who made wine in Sicily in the mid-1800s. You might say that aromatic grape varieties have always been this family's destiny. Back then, it was the muscat of Alexandria; today it's the moscato di Terracina, a specific variant of moscato bianco (white muscat) that has adapted admirably well over time to the unique seaside vineyards of the beautiful Circeo area of southern Lazio. There are three versions of this wine: the off-dry "Templum"; the sticky-sweet "Capitolium"; and my personal preference, the dry "Oppidum"—a remarkably light, enjoyable, balanced wine. My only criticism is that recent vintages seem a bit dilute to me; otherwise, it's a simply delectable wine. I think you'll enjoy its rose petal and grapefruit aromas, and the delicate saltiness and zesty lemon-lime accents that soar out of the glass like a fresh sea breeze. In the mouth it is decidedly dry, with enough acidity to keep it light, lively, and deceptively long, while nicely framing peach, grapefruit, and white pepper flavors. An unbelievably good wine for a price that is almost ridiculously low.

THE WINE

Grape varieties: moscato di Terracina (100%); **Number of bottles:** 30,000; **Alcohol:** 13.5; **Retail price:** $20; **Try it with:** pan-roasted salmon fillet with radish and ginger sauce; curried saffron shrimp; **Imported by:** JK Imports (the Cantina Gabriele kosher wines are imported by Victor Kosher Wines; though the Muscat is somewhat sweet, the Montepulciano and Sangiovese red wines are very good); **Past great vintages:** 2001, 2006

THE PRODUCER: CANTINA SANT'ANDREA

Address: Loc. Borgo Vodice, 04010 Terracina (Latina); **Tel/fax:** 0773 755028/0773 756147; **Web:** www.cantinasantandrea.it; **E-mail:** info@cantinasantandrea.it; **Total bottles:** 200,000; **Total ha:** 70; **Tasting room:** yes; **Visit:** by appointment; **Highway exit:** Frosinone (A1)

OTHER RECOMMENDED WINES UNDER $100 BY CANTINA SANT'ANDREA:
Circeo Rosso "Sogno" (merlot/cesanese—small barrel oaked red), Circeo Rosso "Preludio alla Notte" (merlot/sangiovese—small barrel oaked red), Moscato di Terracina Amabile "Templum" (off-dry white), Moscato di Terracina Passito "Capitolium" (sweet white).

44* | Vernaccia di San Gimignano Vigna Santa Margherita

| PANIZZI • 91/100 • TUSCANY

Giovanni Panizzi is a relatively new producer (his first vintage was in 1989) but has risen to the top of the hierarchy in San Gimignano. He has also done, as president of the consortium of local growers, much important work for Vernaccia, upgrading quality and trying to diminish the sometimes overenthusiastic additions of sauvignon, chardonnay, and even gewürztraminer practiced by some of his colleagues. Vernaccia di San Gimignano is a slightly neutral grape, and so its qualities aren't immediately evident: hence the idea behind "helping" it with other varieties. The trouble is that if one gets carried away by adding too much of the other varieties (all of which usually have stronger personalities than vernaccia), the final wine doesn't taste anything like Vernaccia. Panizzi and other dedicated producers of the area have fought hard against that outcome. Panizzi has also experimented extensively, and his new "Evoé" bottling is a rare, very interesting Vernaccia left to macerate for months on the skins in small oak barrels: it's big and tannic like a red wine, and a truly different taste experience. Although his Vernaccia Riserva can be just a little too oaky, Panizzi's base wine and the Vigna Santa Margherita are top-notch. The latter is usually brilliant straw-green; the nose has pretty floral, citrus, and even tropical fruit scents and a hint of white pepper. Creamy on entry, with butter, vanilla and apricot flavors, it has a wonderful acidic spine. The finish is refined and persistent, with plenty of varietally accurate almond reminders. Remember that Vernaccia di San Gimignano ages splendidly and that Panizzi's wines are fine even eight to 15 years after the harvest.

THE WINE

Grape varieties: vernaccia di San Gimignano (100%); **Number of bottles:** 15,000; **Alcohol:** 13.5; **Retail price:** $15; **Try it with:** seafood risotto; oven-roasted red mullet with prosciutto and sage; **Imported by:** Bacchanal Wine Imports (www.bacchanalwines .com); **Past great vintages:** 1990, 1995, 2004, 2005, 2006

THE PRODUCER: AZ. AGR. GIOVANNI PANIZZI

Address: Loc. Racciano, Podere Santa Margherita 34, 53037 San Gimignano (Siena); **Tel/fax:** 0577 941576/ 0577 906042; **Web:** www.panizzi.it; **E-mail:** panizzi@panizzi.it; **Total bottles:** 200,000; **Total ha:** 45; **Tasting room:** yes; **Visit:** by appointment; **Highway exit:** Valdichiana (A1)

OTHER RECOMMENDED WINES UNDER $100 BY GIOVANNI PANIZZI:

Vernaccia di San Gimignano (unoaked white), Vernaccia di San Gimignano "Evoé" (small barrel oaked white).

45* | Pinot Grigio

DRIUS • 91/100 • FRIULI VENEZIA GIULIA

When you come across a truly good Pinot Grigio such as the one made by Mauro Drius, you begin to understand why the wine deserves to meet with success. Drius is tremendously gifted, and all his other white wines are exceptional as well, in particular the Malvasia, which is a textbook example of the variety. The estate, which is the pretty home of the Drius family, will remind some American visitors of the house they grew up in back home or the house next door: with a picket fence, a backyard, two children, and a dog, it could be in an American neighborhood. The vineyards straddle the Isonzo and the Collio zones, two of the best white wine areas of Italy, and so you know that the producer is starting off on the right foot. The Pinot Grigio comes from grapes grown in the warmer Isonzo DOC, but the wine, with its cool, crisp aromas and flavors, is not at all a product of a warm microclimate. Pale-straw yellow, it has a nose that evokes flowers and yellow fruit such as mandarins and yellow plums, aromas that are nicely lifted by a mineral twist. Very pleasant on entry, with lovely white peach, pear, and tangerine flavors that have a mineral-minty complexity, it proves just how much flavor a mid-weight, unoaked white wine can have. The finish is long and clean, with a lingering almond note. This is the sort of wine that goes with food in a way that many blowsy, overoaked Chardonnays cannot equal.

THE WINE

Grape varieties: pinot grigio (100%); **Number of bottles:** 13,500; **Alcohol:** 13.5; **Retail price:** $21; **Try it with:** spaghetti with radicchio and shrimp; pan-fried catfish with tomato-caraway glaze; **Imported by:** JAO Imports; **Past great vintages:** 2004, 2005, 2006

THE PRODUCER: DRIUS

Address: via Filanda 100, 34071 Cormons (Gorizia); **Tel/fax:** 0481 60998; **E-mail:** drius.mauro@adriacom.itù; **Total bottles:** 70,000; **Total ha:** 11.5; **Tasting room:** yes; **Visit:** by appointment; **Highway Exit:** Palmanova or Villesse (A4)

OTHER RECOMMENDED WINES UNDER $100 BY DRIUS:

Malvasia (unoaked white), Pinot Bianco (unoaked white), Tocai Friulano (unoaked white).

46[*] "Leone d'Almerita"

TASCA D'ALMERITA • **91/100** • SICILY

Lucio Tasca d'Almerita and his sons Giovanni and Alberto brilliantly manage what has long been one of southern Italy's most prestigious wine estates. Indeed, for a very long time the only good-quality Chardonnay and Cabernet Sauvignon in Sicily were theirs, and some historic bottles of these have been produced. Also, the "Rosso del Conte" was for a long time perhaps Sicily's best red wine. The Tasca d'Almeritas never rest on their laurels, and they are always looking toward the future. These facts are best exemplified by their new dessert wine, a Malvasia delle Lipari from their estate called Tenuta Capofaro (a beautiful vacation resort as well); and by the "Leone d'Almerita," which I truly believe is the best new Italian wine for the money in more than twenty years. This wine really is that good: pale straw yellow with golden tones, it has a singularly perfumed nose of lemon-lime, herbs, and ripe yellow melon all complicated by an apricot-mint note. Very juicy and lush on the palate, it has bright acids that give its orange, melon, pineapple, and tangerine flavors lift and focus. It's extremely refreshing, perfectly balanced, and so lip-smackingly good that you'll finish the bottle sooner rather than later. Unfortunately, the most recent vintage does not contain any sauvignon in the blend, and I feel the wine is not as fragrant or refined as before. Hopefully, future vintages will regain its usual citrusy brightness: at Tasca they feel their old vine Cataratto, grown at high altitudes, will supply enough freshness, but I don't think this was the case in such a hot year as 2007.

THE WINE
Grape varieties: cataratto (80%), chardonnay (20%); **Number of bottles:** 300,000; **Alcohol:** 13.5; **Retail price:** $19; **Try it with:** lemon sole; spaghetti with lobster sauce; **Imported by:** Winebow (www.winebow.com); **Past great vintages:** 2004, 2006

THE PRODUCER: TASCA D'ALMERITA
Address: Contrada Regaleali, 90020 Sclafani Bagni (Palermo); **Tel/fax:** 091 6459711/ 091 426703; **Web:** www.tascadalmerita.it; **E-mail:** info@tascadalmerita.it; **Total bottles:** 2.5 million; **Total ha:** 400; **Tasting room:** yes; **Visit:** by appointment; **Highway exit:** Resuttano (A19)

OTHER RECOMMENDED WINES UNDER $100
BY TASCA D'ALMERITA:
Chardonnay (small barrel oaked white), "Rosso del Conte" (nero d'Avola/others—small barrel oaked red), Cabernet Sauvignon (small barrel oaked red), Malvasia Capofaro (sweet white)

47[*] | **"Cirò Bianco"**
LIBRANDI • **91/100** • CALABRIA

Librandi is one of the few high-quality wine estates in Calabria, and it's an example others there would do well to follow. Wineries in the rest of Italy may also want to take a page out of the Librandi handbook and study this estate's extensive work with local, native grape varieties—work that is beginning to succeed. One consequence is a wine such as "Efeso," 100% mantonico, a grape that had been all but forgotten or was used to make rustic, easy-drinking wines that wouldn't last through the summer following the vintage. This state of affairs was a shame, as had been hinted at already by the many excellent sweet Mantonico wines that some small passionate producers were able to make, but it took Librandi's efforts to show just how pleasant a dry mantonico could be (although, frankly, "Efeso" can be too oaky, in some vintages). My personal favorite from Librandi is the Cirò Bianco, an amazingly flavorful yet light wine that is incredibly versatile at the dining table. It is pale straw yellow in color with green tinges, with peach, bitter orange, and pineapple fragrances and more peach, apricot, mint, and thyme flavors on the palate. It has a pleasantly medium-rich texture, but comes across as fresh and crisp on the medium-long finish, thanks to being fermented in temperature-controlled stainless steel tanks, a technique designed to preserve freshness and crispness.

THE WINE
Grape varieties: greco bianco (100%); **Number of bottles:** 250,000; **Alcohol:** 13; **Retail price:** $16–20; **Try it with:** seviche; prosciutto-stuffed flounder fillets; leek and onion omelette; **Imported by:** Winebow (www.winebow.com); **Past great vintages:** 2005, 2006

THE PRODUCER: AZ. VITIVINICOLA ANTONIO E NICODEMO LIBRANDI
Address: C. da San Gennaro, strada statale 106 88811 Cirò Marina (KR); **Tel/fax:** 096231518/0962370542; **Web:** www.librandi.it; **E-mail:** librandi@librandi.it; **Total bottles:** 2.1 million; **Total ha:** 230; **Tasting room:** yes; **Visit:** by appointment; **Highway exit:** Sibari (A3)

OTHER RECOMMENDED WINES UNDER $100 BY LIBRANDI:
"Efeso" (magliocco—small barrel oaked white), Cirò Rosso Riserva "Duca Sanfelice" (gaglioppo—unoaked red), "Magno Megonio" (magliocco—small barrel oaked red).

48[*] | Arneis "Blangé"
CERETTO • 90/100 • PIEDMONT

Ceretto's wines always represent wonderful interpretations of their single vineyards, from standout Barbaresco to Barolo. Their most wildly successful wine is the "Blangé." It is made from the not very highly regarded arneis grape, yet

"Blangé" (a great name for a wine if there ever was one, by the way) was *the* Italian white wine of the 1980s, when no restaurant that wanted to stay in business could afford not to have it on the wine list. You can't say anything bad about it: simply put, it's an immensely enjoyable, lush mouthful of a wine. It is so enjoyable and successful, in fact, that not everyone is sure there really is a grape in it but the arneis. I enjoy its almost excessively deep golden yellow color (it looks almost like a dessert wine); the waxy, floral, cotton candy, citrus nose; and the bright orange and tangerine flavors, which are lifted by a touch of mint and rosemary. Medium-long but richly textured, the silky, layered finish makes you never want to put the glass down. Made for immediate consumption, it should be drunk within a couple of years, at most, after its release. As good as "Blangé" is, don't forget the Barbaresco Bricco Asili, Barolo Brunate, and Barolo Prapò (from the Bricco Rocche estate) among the best in their respective categories in Italy.

THE WINE

Grape varieties: arneis (100%); **Number of bottles:** 600,000; **Alcohol:** 13; **Retail price:** $19; **Try it with:** spaghetti with clams and prawns; deviled eggs; **Imported by:** Moët Hennessy USA (www. mhusa.com); **Past great vintages:** 1986, 1989, 1990, 2001. All these vintages are, however, past their prime now.

THE PRODUCER: CERETTO

Address: Loc. San Cassiano 34, 12051 Alba (Cuneo); **Tel/fax:** 0173 282582/0173 282383; **Web:** www.ceretto.com; **E-mail:** ceretto@ ceretto.com; **Total bottles:** 800,000; **Total ha:** 105; **Tasting room:** yes; **Visit:** by appointment; **Highway exit:** Asti est (A21)

OTHER RECOMMENDED WINES UNDER $100 BY CERETTO:

Barbaresco Bricco Asili (small barrel oaked red), Barbaresco "Bernardot" (small barrel oaked red), Barolo Bricco Rocche Prapò (small barrel oaked red), Barbaresco Bricco Rocche Brunate (small barrel oaked red).

The small barrel oak I refer to is actually the 500-liter tonneau, a slightly bigger barrel than the 225-liter barrique, the vessel usually intended when one speaks or writes of "small barrels."

49 | Chardonnay "Löwengang"
ALOIS LAGEDER • 90/100 • ALTO ADIGE

Alois Lageder's family has been involved in wine making for more than 150 years, and he has two beautiful estates to show for this dedication: Casòn Hirschprunn (from which he produces a separate lineup of wines) and Tenuta Löwengang. About 20 years ago, it was decided to give the estate's name to the top Chardonnay produced, a decision the family has had no reason to regret: "Löwengang" has been amazingly successful and praised over the years. One of the first Chardonnays to be barrel-fermented in Italy, it is still one of the best of its kind today. If anything, it appears to be getting better and better, though the use of oak is not shy. Brilliant yellow with golden highlights, it has a wealth of aromas with ripe melon, yellow plum, and citrus highlights shining through a caramel-mineral veneer. It enters the mouth smooth, and strikes with ripe banana, pear, and pineapple flavors and a lovely English custard and warm apple pie character. It has wonderful elegance and balance, with the not-too-shy oak-derived vanilla flavor nonetheless perfectly fused with the rich, ripe yellow fruit. Beautifully refreshing acidity and wonderfully persistent aromatics make it an absolute winner. For maximum enjoyment, give this opulent, full-bodied white 10 to 12 months in the cellar and then drink it over the next five to eight years. Readers may want to note that Lageder makes a very solid, dependable, and enjoyable dry Riesling.

THE WINE

Grape varieties: chardonnay (100%); **Number of bottles:** 38,000; **Alcohol:** 13; **Retail price:** $43; **Try it with:** roasted chicken with garlic and mushrooms; lobster in tomato-orange sauce; **Imported by:** Dalla Terra (www.dallaterra.com); **Past great vintages:** 1986, 1990

THE PRODUCER: ALOIS LAGEDER

Address: vicolo dei Conti 9, 39040 Magrè (BZ); **Tel/fax:** 0471 809500/0471 809550; **Web:** www.lageder.com; **E-mail:** info@lageder.com; **Total bottles:** 1.2 million; **Total ha:** 63; **Tasting room:** yes; **Visit:** by appointment; **Highway exit:** Egna/Ora (A22)

OTHER RECOMMENDED WINES UNDER $100 BY LAGEDER:

Müller Thurgau (unoaked white), Riesling (unoaked white), Moscato Giallo "Vogelmeier" (unoaked white), Contest Hirschprunn "Mitterberg" (pinot grigio/chardonnay/sauvignon/viognier/many others—small barrel oaked white), Cabernet Sauvignon "Cor Romigberg" (small barrel oaked red).

50 | Verdicchio dei Castelli di Jesi "Podium"
GAROFOLI • 90/100 • MARCHE

Who says Italian white wines don't age well? One taste of older vintages of "Podium" will dispel that myth, at least as regards Verdicchio. Carlo and Gianfranco Garofoli, now capably helped out by their children, were among the first in the area to believe in verdicchio's great potential, investing time and research in the variety, and even creating excellent sparkling wines with it. After four generations and counting, this is one of Italy's most solid estates, with many fine wines to choose from. The "Podium" Verdicchio is a great Italian white wine, and one that ages exceptionally well. With no camouflaging oak, it gives the real taste of verdicchio: a unique grape variety that combines floral, fruit, and mineral elements like none other in Italy. This wine has lovely white flower, lemongrass, almond, and pear aromas, nicely complicated by a mineral touch. The same mineral touch is very obvious on the palate, where the fresh acidity gives this wine great focus and lots of lift. The finish is very long and clean and seems to go on and on, with a lingering almond note. There's a honeyed, stony, mineral quality to this wine's finish that is very intriguing. This complex, layered wine can be enjoyed upon release but is even better after two years of cellaring, and will easily last another 10 after that.

THE WINE
Grape varieties: verdicchio (100%); **Number of bottles:** 50,000; **Alcohol:** 13.5; **Retail price:** $30–45; **Try it with:** rabbit porchetta-style (a local dish—oven-roasted rabbit stuffed with wild fennel and unsmoked bacon); stir-fried squid with asparagus and mushrooms; **Imported by:** Omniwines Distributing (www .omniwines.com), Classic Wine Imports (www.classicwine imports.com); **Past great vintages:** 2001, 2006

THE PRODUCER: CASA VINICOLA GIOACCHINO GAROFOLI
Address: piazzale G. Garofoli, 60022 Castelfidardo (Ancona); **Tel/ fax:** 071 7820162/071 7821437; **E mail:** mail@garofolivini.it; **Web:** www.garofolivini.it; **Total bottles:** 2 million; **Total ha:** 50; **Tasting room:** yes; **Visit:** by appointment; **Highway exit:** Loreto (A14)

OTHER RECOMMENDED WINES UNDER $100 BY GAROFOLI:
Verdicchio dei Castelli di Jesi Classico Superiore Riserva "Serra Forese" (small barrel oaked white), Rosso Conero Riserva "Grosso Agontano" (montepulciano—small barrel oaked red).

51 | Gewürztraminer Baron Salvadori

51* | Gewürztraminer Baron Salvadori
C. P. NALLES MAGRÉ • **90/100** • ALTO ADIGE

This young cooperative, founded in 1985, resulted from the fusion of two much older ones—Nalles (1932) and Magré-Niclara (1893!)—and has been turning out one fine wine after another. It has long-term contracts with more than 130 growers, ensuring a steady supply of high-quality grapes from many different *terroirs*. Its Gewürztraminer "Baron Salvadori" is an excellent example of the very rich style of this wine, high in alcohol. This is always one of Italy's better Gewürztraminers, close to a fine Alsatian wine. Golden yellow, it seduces right from the start with zesty aromas of lychee, ginger, cinnamon, grapefruit, honeyed peach, and apricots. It is stunningly rich yet balanced, with acid-brightened flavors of tangerines, ginger, dried apricot, and more honeyed peach. Though it can be a touch alcoholic, it always has enough acidity to avoid being blowsy. Don't forget to try this co-op's sweet wine "Baronesse," a blend of mainly yellow muscat and a little riesling, which is quite simply one of Italy's 10 best sweet wines but unfortunately is made in small quantities. (Only 1,000 bottles—for the world!) Curiously, Gottfried Pollinger, the cooperative's likable director, feels that the wine gained elegance and improved considerably when the co-op decided to reduce the percentage of riesling in the blend. Its small proportion might make it hard for readers to find, so I have picked the dry Gewürztraminer, which is just as good and is a very cogent example of the great things Italy is capable of doing with this variety. Their Pinot Bianco "Sirmian" and Pinot Grigio "Punggl" are great buys and very good wines.

THE WINE

Grape varieties: gewürztraminer (100%); **Number of bottles:** 13,000; **Alcohol:** 14.5; **Retail price:** $20–30; **Try it with:** baked salmon with mango ginger chutney; pan-roasted trout in mustard and dried fig sauce; **Imported by:** Country Vintner (www .thecountryvintner.com), Elizabeth Imports; **Past great vintages:** 2001, 2005

THE PRODUCER: CANTINA PRODUTTORI NALLES— MAGRÉ

Address: via Heiligenberg 2 39010 Nalles (BZ); **Tel/fax:** 0471 678626 / 0471 678945; **Web:** www.kellerei.it; **E-mail:** info@ kellerei.it; **Total bottles:** 800,000; **Total ha:** 150; **Tasting room:** yes; **Visit:** by appointment; **Highway exit:** Bolzano sud (A22)

Pinot Bianco (Weissburgunder) "Sirmian" (unoaked white), Pinot
Grigio "Punggl" (unoaked white), Moscato Giallo "Baronesse"
(yellow muscat/riesling—sweet white).

Again, this winemaker does use large oak barrels for part
of the aging process of the "Sirmian" and the "Punggl,"
but these are so old and large that there is really no oak
aroma or flavor to speak of when you taste the wines.

52[*] Verdicchio dei Castelli di Jesi "Collestefano"

COLLESTEFANO • 90/100 • MARCHE

Fabio Marchionni is a bright star in the firmament of fine
Italian wine producers, and this Verdicchio is a fantastic
white wine, and has been for some years. It really is a
feather in Fabio's cap, too: before he entered the family
business, his family used to sell the grapes and work with
the local cooperative. Fabio had other goals, and stints in
Alsatian and German wineries helped him decide which
way to take his abilities. He makes only one wine, but it's
a gem. Made with organically grown grapes from the
vineyards surrounding the house and winery, his Verdicchio di Matelica has an incredibly intense and pure nose
redolent of white flowers, citrus, and mineral, and the
mineral gains prevalence with time and bottle age. In the
mouth the wine is extremely fresh and light, yet it has a
wonderful creamy texture and pure flavors that range
from green apple to pear, from tangerine to almonds.
Extremely long, with a focused finish and a luscious ripe
fruit yet mineral edge, it leaves the mouth feeling fresh
and lively. This deceptively lean yet powerful, multilayered wine can be drunk now or held for three to four
years and then enjoyed for another four or five after that.

THE WINE

Grape varieties: verdicchio (100%); **Number of bottles:** 60,000;
Alcohol: 13.5; **Retail price:** $13–15; **Try it with:** mushroom
omelette; pan-roasted scallops; **Imported by:** Selected Estates of
Europe (www.selectedestates.com); **Past great vintages:** 2001,
2006

THE PRODUCER: AZ. COLLESTEFANO

Address: Loc. colle Stefano 3, 62022 Castelraimondo (Macerata);
Tel/fax: 0737 640439/0737 640439; **E-mail:** info@collestefano

.com; **Web:** www.collestefano.com; **Total bottles:** 60,000; **Total ha:** 10; **Tasting room:** yes; **Visit:** by appointment; **Highway exit:** Porto Recanati (A14)

53* | Müller Thurgau "Ritratti"
LA VIS E VALLE DI CEMBRA • **90/100** • TRENTINO

This huge cooperative has more than one production site; it unites 800 members furnishing grapes from different areas of Trentino and even Alto Adige, and these single areas have been studied extensively (soil composition, best exposures, microclimates) in an effort to produce the best possible wines. This attention to detail is clearly shown by the absolutely excellent single vineyard Müller Thurgau Vigna delle Forche, one of Italy's best white wines; and by the Pinot Nero Vigna di Saosent, which—though I feel it relies on a little residual sugar for added charm—is still one of Italy's five or six best Pinot Noirs. Unfortunately both wines are made in extremely small quantities (only about 3,000 bottles each) and are true boutique wines in that you can buy them only at the winery store in Valle di Cembra. Therefore, I have picked another one of their fine Müller Thurgaus, the "Ritratti," which is the name La Vis uses for a high-quality yet fairly priced lineup of wines. The "Ritratti" Müller is creamier, richer, and somewhat more herbal than the Vigna delle Forche. It couldn't be otherwise, since it is made from grapes grown at lower altitudes and in a warmer microclimate. This pretty straw yellow wine with golden highlights has a definite thyme- and marjoram-scented nose, with hints of apricot and pear; its creamy yet pleasantly high-acid texture will remind you of apples and peaches. It has a very long suave finish and is a steal for the price. It's a shame that the best wines La Vis makes, from the single properties called Maso, such as Maso Clinga and Maso Roncador, are not yet imported into the United States. Note that La Vis now also owns the very famous Villa Cafaggio estate in Chianti.

THE WINE

Grape varieties: Müller Thurgau (100%); **Number of bottles:** 20,000; **Alcohol:** 13.5; **Retail price:** $20–25; **Try it with:** sushi; sautéed mussels; **Imported by:** Banville and Jones Wine Merchants (www.banvilleandjones.com), Classic Wines; (www

.classicwines.com), F&F Fine Wines International; **Past great vintages:** 2006

THE PRODUCER: CANTINA LA VIS E VALLE DI CEMBRA
Address: via Carmine 7, 38015 Lavis (Trento); **Tel/fax:** 0461440111/0461440244; **E-mail:** cantina@la-vis.com; **Web:** www.la-vis.com; **Total bottles:** 130,000; **Total ha:** 1,350; **Tasting room:** yes; **Visit:** by appointment; **Highway exit:** Orvieto (A1)

OTHER RECOMMENDED WINES UNDER $100 BY LA VIS E VALLE DI CEMBRA:
Müller Thurgau Maso Roncador (unoaked white), Müller Thurgau Vigna delle Forche (unoaked white), Traminer Aromatico Maso Clinga (white), Müller Thurgau "Dos Caslir" (unoaked white), Ritratti Rosso (red), Pinot Nero Vigna di Saosent (red).

The Maso Roncador, Maso Clinga, Maso Tratta, Vigna delle Forche, and Vigna di Saosent are not yet available in the United States.

54* | Pallagrello Bianco
VESTINI CAMPAGNANO • **91/100** • CAMPANIA

The red wines that the Barletta family makes from native grapes such as pallagrello nero and casavecchia are superlative, with great structure and fine tannins. The Casavecchia wine is a beauty, with a unique, almost aromatic character. But as good as the Casavecchia is, the Pallagrello Bianco is even better—one of the most luscious, juicy, enjoyable white wines you'll ever come across. (This wine does resemble those made with coda di volpe, though the two grapes do not seem to be related.) You'll marvel at the heady, lusty peach, apricot, and citrus aromas, which give way on the palate to similar flavors and an intensely mineral, long, creamy-rich finish. This has plenty of balancing acidity and will undoubtedly also age well. This family deserves credit for having brought to the attention of wine lovers everywhere grape varieties that had been all but forgotten.

THE WINE
Grape varieties: pallagrello bianco (100%); **Number of bottles:** 7,000; **Alcohol:** 14; **Retail price:** $30; **Try it with:** scallops with orange-citrus butter; grilled halibut with pineapple-papaya salsa; **Imported by:** Montecastelli (www.montecastelli.com); **Past great vintages:** 2001, 2004

THE PRODUCER: AZ. AGR. VESTINI CAMPAGNANO
Address: Fraz. Santi Giovanni e Paolo, via Baraccone 5, 81013
Caiazzo (Caserta); **Tel/fax:** 0823 862770/0823 862770; **E-mail:**
info@vestinicampagnano.it; **Web:** www.vestinicampagnano.it;
Total bottles: 37,000; **Total ha:** 6; **Visit:** by appointment; **Tasting
room:** yes; **Highway exit:** Caserta nord–Capua (A1)

OTHER RECOMMENDED WINES UNDER $100
BY VESTINI CAMPAGNANO:
"Le Ortole" (pallagrello bianco—small barrel oaked white),
Pallagrello nero (small barrel oaked red), Casavecchia (small
barrel oaked red), "Connubbio" (pallagrello nero/casavecchia—
small barrel oaked red).

55 | Sauvignon "Ronco delle Mele"

VENICA E VENICA • **90/100** • FRIULI VENEZIA GIULIA

Founded in 1929, the estate led by Gianni and Giorgio
Venica and Giorgio's wife, Ornella, has long been one of
the quality leaders in Italian white wine, and this Sauvignon is one of Italy's most famous wines. One whiff
shouts sauvignon, in an almost exaggerated way: asparagus, tomato leaf, green bell pepper, sage, and grassy aromas jump from the glass, and there's no mistaking it.
Some people may think that its very acidic, lean mouthfeel harks back to an old-fashioned interpretation of very
grassy Sauvignon, as most wines made from this grape
variety today are rich in riper fig, passion fruit, and melon
flavors, but it remains a favorite in Italy. In any case, this
has a highly enjoyable, fresh mouthfeel, and will be greatly
loved by those who appreciate Sauvignons that are grassy,
full of lemony-lime flavors, brightly fresh, and with no
overt tropical fruit aromas or flavors. Other wines made
here also deserve your attention: the Ribolla Gialla, the
Pinot Bianco, and the Malvasia are among the best made
anywhere in the region, and all share a charming,
easy-to-drink quality that makes them highly enjoyable.
This estate is located in one of the most picturesque cor-
ners of Friuli—the cooler, high-altitude area of Dolegna.
There is a wonderful bed-and-breakfast on the property.

THE WINE
Grape varieties: sauvignon blanc (100%); **Number of bottles:**
35,000; **Alcohol:** 13.5; **Retail price:** $32; **Try it with:** crabmeat with
tarragon-dill mayonnaise; asparagus-stuffed sole rolls; **Imported
by:** Martin Scott Wines (www.martinscottwines.com), Wine
Warehouse (www.winewarehouse.com); **Past great vintages:** 2001

Address: Loc. Cerò 8, 34070 Dolegna del Collio (Gorizia); **Tel/fax:** 0481 61264/0481 639906; **E-mail:** venica@venica.it; **Web:** www.venica.it; **Total bottles:** 230,000; **Total ha:** 33.5; **Tasting room:** yes; **Visit:** by appointment; **Highway exit:** Palmanova (A4)

OTHER RECOMMENDED WINES UNDER $100 BY VENICA E VENICA:
Ribolla gialla (lightly oaked white), Malvasia (lightly oaked white), Pinot Bianco (unoaked white), Tocai "Ronco delle Cime" (unoaked white).

56 | Vermentino di Gallura "Capichera"
CAPICHERA • 90/100 • SARDINIA

Italy's best lineup of Vermentinos, with far greater structure than most wines made from this grape, are born here. The estate was founded in the 1920s, when the grandfather of the current owners inherited land around Arzachena, already well known for very fine wines. This Vermentino is rich and long, fuller-bodied than the delectable "Vigna 'Ngena," but easier to drink than the "Vendemmia Tardiva." You'll enjoy its lemony herb and thyme aromas, with luscious tangerine and apricot nuances. Quite fat and mineral on the mouth, it displays a personality bursting with stony, mineral, spicy pineapple, and apricot flavors and exhibits a luscious, long finish that leaves you wanting to drink more. Go ahead and try the other wines made by this estate: all the Vermentinos are top-notch, though they are also unfortunately somewhat more expensive than most. Then again, you owe it to yourself to try these classically structured and authoritatively flavored wines to see just what heights Vermentino can achieve.

THE WINE
Grape varieties: vermentino (100%); **Number of bottles:** 120,000; **Alcohol:** 14; **Retail price:** $47; **Try it with:** penne with lobster and tomatoes; black sea bass with cracked anise and mustard seeds; **Imported by:** Vias (www.viaswine.com); **Past great vintages:** 2001, 2006

THE PRODUCER: CAPICHERA
Address: strada Arzachena—S.Antonio Km 3+500, 07021 Arzachena (Oristano); **Tel/fax:** 0789 80612/0789 80619; **E-mail:** info@capichera.it; **Web:** www.capichera.it; **Total bottles:** 250,000; **Total ha:** 70; **Tasting room:** yes; **Visit:** by appointment; **Highway exit:** none

Vermentino di Gallura "Vigna 'Ngena" (unoaked white),
Vermentino di Gallura "Vendemmia Tardiva" (oaked
white).

57* | Pinot Bianco

ERMACORA • **90/100** • FRIULI VENEZIA GIULIA

This is one of Italy's two or three best unoaked Pinot Bi-
ancos, and it has an amazingly consistent track record for
quality, with one great wine after another. Far removed
from the stereotype of caramelized tropical fruit aromas
and flavors with an ultrarich and buttery mouthfeel, this
is rather lithe and fresh, possibly coming across as thin
and tart to inexperienced tasters. But there is considerable depth and precision to the white flower, green apple,
and pear aromas, nicely complicated by a mineral touch.
There's also more than a whisper of minerality on the
palate, where the bright acids give definition and focus to
the white stone fruit and delicately minty flavors. It finishes long and clean with a pleasant lime and gin nuance.
If you can find them, try some of the other excellent
wines made by Dario Ermacora: the excellent Pignolo, a
red made from a long-forgotten native grape variety that
is making a huge comeback; and especially the Picolit,
one of the four or five best of them all, and a true
world-class sweet wine. Don't miss lunch at Dario's pretty
restaurant and wine bar in the heart of Cividale, where
you'll have an extremely high-class meal in a pleasant,
unpretentious setting and at down-to-earth prices. Congratulations are in order!

THE WINE

Grape varieties: pinot bianco (100%); **Number of bottles:** 11,000;
Alcohol: 13.5; **Retail price:** $25; **Try it with:** marinated swordfish;
artichoke flan; Asian crab and vegetable salad; **Imported by:**
Global Partners International, Vino Terra Imports, Imports Inc./
Chicago, Premier Wine Company; **Past great vintages:** 2004,
2005, 2006

THE PRODUCER: ERMACORA

Address: via Solzaredo 9, 33040 Ipplis (Udine); **Tel/fax:** 0432
716250/0432 716439; **E-mail:** info@ermacora.it; **Web:** www
.ermacora.com; **Total bottles:** 160,000; **Total ha:** 22; **Tasting
room:** yes; **Visit:** by appointment; **Highway exit:** Palmanova
(A4)

Pinot Grigio (unoaked white), Friulano (unoaked white), Pignolo (small barrel oaked red), Picolit (sweet white).

To be precise, about 8% of the total batch of Pinot Grigio does age in small oak barrels, but I defy anyone to pick up the presence of oak in that wine.

58* | "Il Moro"

MARCO CARPINETI • 90/100 • LAZIO

Organically grown native grapes (some of which are extremely rare), manicured vineyards, and a sure hand in the cellar are three secrets of one of Italy's least-known and yet most interesting estates. (That tells you something about the wine guides and publications available on Italy.) This is a simply delectable white wine made from the almost extinct greco moro and greco giallo varieties, yielding a fat and immensely satisfying white that provides an altogether different taste sensation for those weaned on the more classic aromas and flavors of Sauvignon, Chardonnay, and Pinot Grigio. There's a resiny, honeyed tone to the tangerine and peach aromas, nicely complemented by thyme and mineral nuances. Rich and fat on entry, this wine stays light and lively on the palate, thanks to harmonious acids that give focus to the ripe citrus and peach flavors. For added complexity, herbal and minty notes vie with fruit for your attention. The very long finish and the creamy, tactile mouthfeel leave a lasting impression: the latter also explains why this white wine goes remarkably well with white meat dishes. If you can get hold of a bottle, don't hesitate to try the "Ludum," a wonderfully botrytis-affected (see "noble rot" in glossary) sweet wine, which is one of Italy's top dozen dessert wines. And remember, you read it here first.

THE WINE

Grape varieties: greco moro (80%), greco giallo (20%); **Number of bottles:** 7,000; **Alcohol:** 13.5; **Retail price:** $25; **Try it with:** pan-roasted halibut; chicken breast with pineapple-mustard relish; **Imported by:** Bon Vivant (www.bonvivantwines.net); **Past great vintages:** 2003, 2004

THE PRODUCER: AZ. AGR. MARCO CARPINETI

Address: s.p. Velletri-Anzio Km 14+300, 04010 Cori (Latina); **Tel/fax:** 06 9679860; **E-mail:** info@marcocarpineti.com; **Web:** www

.marcocarpineti.it; **Total bottles:** 68,000; **Total ha:** 19; **Tasting room:** yes; **Visit:** by appointment; **Highway exit:** Valmontone (A1)

OTHER RECOMMENDED WINES UNDER $100
BY MARCO CARPINETI:
"Collesanti" (bellone—unoaked white), "Ludum" (bellone—sweet white).

59* | Pecorino
PASETTI • **92/100** • ABRUZZO

The top wines made here belong to the "Testarossa" line, named after the grandparents of the current owners, who were much admired for their fiery red hair and were nicknamed "cocciarosce" (a dialect term meaning the same as the modern-day *testarossa*, "redhead"). The wine I love best from this producer is, however, a less expensive bottling: this lemony fresh Pecorino, made with the native grape of the same name. Bright, fresh herbal-citrusy aromas give way on the palate to more herbal and citrusy flavors with a pleasant soft almond twist and a lively slightly lemony-fresh finish that lasts and lasts. There is a pleasant herbal-mineral quality that lingers and adds to this wine's intrigue. An example of a long-forgotten native variety, pecorino is making a comeback, but unfortunately all is not clear with the variety. In fact, because the grape has been resurrected only recently (10 years ago you wouldn't have found a single bottle of it anywhere in Italy, except perhaps examples made in very small numbers for local consumption), it is still not obvious what exactly the variety can deliver. Hence, the wine comes in a never-ending series of different styles, ranging from lemony-fresh and light, like this one, to overly alcoholic and overly oaked fruit bombs, depending on the choices made by each producer. In brief, it is not really possible to say "I like Pecorino," for only a particular style may appeal to you. I have no doubt that in a few more years it will become clearer to everyone what Pecorino ought to be like, but for the moment it's a bit of a mixed bag.

THE WINE
Grape varieties: pecorino (100%); **Number of bottles:** 100,000; **Alcohol:** 13.5; **Retail price:** $25; **Try it with:** spaghetti with clam sauce; oven-steamed trout with almonds; **Imported by:** Tosco Wine; **Past great vintages:** 2006

THE PRODUCER: AZ. AGR. PASETTI

Address: via San Paolo 21, 66023 Francavilla al Mare (Chieti); **Tel/ fax:** 085 61875/085 4159292; **Web:** www.pasettivini.it; **E-mail:** info@ pasettivini.it; **Total bottles:** 280,000; **Total ha:** 51; **Tasting room:** yes; **Visit:** by appointment; **Highway exit:** Francavilla al Mare (A14)

OTHER RECOMMENDED WINES UNDER $100 BY PASETTI:

Montepulciano Cerasuolo (rosé), Montepulciano d'Abruzzo (lightly oaked red), Montepulciano d'Abruzzo "Testarossa" (small and large barrel oaked red).

Pomino Bianco

60[*]

CASTELLO DI POMINO/FRESCOBALDI
• **90/100** • TUSCANY

Pomino bianco is what a "food wine" ought to be: fresh and tangy (so you keep salivating and enjoying every morsel), floral, mineral, and delicately fruity, with the aromas and flavors neither camouflaged by oak nor too overpowering for the food, and preferably moderate in alcohol so that you can indulge even at lunchtime. This very enjoyable white wine based on pinot bianco is a testament to the importance of a cool microclimate in working with what is essentially a nordic grape variety that in the warm weather of central and southern Italy fares very poorly, giving dull, fat, blowsy wines. The Pomino valley, already considered one of the four best wine-making areas in Tuscany during the times of the Medici family, is northeast of Florence and is characterized by very cool weather and high altitudes. In fact, not just pinot bianco does well there; so do riesling and even pinot noir. The presence of a little riesling in the Pomino bianco blend is instantly recognizable and adds a welcome touch of citrusy freshness and mineral complexity to a lovely, bright white wine. You will have trouble putting the glass down.

THE WINE

Grape varieties: pinot bianco, chardonnay, riesling; **Number of bottles:** 230,000; **Alcohol:** 13–13.5; **Retail price:** $25; **Try it with:** scallops with prosciutto and Pomino Bianco reduction; warm seafood and white bean salad; **Imported by:** Folio Fine Wines (www.foliowine.com); **Past great vintages:** 2004

THE PRODUCER: MARCHESI DE' FRESCOBALDI

Address: via Santo Spirito 11, 50125 (Firenze); **Tel/fax:** 055 27141/055 211527; **Web:** www.frescobaldi.it; **E-mail:** info@frescobaldi.it;

Total bottles: 3 million; **Total ha:** 1,000; **Tasting room:** yes; **Visit:** by appointment; **Highway exit:** Firenze nord or sud or Certosa (A1)

OTHER RECOMMENDED WINES UNDER $100
BY FRESCOBALDI:
Pomino "Il Benefizio" (chardonnay—oaked white), Chianti Rufina Castello di Nipozzano Riserva (sangiovese/others—red), Chianti Rufina "Montesodi" (sangiovese—small barrel oaked red).

THE 15 BEST SPARKLING WINES AND ROSÉS UNDER $100

1 | Franciacorta "Prestige Cuvée"

CA' DEL BOSCO • 94/100 • LOMBARDY

Maurizio Zanella is one of the great names in Italian wine, and this has to be one of the most impressive wineries in the world to visit. If the great wines don't bowl you over, then the modern art, of which Maurizio is a fan, certainly will. All the wines made here are really great, characterized by unbelievably constant and extremely high quality year after year. The still wines, which I feel are underestimated, are exceptional, and the lineup of sparklers is perhaps the best in Italy. The best of the latter is the Anna Maria Clementi, though it is expensive and above our $100 limit. Much more affordable, and comparable to all the common Champagne names you know, is the newly named "Prestige Cuvée," which has taken the place of the old Franciacorta Brut. This wine has a fresher, livelier mouthfeel than its predecessor, with beautiful citrus and very delicate yeasty and truffled scents. It also impresses in the mouth owing to the ripe citrus and strawberry flavors, with a hint of beeswax and hazelnut. It has a lightly creamy quality to which the pinot blanc in the blend no doubt contributes. A wine of wonderful finesse, it shows that the best Franciacortas are close to the best in Champagne.

THE WINE
Grape varieties: chardonnay (70%), pinot nero (20%), pinot bianco (10%); **Number of bottles:** 400,000; **Alcohol:** 12.5; **Retail price:** $40–45; **Try it with:** fried basil prawns with Franciacorta foam; poached cod with mushroom-accented leek and coriander cream sauce; **Imported by:** Paterno Wines International (www.terlatowines.com); **Past great vintages:** nonvintage wine

THE PRODUCER: AZ. AGR. CA' DEL BOSCO
Address: via Case Sparse 20, 25030 Erbusco (Brescia); **Tel/fax:** 030 7766111/030 7268425; **E-mail:** cadelbosco@cadelbosco.com; **Web:** www.cadelbosco.it; **Total bottles:** 1.2 million; **Total ha:** 147; **Tasting room:** yes; **Visit:** by appointment; **Highway exit:** Rovato (A4)

2 | Brut "Perle"

FERRARI • 94/100 • TRENTINO

Without question, Italy's best Blanc de Blancs is the "Giulio Ferrari Riserva del Fondatore," a sparkler of incredible breeding and refinement, but it costs more than our $100 limit. The good news is that the other sparklers of Ferrari are almost as good, and cost far less. The "Perlé," another 100% chardonnay, is beautiful, with a fine and persistent perlage (the tiny stream of bubbles typical of sparkling wines) and a pale gold-green hue. Intense, complex aromas of vanilla, citrus, warm toast, dried apricot, and tangerine peel explode from the glass; in the mouth it packs a load of peach, apricot, and Golden Delicious apple flavors with lovely white chocolate and delicate fresh-baked bread notes to top everything off. Ferrari is one of the class acts in Italian wine, and even though this Ferrari is not related to the famous sports car dynasty, these wines do Italy's name proud just as much as the cars do.

THE WINE
Grape varieties: chardonnay (100%); **Number of bottles:** 480,000; **Alcohol:** 12; **Retail price:** $28–34; **Try it with:** oysters; stuffed chicken Trentino-style, *gröstl* (boiled meat with pan-seared potatoes, onion, and parsley); smoked trout risotto; **Imported by:** Palm Bay International (www.palmbayimports.com); **Past great vintages:** 1996, 1998

THE PRODUCER: FERRARI—FRATELLI LUNELLI
Address: via Ponte di Ravina 15, 38040 Trento; **Tel/fax:** 0461 972311/0461 913008; **E-mail:** info@ferrarispumante.it; **Web:** www.ferrarispumante.it; **Total bottles:** 4.8 million; **Total ha:** 102; **Tasting room:** yes; **Visit:** by appointment; **Highway exit:** Trento centro (A22)

OTHER RECOMMENDED WINES UNDER $100
BY FERRARI:
Trento Brut (sparkling white), Trento Perlé Rosé (sparkling rosé).

3 | Franciacorta Brut "Gran Cuvée"

BELLAVISTA • **93/100** • LOMBARDY

All the wines from Bellavista are fine: this estate is characterized by constant and extremely high quality year after year. The still wines (especially the Chardonnays, though at times these are a touch too oaky) are exceptional, and the sparkling wines, along with those of Ca' del Bosco and Ferrari, are the best in Italy. The "Grand Cuvée" Brut is always, year in, year out, a simply spectacular sparkler that leaves many famous names of Italy and Champagne in the dust. It is a beautiful straw golden-green with its continuous stream of fine bubbles, and it jumps from the glass with fresh floral, citrus, and apricot notes, and hints of freshly baked bread and hazelnuts. One sip pleases the palate no end, with a wonderful acid-extract balance, beautiful precision of fruit and yeasty flavors, and a wonderfully fresh acidic backbone. This is simply a great Franciacorta, with riper and fruitier flavors than its French counterparts. Sybarites reading these pages may want to note that Bellavista is also the owner of l'Albereta, one of the most beautiful wine country resorts of Italy, the restaurant where star chef Gualtiero Marchesi, one of the greatest Italian chefs of all time, weaves his magic.

THE WINE
Grape varieties: chardonnay (72%), pinot nero (28%); **Number of bottles:** 80,000; **Alcohol:** 12.5; **Retail price:** $28–38; **Try it with:** grilled salmon steak with citrus-tarragon mayonnaise; fried catfish with mushroom salad; **Imported by:** Empson USA (www .empson.com); **Past great vintages:** 2001, 2002.

THE PRODUCER: AZ. AGR. BELLAVISTA
Address: via Bellavista 5, 25030 Erbusco (Brescia); **Tel/fax:** 030 7762000/030 7760386; **E-mail:** info@bellavistawine.it; **Web:** www.bellavistawine.it; **Total bottles:** 1 million; **Total ha:** 180; **Tasting room:** yes; **Visit:** by appointment; **Highway exit:** Rovato (A4)

OTHER RECOMMENDED WINES UNDER $100
BY BELLAVISTA:
"Uccellanda" (chardonnay—oaked white), "Convento dell'Annunciata" (chardonnay—oaked white).

4 | Blanc de Morgex et La Salle Brut Metodo Classico

CAVE DU VIN BLANC DE MORGEX ET LA SALLE
• **92/100** • VALLE D'AOSTA

Born in 1983 from the ashes of the Association des Viticulteurs, the largest social cooperative of the region now has more than 100 members and steadfastly supports the upkeep and defense of the local, native prié blanc grape variety, for which there are very few other producers in the valley. This is true mountain viticulture, with vineyards at 1,900 to 3,800 feet above sea level. I have had the pleasure of driving up to and through the vineyards, and I can warn anyone scared of heights against doing so: though the panorama is one of the most beautiful in the world, the heights and steep slopes are dizzying, to say the least. The wines made here are all great—especially the dry still wines and this wonderful sparkler, which is on a par with many a Champagne. You'll love the citrus-yeasty nose, with hints of hazelnut and yeast, as well as the yeasty-buttery flavors, which have a pretty minty-thyme twist on the long, fairly high-acid, but still creamy finish.

THE WINE
Grape varieties: prié blanc (100%); **Number of bottles:** 11,000; **Alcohol:** 12.5; **Retail price:** $25–35; **Try it with:** carpaccio of black sea bass; risotto with clams (www.vinobravo.com); **Imported by:** Doug Polaner Selection (www.polanerselections.com) (note: Vino Bravo imports the very fine Blanc the Morgex et La Salle "Rayon," a still wine); **Past great vintages:** non vintage

THE PRODUCER: CAVE DU VIN BLANC DE MORGEX ET LA SALLE
Address: chemin des Iles 31, La Ruine, 11017 Morgex (Aosta); **Tel/fax:** 0165 800331/0165 801949; **E-mail:** info @caveduvinblanc .com; **Web:** www.caveduvinblanc.com; **Total bottles:** 170,000; **Total ha:** 20; **Tasting room:** yes; **Visit:** by appointment; **Highway exit:** Morgex (A5)

OTHER RECOMMENDED WINES UNDER $100 BY CAVE DU VIN BLANC:
"Fripon" Extra Dry (prié blanc—sparkling white), Blanc de Morgex et La Salle "Vini Estremi" (prié blanc—unoaked white), Blanc de Morgex et La Salle "Rayon"(prié blanc—unoaked white).

5 | Prosecco di Valdobbiadene Sup. di Cartizze Dry

COL VETORAZ • 92/100 • VENETO

Founded in 1992 by Loris dall'Acqua, Francesco Miotto, and Paolo De Bortoli, this is the best producer today of Cartizze, generally considered to be the noblest expression of Prosecco. The grapes for Cartizze grow in vineyards on a hill of the same name, and production therefore ought to be, given the small size of the hill itself, quite small. This being Italy, there seem to be too many bottles labeled Cartizze floating around supermarkets and gas station markets, but we won't go there for now. Suffice it to say that Col Vetoraz owns some of the best-situated parcels in all of Cartizze, and the winery is situated in one of the most picturesque vineyard spots in Italy. This Cartizze is an absolute joy, with aromas of white flowers, talcum powder, cotton candy, mojito cocktail, white peaches, and green apples. The flavors are pure and precise, with more white peach and green apple on the long, pure, mineral finish. The first sip will tell you that this is quite unlike any other Cartizze, or Prosecco, you may have tasted, and its greatness will be immediately apparent to novices and expert wine drinkers alike, even to those who have never heard of it.

THE WINE

Grape varieties: prosecco (100%); **Number of bottles:** 20,000; **Alcohol:** 12.5; **Retail price:** $45; **Try it with:** kiwi fruit sabayon; lemon angel food cake with warm tangerine sauce; **Imported by:** Montecastelli Selections (www.montecastelli.com), North Berkeley Imports (www.northberkeleyimports.com); **Past great vintages:** 2004, 2006

THE PRODUCER:SPUMANTI COL VETORAZ

Address: Fraz. Santo Stefano, via Trenziese, 31040 Santo Stefano di Valdobbiadene (Treviso); **Tel/fax:** 0423 975291/0423 975571; **E-mail:** info@colvetoraz.it; **Web:** www.colvetoraz.it; **Visits:** by appointment; **Total bottles:** 800,000; **Total ha:** 12; **Highway exit:** From Treviso or Conegliano (A27)

OTHER RECOMMENDED WINES UNDER $100 BY COL VETORAZ:

Prosecco di Valdobbiadene Spumante Dry Millesimato (sparkling white).

6[*] | "Vigna Mazzi"

ROSA DEL GOLFO • **92/100** • PUGLIA

Rosa del Golfo has always been a source of great Italian rosés. However, the owner, Damiano Calò, always felt that rosé wines in general could be taken to a much higher level, so the "Vigna Mazzi" is the result of years of experimentation. When it was first presented, years ago, it was a real shock—a unique, new, oak-driven blush wine—and not everyone really understood it: some people found it far too different from anything they had tasted before. Yet it's a wonderful wine, with a medium deep pink hue, and an absolutely lovely nose full of almond blossom, nutmeg, red cherry, strawberry, and vanilla aromas that jump out of the glass. Upon first hitting your palate, it seems soft and sweet, but then it develops into something much more complex. An obvious, but not excessive, oaky vanilla coat wraps up more small red berry, orange zest, marzipan, and raspberry jam flavors, and makes the wine even more interesting. It's a wine of remarkable balance, smooth and surprisingly fleshy, with a long suave finish that adds to its charm. If you are looking for a fresher, lighter style of rosé or blush wine, don't hesitate to try the "Rosa del Golfo" bottling, which may well be Italy's best rosé wine of its kind. This estate also makes solid whites and reds, but the latter seem less interesting and less successful to me.

THE WINE

Grape varieties: negro amaro (90%) and malvasia nera (10%); **Number of bottles:** 5,000; **Alcohol:** 13; **Retail price:** $25; **Try it with:** rabbit with olives, capers, and rosemary; tuna and scallops with a thyme-raspberry reduction; **Imported by:** Vinifera Imports (www.vinifera-il.com); **Past great vintages:** 2006

THE PRODUCER: ROSA DEL GOLFO

Address: via Garibaldi 56, 73011 Alezio (Lecce); **Tel/fax:** 0833 281045/0331 992365; **E-mail:** calo@rosadelgolfo.com; **Total bottles:** 350,000; **Total ha:** 30; **Tasting room:** yes; **Visit:** by appointment; **Highway exit:** Bari or Taranto nord (A14)

OTHER RECOMMENDED WINES UNDER $100 BY ROSA DEL GOLFO:

Verdeca "Bolina" (white), "Rosa del Golfo" (rosé).

7* | Moscato d'Asti "Bricco Quaglia"

LA SPINETTA • **92/100** • PIEDMONT

Some of Italy's finest sparkling sweet wines come from this estate, which is famous for Barbaresco, Barolo, and Barbera. Almost everyone likes Moscato d'Asti, but there are some less than successful examples that tend to be cloying and boring. The "Bricco Quaglia" by La Spinetta is a benchmark, with a long history of great bottles, vintage after vintage. Still at an extremely high level of quality today despite the very large number of bottles made, it's a wine that will put a smile on the faces of all your guests and close off an evening perfectly. It is pale straw-green with a stream of pretty, busy little bubbles and copious froth and an absolutely fragrant, lovely nose of white peach, apricot, green apple, rose petals, and white flowers. Wonderfully creamy and fresh in the mouth, it has a silky, sweet texture and taste; it's impossible to resist, and you'll find yourself gulping it down. Though some vintages could use a bit more acidity to cut through all the sweetness, you'll never be disappointed by this wine. The "Biancospino" Moscato is nearly as good.

THE WINE
Grape varieties: moscato bianco (100%); **Number of bottles:** 110,000; **Alcohol:** 5.5; **Retail price:** $18; **Try it with:** tiramisù; peach-apple cobbler with a Moscato sabayon; **Imported by:** Marc de Grazia Selection (www.marcdegrazia.com), numerous importers; **Past great vintages:** 2001, 2006

THE PRODUCER: AZ. AGR. LA SPINETTA
Address: via Annunziata 17, 14054 Castagnole Lanze (AT); **Tel/fax:** 0141 877396/0141 877566; **E-mail:** info@la-spinetta.com; **Web:** www.la-spinetta.com; **Total bottles:** 600,000; **Total ha:** 165; **Tasting room:** yes; **Visit:** by appointment; **Highway exit:** Asti est (A21)

OTHER RECOMMENDED WINES UNDER $100 BY LA SPINETTA:
Barbera d'Alba "Gallina" (red), Moscato d'Asti "Biancospino" (sweet sparkling white).

8*
Prosecco di Valdobbiadene Dry Vigneto Giardino
ADAMI • 92/100 • VENETO

The Giardino vineyard is the site at which Abele Adami, the grandfather of the current owners, started the company in 1920. He obviously had a clinical eye, as this particular amphitheater of vines is one of the best possible places to grow prosecco grapes, a *grand cru* for the variety. This is almost always the best wine made by Adami, an ode to all wines nice and good. You'll fall in love with its pretty straw-green hue, the effortless stream of tiny persistent bubbles, and the lovely yeasty bread, powdered stone, green and yellow apple aromas. (The yellow apple is more evident in particularly warm years; otherwise, green apple always dominates.) On the palate it's a little leaner and less rich than other "dry" Proseccos, though it has impeccable balance with just the right amount of acidity necessary to counteract the resdiual sugars present. Still, it really doesn't come across as very sweet. Hence, it's a perfect wine for aperitifs or even for a whole meal, and an excellent example of what a "serious" Prosecco is all about.

THE WINE
Grape varieties: prosecco (100%); **Number of bottles:** 25,000; **Alcohol:** 12.5; **Retail price:** $19; **Try it with:** Tempura-style fried oysters; crab salad; scallops with shiitake and enoki mushrooms; **Imported by:** Dalla Terra (www.dallaterra.com); **Past great vintages:** nonvintage

THE PRODUCER: ADAMI
Address: Fraz. Colbertaldo, via Rovede 17, 31020 Vidor (TV); **Tel/fax:** 0423 982110/0423 982130; **E-mail:** info @adami spumanti.it; **Web:** www.adamispumanti.it; **Total bottles:** 450,000; **Total ha:** 8; **Tasting room:** yes; **Visit:** by appointment; ask for Franco or Armando Adami; **Highway exit:** Conegliano (A27)

OTHER RECOMMENDED WINES UNDER $100 BY ADAMI:
Prosecco di Valdobbiadene Brut "Bosco di Gica" (sparkling white).

9*
Rosato del Salento "Five Roses"
LEONE DE CASTRIS • 91/100 • PUGLIA

Leone de Castris was the first to produce a rosé in Italy, and his innovative spirit is still very much present today, even though this 300-year-old estate also continues to produce wines that are faithful to tradition. The estate is best known for its inexpensive, fine Salice Salentino Riserva, but you can't go wrong in choosing the "Messapia," as delightful a fresh white wine as there is in Italy today; or the "Donna Lisa" Rosso Riserva, a testament to all things great about negro amaro. Negro amaro is also the grape used to make two of Italy's best rosé wines, the "Five Roses" and the "Five Roses Anniversario." The latter contains a bit more of the softer malvasia nera grape (the softness seems to be due to a little more residual sugar as well, though I could be wrong about that) but both wines are great. "Five Roses" has a pretty salmon pink hue, with plenty of almond flower, strawberry, and sour red cherry aromas that have a delicate lemon zest twing. Your taste buds will be won over by the explosively juicy red berry fruit and the touches of mineraly almond and candied orange peel that linger on and on in the fresh, savory finish. Excellent.

THE WINE
Grape varieties: negro amaro (90%), malvasia nera (10%); **Number of bottles:** 160,000; **Alcohol:** 12.5; **Retail price:** $15–20; **Try it with:** prosciutto and melon; mushroom omelette; smoked pheasant breast with red currant jelly; **Imported by:** A.V. Imports (www.avimports.com); **Past great vintages:** 2001, 2006

THE PRODUCER: LEONE DE CASTRIS;
Address: via Senatore de Castris, 26—73015 Salice Salentino (LE); **Tel/fax:** 0832/731112/0832/731114; **E-mail:** info@ leonedecastris.com; **Web:** www.leonedecastris.com; **Total bottles:** 2.1 million; **Total ha:** 300; **Tasting room:** yes; **Visit:** by appointment; **Highway exit:** Bari (A14)

OTHER RECOMMENDED WINES UNDER $100 BY LEONE DE CASTRIS:
"Messapia" (verdeca—white), "Five Roses Anniversario" (negro amaro/malvasia nera—rosé), Negro Amaro "Eloveni" (red), Salice Salentino Riserva (negro amaro/malvasia nera—red), Moscato "Pierale" (white muscat—sweet white).

10* | Prosecco di Valdobbiadene "Crede"
BISOL • **91/100** • VENETO

Without doubt, considering the large amount produced, this is Italy's best Brut Prosecco, of rare creaminess and drinkability. It's the creaminess that differentiates a good Prosecco from a bad one: when you sip a Prosecco that is lean, tart, and acidic, you know you're not getting the real deal. Bisol has been making wine since the sixteenth century, so you know it's doing something right. This producer started with beautifully situated vineyards in the Santo Stefano subzone of Valdobbiadene, known for Prosecco of great fruitiness and wondrous perfumes, as opposed to those of Conegliano, which confer structure and size on the finished wines. Pale straw-green with a delicate frothy stream of bubbles, the Crede has an absolutely delicious, mouthwatering nose reminiscent of green apples and white peaches, with a refreshing delicate spearmint twist. This is followed up by a creamy soft texture with gobs of ripe peachy fruit, green apples, and an almost sweet sensation on the immensely pleasing, deceptively soft (though it's a dry wine) finish that will have you refusing to put the glass down.

THE WINE

Grape varieties: prosecco (100%); **Number of bottles:** 80,000; **Alcohol:** 12.5; **Retail price:** $24; **Try it with:** soft-shell crabs; risotto with peas and prosciutto; **Imported by:** Vias (www.viaswine.com); **Past great vintages:** nonvintage

THE PRODUCER: AZ. AGR. DESIDERIO BISOL E FIGLI;

Address: Fraz. Santo Stefano, via Fol 33, 31040 Santo Stefano di Valdobbiadene (Treviso); **Tel/fax:** 0423 900138/0423 900577; **E-mail:** info bisol@bisol.it; **Web:** www.bisol.it; **Total bottles:** 300,000; **Total ha:** 55; **Visits:** by appointment; **Highway exit:** From Treviso or Conegliano (A27)

OTHER RECOMMENDED WINES UNDER $100 BY BISOL:

Prosecco di Valdobbiadene "Selezione Jeio" (sparkling white), Prosecco di Valdobbiadene Spumante Superiore di Cartizze Dry (sparkling white).

11* Lambrusco di Sorbara "Vigna del Cristo"

| CAVICCHIOLI • **90/100** • EMILIA ROMAGNA

If you don't think Lambrusco can be a serious wine, think again. Cavicchioli is one of the best names in Lambrusco, and all its wines are at the top or close to the top of their respective categories. This "Vigna del Cristo" is a remarkably serious effort, the first Lambrusco made in Italy from the grapes of a single *cru*, and a very good *cru* at that. It has all the trademark characteristics of the Lambrusco di Sorbara, a lighter, more fragrant Lambrusco that may disappoint those looking for larger volume and structure. Nonetheless, you'll greatly appreciate the delicate strawberry, citrus peel, almond flower, and rose petal aromas, as well as the citrus and red berry flavors that abound on the palate. Its has high acids that are harmonious enough not to turn this into yet another example of a shrill, tart Lambrusco—of which there are already far too many examples. The rosé version of this wine is made according to the Metodo Classico refermentation technique in the bottle in the manner of Champagne, and is extremely fine: three years sitting on its lees have given it a creamy, rich feel that is unmistakable. Don't miss it, though not many bottles are made (roughly 3,000).

THE WINE
Grape varieties: lambrusco di Sorbara (100%); **Number of bottles:** 80,000; **Alcohol:** 12–12.5; **Retail price:** $15–20; **Try it with:** fried eggplant and zucchini; polenta and sausages; **Imported by:** Lambrusco Imports; **Past great vintages:** 2001

THE PRODUCER: CANTINE CAVICCHIOLI E FIGLI
Address: via Canaletto 52, 41030 San Prospero sulla Secchia (Modena); **Tel/fax:** 059 812411/059 812424; **E-mail:** cantine@cavicchioli.it; **Web:** www.cavicchioli.it; **Visits:** by appointment; **Total bottles:** 17 million; **Total ha:** 150; **Highway exit:** Modena Nord or Carpi (A1)

OTHER RECOMMENDED WINES UNDER $100 BY CAVICCHIOLI:
"Rosé del Cristo" Spumante (lambrusco di Sorbara—sparkling rosé), Lambrusco Salamino di Santa Croce Semisecco "Tre Medaglie" (sparkling red—off dry), Lambrusco Grasparossa di Castelvetro Secco "Contessa Matilde" (sparkling red).

12* | Erbaluce di Caluso "San Giorgio"
CIECK • **90/100** • PIEDMONT

The name is enough to make you love Erbaluce: legend has it that it derives from Albaluce, a gentle fairy who donated the pretty vines to the inhabitants of the little village of Caluso. According to an alternative legend, the variety is so called because it is planted high up the slopes of the hills and is the first grape to see the dawn—*alba* in Italian. Though there may be doubts as to the exact origin of the name, there is no doubt in my mind that Cieck is the best producer of Erbaluce wines. The estate was born in 1985, when Remo Falconieri and Lodovico Bardesono decided to unite their vineyards and professional capabilities. Since then, the estate has risen to the top among the producers of Erbaluce. Its vineyards are situated on gravelly-sandy soils in the hills around the towns of Agliè, San Giorgio, and Cuceglio, and the wines it makes are very fresh, high-acid, and clean, though they have more body and intensity than many others made in the area. I thoroughly recommend Cieck's excellent sparkling wines (erbaluce is a high-acid variety and so is ideal for making sparkling wine), though I am always quite taken by the "Misobolo," an Erbaluce that has a lovely, delicate nose of white flowers, green apples, and almonds. The "San Giorgio" vintage sparkler is the wine I pick as the best of the estate, as it combines remarkable freshness and body with uncharacteristic complexity. Fresh and bright on the palate, it has a surprisingly rich mouthfeel. You'll love the delicate hazelnut and fresh-baked bread scents as well as the citrus and pear flavors that go on and on in the long, mineral finish.

THE WINE
Grape varieties: erbaluce di Caluso (100%); **Number of bottles:** 10,000; **Alcohol:** 13; **Retail price:** $25–30; **Try it with:** fried calamari and orange-lemon mayonnaise; grilled chicken breast with a sparkling wine mushroom-accented cream sauce; **Imported by:** Rosalie Sendelbach Imports (www.rosaliesendel bach.com); **Past great vintages:** 2001

THE PRODUCER: AZ. AGR. CIECK
Address: Fraz. San Grato, Cascina Cieck, 10011 Agliè (Torino); **Tel/fax:** 0124 330552/0124 429824; **E-mail:** info@cieck.it; **Web:** www.cieck.it; **Total bottles:** 90,000; **Total ha:** 17; **Tasting room:** yes; **Visit:** by appointment; **Highway exit:** San Giorgio (A5)

OTHER RECOMMENDED WINES UNDER $100 BY CIECK:
Erbaluce di Caluso Spumante "San Giorgio" (sparkling white), Erbaluce di Caluso Spumante "Calliope" (sparkling white), Neretto (red).

13[*] | Montepulciano d'Abruzzo Cerasuolo
CATALDI MADONNA • 90/100 • ABRUZZO

You might think that an area known as the "Abruzzo oven" would not be indicated for growing high-quality grapes, but the wines of Cataldi Madonna prove otherwise. Though the area where the vineyards are located (27 hectares right below the town of Ofena and another 3 hectares on the slopes leading to the Gran Sasso mountain) is so called because of its large amounts of sunlight and high temperatures, these wines are among the best of central Italy. Two rosés are made: the stellar Pié delle Vigne and the user-friendly, easygoing, absolutely delicious base version I describe here. This is a wine, by the way, that will go well with both the heartier dishes of winter and the lighter fare of summer; I suggest that in summer you try it slightly chilled. A panoply of aromas greets the nose, starting with notes of wild strawberries, but you'll quickly also pick up hints of bergamot, yeast, almond, and cinnamon. Bright and fresh on entry, it has a pleasant creaminess that is accentuated in the warm vintages such as 2007. The flavors are similar to the aromas and there's a wonderful saline, mineral tinge to the long finish. Cataldi Madonna makes many fine wines, and its Montepulciano "Toni" is a really fanatstic wine that I urge you to try. In fact, had I not wished to shine a little light on the pleasant but often forgotten rosés of Abruzzo, I would have certainly included the "Toni" in the 200 Best rankings.

THE WINE

Grape varieties: montepulciano (100%); **Number of bottles:** 38,000; **Alcohol:** 12.5; **Retail price:** $16–20; **Try it with:** prosciutto and melon; veal sweetbreads with black morels and gazpacho salsa; **Imported by:** Vias (www.viaswine.com); **Past great vintages:** 2006

THE PRODUCER: CATALDI MADONNA

Address: Loc. Piano, 67025 Ofena (Aquila); **Tel/fax:** 0862 954252/0862 954839; **E-mail:** cataldimadonna@virgilio.it; **Total bottles:** 240,000; **Total ha:** 30; **Tasting room:** yes; **Visit:** professionals only; **Highway exit:** Bussi Popoli (A25)

OTHER GREAT WINES UNDER $100
BY CATALDI MADONNA:

Montepulciano d'Abruzzo Cerasuolo "Piè delle Vigne" (rosé), Montepulciano d'Abruzzo (red), Montepulciano d'Abruzzo "Toni" (red).

14* | Moscato d'Asti
SARACCO • **90/100** • PIEDMONT

According to an ancient legend, Eliar, a young Greek from the Aegean islands, moved to this corner of Italy, overcome by its beauty. He brought along the white muscat vine, from which he made wonderful wine that quickly became famous. It was served at a banquet in honor of the patriarch of the most important family of the area, the Aleramo, believed to be on his deathbed; it proved a smashing success, and the patriarch himself lived, unexpectedly, for many more years in fine health after tasting a glass of the wonderful nectar produced by the "Greek man." The wine made by Paolo Saracco, also a white muscat, is one descendant of that original Greek wine, and it does its famous ancestor proud. This has always been one of Piedmont's best Moscatos d'Asti, a leader in quality recognized by all those in the know. Paolo Saracco has tried hard to capture the essence of the Castiglione Tinella *terroir*, always one of the best for Moscato d'Asti. This wine is bright and light on its feet, with just enough creamy sweetness to its bright, nose-tickling bubbles to make it immensely enjoyable and satisfying; it also has above-average complexity on its long, refined finish. It ages fairly well; you'll be surprised at how fresh it remains even after a few years in the bottle. I am not sure that drinking Saracco's Moscato regularly will guarantee longevity and health for the wine lovers of today, but they are certain to be much happier, and this may well be the key to a long, hearty life.

THE WINE
Grape varieties: moscato bianco (100%); **Number of bottles:** 350,000; **Alcohol:** 5; **Retail price:** $20; **Try it with:** fruit cocktail; bananas Foster; **Imported by:** Dalla Terra (www.dallaterra.com); **Past great vintages:** 2004

THE PRODUCER: AZ. AGR. SARACCO
Address: via Circonvallazione 6, 12053 Castiglione Tinella (Cuneo); **Tel/fax:** 0141855113/0141855360; **E-mail:** info@paolosaracco.it; **Visits:** by appointment; **Total bottles:** 380,000; **Total ha:** 35; **Highway exit:** Asti est (A21)

OTHER RECOMMENDED WINES UNDER $100 BY SARACCO:
Monferrato Bianco Riesling (white), Moscato d'Asti d'Autunno (sweet white).

15 | **Lambrusco Reggiano Secco Frizzante "Arte E Concerto"**
MEDICI ERMETE E FIGLI •
90/100 • EMILIA ROMAGNA

You won't find a better Lambrusco than the ones made here, wines of uncommon depth and creaminess whereas other Lambruscos are all too often thin, tart, and unpleasant. The Medici family has been involved with Lambrusco for more than 100 years and today looks after 60 hectares of vineyards subdivided among three main properties (Tenuta Rampata, Tenuta Quercioli, and Villa Giada), doing considerable work on its grape varieties. The lambrusco family of grapes is large, and not all grapes are at the same level of quality. The "Concerto" by Medici Ermete is made with the superior lambrusco salamino variety, which tends to give Lambruscos more immediate appeal and is easier to understand for wine lovers who do not find fizzy red wines to their liking. This wine is crimson-purple in color, with loads of wild strawberry, raspberry, and ripe cherry aromas and a touch of red roses; it enters rich and round, with lots of lively acidity, delineating flavors similar to the aromas. The very long and unapologetically dry finish leaves the mouth fresh and salivating, and ready for another glass immediately. The "Solo" bottling (see the "10 Best Sparkling and Rosé Wines at $25 or Less" list in section 2) is also very fine, but altogether different from the wine described here, due to the presence of the ancelotta grape variety (as well as the lambrusco salamino, quite different from the Marani subvariety), which makes the latter wine much smoother and almost sweet.

THE WINE
Grape varieties: lambrusco Marani, others (100%); **Number of bottles:** 120,000; **Alcohol:** 12.5; **Retail price:** $16–20; **Try it with:** veal saltimbocca; lentil stew; **Imported by:** JK Imports; **Past great vintages:** 2006

THE PRODUCER: MEDICI ERMETE E FIGLI
Address: Fraz. Gaia—via Newton 13/a, 42020 Reggio Emilia; **Tel/fax:** 0522 942135/0522 941641; **E-mail:** medici@medici.it; **Web:** www.mediciermete.it; **Total bottles:** 800,000; **Total ha:** 60; **Tasting room:** yes; **Visits:** by appointment; **Highway exit:** Reggio Emilia (A1)

OTHER RECOMMENDED WINES UNDER $100
BY MEDICI ERMETE:
Malvaisa Frizzante Secco "Daphne" (malvasia aromatica di Candia—sparkling white), Lambrusco reggiano Secco Frizzante "Solo" (ancellota/lambrusco salamino—sparkling red), Rosé Brut Metodo Classico (lambrusco Marani—sparkling red), Malvasia Dolce "Nebbie d'Autunno" (sweet white).

THE 25 BEST SWEET WINES UNDER $100

1 | Vin "San Giusto"

SAN GIUSTO A RENTENNANO • **96/100** • TUSCANY

Not counting the two made by Avignonesi—fantastic but unfortunately too expensive—this is Italy's best Vin Santo. Take note that since the 2000 vintage it is no longer labeled Vin Santo, as it does not reach the alcohol level (14%) required by the Italian legislature for a wine to be so called. No matter, the wine is a Vin Santo in everything but its name. It is also a true work of art, and has been exceptional right from the start. I have tasted bottles from the 1950s that are still thrilling; and recent vintages, which are just as brilliant, promise to last at least as long. The deep bronze hue clings to the sides of the glass as a smorgasbord of milk chocolate, citrus fruits, caramel, almond, hazelnut, and roasted coffee bean aromas emerge from the thick, syrupy liquid. One sip and you'll find yourself sweetly surrendering to ultra-date, dried fig, peach, caramel, and traditional balsamic vinegar flavors, which go on forever. Still, it's not so rich that it'll glue your gums together after the first sip.

THE WINE
Grape varieties: trebbiano (10%) and malvasia toscana (90%); **Number of bottles:** 1,800–2,000 (roughly), depending on the vintage; **Alcohol:** 11; **Retail price:** $60; **Try it with:** aged Gorgonzola or taleggio; warm chocolate-almond torte; **Imported by:** Marc de Grazia Selection (www.marcdegrazia.com) and numerous importers; **Past great vintages:** 1990, 1995, 1998, 1999, 2003

THE PRODUCER: FATTORIA SAN GIUSTO A RENTENNANO
Address: Loc. San Giusto 20, 53013 Gaiole in Chianti (SI); **Tel/fax:** 0577 747121/0577 747109; **Web:** www.fattoriasangiusto.it; **E-mail:** info@fattoriasangiusto.it; **Total bottles:** 83,000; **Total ha:** 30.5; **Tasting room:** yes; **Visit:** by appointment; **Highway exit:** Valdarno or Val di Chiana (A1)

Chianti Classico (large barrel oaked red), "Percarlo" (sangiovese—small barrel oaked red), "La Ricolma" (merlot—small barrel oaked red).

2 | Picolit Riserva

LIVIO FELLUGA • **96/100** • FRIULI VENEZIA GIULIA

This is one of Italy's—and the world's—greatest grape varieties, but its reputation has been tarnished by, among other causes, countless bad, false, and superexpensive wines. It's not possible to produce a Picolit that costs only a few euros, nor is it possible to produce tens of thousands of bottles of this wine. The reason is that, as the name implies (picolit derives from *piccolitto*, "small"), the variety has a scrawny cluster with 10 to 30 berries rather than the normal 200. Felluga's Picolit is an extremely refined wine that is not of a concentration for concentration's sake, unlike far too many other sweet wines today, which have all the subtlety of a woodpecker. It is deep gold with bronze strokes and has powerful aromas of acacia honey, dry figs and dates, apricots, and peaches that will blow you away, and a gazillion different flavors including peach, dried apricot, orange peel, tangerine, and nutmeg. Some vintages have a pleasant resiny quality. Its texture is lovely and rich with huge buffering acidity to keep it long and lively on the finish, which has some beautiful mineral hints.

THE WINE

Grape varieties: picolit (100%); **Number of bottles:** 2,000; **Alcohol:** 13.5; **Retail price:** $95–100; **Try it with:** pan-seared foie gras; fresh Gorgonzola and acacia honey; **Imported by:** Moët Henessy USA (www.mhusa.com); **Past great vintages:** 1982, 1985, 1996, 1999, 2001, 2003

The '82 has a nose of acacia honey, has citrus and apricot aromas and flavors, and is a very good example of lighter-styled Picolit (93/100). The '99 is amazingly rich and almost resiny with cardoon honey and dried apricot, fig, and date aromas and flavors (96/100). The '01 is almost as rich, a touch more elegant, but not as long (95/100).

THE PRODUCER: EREDI AZ. AGR. LIVIO FELLUGA

Address: Fraz. Brazzano, via Risorgimento 1, Cormons (Gorizia); **Tel/fax:** 0481 60203/0481630126; **Web:** www.liviofelluga.it; **E-mail:** info@liviofelluga.it; **Total bottles:** 650,000; **Total ha:** 135; **Tasting room:** yes; **Visit:** by appointment; **Highway exit:** Palmanova or Villesse (A4)

OTHER RECOMMENDED WINES UNDER $100
BY LIVIO FELLUGA:
Pinot Grigio (unoaked white), Tocai Friulano (unoaked white),
"Terre Alte" (tocai/sauvignon—oaked white), "Sossò" (refosco—
small barrel oaked red).

3 | Cinque Terre Sciacchetrà

BURANCO • 95/100 • LIGURIA

Sciacchetrà is one of Italy's most famous sweet wines, but if truth be told, few examples are worth getting excited about. However, the version by Buranco is certainly worth getting into some mischief for (even more so after you've enjoyed drinking it). The name of this lovely estate comes from the little Buranco, a stream that cuts a swath through the valley where the estate is situated. The wine differs from most other Sciacchetràs, which tend to resemble poor-quality Vin Santos. By contrast, a good Sciacchetrà like this one is a thing of beauty. Lusciously golden-yellow, it has perfumes of sea breeze, herbs, citrus, and some very ripe tropical fruit (pineapple, papaya, passion fruit); the flavors speak mainly of acacia honey, tangerines, pineapple, and more marine mist. Creamy, rich, and very sweet, it keeps light and lively despite high levels of residual sugar, thanks to fine acidity. Its only problem is that not very much is made.

THE WINE
Grape varieties: bosco (70%), vermentino (25%), albarola (5%); **Number of bottles:** 5,300; **Alcohol:** 14.5; **Retail price:** $60; **Try it with:** carrot cake; lemon and blueberry tiramisù; **Imported by:** **Past great vintages:** 2003, 2004, 2005

THE PRODUCER: AZ. AGR. BURANCO
Address: via Buranco 72, 19016 Monterosso al Mare (La Spezia); **Tel/fax:** 0187 817677 / 0187 802084; **E-mail:** info@buranco.it; **Web:** www.buranco.it; **Total bottles:** 6,500; **Total ha:** 1; **Tasting room:** yes; **Visit:** by appointment; **Highway exit:** Carrodano (A12)

OTHER RECOMMENDED WINES UNDER $100
BY BURANCO:
Cinque Terre (vermentino/bosco/albarola—unoaked white).

4 | Recioto Classico della Valpolicella

TOMMASO BUSSOLA • 94/100 • VENETO

After the wines of Quintarelli and Dal Forno, the two cult-wine producers of Amarone, there's no doubt that wine collectors everywhere clamor for those of Bussola. His wines had been, until recently, divided into two groups: the BG (more traditional, named after Tommaso's uncle Giuseppe) and the TB (more modern, very concentrated, and named after Tommaso himself). However, with the '04 vintage, the BG was dropped, because it had been engendering confusion among wine buyers, some of whom thought the wines were being made by a different Bussola altogether. The new name of the BG wine is Recioto della Valpolicella Classico; TB wines have kept their old name. In any case, I always prefer the former BG version of Recioto: easier to drink and very fruity, but concentrated, it is a fine example of why many people feel Bussola is the best of them all at Recioto. Deep ruby-black, it has an intense port-like nose of cherry jam, raspberries macerated in alcohol, bitter chocolate, graphite, bay leaf, and a hint of vinegar and cassis. There are chocolate and cherry jam flavors on the palate with touches of traditional balsamic vinegar and herbs, and enough acidity to keep it buoyant and lively.

THE WINE
Grape varieties: corvina, corvinone, rondinella (and molinara, merlot, and cabernet in small quantities); **Number of bottles:** 4,000 (375 mL); **Retail price:** $55–60; **Try it with:** chocolate truffles; Roquefort-stuffed pears poached in red wine; **Imported by:** Doug Polaner Selection; (www.polanerselections.com), Rare Wine Company (www.rarewineco.com); **Past great vintages:** 2001

THE PRODUCER: AZ. AGR. TOMMASO BUSSOLA
Address: via Molino Turri 30, 37024 Negrar (VR); **Tel/fax:** 045 7501740/045 6011363; **E-mail:** info@bussolavini.com; **Web:** www .bussolavini.com; **Total bottles:** 90,000; **Total ha:** 9.5; **Tasting room:** yes; **Visit:** by appointment; **Highway exit:** Verona nord (A22) or Verona sud (A4)

OTHER RECOMMENDED WINES UNDER $100 BY TOMMASO BUSSOLA:
Valpolicella Superiore TB (red), Recioto della Valpolicella Classico TB (sweet red).

There were always many versions of Picolit, depending mainly on whether air-drying of the grapes was used (this method is now obligatory under the newly created DOCG) or the grapes were late-harvested *tout-court*. More important still was the particular subzone of Friuli the grapes were grown in. Of the three main *grand cru* sites for the variety—Rosazzo, Rocca Bernarda, and Cialla—it is Cialla that gives the most elegant, almost dainty wines, a consequence of its cool climate. The result is a Picolit for connoisseurs, one based on finesse and refinement, rather than sheer force or ultra-ripe fruit. That being said, some particularly warm vintages, such as 1999 and 2003, gave surprisingly rich, almost viscous Picolits for Cialla. Usually, this wine is pale golden yellow in color, with echoes of acacia honey, white flowers, and yellow plums on the nose, and more delicately honeyed citrus fruit flavors on the long finish. It is a lightweight to mid-weight sweet wine; most vintages won't give you bragging rights at the dinner table, and its daintiness usually precludes it from obtaining high scores in blind tastings. However, points aren't everything in life, and we'll just sit back and enjoy a glass of this nectar at any time. The Rapuzzi family, owners of Ronchi di Cialla, have many merits. They single-handedly saved the schioppettino grape from extinction and were the first in Italy to use the barrique for the aging of sweet wines. Every wine made here is an absolute benchmark for the grape variety.

THE WINE
Grape varieties: picolit (100%); **Number of bottles:** 1,100 (375 mL); **Alcohol:** 13.5; **Retail price:** $60 (375 mL); **Try it with:** sweet pumpkin and scallop soup; pineapple fritters with Picolit-Piñacolada sauce; **Imported by:** Bacchanal Wine Imports (www.bacchanalwines.com); **Past great vintages:** 1982, 1983, 1985, 1990, 1999, 2003

THE PRODUCER: AZ. AGR. RONCHI DI CIALLA
Address: Fraz. Cialla 47, 33040 Prepotto (Udine); **Tel/fax:** 0432 731679/0432 709806; **E-mail:** info@ronchidicialla.it; **Web:** www.ronchidicialla.com; **Total bottles:** 60,000; **Total ha:** 20; **Tasting room:** yes; **Visit:** by appointment; **Highway exit:** Palmanova (A4) or Udine sud (A23)

Ribolla gialla (unoaked white), Refosco del Peduncolo Rosso (small barrel oaked red), Schioppettino (small barrel oaked red), Verduzzo (sweet white).

6 | "Tal Luc"

LIS NERIS • 94/100 • FRIULI VENEZIA GIULIA

That the river plain of the Isonzo could be an ideal site for fantastic sweet wines had been shown in the 1970s with Picolit, made at the time by a small maverick producer, but it seemed that nobody else had realized the area's exact potential. (Much the same happened with Bolgheri, where it took 20 years for people to realize that Sassicaia wasn't a fluke.) Then Alvaro Pecorari came along and started air-drying verduzzo grapes, thereby creating Tal Luc, which is, quite simply, one of Italy's greatest wines. One glance at this wine's deep golden-bronze hue and its viscous, thick appearance will tell you that concentration won't be lacking, and this is exactly the case. Very intense tropical fruits dominate the wine's heady aromas, with amazingly rich apricot, peach, mango, guava, and baked apple fragrances. Riesling's contribution to the package is highlighted by a certain citrusy and faint mineral character. It is extremely fat and opulent, with unbelievable sweetness that is never cloying—thanks to humongous quantities of acids—and its apricot jam, pineapple, peach oil, honeyed minerality, and caramel flavors go on and on.

THE WINE

Grape varieties: verduzzo (and very small amount of riesling); **Number of bottles:** 1,800 (90 magnums—that is, 1.5-liter bottles); **Alcohol:** 14; **Retail price:** $70; **Try it with:** apple crumble; foie gras with mango chutney; **Imported by:** Dancing Bear Cellars (www.dancingbearcellars.com), Lis Neris Estate (www.lisneris.it); **Past great vintages:** 1999, 2001, 2004

THE PRODUCER: LIS NERIS

Address: via Gavinana 5, 34070 San Lorenzo Isontino (GO); **Tel/fax:** 0481 80105/0481 809592; **E-mail:** lisneris@lisneris.it; **Web:** www.lisneris.it; **Total bottles:** 300,000; **Total ha:** 50; **Tasting room:** yes; **Visit:** by appointment; **Highway exit:** Villesse (A4)

"Gris" (pinot grigio—small barrel oaked white).

The "small barrels" I refer to here are the 500-liter tonneaux, rather than the 225-liter *barriques* that one usually means by small barrels.

7 | Vernaccia di Oristano "Antico Gregori" n.v.

CONTINI • 93/100 • SARDINIA

Like Vernaccia of San Gimignano, Vernaccia di Oristano is a name that applies both to a grape variety and to a wine. The latter is a wine that resembles Sherry, and as with Sherry the styles of Vernaccia di Oristano can vary from lighter, drier Fino- to richer Oloroso-style wines. Hats off to the Contini family and its "Antico Gregori," by far one of Italy's best and most complex wines. The name "Gregori" refers to the light sandy soils, typical of the Tirso valley, that are best for this particular vernaccia grape. Amber-gold in color, with very intense thyme, date, hazelnut, and almond aromas, which are followed up by complex flavors of dark honey, toffee, orange peel, and dates, it reveals a splendid acid backbone and a never- ending finish. Not syrupy or sticky-sweet, it will remind you of a very high-quality Amontillado or a lighter Oloroso Sherry, though it is less characterized by flor, the yeast that is specific to Sherry and that gives it many of its qualities. Vernaccia di Oristano relies more on desired oxidative characteristics. It is made by the *solera* system, using the estate's best Vernaccias, the oldest one in the blend being close to 100 years old. It's not the easiest wine to understand, but it's a beauty.

THE WINE
Grape varieties: vernaccia di Oristano (100%); **Number of bottles:** 4,000 (500 mL); **Alcohol:** 18; **Retail price:** $90 (500 mL); **Try it with:** amarettus (the dry almond cookies of Oristano are quite famous); pan-roasted rabbit with olives; **Imported by:** Domaine Select (www.domaineselect.com)

THE PRODUCER: AZ. VINICOLA ATTILIO CONTINI
Address: via Genova 48/50, 09072 Cabras (Oristano); **Tel/fax:** 0783 290806/0783 290182; **E-mail:** vinicontini@tiscali.it; **Web:** www.vinicontini.it; **Total bottles:** 500,000; **Total ha:** 60; **Tasting room:** yes; **Visit:** by appointment; **Highway exit:** none

OTHER RECOMMENDED WINES UNDER $100 BY CONTINI:
Nieddera Rosso (small barrel oaked red).

8 | Marsala Superiore 10 Anni

MARCO DE BARTOLI • 93/100 • SICILY

If you haven't yet found a Marsala you like, this estate is a good place to look. In fact, a number of its bottlings are nothing short of amazing, and Marco De Bartoli has to be considered the address for high-quality Marsala. However, Marco, whom I find to be an extremely likable and engaging fellow, is anything but soft-spoken, and tends to tell it like it is, rubbing more than a few people the wrong way. It may well be true that the majority of Marsalas made today (including some of the more famous names of Passito di Pantelleria) are not up to snuff and discredit this once glorious name, but some people tend to hold grudges. To be blunt, this is why De Bartoli's wines have been overlooked by some. Nevertheless, Marco's wines are much sought after by wine lovers everywhere, and in fact are so good that it is hard to pick the best one. Though his dry wines are just fine, it is Marsala for which Marco is most famous, and the 10 Anni bottling is dandy. It is made by the ancient *solera* system (also applied to make Sherry): small amounts of younger wines are added to top off barrels containing older wines, from which wine is drawn off and bottled. This technique guarantees a continuous and harmonic blending of wines in each barrel over time; the resulting wines are nectars of a rare complexity. The 10 Anni is a beautiful amber in color and ravishes the olfactory mucosa with wave after wave of aromatic field flowers, thyme, almond, hazelnut, marzipan, and white chocolate aromas. On the palate it reveals appealing honeysuckle and butterscotch flavors, with hints of dried apricot, orange peel, and mounting dried fig, date, and hazelnut nuances on the long, saline finish. A wonderfully acidic spine keeps it light and lively.

THE WINE

Grape varieties: grillo (100%); **Number of bottles:** 4,000; **Alcohol:** 18; **Retail price:** $30–40; **Try it with:** mature Canestrato cheese; chocolate-covered almond biscotti; **Imported by:** Vias (www.viaswine.com); **Past great vintages:** nonvintage wine

THE PRODUCER: AZ. AGR. VECCHIO SAMPERI/ CANTINE MARCO DE BARTOLI

Address: Contrada Fornaia Samperi 292, 91025 Marsala (Trapani); **Tel/fax:** 0923 962093/0923 962093; **Web:** www.marcodebartoli.it; **E-mail:** info@marcodebartoli.com; **Total bottles: Total ha:** 20; **Tasting room:** yes; **Visit:** by appointment; **Highway exit:** Mazara del Vallo (A29) or Marsala (A29)

OTHER RECOMMENDED WINES UNDER $100
BY MARCO DE BARTOLI:
"Pietranera" (moscato d'Alessandria—unoaked white), "Grappoli
del Grillo" (grillo—unoaked white), Marsala "La Miccia"
(oxidized white), Marsala Vergine Riserva "Vecchio Samperi"
(oxidized white), Passito di Pantelleria "Bukkuram" (moscato
d'Alessandria—sweet white).

9 | Passito di Pantelleria "Ben Ryé"

DONNAFUGATA • 94/100 • SICILY

True wine lovers owe it to themselves to visit, if but once
in their lives, the island of Pantelleria and the estate
owned by the Rallo family of Donnafugata. The sheer
rugged beauty of the island, with its black volcanic soils
and lunar landscapes (some scholars believe it to be the
last vestige of Atlantis) would be reason enough for a visit,
but the quality of the "Ben Ryé" and its unique production
process add to the magic of the place. There are several
subzones on the island, each with its particular soil, exposure, altitude, and subvarieties of moscato di Alessandria,
and the wines made from these areas are very different.
For example, Khamma is a warm area and promotes early
ripening; Barone is higher up and has a cooler climate;
and the somewhat overrated Martingana falls somewhere
between these two extremes. Donnafugata uses grapes
from these various locations (in some vintages from as
many as eight subzones), and this fact goes a long way toward explaining the high quality of "Ben Ryé," which is
unmatched by any other Passito di Pantelleria. The wine
is of a beautifully luminous golden yellow color; has a
nose full of tantalizing aromas of apricots, peaches, dates,
figs, and honey; and has a wonderfully exotic palate full of
waves of apricot jam, ripe peaches, orange marmalade,
dried apricot, and spices. The aromatic finish lingers on
with a gentle sweetness, but is lighter on your taste buds
than the rich nose would suggest.

THE WINE

Grape varieties: moscato di Alessandria or zibibbo (100%);
Number of bottles: 50,000; **Alcohol:** 14.5; **Retail price:** $35; **Try it
with:** mango and passion fruit salad with Passito sabayon; apricot
and papaya pizza with a sweet lemon ricotta crust; **Imported by:**
Folio Fine Wine Partners (www.foliowine.com); **Past great
vintages:** 2000, 2001

Address: via Sebastiano Lipari 18, 91025 Marsala (Trapani); **Tel/fax:** 0923 724200/0923 722042; **E-mail:** info@donnafugata.it; **Web:** www.donnafugata.it; **Total bottles:** 2.4 million; **Total ha:** 302; **Tasting room:** yes; **Visit:** by appointment; **Highway exit:** Mazara del Vallo (A29) or Marsala (A29)

OTHER GREAT WINES UNDER $100
BY DONNAFUGATA:

"Anthilia" (ansonica/cataratto—unoaked white), "Lighea" (zibibbo/inzolia/cataratto—unoaked white), "Polena" (viognier—white), Sedara (nero d'Avola—unoaked red), "Mille e Una Notte" (nero d'Avola—small barrel oaked red), Moscato di Pantelleria "Kabir" (light sweet white).

10 | Picolit

DORIGO • **94/100** • FRIULI VENEZIA GIULIA

The Rosazzo subzone, a *grand cru* for Picolit, is a warmer area of the Colli Orientali del Friuli that gives rich wines in general, and Picolit is a grape that likes well-exposed sites. For more than 20 years, Girolamo Dorigo, a young 80-year-old who will outrun you every time to the top of the hill to the vineyard, has been producing some of the best wines in the area. Sweet or dry, white or red, wine holds few secrets for him; he's now even making an acceptable Gewürztraminer, no easy feat in Friuli. Above all, he makes a very fine Picolit from air-dried grapes. True Picolit was always a late-harvest wine, but air-drying can effectively increase its overall power. Dorigo's wine, creamy-sweet and rich, is undoubtedly the best of all the Passito versions of Picolit (he air-dries the grapes anywhere from two to three months). It manages to maintain the elegance so characteristic of this wine (no small achievement, as air-drying grapes tends to give richer, more structured wines that often lack finesse). You understand a lot about the difficulties and the expense of making Picolit when you learn that at Dorigo it takes eight vines to make one liter of this wine!

THE WINE

Grape varieties: picolit (100%); **Number of bottles:** 2,000; **Alcohol:** 13; **Retail price:** $50 (375 mL); **Try it with:** Gorgonzola; pan-seared foie gras with peach-mango relish; *perseghini* (a dry doughnut-shaped cookie typical of the town of Cividale, made with flour, salt, and sugar), served warm with an English custard cream sauce; **Imported by:** Panebianco (www

.panebiancowines.com); **Past great vintages:** 1985, 2003, 2004, 2005

THE PRODUCER: AZ. AGR. GIROLAMO DORIGO
Address: via del Pozzo 5, 33042 Buttrio (Udine); **Tel/fax:** 0432 674268/0432 673373; **E-mail:** info@montsclapade.com; **Web:** www.montsclapade.com; **Total bottles:** 180,000; **Total ha:** 32; **Tasting room:** yes; **Visit:** by appointment; **Highway exit:** Udine sud (A23)

OTHER RECOMMENDED WINES UNDER $100 BY DORIGO:
Dorigo Brut (chardonnay—sparkling white), Ribolla Gialla (white), Pinot Grigio (white), Pignolo (red), "Montsclapade" (cabernet sauvignon/merlot—red).

11 | Malvasia Puntinata "Stillato"
PALLAVICINI • **93/100** • LAZIO

"Stillato" is one of Italy's greatest dessert wines, as Lazio's best native grape, malvasia del Lazio, is world-class. On the label you'll find only the variety's folk name, malvasia puntinata (*puntinata* means mottled), there at my insistence and something I am proud of, rather than the official name malvasia del Lazio. As the lower-quality malvasia of Candia also grows there, the possibilities for clever labeling "mistakes" were endless. Pallavicini, greatly to their credit, believed in a difficult variety of great potential and then produced one of Italy's great wines. It was originally a pure late harvest, but since the '06 harvest it has also been made from air-dried grapes. It is golden yellow, and memories of saffron, resin, apricot, tangerine, and acacia honey aromas echo through your mind while similar flavors caress your taste buds. Ultra-sweet, with a smooth-as-silk texture and vibrant acidity, it leaves a long-lasting impression.

THE WINE
Grape varieties: malvasia puntinata or del Lazio (100%); **Number of bottles:** 6,000 (375 mL); **Alcohol:** 14; **Retail price:** $20 (500 mL); **Try it with:** ricotta tart with chestnut honey; raisin sponge cake with honeyed goat cheese; **Imported by:** Verdoni Imports (www .verdoniimports.com); **Past great vintages:** 2003, 2004

The 2004 is golden yellow, rich, and perfumed, with lots of acacia honey, grapefruit, banana, and pineapple; a suave texture; and a very sweet yet high-acid palate. It's one of the greatest sweet wines ever made in Italy (97/100). The '03 is golden-bronze, with a very sweet nose redolent of honey, and with mango and papaya aromas and flavors (93/100).

THE PRODUCER: PALLAVICINI

Address: Fraz. Colonna, Via Casilina, Km 25.5 00030 Roma; **Tel/ fax:** 069438816/069438027; **E-mail:** saitacolonna@vinipallavicini .it; **Web:** www.vinipallavicini.com; **Total bottles:** 600,000; **Total ha:** 80; **Tasting room:** yes; **Visit:** by appointment; **Highway exit:** Monte Porzio Catone (A1)

OTHER RECOMMENDED WINES UNDER $100 BY PALLAVICINI:

"Pagello" (falanghina/greco/grechetto—unoaked white), "Soleggio" (cabernet sauvignon—small barrel oaked red).

About 25% of "Pagello" ages in acacia barrels, but the wood presence isn't noticeable.

12 | "Angialis"

ARGIOLAS • 93/100 • SARDINIA

Angialis is a perfect example of a clever wine, one in which a perfect match has been found between the naturally wild side of a native grape called nasco and the gentler, sweet malvasia di Sardegna, another native. Though the declared percentage of malvasia is low, my gut feeling is that just a bit more than this finds its way in, though of course I could be wrong. This is because pure Nascos (you can still find artisanal, well-made examples on the island) are pungent, herbal, musky wines (in fact, the name of the grape is derived from the Latin *nusus*, "musk"). "Angialis" is not all that musky, though it certainly has an aromatic nose. Nevertheless, this is one of Italy's really great wines. It has a deep golden-amber tone, with a wonderfully exotic nose blasting forth with waves of mango and peach and spicy mountain herbs; then it settles down a little on the palate, where its soft acids still manage to nicely frame thyme, caramel, peach, and apricot jam flavors. And there is just enough citrus acidity to keep everything in balance on a long rich, extremely sweet finish.

THE WINE

Grape varieties: nasco (95%), malvasia (5%); **Number of bottles:** 14,000 (375 mL); **Alcohol:** 14.5; **Retail price:** $35–50; **Try it with:** foie gras toast; Roquefort flan; or, for something with a local touch, timballetti (small pies stuffed with both sweet and bitter almonds, eggs, sugar, and flour); sabadas (large fried ravioli containing melted cheese and smothered in honey—beyond heavenly!); **Imported by:** Winebow (www.winebow.com); **Past great vintages:** 2001, 2003

THE PRODUCER: ARGIOLAS
Address: via Roma 56/58, 09040 Serdiana (Cagliari); **Tel/fax:** 070 740606/070 743264; **E mail:** info@cantine-argiolas.it; **Web:** www.cantine-argiolas.it; **Total bottles:** 2 million; **Total ha:** 230; **Tasting room:** yes; **Visit:** by appointment; **Highway exit:** none

OTHER RECOMMENDED WINES UNDER $100 BY ARGIOLAS:
"S'elegas" (nuragus—unoaked white), "Turriga" (mainly cannonau—small barrel oaked red).

13 | Vin Santo di Carmignano Riserva
CAPEZZANA • **93/100** • TUSCANY

The Vin Santo by Capezzana is one of Italy's three or four best, and this producer's one true world-class wine, though the red Carmignanos are no slouches (especially the base white-label "Villa di Capezzana" Carmignano, which is a steal for the price). The Vin Santo is medium golden yellow with glimmers of mahogany and copper; you'll find the nose absolutely enchanting with all of its lovely, low-key, yet pure and precise aromas of yellow field flowers, marzipan, hazelnut, white chocolate, yellow melon, and peach. The flavors remain elegantly restrained, avoiding showiness, but you won't remain indifferent to the almond and hazelnut nuances as well as the candied citrus fruit and lavender hints you'll pick up on the long, high-acid, very intense finish. All in all, this Vin Santo relies not on opulence or power but rather on grace and refinement. You'll remain enchanted by the sheer balance of the wine.

THE WINE
Grape varieties: trebbiano (90%), San Colombano (10%); **Number of bottles:** 5,600 (375 mL); **Alcohol:** 15; **Retail price:** $35–50 (375 mL); **Try it with:** veal spleen crostini; mocha-almond torte with orange liqueur vanilla sauce; **Imported by:** Moët Hennessy USA (www.mhusa.com); **Past great vintages:** 2000, 2001

THE PRODUCER: TENUTA DI CAPEZZANA
Address: Loc. Seano, via di Capezzana 100, 59015 Carmignano (Prato); **Tel/fax:** 055 8706005–8706091/055 8706673; **E-mail:**

capezzana@capezzana.it; **Web:** www.capezzana.it; **Total bottles:** 600,000; **Total ha:** 100; **Tasting room:** yes; **Visit:** by appointment; **Highway exit:** Prato ovest (A11)

OTHER RECOMMENDED WINES UNDER $100 BY CAPEZZANA:
Carmignano "Villa di Capezzana" (small barrel oaked red).

14 | Recioto della Valpolicella Classico "Capitel Monte Fontana"
TEDESCHI • 92/100 • VENETO

Tedeschi's history in wine making goes back to the seventeenth century, so it must be doing something right. In fact, Tedeschi is one of the better sources for Valpolicella and Amarone, available in various styles and prices. Their three Valpolicellas are fine, as are the various Amarones, from the perfectly acceptable entry-level wine to the very fine "Capitel Monte Olmi" bottling right up to the mega-expensive and downright seductive "La Fabriseria," which, though a treat, carries a little too much residual sugar. In fairness, residual sugar is a problem with many famous name Amarones today, as producers feel that consumers prefer red wines with a little extra sweetness. The Recioto by Tedeschi is one of the best, and a wine you really ought to try. It is violet ruby in color, with ripe plum, fig, and balsamic aromas and nutty overtones, medium-bodied with excellent balance. The cherries macerated in alcohol, chocolate, and delicately herbal-raspberry jam flavors are not overbearing, and have a rich, decadent mouthfeel. There's a pretty floral and mineral quality to the long, sweet, and very balsamic finish. Few wines match better with desserts containing dark chocolate than this one. It will do splendidly with blue cheeses as well.

THE WINE
Grape varieties: corvina (30%), corvinone (30%), rondinella (30%), others (10%); **Number of bottles:** 3,000; **Alcohol:** 15–15.5; **Retail price:** $70; **Try it with:** Roquefort; chocolate brownies; chocolate cherry soufflé omelet; **Imported by:** Dreyfus Ashby and Company (www.dreyfusashby.com); **Past great vintages:** 1988, 1990, 1995, 1997, 1998, 2001, 2003

The '97 has figgy-balsamic and nutty nuances complementing the black cherry aromas and is rich and thick on the palate with smooth tannins (93/100). The '98 was particularly fine for Tedeschi, refined in its floral and fresh raspberry aromas, and in its cocoa, coffee, and cherry jam flavors (92/100).

THE PRODUCER: AGRICOLA FRATELLI TEDESCHI
Address: Fraz. Pedemonte, via Verdi 4, 37020 San Pietro in Cariano (Verona); **Tel/fax:** 045 7701487 / 045 7704239; **E-mail:** tedeschi@tedeschiwines.com; **Web:** www.tedeschiwines.com; **Total bottles:** 500,000; **Total ha:** 67; **Tasting room:** yes; **Visit:** by appointment; **Highway exit:** Verona nord (A22)

OTHER RECOMMENDED WINES UNDER $100 BY TEDESCHI:
Valpolicella Superiore Ripasso Capitel San Rocco (large barrel oaked red), Amarone della Valpolicella Classico Capitel Monte Olmi (large barrel oaked red).

15 | "Essenzia"
POJER E SANDRI • 92/100 • TRENTINO

For my money there is probably no better wine making duo in all of Italy than Mario Pojer, winemaker, and Fiorentino Sandri, agronomist. The former takes care, brilliantly, of cellar matters, while the latter looks after the vineyards, and the end result of their teamwork is splendidly manifest when you open any of the bottles made by them. These include a fantastic Müller Thurgau, an above-average (for Italy) Pinot Nero, a very fine Gewürztraminer and Nosiola—the list goes on and on. The Essenzia is one of Italy's best sweet wines, with a strong aromatic character deriving from the kerner, riesling, and traminer, and with waterfalls of flavors hitting your tongue and palate right at the first sip. I am willing to bet that you will find the mango, passion fruit, peach, and spicy citrus aromas more than just a little appealing, and the rich honeyed texture is one you won't soon forget. Very fine acidity keeps this very sweet wine from being cloying or too opulent. Pojer and Sandri are also conducting extensive research on rare, forgotten local native grape varieties such as the groppello di Revò and the negrara trentina, and I, for one, am eager to see what else they will soon have in store for us all.

THE WINE
Grape varieties: kerner and chardonnay (60%), sauvignon, gewürztraminer, and riesling (40%); **Number of bottles:** 40,000; **Alcohol:** 9.5; **Retail price:** $35–45 (375 mL); **Try it with:** strawberry tart; fruit cocktail; **Imported by:** Lauber Imports (www.lauber imports.com), M. S. Walker; **Past great vintages:** 2005

THE PRODUCER: AZ. AGR. POJER E SANDRI
Address: via Molini 4, 38010 Faedo (Trento); **Tel/fax:** 0461 650342/0461 651100; **E-mail:** info@pojeresandri.it; **Web:** www .pojeresandri.it; **Total bottles:** 250,000; **Total ha:** 24; **Tasting room:** yes; **Visit:** by appointment; **Highway exit:** Villanova d'Asti (A21)

OTHER RECOMMENDED WINES UNDER $100
BY POJER E SANDRI:
Müller Thurgau "Palai" (unoaked white), Traminer Aromaico (unoaked white), Nosiola (white), "Vin dei Molini" (rotberger—rosé), Pinot Nero "Rodel dei Pianezzi" (red), Rosso "Fayé" (cabernet sauvignon/cabernet franc/merlot/lagrein—red).

16 | "I Capitelli"

ANSELMI • **92/100** • VENETO

Anselmi is a name recognized the world over—a well-deserved reward for many years of dedicated hard work on behalf of high-quality Soave. There is no question that Roberto Anselmi's efforts, along with those of Nino Pieropan, helped establish Soave as one of the world's great dry white wines, and Recioto as an outstanding dessert wine. Anselmi's drive for quality is such that, years ago, he opted out of the DOCG, in the belief that the government guidelines for the production of Soave were inadequate and had been drawn up with volume, rather than quality, in mind. Therefore, it is the name Anselmi, not Soave or Recioto, that stands out on the labels, and this is as good a guarantee of quality as there is. Anselmi's emergence is all the more remarkable because he comes from a family that was as much to blame as anyone else for the poor-quality stuff being churned out in Soave. His father was content to bottle large volumes of wine without owning any vineyards, and this was just one of the aspects that Roberto sought to change when he entered the family business in 1974. He bought great parcels of vines in top-quality areas in the Classico area of Monteforte, and he introduced yield reductions, small oak barrels, and even a foreign grape such as chardonnay, believing a small percentage of it could help garganega make a better wine. His sweet I Capitelli wine is a real work of art: golden-orange in hue, extremely rich and viscous, it coats the glass while releasing fantastic aromas of ripe peaches, apricot jam, dates, barley, and chestnut honey. On the palate it is thick and almost oily, and immensely sweet, but usually with enough acidity to keep it lively and far from cloying. The tidal waves of honeyed ripe tropical fruit are never-ending, and the flavors will last in your mouth for many minutes after you've finished the glass.

THE WINE
Grape varieties: garganega (100%); **Number of bottles:** 30,000; **Alcohol:** 12.5; **Retail price:** $34–48; **Try it with:** grated apple tart; lemon pound cake with coriander-vanilla sauce; **Imported by:** Palm Bay International (www.palmbayimports.com); **Past great vintages:** 1990, 1996, 2001

THE PRODUCER: ANSELMI
Address: via San Carlo 46, 37032 Monteforte d'Alpone (Verona); **Tel/fax:** 045 7611488/045 7611490; **E-mail:** capitelfoscarino@internet.net; **Web:** www.robertoanselmi.com; **Total bottles:** 700,000; **Total ha:** 70; **Tasting room:** yes; **Visit:** by appointment; **Highway exit:** Soave or Montebello (A4)

OTHER RECOMMENDED WINES UNDER $100 BY ANSELMI:
"Capitel Foscarino" (garganega/chardonnay—unoaked white), "Capitel Croce" (garganega—oaked white).

17 | "Rhea"
GRITTI • **93/100** • UMBRIA

Unfortunately available only in small amounts, this dessert wine is relatively unknown even in Italy, but it has been turning more and more heads with each new vintage. Supersweet, rich yet lithe, it will leave you with a delightful impression of lightness, and of lip-smacking acidity that makes it seem a great deal less sweet than it is (it has over 300 g/L of residual sugar). It comes from 10- to 25-year-old vines of native grapes that are traditionally used in the area to make sweet wines. You'll love the aromas of figs, peaches, dates, caramel, vanilla, toffee-caramel, and white chocolate. There are more peaches and apricots on the palate, with plenty of figs, clover honey, and caramel on the long smooth finish. Make sure you also stop at the winery restaurant, where you'll feast on local dishes prepared with real skill; the estate has a vegetable garden and raises both Chianina and Limousin cattle, so most of the herbs, vegetables, and meats you'll eat here are grown or raised on the premises. When you're done, drive a short distance to the fine butcher shop of the estate.

Grape varieties: grechetto (33%), trebbiano toscano (33%), malvasia bianca (33%); **Number of bottles:** 2,000; **Alcohol:** 9; **Retail price:** $40 (375 mL); **Try it with:** tiramisù; pumpkin bread pudding with lemon-hazelnut vanilla sauce; **Imported by:** DKR Imports (www.dkrimports.com); **Past great vintages:** 2001

THE PRODUCER: CARLO MASSIMILIANI GRITTI
Address: Loc. Molino Vitelli, 06010 Umbertide (PG); **Tel/fax:** 075 9410798/075 9427114; **Web:** www.vitiarium.it; **E-mail:** info@vitiarium.it; **Total bottles:** 60,00; **Total ha:** 40; **Tasting room:** yes; **Visit:** by appointment; **Highway exit:** Val di Chiana or Chiusi (A1)

OTHER RECOMMENDED WINES UNDER $100 FROM GRITTI:
Malvasia nera (large barrel oaked red), "Ca'Andrea" (large barrel red), "Muda" (small barrel oaked red).

18 | "Torcolato"
MACULAN • 93/100 • VENETO

Fausto Maculan is the owner and winemaker of his family estate, which he single-handedly turned around in the 1970s. In fact, the Maculan estate was at the forefront of the revolution in quality and technology that took Italy by storm during those years. There are a number of very fine wines made here, and as good as the "Fratta" is, I feel that the sweet wines are the estate's best work. The excellent "Acininobili" is not unlike a rich Sauternes, but the "Torcolato" is a more accessible and almost as good stickie that also has remarkable aging potential (vintages of the '80s and '90s are still very fine today). Deep golden yellow with some bronze highlights, it has scents of apricots, honey, and crushed stones with a beautiful interplay of citrus and ripe honeyed stone fruits. The luscious, viscous texture is nonetheless wonderfully balanced and fine, and the wine almost always has an exquisitely long finish where the refinement and balance become even more apparent.

THE WINE
Grape varieties: vespaiola (85%), tocai (10%), garganega (5%); **Number of bottles:** 25,000; **Alcohol:** 13; **Retail price:** $40; **Try it with:** lemon-caramel custard; buttery orange shortbread cookie dough with apricot-peach sauce; **Imported by:** Winebow (www.winebow.com); **Past great vintages:** 1990, 1998

THE PRODUCER: AZIENDA AGRICOLA MACULAN
Address: via Castelletto 3, 36042 Breganze (Vicenza); **Tel/fax:** 0445 873733/0445 300149; **E-mail:** fausto@maculan.net; **Web:** www.maculan.net; **Total bottles:** 850,000; **Total ha:** 40; **Tasting room:** yes; **Visit:** by appointment; **Highway exit:** Dueville (A31)

OTHER RECOMMENDED WINES UNDER $100
BY MACULAN:
"Ferrata" Bianco (chardonnay/sauvignon—small barrel oaked white), "Fratta" Rosso (cabernet sauvignon/merlot—small barrel oaked red), "Dindarello" (yellow muscat—sweet white), "Acininobili" (sweet white).

19 Recioto Classico della Valpolicella "Acinatico"

STEFANO ACCORDINI • **92/100** • VENETO

This wine is a testament to the talents of the Accordini family. Their dry Amarones are just fine, too: both the "Acinatico" and especially the top-of-the-line "Il Fornetto" are mesmerizingly good. Just a sip of this sweet Recioto will capture your attention and wow you no end. The color is deep ruby with splashes of ink; the nose is so rich and racy in its ripe red fruit that it is almost immoral. An orgy of red cherry, spicy plum, balsamic strawberry-rhubarb, and milk chocolate aromas greets your nose, and the flavors follow along much the same lines. The lively, mouthwatering acidity adds to the many charms of this wine. Sweet and just slightly syrupy on the long creamy, intense finish, this is a very refined sweet red wine that just glides and glides over the palate with remarkable freshness. Once you realize that your mouth is empty, it immediately makes you want to take another sip.

THE WINE

Grape varieties: corvina (55%), corvinone (30%), rondinella (10%), molinara (5%); **Number of bottles:** 7,000; **Retail price:** $45; **Try it with:** marble fudge brownies; caramelized roasted fig tart with dark chocolate sauce; **Alcohol:** 13; **Imported by:** Vinity Wine Company (www.vinitywinecompany.com), Elizabeth Imports, Omniwine Distribution (www.omniwines.com); **Past great vintages:** 2001, 2003

THE PRODUCER: AZ. AGR. STEFANO ACCORDINI
Address: Fraz. Pedemonte, via Alberto Bolla 9 37020 San Pietro in Cariano (VR); **Tel/fax:** 0457701733/04577001733; **E-mail:** stefano.accordini@tin.it; **Web:** www.accordinistefano.it;

Total bottles: 55,000; **Total ha:** 8; **Tasting room:** yes; **Visit:** by appointment; **Highway exit:** Verona nord (A22)

OTHER RECOMMENDED WINES UNDER $100 BY STEFANO ACCORDINI:
Valpolicella Classico (unoaked red), Valpolicella Classico Superiore Ripasso "Acinatico" (small barrel oaked red), Amarone della Valpolicella "Acinatico" (small barrel oaked red).

The Amarone "Il Fornetto" is Stefano's best wine but will cost more than $100 a bottle.

20 | "Muffato della Sala"
CASTELLO DELLA SALA • 92/100 • UMBRIA

Few wines in Italy have improved this much over the years. When Muffato was first released, in the 1980s, though perfectly fine, it was not an outstanding wine—it lacked complexity and concentration. This is no longer the case, and hasn't been for some time: Muffato is now not just one of Italy's best sweet wines but one that can compete with the best from the rest of the world. Medium deep straw yellow with tinges of gold, it lunges out of the glass with wonderful aromas of pineapple, banana, ginger, lemon custard, and cinnamon. Creamy- textured with loads of pretty grapefruit, lychee, and more pineapple and banana flavors on the palate, it has a full-bodied medium-long finish that is fresher and less caramely sweet than before. There's a very fine use of oak here, evident in a pleasant touch of finishing vanilla. This manages to be light yet concentrated at the same time, no easy feat for a sweet wine. A wonderful result indeed. *Bravi!*

THE WINE
Grape varieties: sauvignon (60%), grechetto, gewürztraminer, riesling (40%); **Number of bottles:** 45,000; **Alcohol:** 12; **Retail price:** $40 (500 mL); **Try it with:** apple strudel; lemon and tangerine–goat cheese cheesecake; **Imported by:** Château Ste. Michelle Wine Estates (www.stimson-lane.com); **Past great vintages:** 2004, 2005

THE PRODUCER: TENUTA CASTELLO DELL SALA
Address: Loc. La Sala, 05016 Ficulle (Terni); **Tel/fax:** 0763 86051/0763 86491; **E-mail:** antinori@antinori.it; **Web:** www. antinori.it; **Total bottles:** 615,000; **Total ha:** 160; **Tasting room:** yes; **Visit:** by appointment; **Highway exit:** Fabro or Orvieto (A1)

OTHER RECOMMENDED WINES UNDER $100
BY CASTELLO DELLA SALA:
"Conte della Vipera" (sauvignon—large barrel oaked white),
"Cervaro della Sala" (chardonnay—white).

21 Montefalco Sagrantino Passito "Colle Grimaldesco"

TABARRINI • 92/100 • UMBRIA

Gianpaolo Tabarrini was born into a family with a long tradition of wine making and he is passionate about the subject. In the 1990s he decided to produce high-quality wines, and one has to admit he has been extremely successful, catching the eye, and the palate, of critics everywhere. His Passito, unfortunately made in small quantities, is excellent—in fact one of the more balanced and better Sagrantino Passitos, with plenty of acidity and alcohol to keep the flavors fresh and appealing. On the palate, the flavors range from a hint of black and red cherries macerated in alcohol to caramely peanut brittle, crème de cassis, and plenty of dark chocolate. A highly impressive and lovely balsamic menthol note on the long, slightly warm, but ultimately suave finish only adds to the many charms of this very successful wine. Like the other wines by Tabarrini, it will greatly benefit from two to three years of bottle age, which will allow it to shed its oaky veneer.

THE WINE

Grape varieties: sagrantino (100%); **Number of bottles:** 2,000; **Alcohol:** 15; **Retail price:** $40; **Try it with:** dark chocolate cake with raspberry sauce; plum tart with chocolate-almond sauce; **Imported by:** Jan D'Amore Wines; Vini Veris; Vitis Imports; **Past great vintages:** 2004

THE PRODUCER: TABARRINI

Address: Fraz. Turrita, 06036 Montefalco (Perugia); **Tel/fax:** 0742 379351/0742 379351; **E-mail:** info@tabarrini.com; **Web:** www .tabarrini.com; **Total bottles:** 50,000; **Total ha:** 11; **Tasting room:** yes; **Visit:** by appointment; **Highway exit:** Fabro or Orvieto (A1)

OTHER RECOMMENDED WINES UNDER $100
BY TABARRINI:
Sagrantino Montefalco "Colle Grimaldesco" (small barrel oaked red).

22 | Recioto della Valpolicella Cl. "Le Calcarole"

ROBERTO MAZZI • 92/100 • VENETO

Our family has always enjoyed the wines of the Mazzi estate, and we're obviously not the only ones—the estate has been making wine since the early twentieth century. Le Calcarole is only one of the great vineyard sites of the Mazzi family (other *crus* being Poiega and Villa), but it's the one that most often gives the grapes used to make the sweet wine. This wine is deep violet-ruby with a hint of amber at the rim; there's a certain autumnal quality in its aromas of faded flowers, dried tea leaf, quinine, red berry syrup, cinnamon, and figs steeped in balsamic vinegar. The flavors are pure and precise and call to mind blackberry jam, red berries macerated in alcohol, milk chocolate, and still more balsamic vinegar, cloves, and cinnamon. A relatively lighter style of Recioto, it finishes long and smooth, with a wonderfully smooth texture that eschews needless muscularity.

THE WINE
Grape varieties: corvina (65%), rondinella (25%), croatina e molinara (10%); **Number of bottles:** 4,000 (375 mL); **Alcohol:** 15; **Retail price:** $25–30 (375 mL); **Try it with:** chocolate mousse with cherry sauce (the cherries of Negrar are famous, so in an ideal world you'd use those for the sauce, since that's where this estate is located); **Imported by:** Marc de Grazia Selection (www .marcdegrazia.com) and numerous importers; **Past great vintages:** 2003

THE PRODUCER: AZ. AGR. ROBERTO MAZZI E FIGLI
Address: Fraz. Sanperetto, via Crosetta 8, 37024 Negrar (Verona); **Tel/fax:** 045 7502072/045 8266150; **E-mail:** info@ robertomazzi.it; **Web:** www.robertomazzi.it; **Total bottles:** 45,000; **Total ha:** 6.5; **Tasting room:** yes; **Visit:** by appointment; **Highway exit:** Verona nord (A22) o Verona sud (A4)

OTHER RECOMMENDED WINES UNDER $100 BY MAZZI:
Valpolicella Classico Superiore (large barrel oaked red), Amarone della Valpolicella Classico "Punta di Villa" (small barrel oaked red).

23 | Recioto di Soave Vigna Marogne

TAMELLINI • **92/100** • VENETO

The brothers Pio Francesco and Gaetano Tamellini produce only three wines, and have been doing so only since 1998, even though they were born into a family with a long tradition of wine making. They have been remarkably successful ever since they started, with each of their wines quickly rising to the top of the hierarchy of Soave, as they devote a great deal of attention and dedication to their pet project. This Recioto is a stunningly rich yet balanced dessert wine, starting with a beautiful bright topaz yellow color, and then proceeding to almost decadent aromas of orange jam and ripe apricots, mixed in with hints of burned almonds, beeswax, and honey. Despite the intense, honeyed sweetness and the seemingly endless tsunami-like waves of pineapple, candied papaya, and baked cinnamon apple flavors that smother the palate in a magically mouth-coating way, there is enough lemony-lime acidity to keep this wine fresh and buoyant on your taste buds. A caveat for purists is the rather intense notes of noble rot that are often present on this wine's nose: as enjoyable and wonderful as these may be, further adding to the wine's immense complexity, it should be clear to readers that the presence of noble rot is *not*, and has never been, a typical feature of Recioto di Soave, historically always just the product of air-drying grapes. That small point aside, the wine is mesmerizingly good.

THE WINE

Grape varieties: garganega (100%); **Number of bottles:** 6,000; **Alcohol:** 13; **Retail price:** $45 (375 mL); **Try it with:** pumpkin bread pudding with Bourbon vanilla cream; lemon chiffon cake with apricot-orange liqueur sauce; **Imported by:** Marc de Grazia Selection (www.marcdegrazia.com) and numerous importers; **Past great vintages:** 2000, 2004

THE PRODUCER: TAMELLINI

Address: via Tamellini 4, Fraz. Costeggiola—37038 Soave (Verona); **Tel/fax:** 045 7675328/045 7675328; **E-mail:** piofrancesco.tamellini@tin.it; **Web:** www.marcdegrazia.com; **Total bottles:** 200,000; **Total ha:** 70; **Tasting room:** yes; **Visit:** by appointment; **Highway exit:** Soave (A4)

OTHER RECOMMENDED WINES UNDER $100 BY TAMELLINI:

Soave Classico "Le Bine di Costiola" (garganega—unoaked white).

24 | Verduzzo Friulano

LA TUNELLA • **91/100** • FRIULI VENEZIA GIULIA

Massimo, Gabriella, and Marco Zorzettig have created, with the very capable help of Luigino Zamparo in the cellar, one of Italy's most dependable wineries, in that you will never be disappointed by any bottle from La Tunella you decide to try. La Tunella is also one of the area's more beautiful wineries, and is certainly worth visiting. There are some very fine white wines such as the "RJ," a Ribolla that is fresh and enjoyable, delicious red wines that are all fairly soft and smooth (the small oak helps to smooth some of the harsher tannins of Friulian native varieties such as schioppettino and refosco) and absolutely splendid sweet wines. The latter may well be this estate's strongest suit, with three beauties that couldn't be any more different from one another: the lighter Verduzzo, the sweeter Picolit, and the intensely sweet, downright sticky "Noans." The Verduzzo is an often overlooked wine by those who prefer sheer power and sweetness, but I feel it is a wonderfully lighter, medium-sweet white wine that is ideal after a long meal: actually, it can be enjoyed at the start of a meal with gorgonzola or paté or foie gras hors d'oeuvres. Verduzzo is never actually too "light," since it is a slightly tannic white grape that gives wines you can almost chew on, but La Tunella's example is one that is less heavy than others. When Verduzzo is grown in the specific subzone of Ramandolo, it takes that name, but there are plenty of very fine Verduzzos available that don't come from what is supposedly the best area for the variety.

THE WINE

Grape varieties: verduzzo friulano (100%); **Number of bottles:** 2,500 roughly, depending on the vintage; **Alcohol:** 13; **Retail price:** $40; **Try it with:** pear-hazelnut crisp with apricot yogurt sauce, almond biscotti; **Imported by:** Quintessential wines (www .quintessential.com); **Past great vintages:** 2005, 2006

THE PRODUCER: AZ. AGR. LA TUNELLA

Address: fraz. Ipplis, via del Collio 14, 33040 Premariacco (Udine); **Tel/fax:** 0432 716030/0432 716494; **E-mail:** info@ latunella.it; **Web:** www.latunella.it; **Total bottles:** 450,000; **Total ha:** 70; **Tasting room:** yes; **Visit:** by appointment; **Highway exit:** Palmanova (A4) or Udine Sud (A23)

Pinot Grigio (unoaked white), "RJ Selenze" (ribolla
gialla—unoaked white), Schioppettino (small barrel oaked red),
Refosco del Peduncolo Rosso (small barrel oaked—red), Picolit
(small barrel sweet white), "Noans" (sauvignon/riesling/
gewürztraminer—small barrel oaked sweet white).

25 | Grechetto "Muffo"

SERGIO MOTTURA • 91/100 • LAZIO

It didn't take long for Sergio Mottura to figure out that the
grechetto grapes he made his wines with were altogether
different from those used to make Orvieto across the regional border. He decided to look into the matter, even
financing university studies to determine the exact family
history and origins of the grapes in his vineyards. Those
studies revealed that the true grechetto is the one he
grows, whereas the grechetto used to make Orvieto is
most likely related to the trebbiano family, and hence not
a grechetto at all (and neither is it related to the various
greco grapes found all over Italy, the best known of which
is the one used to make the famous Greco di Tufo wine).
This being Italy, you'd expect this revelation to be a source
of never-ending arguments, and of course you would be
right. Frankly, even without the benefit of scientific studies, one taste of the various wines tells everyone with taste
buds that they're completely different. The late-harvest
version, "Muffo" (recalling the italian word *muffa*, as in
rot, and of course they mean the noble one!), is a little
jewel. It is bright yellow with gold highlights and has a
floral-citrus nose with banana and peach undertones. Citrus and exotic fruit flavors abound on the palate, where
tantalizing hints of burned almond, caramel, and dried
pineapple add interest. A lovely, delicious lightweight with
a finish of medium length but with fine acids keeping it
light and lively.

THE WINE

Grape varieties: grechetto (100%); **Number of bottles:** 2,000;
Alcohol: 14; **Retail price:** $45; **Try it with:** lemon panna cotta;
apricot-ginger tart; **Imported by:** Chambers and Chambers (www
.chamberswine.com); **Past great vintages:** 1999, 2001

THE PRODUCER: SERGIO MOTTURA

Address: poggio della Costa 1, 01020 Civitella d'Agliano
(Viterbo); **Tel/fax:** 0761 914533/0761 915783; **E-mail:** vini@

motturasergio.it; **Web:** www.motturasergio.it; **Total bottles:** 100,000; **Total ha:** 45; **Tasting room:** yes; **Visit:** by appointment; **Highway exit:** Attigliano or Orvieto (A1)

OTHER RECOMMENDED WINES UNDER $100 BY SERGIO MOTTURA:

Orvieto "Tragugnano" (unoaked white), Grechetto "Poggio della Costa" (unoaked white), Grechetto "Latour a Civitella" (small barrel oaked white).

The "Best Of" Lists

WINES AT $25 OR LESS

ITALY MAKES SOME TREMENDOUSLY FINE wines that are amazingly inexpensive, and that will often surprise your guests who may have never heard of them. This is because once you step away from the tried-and-true, such as Barolo or Brunello, or the top bottlings by ambitious producers, many Italian wines are remarkably affordable. I give you here a can't-fail list of wines any one of which is sure to be a crowd-pleaser. Some of these wines are made from grape varieties you may never have heard of before; others will sound more familiar. Not surprisingly, you will find many Chiantis on this list, for when Chianti is what it should be—that is, a lovely, floral, mouthwatering fruit cocktail—it really is one of the best buys on the planet. What all the wines on this list have in common is the men and women behind them, individuals who are passionate about their work and who are able to turn out perfectly fine wines that do not require you to break the bank. These wines will taste good even when you are back home after a memorable, wonderful vacation, when just about anything you might have tried while looking over bucolic Italian countryside would have tasted great. Just one more of the many charms of the wines that follow: ensuring that eating dinner in the kitchen after what might have been a dog day afternoon at the office makes you think of the brighter, better things in life.

15 Best Red Wines at $25 or Less

1. VALPOLICELLA CLASSICO SUPERIORE ROBERTO MAZZI
(VENETO)—90/100; $18

Valpolicella can be one of Italy's most disappointing wines, but in the hands of a serious producer such as Mazzi it will turn more than a few heads. It's hard to argue with this wine's up-front juicy fruitiness.

2. CHIANTI RUFINA TRAVIGNOLI
(TUSCANY)—90/100; $15

Near the little hamlet of Pelago in Chianti's Rufina district, Travignoli is one of the more dependable names for well-made, consistent Chianti. Owner Giampiero Busi makes an excellent base wine that is quite inexpensive, given the quality in the bottle, but the Riserva costs only a fraction more and is even better. Keep in mind that Travignoli, just like almost every other producer in Rufina, makes an outstanding Vin Santo.

3. DOLCETTO DI DIANO D'ALBA "COSTA FIORE"
CLAUDIO ALARIO (PIEDMONT)—90/100; $18

Claudio Alario has a name linked to an excellent Barolo from the Riva *cru*, and yet he really deserves to be complimented for two of the most enjoyable Dolcettos around, wines so good that you'll have trouble letting go of the glass. The Dolcetto "Montagrillo" is often considered the better of the two, but I prefer the "Costa Fiore," a wine that admirably represents the essence of the dolcetto grape: vinous, fragrant, and wonderfully yummy, with amazingly pure aromas and flavors of fresh blackberries and grapes. Alario's is one of the most beautiful estates in the area, and well worth a visit.

4. CHIANTI RUFINA SELVAPIANA (TUSCANY)—90/100; $16

This is another Chianti that will make you think all the bad stuff out there really shouldn't be allowed to share the same name: it is pure sangiovese at its best, absolutely crammed with violet, red currant, and licorice aromas and flavors, and high acids to keep everything light and lively on your palate. Francesco Giuntini is passionate about Rufina, which is less well known than Chianti Classico but capable of simply great wines, characterized by an intense vinous and smoky black currant quality unique to the area. That Rufina was a high-quality vine-growing area was evident in medieval times, and in the eighteenth century Cosimo of the Medicis classified it as one the four best wine making areas in Tuscany.

5. VELLETRI ROSSO RISERVA "TERRE DEI VOLSCI"
CONSORZIO PRODOTTORI VINI (LAZIO)—88/100; $16

A successful blend of montepulciano, sangiovese, cesanese, and merlot, this is never less than delicious. It is instantly recognizable on shelves, owing to the curious shape of the bottle, nicknamed *collo storto* ("crooked neck" in Italian): the neck is bent slightly to the side. Produced by a cooperative in the town of Velletri (Julius Caesar's birthplace), just a 30-minute drive from Rome, this wine is a good example of the fact that one does not need to spend an arm and a leg to drink well. It goes well with food—far better than many wines commanding big bucks do.

6. GRIGNOLINO D'ASTI BRAIDA (PIEDMONT)—90/100; $16

Grignolinos are rarely better than this one, a good example of the perfumed heights this variety can reach in the sandier soils of Asti, as opposed to the soils of the Monferrato Casalese. Pretty red cherry and raspberry fruitiness and high acids give this lightweight rapport with many dishes: deviled eggs, vitello tonnato, cold cuts of all kinds. The Bologna family deserves to be commended for the effort and research it has put into Grignolino. This is a wine others have abandoned because of its lightish color and tannic structure, yet it is a lovely light, pale-hued red wine that can be enjoyed lightly chilled. Its pretty strawberry and red currant aromas and flavors and low alcohol are sure to be appreciated by all who try it.

7. CHIANTI "CASTELROTTO" GIACOMO MORI (TUSCANY)—90/100; $16

Another beauty here: juicy-fruity, bright, and fresh, it goes down almost too easily, as a disapproving mother-in-law may be quick to point out. Soft and effusively fruity, this has immense appeal, especially since its lower acidity makes it seem sweeter and gentler on the palate. It also shows how a wine simply labeled Chianti may be well made and enjoyable: most often, one needs to be careful with bottles labeled this way, because far too many unpleasant and very poorly made wines are sold by relying solely on the magical name Chianti. In general, it is almost always better to opt for a Chianti whose label includes other qualifications, such as "Classico" or "Rufina" or "dei Colli Fiorentini." Such terms indicate that the wines are made according to stricter guidelines and from grapes grown in specific areas, whereas bottles labeled just Chianti can offer a very mixed bag.

8. VALPOLICELLA SUPERIORE RIPASSO CECILIA BERETTA (VENETO)—88/100; $18

This is the top brand name for the venerable house of Pasqua, and wines like it—bright, fresh, and fruity—deserve your encouragement. Valpolicellas that are labeled "ripasso" are usually richer and fleshier than others: the Italian word *ripasso* means "passed over again" and refers to the fact that the wine has been passed over the grape skins so as to gain in structure and sweetness. Valpolicella has always produced interesting and enjoyable wines, but many bad wines are also made, so a little care has to be taken in choosing one. That the area could make great wines was evident in ancient Roman times:

the name Valpolicella comes from the Latin *polis cellae*, "many cellars," a reference to the intense wine making in this territory.

9. CHIANTI RUFINA FRASCOLE (TUSCANY)—90/100; $15–20

Another Chianti Rufina; another enjoyable, refreshing wine. This wine is sleek, lithe, and filled to the brim with small, crunchy red berry and floral aromas. The people at Frascole try to make wines that speak of the land, and this area—the northernmost and coolest of the Rufina zone—does give wines that are different, with higher-acid structures and fresher fruit aromas and flavors. The more concentrated Riserva bottling (from older vines) is very fine too.

10. DOLCETTO DI DOGLIANI BRICCOLERO QUINTO CHIONETTI (PIEDMONT)–90/100; $20

This wine has a lovely nose that smells of fresh violets, irises, and especially grapes, and you will find that the very grapey aroma is an absolute charmer. Chionetti also packs in ripe blackberry and plum flavors, with enough bright acids to make you wish, after every glass, for just one more. A wine of truly irresistible appeal that is made from grapes grown in the producer's best vineyard, situated on the hill right above his house—an easily recognizable site because of a large pine tree standing at the top of the hill. A quick glance at the lightly colored, almost whitish soil helps explain, at least in part, the lighter, more elegant structures of the Dolcettos from the Briccolero vineyard (and of all those produced from sites located above the local church of San Luigi) compared with Dolcettos produced in other areas of the Dogliani zone—such as those nearer the village of Monforte, where the higher clay content gives darker-looking soils and heavier, more structured wines.

11. CESANESE DI OLEVANO ROMANO "ATTIS" COMPAGNIA DI ERMES (LAZIO)—88/100; $25

This relatively new estate is the brainchild of Mariano Mampieri, who was at the helm of the local cooperative for 10 years and knows the area around Olevano as few others do. The years he spent walking through the vineyards have helped him identify some of the oldest and best situated, which he has tried to buy or rent in order to create his own boutique winery. There are few more enjoyable red wines made in Italy than Cesanese: ripe red cherry fruit, a touch of smoke and tobacco on both nose and palate, and fine but assertive tannins make this wine perfect with food.

12. MORELLINO DI SCANSANO LA MOZZA (TUSCANY)—88/100; $20

Morellino as it should be: hearty, chewy, and full of herbal-scented roasted red and black fruit aromas and flavors. This Morellino also has a telltale saline quality typical of the vine-growing area, which is not that far from the sea. An absolutely great wine with pizza, sausages, stews, and Sunday barbecues.

13. BIZANTINO PERVINI (PUGLIA)—88/100; $20

Pervini is part of the Accademia dei Racemi group, and one of the more famous domains under that umbrella. There have been a number of very good wines made by Pervini throughout the years, and "Bizantino" is one of its lighter-styled, less complex creations. Still, the delivery of chunky tannins and sweet ripe fruit is just what the palate looks for, and this hearty red will go well with foods as diverse as sandwiches and slow-cooked stews.

14. "POGGIO ALLA GUARDIA" ROCCA DI FRASSINELLO (TUSCANY)—88/100; $16

A very successful blend of 45% merlot, 40% cabernet sauvignon, and 15% sangiovese, this wine exudes plenty of up-front charm and luscious fruit, with a pretty mineral note that lingers on the suave finish. Made by a relatively new estate that is a joint venture between two of the biggest names in wine, Paolo Panerai in Tuscany and Baron Eric de Rothschild in Bordeaux. The cellar was designed by Renzo Piano and is a marvel to behold.

15. MERLOT CASALE DEL GIGLIO (LAZIO)—87/100; $20

Few producers in Italy offer so many good wines at such low prices. The merlot is particularly successful, and in fact some important Tuscan producers buy grapes regularly from Antonio Santarelli, knowing that they can always count on his quality. Soft and effusively fruity, this is a mid-weight wine that packs in lots of violet, chocolate, and coffee aromas and flavors and has a pleasant smoth, long finish.

10 BEST WHITE WINES AT $25 OR LESS

1. FALANGHINA CANTINA DEL TABURNO (CAMPANIA)—91/100; $16–20

This producer's Coda di Volpe "Amineo" is in the list of the 60 Best whites, and the Falanghina Cantina del

Taburno isn't far behind in quality. Falanghina doesn't get any better, though this one has a touch of clever residual sweetness; bright acids give lift to the gobs of tropical fruit flavors and the fat luscious texture. Falanghina is a wine available in many styles, because the vines are grown in very different soils; so keep in mind that this is one wine that can vary tremendously from one producer to the next. It is believed that falanghina was the grape from which the ancient Romans made Falernum, considered the greatest wine in antiquity, and that the poet Horace enjoyed drinking it when it was at least 20 years old, though he was quick to point out that 100-year-old examples were even better. Unfortunately, it is safe to say that no modern-day Falanghina can live that long. Again, other experts believe Falernum was made with aglianico, a red grape.

2. SOAVE CAPITEL FOSCARINO ANSELMI (VENETO)—91/100; $20

Anselmi is a master of Soave, and this is a wonderfully modern example of this wine, as it receives no oak treatment and has 10% chardonnay added to the garganega. The use of chardonnay, a foreign grape, in Soave wines is much decried (though it is legal, in small amounts) by old-timers faithful to tradition. I am not sure I like chardonnay in my Soave, having always felt that the garganega didn't need it to shine, but there is no denying that this is an extremely successful wine. Pretty flint-citrus aromas and a fresh mouthfeel give this deceptively simple white a charming easy-to-drink quality, but there is considerable concentration lurking beneath a seemingly light frame. The Monforte d'Alpone area, where Anselmi is situated, is in the middle of the Classico production zone of Soave and the soils are full of marine fossils, indicating that the area was once beneath the sea. This fact also explains the mineral and lightly saline quality of Soave wines.

3. TOCAI FRIULANO BASTIANICH (FRIULI VENEZIA GIULIA)—91/100; $18

The Tocai Plus is a fantastic wine, and though this may be only its little brother, it's a great introduction to the house style. Mineral, almondy, flinty, slightly grassy, bright, fresh, and surprisingly long, it is made from bought grapes, but is as good as if not better than many more famous Tocais. As tocai is actually the sauvignon vert or sauvignonasse grape, you won't have any trouble recognizing some grassiness, thyme, and sage notes in this wine, and actually these are descriptors you should associate with all Tocais made in

Italy. Also note that the Premariacco area, where the Bastianich estate is situated, has always been associated with good-quality Pinot Bianco as well.

4. BLANC DE MORGEX ET LA SALLE "RAYON" (VALLE D'AOSTA)—91/100; $25

This usually extremely high-acid wine has been somewhat tamed by the talented winemaker Gianluca Telolli, who turns out a series of different Vin Blancs from the high-acid "Vini Estremi" to this much richer, creamier, and ultimately more complex version, called "Rayon." It has a pale straw-green hue with some golden highlights and is always characterized by a light, airy quality but with a rich creaminess to the green apple, banana, and apricot aromas and flavors. Very long and very mineral on the finish, this is easy to drink and has the breezy quality of a breath of fresh mountain air. The cooperative makes about 90% of all the Blanc de Morgex et La Salle wine in the region, also offering it in a sparkling version and a relatively sweet version.

5. RIBOLLA GIALLA TORRE ROSAZZA (FRIULI VENEZIA GIULIA)—91/100; $16

Torre Rosazza's Tocai is just great, and often underestimated, but the truth is that its Ribolla is just as good. Insiders know that Torre Rosazza always excels with this wine, and they look for it avidly. Bright mandarine and lemon-lime aromas with fresh citrus-mineral flavors make it an absolute winner, and I guarantee that just about anyone you try it with will appreciate it. Try it as a predinner drink, or match it with simply prepared vegetable and seafood appetizers, and get ready to be happy. Rosazzo, where this estate is located, is a particularly warm part of Friuli, and has always been considered one of the best sites, if not *the* best site, for growing ribolla grapes.

6. VERNACCIA DI SAN GIMIGNANO VIGNA CASANUOVA FONTALEONI (TUSCANY)—90/100; $18

Along with Panizzi's, this is the best Vernaccia out there. Its fragrant, citrusy style speaks clearly of the terroir of Ulignano in the northern section of San Gimignano, where cooler, more humid weather gives wines with a lighter frame but greater perfume. You'll find that this Vernaccia has a surprisingly luscious texture and a lovely lingering grapefruit and mineral aftertaste. Because there are quite a few nondescript, neutral Vernaccias di San Gimignano, be sure to try this one, and get ready to be amazed by how much flavor it can throw at you. A very small percentage of chardonnay is added in, but you'll hardly notice it.

7. "MARESE" RIVERA (PUGLIA)—90/100; $18

The bombino bianco variety is coming back from oblivion, and this is yet another example of a great, highly enjoyable little wine that has recently appeared on the scene. Its creamy, almost sweet texture delivers loads of ripe apricot, pineapple, and apple flavors with finely integrated acids. An altogether different wine from the thin watery efforts that used to be associated with this variety, it delivers such a soft-textured, almost sweet mouthfeel that I have yet to meet anyone who wasn't smitten with it at first sip.

8. MOSCATO GIALLO MANINCOR (ALTO ADIGE)— 90/100; $18

If you like aromatic wines and want to try something other than Riesling or Gewürztraminer, this is the best dry Moscato Giallo (Yellow Muscat) of Italy. Do note the word "dry" in the previous sentence: be aware that some Moscato Giallos by other producers, though perfectly fine, can actually carry quite a bit of residual sugar and seem sweet. Not this one, however; you'll be thrilled at the delicious white pepper, cinnamon, and citrus aromas and flavors. I guarantee that this wine will bowl you and your guests over, especially if you serve it with Chinese dishes such as lemon chicken or sweet-and-sour pork. It will also go just fine with dishes of many other ethnic cuisines.

9. "INCÒ" LA VIARTE (FVG)—90/100; $18

This blend of tocai and other varieties is an extremely well-balanced lightweight that's so enjoyable it goes down like water: a nose like a spring day and pretty lemony and apricot flavors will make you a believer. It comes from the well-respected producer La Viarte, whose wines are generally not at all expensive. With this wine La Viarte has achieved a true masterpiece: quality this high for the price is really not easy to come by, in Italy or anywhere else.

10. FRASCATI CASTEL DE PAOLIS (LAZIO)—90/100; $20

With so many Frascatis to choose from and with so many bad ones turning people off, it's a joy to be able to write about one of the many good ones. This is richer than most, thanks to a healthy dose of the malvasia puntinata grape, which gives a fatter, more resiny mouthfeel. Though Frascati doesn't age particularly well, this one does, with bottles from 1995 still in fine shape. It is a wine of great charm and a real palate pleaser: its creamy texture and bright acids nicely delineate the herbal and ripe fruit aromas and flavors.

10 BEST SPARKLING AND ROSÉ WINES AT $25 OR LESS

1. ETNA ROSATO TENUTA DELLE TERRE NERE (SICILY)—90/100

Without question, this is one of the world's great rosés, and the 2006 is simply spectacular, as good as any other made anywhere in the world. The nerello mascalese grape has always been known to give almost pinot noir–like aromas and flavors, but this rosé is the first that also manages to showcase them to full effect. The strawberry, mineral, and floral aromas are enchanting and the balance is impeccable. Finishes very long and clean, with a great deal more concentration than is usual with rosés. A really great wine.

2. MONTEPULCIANO D'ABRUZZO CERASUOLO LEPORE (ABRUZZO)—88/100

Lepore's wines are fairly traditional in style (some more internationally styled, softer wines are in the lineup) but this rosé will appeal to any wine lover. Made from clay-rich soils in the area of Teramo, not far from the sea, this has considerable body and depth.

3. REGGIANO LAMBRUSCO "SOLO" FRIZZANTE SECCO MEDICI ERMETE (EMILIA ROMAGNA)—88/100

This is a blend of 55% ancellotta and 45% lambrusco salamino, and it is remarkably different from the "Concerto" wine I listed in the "15 Best Sparkling and Rosé Wines" rankings. The ancellotta adds a tremendous amount of color, making the wine almost black (in fact, ancellotta is a variety that has long been a favorite of sangiovese producers who need to kick up the color of their wines a bit) and also adds softness and an apparent sweetness. Those who find lambrusco a bit too tart will undoubtedly prefer this version, which has a creamy, smooth mouthfeel.

4. CIRÒ ROSATO LIBRANDI (CALABRIA)—87/100

Antonio and Nicodemo Librandi have been doing extensive work on their native grapes, and this rosé is one of their most improved wines. It is made with the gaglioppo grape—not an easy one to work with, due to rustic tannins and its lack of color and fruit, but is well suited to excellent, enjoyable rosés that have been scarce in Italy only because of Calabria's retrograde enological practices.

There are signs, though, that Calabria, a region second to none when it comes to terroir and climate, is now coming out of its doldrums, so perhaps we will have many more fine wines such as this to look forward to.

5. PROSECCO DI VALDOBBIADENE EXTRA DRY "DEI CASEL" ADAMI (VENETO)—87/100

Adami is one of the most reliable names in Prosecco. The "Bosco di Gica" bottling is also very good, though a little drier than most, while this extra-dry wine has a soft, creamy, and effusively fruity appeal.

6. COLLI PIACENTINI "VALNURE" FRIZZANTE LA TOSA (EMILIA ROMAGNA)—87/100

A complicated blend of 45% malvasia di Candia, 40% ortrugo, and 15% trebbiano, this golden-tinged wine has aromas of yellow plums, grapefruit, and hazelnuts. It finishes bright and fresh, with a slight hint of almonds. La Tosa makes many wonderful wines, and I urge you to try its various malvasia bottlings, ranging from dry to frankly sweet, which undoubtedly will appeal to most readers.

7. COLLI PIACENTINI GUTTURNIO FRIZZANTE LA STOPPA (EMILIA ROMAGNA)—87/100

Made from a blend of 60% barbera (which gives freshness) and 40% bonarda (which gives structure and body), this is an excellent Gutturnio, a locally famous wine that is one of the many bubbly reds Italy is famous for and that are absolutely ideal with cold cuts and sandwiches of all kinds. Strawberry, pomegranate, and raspberry aromas give way to similar flavors on the palate and a touch of warmth on the finish.

8. PROSECCO DI VALDOBBIADENE BRUT COL VETORAZ (VENETO)—87/100

One of the really great names in Prosecco, though Col Vetoraz has always been linked to Italy's single best Cartizze. The Brut Prosecco is just as fine, and its pretty white peach and green aromas and flavors will make you just wish summer would never go away.

9. MONTEPULCIANO D'ABRUZZO CERASUOLO "VERMIGLIO" ORLANDI CONTUCCI PONNO (ABRUZZO)—87/100

This is Contucci Ponno's most improved wine, and now ranks with the best of the rosé wines made in Italy today. Made in a lighter, more immediate style, it will be ideal for summer sipping, slightly chilled, and matches well with just about any uncomplicated pizza or pasta dish you'll be serving.

10. ESSÉ BRUT VALLONA (EMILIA ROMAGNA)—87/100

Vallona is most adept at turning the local grape variety pignoletto into something really special, and though his best wines are undoubtedly the still ones, it is remarkable how much flavor he packs into this sparkling version. Pignoletto, a high-acid variety, is ideal for making sparkling wines. There are plenty of pretty citrus and apple aromas and flavors here, with a lingering herbal note on the finish. It makes an absolutely ideal start to any meal, one that shall allow you to get away from the usual glass of Prosecco or Champagne.

10 BEST SWEET WINES AT $25 OR LESS

Unfortunately, because of the process by which sweet wine is made, which most often involves the dehydration of grapes, it is virtually impossible to produce these wines inexpensively. Dehydrated grapes contain less water than normal grapes, and this results in smaller volumes of wine being produced. In addition, the production of sweet wines is very labor intensive (taking care of the sweet, dehydrating grapes is a lot of work, as there is a greater chance they may rot) and therefore the wines are more expensive than many whites or reds. There really are not that many sweet wines of real quality available at less than $25: in fact, most are far more expensive. However, there are some interesting sweet wines made in Italy that do not cost an arm and a leg: you can try the Sangue di Giuda by Bruno Verdi, an off-dry red from Lombardy, or the "Primo Amore," an excellent Primitivo Dolce made by Pervini in Puglia.

CULT WINES

25 DON'T ASK CULT WINES

All the wines listed below are routinely thought of as the best Italy has to offer, wines that for the most part have a proven track record going back 20 or 30 years. They have retail prices of about $150 or more. Moreover, specific vintages may now fetch more than $1,000, if provenance can be guaranteed, meaning that the bottles were well kept throughout their lifetime (in other words, kept in a temperature-controlled cellar). In fact, the "Sassicaia" from the 1985 vintage, arguably Italy's most famous and most successful wine of all time, routinely sells at auction for $3,000 a bottle. Though I shudder at the thought, preferring to maintain a more romantic, if hopelessly outdated, vision of wine, these are the ideal wines to buy as an investment, because they all age beautifully and have repeatedly increased in price over the years. Personally, I don't believe that all of them are worth the stratospheric prices they command, and I find some slightly overrated. That being said, the vast majority, including Sassicaia 1985 and Brunello Case Basse Riserva 1983, do rank with the greatest wines in the world, and of all time. One note: all but one of the entries on this list are red wines, and it could not be otherwise: all over the world, reds always fetch the highest prices, in stores or at auctions. This is because red wines age well and long, something that cannot usually be said of white wines (certainly not of Italy's, though fine German Rieslings, which are among my favorite wines, age extremely well). Of course, sweet white wines do age well, and the lone non-red wine on this list is in fact a dessert wine.

1. BAROLO RED LABEL "VIGNA RIONDA"
BRUNO GIACOSA (PIEDMONT)

For my money, this is Italy's single greatest wine: not just one mesmerizing year like the Sassicaia '85 or the Case Basse Riserva '83, but a never-ending string of successes, 1971, 1978, and 1982 foremost above them. The term "red label," which you will not find on the label, refers to the color the label uses for the Riserva wines; the base wines have a white label. Prior to 1978 the red labels were often Riserva Speciale wines (that is, with even one more year of wood aging) rather than just Riserva. No matter—they're all great, and you should never pass up an opportunity to taste one. The Vigna Rionda is the greatest of all Barolo vineyards, but Giacosa didn't own it and now most of those grapes are being used by others—unfortunately, as Giacosa is Italy's single greatest winemaker. The '71 is beyond words (100/100); the '78 is the best Barolo of that great vintage (99/100); and the '82 is slightly softer than most (98/100).

2. SASSICAIA TENUTA SAN GUIDO (TUSCANY)

The 1985 is Italy's most famous and perhaps best-ever wine (100/100). I have enjoyed it exactly 33 times over the years since its release (having bought 12 bottles a few days after it was released for the equivalent of about $20 a bottle). It has never been anything less than stellar, save for one prematurely evolved bottle that I drank in Toronto in the late 1980s. It is one of those wines that can easily last more than 100 years, as some of the great Bordeaux of the nineteenth century have. It's the stuff not just of dreams but of legends. Another vintage worth seeking out is the '88, almost as good (97/100) but nowhere near the same price level ($750). The '90, though a very fine wine (95/100), has always been a bit of a disappointment, considering the stellar vintage. It lacks the depth and complexity of the '85 and the '88.

3. BAROLO MONFORTINO GIACOMO CONTERNO (PIEDMONT)

This wine is made only in the better vintages, and in the past it received as much as 12 years of wood aging prior to release (most Barolos are aged in oak barrels for three years at most). The '64 and '67 are so good that words can't do them justice; I've also had the '37, and it's not bad, either. Simply put, this Barolo has a longevity unmatched by any other, and may well be, in the minds of many experts, Italy's best wine. The '67 was a 100-point wine at the end of the 1990s, but a recent bottle was beginning to fade (96/100). The '82 and '85 are both 98-point wines and will easily last another 30-plus years. The estate is now being very capably managed by Roberto Conterno, who distinguished himself by bottling the '02 vintage. That vintage was generally considered horrible by everyone else, yet the magic of Monfortino is such that it can give mesmerizing results even when you would think the conditions are impossible.

4. BRUNELLO DI MONTALCINO RISERVA CASE BASSE (TUSCANY)

If it weren't for the Sassicaia '85, the '83 Riserva of this wine would be considered Italy's best ever (100/100). It is a wine of unbelievable depth and perfume, like no other Brunello you have ever tried or ever will try. It is almost unfindable, since not much was made to begin with. The '81 has lovely perfumes but a thinnish body (92/100), and it may be starting to fade. The '82, chunkier from the start but with plenty of fruit and a rich mouthfeel, is still lovely (95/100). I have been less of a fan of some of the wines of the '90s, but recent vintages have shown this estate to be in top form again. A must-try for all those who have never been fans of sangiovese: if this wine does not get them thinking otherwise, nothing will.

5. "MASSETO" ORNELLAIA (TUSCANY)

American readers might like to know that one of Italy's greatest wine estates, Ornellaia (also the name of a wine), used to be partly owned by Napa's famous wine producer Robert Mondavi. The estate was originally founded by Ludovico Antinori, who had inherited land in the corner of the Bolgheri area and had a real passion for fine wines. It has also involved wine luminaries such as André Tchelistchev, one of the men responsible for turning Napa into a great wine making area. Ornellaia is now the property of the Frescobaldi family, and the wines continue to be splendid. "Masseto," first made with the 1986 vintage, is a modern, rich, ripe Merlot that eschews jamminess and exaggerated flavors and aromas. There's a velvety opulence to its texture that is really hard to describe, and that you will find in only a very few of the world's best wines. This is a wine of amazing grace and power, and in my opinion the world's single greatest Merlot made outside France. The '01 is the best yet made (99/100).

6. AMARONE DELLA VALPOLICELLA DAL FORNO (VENETO)

Romano Dal Forno's wines always walk a fine line between genius and exaggeration. This Amarone is one of Italy's four or five wines most sought after by collectors with deep pockets everywhere, a super-concentrated wine that has reached amazing prices per bottle on release (it usually starts at $400). But as good as it is, and as nice a man as Romano Dal Forno is, I think it's something of a trophy wine. In fact, it is so thick and powerful that drinking the stuff is one thing but eating with it is another matter altogether, and matching it to food is very difficult. For my taste, the tannins are just a little too much, and the wine always seems to finish with a hint of lingering bitterness that is not for me. The 1999 is a case in point (89/100): almost black, thick and viscous like motor oil, it is loaded with inky quinine, blackberry, and plum jam aromas and flavors, with a never-ending iodine and balsamic aftertaste. It is a very impressive wine, thanks to its sheer force—one glass takes your palate places where you haven't been before. However, just being taken for a ride doesn't mean you enjoyed the trip. Fairness demands that you try this wine and see for yourself: remember that it scores extremely high with just about every other wine writer, so I am in a very small minority.

7. AMARONE DELLA VALPOLICELLA QUINTARELLI (VENETO)

From the old master of Amarone, a more refined wine than Dal Forno's, though it will appeal less to those who prefer size over elegance. Giuseppe Quintarelli is now the third generation of the Quintarelli family, which has lavished attention and dedication on its Monte Ca' Paletta vineyard since 1924. Try the Amarone 1979, a lesser year, but in the hands of a genius such as Quintarelli a true work of art (99/100). In fact, never turn down a chance to drink *any* vintage of this wine, though the '98 is a little less stellar than usual (93/100). Be warned: you need to accept a touch of volatile acidity here and there. Some people will criticize this aspect of Quintarelli's wines, just as I find the exaggerated tannic strength of Dal Forno's wines a little difficult to live with; it really is a matter of taste. Quintarelli, a staunch traditionalist who has also experimented successfully with cabernet franc, cabernet sauvignon, and other grapes, makes many other fine wines, but unfortunately the only great one that is reasonably priced is the Valpolicella.

8. "REDIGAFFI" TUA RITA (TUSCANY)

When you see the most recent vintage of a wine on restaurant lists in the United States at $700 a bottle, you realize you're in cult wine territory. And so it should be, as this is one of the world's greatest Merlots: you'll be thrilled by its smooth-as-silk tannins, which are rare in any but the greatest of the world's wines. Take note of Redigaffi's typical licorice flavor mixed in with all the coffee, chocolate, and ripe blackberry-plum fruit you could wish for. The owner, Stefano Frascolla, is so attentive to this wine's quality that he won't use any barrels he feels are even very slightly below his usual exalted level of quality: he passed on four barrels of the '04 vintage that only a robot programmed to taste wine, or less than 1% of the world's wine experts, could ever have thought of as being less than stellar. The '01 is a 100-point wine, and the '04 is close (98/100).

9. "MESSORIO" LE MACCHIOLE (TUSCANY)

Another of Italy's greatest wines and yet another fine Merlot from Tuscany, this one comes from a cooler microclimate than the "Redigaffi" and usually has a more savage roast coffee bean and herbal note. The estate, founded in 1981 by Eugenio Campolmi, is right next to Ornellaia, so you know the *terroir* here is more than just a little special. Messorio also goes for about $700 on some restaurant lists in the United States, and is one of Italy's most coveted cult wines. Its greatness lies in the fact that it never comes across as jammy or heavy-handed, even in hot years, when merlot vines (the wrong grape to plant in areas with very hot climates) tend to shut down the physiological ripening process of the grapes, giving green, vegetal wines marked by harsh tannins. The '01 (99/100) and the '04 (98/100) are the best recent efforts. The '97 and '98 are very fine, too (both 97/100), and have a noticeable mineral-herbal quality that the more recent vintages don't exhibit, at least not to the same degree.

10. "SOLAIA" ANTINORI (TUSCANY)

One of Italy's greatest wines, this is remarkably dependable year after year. Some experts feel there are many better cabernets for the price, but one taste of the '85, '88, or '90 will make a believer of anyone. Solaia is a true super-Tuscan, exuding refined tannins, depth of concentration, elegant oak touches, and very pure black currant and plum aromas and flavors that in better years can all add up to a truly memorable drinking experience. In my opinion, Solaia's greatest asset is that it is usually endowed with unbelievably silky tannins, of a quality only the Bordeaux first growths and some of the very best in Napa attain. The 1985 is a fantastic, unforgettable wine, less thought of only because it had the misfortune to be made the year the unbelievable "Sassicaia" was also produced, but I can guarantee that when these two first came out there was only a minimal difference between them. In fact, being a penny-conscious university student at that time, I remember agonizing at length over which one of the two I should have bought (as luck would have it, I picked "Sassicaia," but I would have been very happy with this wine as well). Today it's still a fantastic bottle of wine (98/100). The '78, the first ever made, is also a work of art (97/100), and the '97, '98, and '01 are all 96-point wines.

11. SYRAH "SCRIO" LE MACCHIOLE (TUSCANY)

Syrah hasn't yet reached the heights of Italy's Merlots, but this is the best Syrah of them all and in some vintages it can hold its own with the greatest from the Rhône. In fact, it was the first Syrah of note to be made in the Bolgheri area; and this little-known first is one of a long line of credits for Eugenio Campolmi. His wife, Cinzia, carries on the fine work and never misses a beat. I am sure you will love this wine's spicy nose and lush fruity personality. The '03 and '04 are beautiful and are two of the greatest Italian wines (both 97/100) to drink while they are still young: the sheer opulence of the spicy red and black fruits with generous hints of smoky bacon fat make this wine unbelievably fun to drink. Because of global warming, syrah is very well suited to this part of Italy and this wine can only get better and better as the relatively young vines (planted in the 1980s) come of age.

12. "TENUTA DI TRINORO" TENUTA DI TRINORO (TUSCANY)

Andrea Franchetti is an amazingly talented man, a former wine broker who founded his estate in the town of Sarteano in the 1990s, planting cabernet sauvignon, merlot, and cabernet franc (plus other varieties) on clay-gravel soils not unlike those of his beloved Bordeaux. His wines have more than a passing resemblance to those of Jean-Luc Thunevin, the maverick winemaker who has risen to the top of the heap in the Saint Emilion area with his own wines as well as helping fashion those of many now wildly popular estates. However, a sip of Franchetti's wines reveals that they have a great deal more personality than those made by Thunevin, which all too often tend to resemble each other. In fact, a sip of the Tenuta di Trinoro will convince you that there's a genius at work. A wine of remarkable creaminess (you really do have to taste it to see just what I mean), and with especially silky ripeness in its fruit. The '01 is the best ever (99/100), but the '98 is not far behind (98/100). For something completely different, try the '04, which is top-heavy in merlot, unusually for this wine (94/100). Don't forget to try this estate's Cincinnato bottling—a 100% cesanese that Franchetti has almost given up on because the grape never seems to ripen fully except in very hot years, but the '03 and the '99 are very memorable wines (both 98/100).

13. BARBARESCO RED LABEL "SANTO STEFANO" RISERVA BRUNO GIACOSA (PIEDMONT)

This is another wine that Giacosa makes less of nowadays (again, he didn't own the vineyard), but the '71, '78, '82,

'88, '89, and '90 are worth breaking the piggy bank for. If you bought only six wines in your life, you could hardly do better than choose this set. Unbelievably long-lasting and penetrating on the palate, they are remarkably concentrated yet refined Barbarescos that have the larger frame and ripe fruit typical of the Neive subzone. The '71 is the greatest of the lot and one of my five best Italian wines of all time (100/100), but the '82 is almost as great (98/100). In some years, Giacosa also produced an "Albesani" bottling, using grapes that came from the same vineyard as the Santo Stefano version but that weren't used for the latter, better, wine. Still, the 1971 was a thing of beauty as well.

14. BAROLO "BRUNATE" ROBERTO VOERZIO (PIEDMONT)

This producer is a modern-day icon, offering deep, dark wines that have intense ripe aromas and flavors and fetch extremely high prices. These rich, brooding wines do not represent my preferred style of Barolo (I opt for a more refined, perfumed expression of the grape, but to each his own); still, it's hard to argue with success. Voerzio's estate was born when his father's original domain, founded in the 1950s, was split in two (his brother Gianni has created an estate with the other half). Roberto is a perfectionist, and people who have worked with him in the vineyards will tell you they've never seen anyone work as hard and take as good care of the vines. There are many different Barolos to choose from, and though he is perhaps most famous for the bottling from the Cerequio *cru*, they are all just as grand in their own ways. My pick is actually the Brunate, another of the great vineyard sites of Barolo: it will give you a good idea of what Voerzio can achieve from a vineyard that many others farm but with very different, and often lesser, results. You won't even get near a bottle of any vintage with less than $250, and that's just the starting price.

15. BAROLO "CANNUBI BOSCHIS" LUCIANO SANDRONE (PIEDMONT)

The '85, the '89, and especially the '90 of this wine are unforgettable. The prices are unforgettable, too. A magum of '85, a fantastic wine (99/100), goes for $1,500 or more; the '90, perhaps Sandrone's best wine ever (100/100), used to sell for $250 in 1999. A good example of Sandrone's immense talent, which he honed as the acting winemaker at the venerable Marchesi di Barolo estate in the 1970s, is what he was able to achieve with the 1984. This was an outright lousy year, but his was the wine of the vintage (the bottle still carried the old white label and the name "Monghisolfo dei Cannubi" rather than the newer "Cannubi Boschis"). It was a very fine though lighter-styled Barolo that displayed impeccable balance considering the poor weather and was a clear example of what a great winemaker can achieve even in poor years. Experiencing mounting success, Sandrone left the Marchesi di Barolo estate in the early 1990s to dedicate himself full-time to his own estate.

16. BAROLO RED LABEL "LE ROCCHE DEL FALLETTO" RISERVA BRUNO GIACOSA (PIEDMONT)

As I mentioned previously, an unexpected and serious problem for Giacosa was that he had never owned any of his famous Barolo or Barbaresco vineyards. It had never been necessary to own vineyards in this part of Italy, as the larger producers had always either bought grapes or arranged for long-term rentals of choice land. However, with the economic wine boom of the 1980s and 1990s, many vineyard owners decided to try their hand at making and bottling their own wines, leaving those who had always counted on them for grapes to scramble around once the contracts expired. Giacosa quickly remedied this situation by buying parcels at other wonderful sites, such as Asili. Le Rocche is a great Barolo made from grapes grown in the Serralunga area, which gives, potentially, the sturdiest and longest lived of all Barolos. Less perfumed and refined than those of La Morra, and never as initially balanced as those of Castiglione Falletto, these are quintessential Barolos of great balance and breeding. Giacosa's "red label" version is made from the best grapes grown at the highest point of this hillside parcel, and has a characteristic tobacco nuance that sets it apart from the more licorice-endowed Vigna Rionda bottlings. The '01 is the best Le Rocche yet (98/100).

17. BAROLO "GRANBUSSIA" ALDO CONTERNO (PIEDMONT)

The estate of Aldo Conterno has always made two of the best Barolos from the Cicala and Colonnello vineyards in the Bussia area of Monforte d'Alba. Yet as good as these two are, the wine everybody looks for is the "Granbussia," made from grapes grown mainly in another vineyard, Romirasco, though this wine often contains small additions of grapes from Colonello and Cicala as well. This is a great, traditionally made Barolo that undergoes fairly long skin contact and is aged in large oak barrels for at least four years. The '89 and '90 are to die for (both 99/100) and the '85 is just a hair beneath their quality

(97/100). The 1982 is also a great wine (96/100), less rich and ripe than the others but with a more elegant, refined feel. Aldo Conterno is one of the greatest names in Italian wine. He separated from his ultratraditionalist brother, the winemaker Giovanni Conterno, in 1969 in order to found his own winery, but he has never become a modernist, preferring to take a balanced approach in his vineyards and cellar. The same exemplary balance is always shown by his fantastic wines.

18. LANGHE ROSSO "SORÌ TILDIN" GAJA (PIEDMONT)

Angelo Gaja, whose personality is almost larger than life, has single-handedly put Barbaresco on the map, and all his wines fetch extremely high prices nowadays. Of Gaja's many great wines, this is his best, at least to my taste. The '82 is fantastic (99/100), the '85 is almost as good (97/00), and there's never been one that was less than outstanding. This is a wine that gives new meaning to the words "smooth as velvet," and it always has a deep rich red cherry flavor that is impossible to resist. Many people might not know that the "Sorì Tildin" wine comes from a vineyard called Roncagliette, whose quality was described accurately centuries ago but which had gone unnoticed or forgotten in modern times—that is, until Gaja came along. Talent can be measured in many ways, and being able to recognize what others miss is one of them.

19. LANGHE ROSSO "SORÌ SAN LORENZO" GAJA (PIEDMONT)

Gaja's other great wine is more austere, less charming, and less fleshy than the Sorì Tildin but beautiful in its own way: more Modigliani than Rubens, if you will. This wine is made of grapes from a different *cru*, Secondine, a south-facing site at the foot of the town of Barbaresco. It was never considered a star site, until Gaja came along to show otherwise (though I still feel that Roncagliette, the *cru* from which "Sorì Tildin" is made, is the better of the two). The '85 and '90 rank among the world's greatest wines of all time (both 98/100), with nearly perfect balance and depth of flavor. There is an intensity to the rose petal and sour red cherry aromas that you won't soon forget, and the wine has been praised by just about everyone in the know. Gaja's tireless public relations on behalf of his wines have also greatly benefited others in Piedmont and Italy, something everyone gives him credit for.

20. "MONTEVETRANO" MONTEVETRANO (CAMPANIA)

This is what put Campania on the map of "serious" wines and made the winemaker Riccardo Cottarella's career. An elegant cabernet-merlot blend that has much of the sunny south in it, with small amounts of the local aglianico added in, the wine is the pride and joy of the charming Silvia Imparato, who leads her estate with passion and style. To her credit, Montevetrano changes, twisting and turning over time—unlike many so-called great wines, which never seem to change with the different vintages. This is something more people, especially wine writers, would do well to reflect on. The most enjoyable one for current drinking is the '95, a lovely delicate refined cabernet-merlot (95/100); the '97 remains the best ever made (98/100). The '05 is underrated but is a magnificently refined bottle (95/100). The '04 will appeal more to those who prefer muscle in a wine (94/100). The '91, which was never sold by the estate, is still a singularly beautiful wine and offers a taste of Italian wine history with every sip (94/100). There's a bed-and-breakfast on the estate grounds that should not be missed if you visit. Not far from the winery, you'll find one of the best producers of buffalo milk mozzarella.

21. "ORNELLAIA" ORNELLAIA (TUSCANY)

During a highly enjoyable meal in the late 1980s at the wonderful (but unfortunately no longer extant) Il Dito e la Luna restaurant in Rome's trendy San Lorenzo district, I drank my first bottle of the Ornellaia 1985. The vines it was made from were then very young, so I was amazed by just how wonderful it was, and how much promise it held. If at that time the wines of Ornellaia were already showing great promise, it is fair to say that the promise was kept. Almost everyone agrees there are few finer wines made in Italy today. In fact, now that the vines are no longer young, just about every vintage is spectacular, exhibiting the typical Ornellaia sweetness and smoothness, truly a wine turned satin. Most important, Ornellaia has an uncanny ability to be great even in lesser vintages like 2002 and 2003, something that cannot be said of its more important stablemate, the 100% merlot called Masseto. The Ornellaia '97 and '98 are both 98/100 wines; the 1985 scores 92/100; and the 1988 is even better (94/100).

22. MERLOT L'APPARITA CASTELLO DI AMA (TUSCANY)

This is Italy's best cool-climate Merlot, a wine of unparalleled finesse and elegance. It comes from vines planted on a clay-rich section of the Bellavista vineyard, where one of this estate's best single vineyard Chiantis of the same name is made, high up in the hills of Gaiole in the heart of Chianti. When it first appeared in the 1980s, it quickly earned almost as much respect as Sassicaia, and deservedly, as there has never been a less than wonderful version. There are lovely coffee and milk chocolate flavors, with bright acids that always keep this wine light and lively on the palate. Insiders know that L'Apparita can be particularly good in lesser vintages, such as the rain-plagued 1992 or the rather cold 1987. Why this should be so is not completely clear, but great attention to quality in the vineyard, with lower yields and brutal selection of only the best berries, certainly helps. In any case, it is something the Castello di Ama shares with other famous estates such as Château Latour in Bordeaux. The '87 and the '92 L'Apparitas are two of the finest Merlots ever made in Italy (both 98/100).

23. VIGNA D'ALCEO CASTELLO DEI RAMPOLLA (CABERNET SAUVIGNON/PETIT VERDOT; TUSCANY)

Ironically, although it is situated in perhaps the single best area of Chianti for growing sangiovese—known as the "golden amphitheater of Panzano"—Castello dei Rampolla has achieved its greatest success with cabernet and other international varieties. A perfectly acceptable Chianti Classico is made from vines grown in this "golden amphitheater," but there can be no doubt that the two best wines of the estate are the super-Tuscans Sammarco (cabernet sauvignon, merlot, and sangiovese) and Vigna d'Alceo, a remarkably successful blend of cabernet sauvignon and petit verdot. In fact, the latter was the first wine in Italy to show just how successful the petit verdot could be, especially in Tuscany's warmer climate, which allows it to ripen fully. The Vigna d'Alceo is named in honor of Alceo di Rampolla, a noble gentleman who brought in cuttings from Château Lafite-Rothschild and enlisted the highly talented Giacomo Tachis (of Sassicaia fame) to make the wines. Though he enjoyed the great wines of Bordeaux, his real goal in planting the French varieties was to ensure a viable alternative in years such as 1984 when sangiovese failed to ripen completely or well. This wine is a modern masterpiece, and you will be seduced by its unparalleled elegance and poise, and its great concentration of blackberry, black currant, and lead pencil aromas and flavors.

24. FIORANO PRINCIPE LUDOVISI BONCOMPAGNI PRINCIPE DI VENOSA (LAZIO)

Few people may have heard of this wine, yet it had everything in place to become the next Sassicaia and only a difficult ownership situation kept it from reaching that level. It is a cabernet-merlot blend made in an area just outside Rome, which has been associated with the production of great wines throughout history; and it is one of Italy's greatest red wines of all time, very much on a par with the best of Bordeaux. I should point out that because the wine was bottled separately from each cask, depending on the state of the particular barrel chosen, the bottled wine could prove more or less great. Attention to detail and hygiene has not always been as intensive as it is today, so there is quite a bit of variation in quality between bottles, and not all are equally great. Still, the 1961 is usually to die for (98/100), and the 1971 and the 1978 were almost as good (96/100). Fiorano is, unfortunately, no longer made. Piero Antinori, who was related to Fiorano's owner, Prince Ludovisi Boncompagni, tried long and hard to bring this great wine into the hallowed Antinori fold, but to no avail. Still, Fiorano remains a testament to what could be achieved in Italy even in the years when wine making wasn't as up-to-date as it is today.

25. VIN SANTO OCCHIO DI PERNICE AVIGNONESI (TUSCANY)

This sweet wine is in a league apart. It is Italy's best sweet wine and arguably Italy's best wine. Like Château d'Yquem, the lone Bordeaux wine to be designated *hors classe* in the famous classification of 1855, Avignonesi's Vin Santos are in a category of their own. Two distinct Vin Santo wines are made: one labeled simply Vin Santo di Montepulciano, made from white grapes, and this "Occhio di Pernice," made from sangiovese grapes. The intensity, texture, and complexity of the latter defy description, and the Vin Santo is almost as good. If you have a sweet tooth, you owe it to yourself to try the panoply of aromas and flavors, which will remind you of dates, figs, apricots, peaches, caramel, balsamic vinegar, vanilla, and more. Every recent vintage save for the 1994 is at least a 95-point wine (the '95 is a 99-point wine). The '94 Occhio di Pernice may be only a 90-point wine, but the Vin Santo 1994 is nearly perfect (99/100). On a number of occasions I have actually given it 100 points (two different bottles I opened recently were a little short on acidity, hence the 99 points as its definitive score).

WINES MADE FROM NATIVE GRAPE VARIETIES

AS I MENTIONED ELSEWHERE IN THIS BOOK, native grapes are all important for Italy since they represent a means by which to offer jaded palates everywhere new fragrances and flavors. As more about these often long forgotten varietals is learned, it is likely that more exciting wines from Italy will reach store shelves all over the world. In fact, new grapes are being planted all the time, with new wines popping up every year. The following wines are the best wines made in Italy from native grape varieties, other than those already included in the 200 Best list or the cult wines described above. These are not lesser or runner-up wines, but since there are so many different estates in Italy making fine wines, I wished to place a one-estate limit on the wines to be included in the 200 Best, to give you many more names to choose from. In the list that follows you'll find many wines made by estates that have already placed one of their wines in the 200 Best, but I feel these other wines should not be missed, and I would be doing you a disservice if I didn't tell you about them. Some of the wines listed here will cost in excess of $100 a bottle (but not much more) and are among the very best Italy has to offer. However, most of the wines in this list cost less than $100 and are relatively easy to find as they are made in large enough numbers.

15 BEST RED WINES UNDER $100 MADE FROM NATIVE GRAPES

1. BRUNELLO DI MONTALCINO POGGIO DI SOTTO (SANGIOVESE; TUSCANY)

The pretty light ruby hue is the color Brunello ought to be. This wine is so light-hued, in fact, that many people used to say it was prematurely oxidized and wouldn't last; but the owner, Piero Palmucci, has had the last laugh. If this wine didn't cost more than $100, it would have been among the top five red wines in this guide. The 1999 Riserva and the 2001 Riserva are both 98-point wines.

2. AMARONE DELLA VALPOLICELLA TOMMASO BUSSOLA "TB" (CORVINA, OTHERS; VENETO)

This is Bussola's most important dry wine and is generally considered Italy's best Amarone after those of Quintarelli and Dal Forno. It is so concentrated and rich that it gives real meaning to the saying "So good it's almost painful." Clearly, it is quite unlike any other wine you might have tried, and it is a taste experience I heartily recommend. Loaded with aromas and flavors of red cherries macerated in alcohol, balsamic vinegar, dark chocolate, and herbs, it's a wine you won't soon forget. It is also amazingly well balanced—no easy feat at 16 degrees alcohol.

3. BAROLO BRICCO ROCCHE BRICCO ROCCHE CERETTO (NEBBIOLO; PIEDMONT)

I may have been somewhat unfair to Ceretto when I listed its Blangé among Italy's 200 Best wines, because it is one of *the* names in Barolo and Barbaresco. Then again, the Blangé is so delightful, and holds such an important place in the history of Italian wine, that I really couldn't pass on it. I'll make amends here by stating as clearly as possible that one of Italy's five greatest Barolos is the Barolo Bricco Rocche Bricco Rocche. (That's not a typo, and there are also Barolo Bricco Rocche Brunate and Barolo Bricco Rocche Prapò: Bricco Rocche is the name of the estate but also of a vineyard site.) The 1982 is the stuff of legends (99/100).

4. BRUNELLO DI MONTALCINO RISERVA BIONDI SANTI (SANGIOVESE; TUSCANY)

This is like the base or entry-level Brunello, but with considerably more power and intensity. It nonetheless remains true to the Biondi Santi mantra: high acidity and refined sour red cherry and red currant fruit aromas and flavors. These wines keep forever, by the way, as the Brunello 1891 and 1898 still in the estate cellars have shown. The 1975 Riserva is very close to a perfect wine (99/100). The 2001 Riserva may well be the best made since that one (97/100): it seems to be a little plumper and to have greater depth than other recent vintages.

5. MONTEPULCIANO D'ABRUZZO VILLA GEMMA MASCIARELLI (MONTEPULCIANO; ABRUZZO)

This wine is made only in the better years and has perhaps just a touch too much oak when still young, but it is one you won't soon forget. It is so rich and wonderful that you'd never guess it spends an average of 18 months in small oak barrels; and the oaky veneer does wear off over time, leaving a truly great Italian red wine for you to enjoy. It ages splendidly, by the way. The '95 is one of the best Villa Gemmas ever, still splendid, with a slightly garnet rim and a unique satiny-smooth red cherry rich finish (97/100). Also very fine are the '98 and the '99: the former has a riper personality, with a tomato paste and earthy note to go along with the rich red fruit aromas and flavors; the latter is more elegant, with higher acidity delineating the blueberry, plum, and red cherry notes (both 93/100). The '01 is currently quite closed on the nose but is showing amazing depth of clove, rhubarb, chocolate-covered cherry, and black pepper flavors (95/100). The '00 has a more aromatic, spicy quality to its nose than most other vintages and also has a hint of overripeness, but is very refined on the palate, with silky tannins (94/100).

6. BAROLO SORÌ GINESTRA CONTERNO FANTINO (NEBBIOLO; PIEDMONT)

Claudio Conterno and Guido Fantino turn out one great Barolo after another, and the prized vineyard of Ginestra, between the other *crus* of Grassi and Mosconi south of Castelletto Monforte, is an absolutely stellar site not just for nebbiolo but for barbera and freisa as well. The nebbiolo in this area is of such high quality that the most famous wines made from it are the Barolos, and none is better than Conterno Fantino's. The splendidly situated hilltop winery is a must to visit, and you'll be thrilled by the silky-sweet, profound Barolo, with its immense fruit-forward style and its never-ending flavors of blackberry and balsamic plum. The 2003 was the best Barolo of that difficult, much too hot vintage (93/100). The '01 is starting to open up and blossom into a very fine, textbook Barolo rich in tar and rose petal aromas, and with the balsamic touches typical of this wine (94/100).

7. BAROLO BRICCO GATTERA MONFALLETTO (NEBBIOLO; PIEDMONT)

The Cordero di Montezemolo family is one of the great names of Barolo, among the first in the 1960s to produce cleaner, more modern red wines. Today there are four different Barolos to choose from, and while the Enrico VI from the Villero vineyard, situated farther away, near the town of Castiglione Falletto, is usually their best wine, the Bricco Gattera, a small plot to the left of the house in La Morra, is capable of giving a wonderfully perfumed, aristocratic, if less fleshy Barolo. The first ten or so rows of wines right behind the house (literally their backyard) actually belong to another grower, who is so attached to his land that over the years has resisted selling them the parcel of vines or even accepting an exchange. This too is Italy.

8. TAURASI VIGNA CINQUE QUERCE RISERVA SALVATORE MOLETTIERI (AGLIANICO; CAMPANIA)

This traditionally made Aglianico gives modernists fits: so good and yet so old-style, it can seem slightly abrasive when young, as its not-shy tannins can be quite a jolt to less experienced tasters weaned on softer, plumper wines. Yet the Taurasi of Molettieri repays handsomely those who are willing to wait patiently for it to release its charms (admittedly, it does this slowly). It is highly scented with mineral, plum, raspberry, and tobacco—the last aroma verges on the vegetal without actually tipping over the edge. There is plenty of complexity on the palate as well, with flavors ranging from cola to sassafras, red cherries, mushrooms, leather, and earth. The 2001 is a big, earthy wine with plenty of fruit, lots of personality, and chunky tannins that still need years to resolve fully (94/100).

9. AMARONE DELLA VALPOLICELLA "MAZZANO" MASI (CORVINA, OTHERS; VENETO)

There's a lot to be said for a giant house that makes a gazillion bottles a year (and not just in Italy, as it owns vineyards and makes wine in Argentina as well) and is still able to turn out great wines such as these. Both the "Mazzano" and the "Campolongo di Torbe" are single vineyard bottlings that do their region and their owners proud. Mazzano's aromas are enticing, with nuances of black cherries macerated in alcohol, dark chocolate, espresso coffee, and a forest-floor note that is becoming more and more apparent in the most recent vintages and that I am beginning to find excessive of late. Nonetheless, it has huge amounts of roast nut, black cherry, and plum flavors and formidable tannins that are not for the faint of heart. The 1979 was a 98-point wine during the late 1980s, and though still fine it has faded just a touch (93/100).

10. SAGRANTINO "25 ANNI" ARNALDO CAPRAI (SAGRANTINO; UMBRIA)

This wonderfully powerful wine is able to age with the best of them and acquires grace with bottle age. Very tannic and a little too much for me in the early years, it softens somewhat with time. The coffee, plum, and cherry aromas and flavors are alluring, and along with similar flavors they form a seamless whole with a mouthwatering if chewy succulence and leave you with a very polished feel on the nearly interminable finish. A very fine wine that has garnered medals and honors all over the world.

11. PIGNOLO ERMACORA (FRIULI VENEZIA GIULIA)

Pignolo is a recently rediscovered variety, and in the past 20 years more and more producers have been starting to bottle it, as the vines age. It is generally considered potentially the best of all the native red varieties in Friuli Venezia Giulia, but I think this idea is based mostly on the fact that it gives wines of huge tannic structure. Still, Pignolo also has high natural acidity and lots of silky refinement to make it more enjoyable. Ermacora's version is a particularly good one, and softer than most. Rich and suave, it is tremendously rich in coffee, blackberry, and smoky plum aromas and flavors.

12. CERASUOLO DI VITTORIA PLANETA (SICILY)

This is absolutely lovely, a compact sleek wine that will also do well lightly chilled. Made from a blend of nero d'Avola (for body and structure) and another, lesser-known native called frappato (which adds perfume), it is so crammed with ripe red cherry fruit that it is irresistible from the first sip. The floral, slightly saline finish speaks of the frappato and the seaside vineyards.

13. TEROLDEGO FORADORI (TRENTINO)

Teroldego is a difficult grape to grow and to make wine from, and doesn't seem to adapt well in other parts of the country (though there have been some successful tries by experimentally-minded producers in both Sicily and Tuscany). Yet the charming Elisabetta Foradori is a wizard with this grape, and has been turning out one fine wine after another during the years. I have fond memories of the single vineyard "Sgarzon," no longer made, but this entry-level Teroldego, which has taken its place, is just as lovely. Each glass is filled with herb, spice, strawberry, and bell pepper aromas and flavors. It finishes long and saline, with a touch of ink and black pepper, the latter note reminding you that teroldego is a distant relative of syrah.

14. REFOSCO DEL PEDUNCOLO ROSSO GIROLAMO DORIGO (FRIULI VENEZIA GIULIA)

In addition to its name, which is very long and almost impossible to pronounce (at least for native English-speakers), Refosco has long been plagued by uneven quality and some overly vegetal examples. Yet when well made, it is a very enjoyable mid-weight wine not unlike a well-made cabernet franc of similar structure. Dorigo's is always one of the best, with plenty of sassafras and bay leaf aromas to go along with the ripe blackberry and blueberry aromas and flavors. It has very refreshing acids on the long mineral finish. The Riserva bottling of which not much is made, is even better.

15. BRUNELLO DI MONTALCINO SALVIONI (TUSCANY)

Giulio Salvioni is a master of Brunello, and his is one of the more concentrated, richer versions of the wine. He uses new clones that give his wine a darker hue, but the aromas and flavors are all typical of sangiovese. The nose has lovely scents of fresh violet, tea leaf, and red currant and gives way on the palate to rich, mouth-coating milk chocolate, coffee, and smoky plum flavors and silkier-than-silk tannins. This wine ages extremely well.

10 BEST WHITE WINES UNDER $100 MADE FROM NATIVE GRAPES

1. TOCAI PLUS BASTIANICH (FRIULI VENEZIA GIULIA)

A great wine, and one for which no expense is spared: I remember, years ago, a young winemaker in training marveling at all the care taken at Bastianich to make this wine, and the result in the bottle shows this very well. It is a fat, almost oily Tocai of great breeding and length; its only problem is that too few bottles are available. A very fine wine making team—Andrea Brunisso, with the consultants Emilio Del Medico and the great Maurizio Castelli—ensures that virtually every wine made at Bastianich is at the top of the game.

2. MALVASIA SELEZIONE BORGO DEL TIGLIO (FRIULI VENEZIA GIULIA)

Some people find this wine's sweet, oak-derived vanilla aroma and flavor a little overpowering and feel it camouflages the delicate mineral, white peach, and pear aromas and flavors of malvasia Istriana. Still, I feel there's plenty of pretty mineral fruit shining through the oaky veneer to make this a highly enjoyable, elegant wine of real class. It is also the best example of oak-aged Malvasia from Friuli made today. One sip will leave you grinning from ear to ear.

3. RIBOLLA MIANI (FRIULI VENEZIA GIULIA)

A super-concentrated but beautifully drinkable wine by Enzo Pontoni, and really quintessential Ribolla, of a purity and intensity unmatched by any other Ribolla made today. I have no problem saying that I consider this one of Italy's 10 best white wines, but it is unfortunately made in very small quantities and has become extremely expensive of late, with bottles regularly fetching $100, so I couldn't include it in the best 200. There are incredibly pure, lovely, intense lemon-lime, mineral, and apricot aromas that explode from the glass, and there is a a decadently rich, almost viscous character to the flavors of apricot, honey, and crushed stone. This wine is concentrated yet brightly acid and fresh; you'll be mesmerized by the wonderful interplay of stone fruits and ripe citrus in the long, pure mineral finish.

4. PASSERINA DEL FRUSINATE "COLLE BIANCO" CASALE DELLA IORIA (LAZIO)

Yes, this is an outsider, but one you are sure to hear more about in the next few years. Depending on exactly when the grapes are picked, Passerina can be a very high-acid and lemony wine or a flat, flabby wine sorely in need of more acidity, and in either case it rarely has much appeal for wine lovers. This is because passerina, a difficult grape when not picked at exactly the right moment of ripeness, quickly loses all its acidity, and the resulting wines are flabby and uninteresting. However, when the producer gets Passerina right, the wine is delectable, with lemony and tropical fruit aromas and a riper-than-expected mouthfeel that offers a welcome change from the usual Chardonnays and Sauvignons. There is also something to be said for these less expensive "new" wines, made from ancient varieties that have recently been resurrected.

5. COLLI DI LUNI VERMENTINO "SARTICOLA" LAMBRUSCHI OTTAVIANO (LIGURIA)

For more than 50 years the Lambruschi family—first with father, Ottaviano, and now with the son, Fabio—has been cultivating the mountaintop vineyards of the Lunigiana area of Liguria. This is truly heroic viticulture, given the slopes and altitudes one has to work with. The "Sarticola" is the family's best Vermentino, but it is made only in the better years. It usually starts off with scents of crushed stone, lime, and apple, with noticeable hints of thyme and almond. Medium-bodied with enough crispness to keep the flavors lively on the tongue, it finishes long and pure with a definite salty edge.

6. SOAVE CLASSICO LA ROCCA PIEROPAN (VENETO)

Barrel-fermented Soave does not get any better than this wine, which has won trophies, medals, and awards everywhere it competes. The wonderfully exotic nose blasts forth with waves of vanilla, mango, and peach, then settles down a bit on the palate to reveal more creamy vanilla and tropical fruit characteristics and a long suave finish. Long and rich, it has just enough apple and citrus notes to keep everything in balance.

7. CODA DI VOLPE LA RIVOLTA (CAMPANIA)

The area of Torrecuso in the province of Benevento is the home of coda di volpe, one of Italy's most interesting if lesser-known white grape varieties and one you will undoubtedly hear more of over the next few years. The owner, Paolo Cotroneo, turns out a fine lineup of wines, and this wine always hits home, absolutely true to type in its citrus, honeyed, and earthy scents, which are mirrored on the palate. Rich and creamy, it wraps itself around your taste buds and doesn't let go for what seems like minutes.

8. "KRATOS" LUIGI MAFFINI (CAMPANIA)

A 100% pure Fiano aged in stainless steel, this is as good an example of Fiano as there is. A strongly mineral wine on both nose and palate, it usually starts off with beautiful citrus and herbal aromas, then follows up with invigorating flavors of apple, pear, and lime. It finishes long and very well balanced with a pretty mineral, almost saline character. A barrel-fermented version of Fiano is also made here, called "Pietraincatenata," but as good as it is, I find the oak treatment a little excessive at times.

9. RIVIERA LIGURE DI PONENTE PIGATO
"U' BACCAN" BRUNA (LIGURIA)

Riccardo Bruna is one of the best winemakers in Liguria, and this is the most concentrated and interesting of all Pigatos made in the region. Dry and very elegant in its intensely herbal and fruity nose, it opens slowly in the glass at first, then gains complexity with stone, iodine, and spice aromas emerging. Always fairly ripe and herbal on the palate, this Pigato has plenty of ripe tangerine, pear, and minty spicy flavors and a nice creamy and definitely salty finish that speaks of its marine origins (the vineyards are situated next to the sea).

10. GRECO DI TUFO PIETRACUPA (CAMPANIA)

This interesting and extremely well made Greco comes from a producer perhaps more famous for his Fiano. Nonetheless, I think it's his Greco that is the truly memorable wine, and one that has few rivals (whereas there are plenty of great Fianos to choose from). It is very mineral on the nose, with scents of smoke and stone that mingle with white peach, oregano, and pear. On the palate it delivers plenty of zippy acidity and tropical fruit flavors wrapped around a core of minerals and herbs. It is rich and creamy on the long, iodine finish.

10 Best Sparkling and Rosé Wines Under $100 Made from Native Grapes

Note that some of these wines, such as Moscato or Prosecco, can be a little sweet, because the native grape varieties, such as moscato bianco, always give wines that are best with a litle sweetness. I indicate at the end of each description if the wine is dry or sweet.

1. ASTI METODO CLASSICO "DE MIRANDA" CONTRATTO (MOSCATO BIANCO; PIEDMONT)

You may never have thought Moscato could make so interesting a sparkler, and yet this has a honeyed creaminess that is to die for, and wonderful pure length. It is made in the manner of Champagne (the bubbles form directly in the bottle), and therefore has greater complexity than other Astis. The result, a far deeper and richer Moscato, of considerable complexity, is truly memorable. This sparkler is not yet imported into the United States, probably because an "important," more expensive Asti might not be easily understood and might fail to to win customers. (Sweet.)

2. MALVASIA DI CASTELNUOVO DON BOSCO CASCINA GILLI (MALVASIA DI SCHIERANO; PIEDMONT)

Here is another absolute gem that is not currently being imported into the United States. It was imported until quite recently, but sales were so poor that it was unfortunately let go, even though few more enjoyable wines are produced in all of Italy. Made from the little-known native grape malvasia di Schierano, this wine is absolutely brimming with red berry, almond flower, and cinnamon aromas, and it has a creamy, sweet texture. Think of it as a lightly alcoholic cream soda and you won't be too far of the mark. It's one of my favorite Italian wines. (Sweet.)

3. GAVI SOLDATI LA SCOLCA BRUT D'ANTAN (CORTESE; PIEDMONT)

La Scolca, owned by the Soldati family, is a revered name in Italian wine and is known the world over. When Tom Cruise married Katie Holmes, wines of La Scolca were served; the event war fairly typical of the carefully orchestrated and extremely successful public relations of this house. Also, it was Vittorio Soldati who first showed, in the 1960s, that cortese could be used to make very good still wines: until then, it had been used only to make fine sparklers. That said, all the public relations and historic firsts in the world cannot help you sell a wine or acquire worldwide respect unless the wines you make are good. At La Scolca, all the wines are very competently made, and the sparklers are undoubtedly the best in Gavi. This is the producer's most complex bottling, a smorgasbord of apricot, thyme, lemon, caramel, and hazelnut aromas and flavors. The wine's finish goes on for minutes. (Dry.)

4. PROSECCO DI VALDOBBIADENE BRUT "VECCHIE VITI" RUGGERI (PROSECCO; VENETO)

The prosecco grape variety probably originated around the city of Trieste, in Friuli Venezia Giulia, but it has adapted remarkably well in Veneto, particularly around the city of Treviso on the hills surrounding the hamlets of Conegliano and Valdobbiadene. Prosecco is usually made either from prosecco grapes alone or with a small addition of verdiso, but the "Vecchie Viti" bottling by Ruggeri also contains two much rarer varieties: bianchetta and perera. This lovely Prosecco, made from the old vines situated around the winery, is bright, fresh, and surprisingly full-bodied. Chock-full of varietally accurate green apple and white peach aromas, it exhibits more complexity than most proseccos on the palate, where some yeasty and hazelnut flavors are also evident. It's just what the doctor ordered for a hot summer day, but it has enough body to stand up to important salmon and chicken preparations. (Dry.)

5. MOSCATO D'ASTI CASCINA FONDA (MOSCATO BIANCO; PIEDMONT)

Situated in the very high-quality area of Mango, a true *grand cru* for the moscato bianco grape, Cascina Fonda has always been considered a star among Moscato producers, and rightly so. More than 20 years' experience has given Massimo and Marco Barbero a sure hand with the variety and the wine, and you will never find anything less than good from their estate. With loads of pretty white flowers and peaches on the nose, and a hint of grapefruit and white pepper on the palate, this wine has a lovely creaminess that keeps you company long after you've finished the glass and the lights have gone out. (Sweet.)

6. PROSECCO DI VALDOBBIADENE SUPERIORE DI CARTIZZE DRY ASTORIA (PROSECCO; VENETO)

The Polegato brothers launched their winery in 1987, and the estate has always distinguished itself for solidly made, dependable, fairly priced wines. What I really enjoy from Astoria is its Passito di Refrontolo called "Fervo," a sweet red dessert wine that deserves to be better known; however, as it is made in small quantities, it may not be easy to find. On the other hand, the Polegatos make about 30,000 bottles a year of this Cartizze, a very fine, off-dry bubbly that will impress you and your friends no end. It has very pretty green apple and yellow plum nuances and not unpleasantly tart acidity on the palate, with a medium-long clean finish. This wine has enough body to stand up to salmon and other fish dishes. (Sweet.)

7. MOSCATO D'ASTI LA CALIERA BORGO MARAGLIANO (MOSCATO BIANCO; PIEDMONT)

Carlo Galliano has gained fame in Italy for his talent at producing sparkling wines, both dry and sweet, and I for one feel he is particularly gifted with the sweet Moscato-based sparklers. The La Caliera is a case in point, with its pretty apricot and ripe pear aromas and flavors and its lovely honeyed, creamy texture that keeps you going back to the glass time and again. This producer's late-harvest Loazzolo is also a very good dessert wine. (Sweet.)

8. CALUSO SPUMANTE CUVÉE TRADIZIONE GRAN RISERVA ORSOLANI (ERBALUCE DI CALUSO; PIEDMONT)

Gianluigi and Francesco Orsolani are dedicated to the erbaluce variety, and they achieve a great deal more complexity from it than almost anybody else except Cieck and Ferrando. This sparkling wine is a thing of beauty, with an effortless stream of steady bubbles tickling your nostrils while you appreciate the warm biscuit, hazelnut, and green apple aromas and flavors. Sharp acidity keeps this wine dancing on your taste buds and will make it a perfect foil even for pasta based on a rich cream sauce. (Dry.)

9. MALVASIA DOLCE FRIZZANTE MONTE DELLE VIGNE (MALVASIA DI CANDIA AROMATICA; EMILIA ROMAGNA)

Andrea Ferrari and Paolo Pizzarotti are partners in an extremely fine estate that employs real talent everywhere: its agronomist Federico Curtaz and its winemaker Attilio Pagli are two of the very best in Italy at what they do. The wines show this, and it is hard to choose among a number of simply excellent bottles. This sweet malvasia, available also in a dry version that is just as enjoyable, is loaded with peach and apricot aromas and flavors, with delicate grapefruit, rosemary, and marjoram notes for added complexity. (Sweet.)

10. GARDA CHIARETTO ROSAMARA COSTARIPA (GROPPELLO, MARZEMINO, BARBERA, SANGIOVESE; LOMBARDY)

Italy's beautiful Lake Garda (a heavenly tourist spot) has a unique microclimate, so that this rather northern Italian area is actually more Mediterranean than alpine, with olive and citrus trees standing alongside the vines. This part of Italy is also famous for Chiaretto, a light rosé unlike any other, with delicate rose petal and mineral nuances. It is believed to have been first made in 1896 by a Venetian senator, Pompeo Gherardi Molmenti, after whom is named another Chiaretto made here, one that sees a little oak in its aging process. Though very good, the RosaMara is the more typical Chiaretto, and I signal it here. Costaripa is a quality estate owned by the Vezzola family (Mattia Vezzola is the winemaker for Bellavista, one of Italy's premier sparkling wine houses).

10 BEST SWEET WINES UNDER $100 MADE FROM NATIVE GRAPES

1. MALVASIA PUNTINATA "PASSIONE" CASALE PILOZZO (LAZIO)

There is no better sweet wine in Italy, but it is not yet imported to the United States—a state of affairs I hope will soon change. Often amazingly concentrated, rich, and downright viscous wine with a pretty golden, almost orange hue, Malvasia Puntinata is an extremely high-quality native varietal of Lazio that—like riesling—has the ability to give both interesting dry and sweet wines. (Even chardonnay, a truly great grape, cannot do this—sweet wines made from chardonnay usually don't hold much interest.) Unfortunately, the wine is not made in very large quantities, but it is not impossible to find. This is a wine that, though made with a little-known variety and hence receiving little if any press, is so good that just one sip will make a believer of you, though the wine can be very different from year to year, depending on vintage characteristics.

2. GRECO DI BIANCO STELITANO (GRECO BIANCO; CALABRIA)

This simply mesmerizing wine is not just one of Italy's best sweet wines but one of its best wines in general. Made from the greco bianco variety (do not confuse this with the many other greco varieties growing in Italian soil), the wine has an unbelievable olfactory and gustatory complexity that not many other sweet wines made anywhere achieve. There's an amazing honeyed quality to the rich tangerine, grapefruit, mango, and peach aromas and flavors, beautifully underpinned by a mineral streak and high acidity of rare balance and beauty.

3. COLLI PIACENTINI ALBAROLA VAL DI NURE VIN SANTO CONTE BARATTIERI DI SAN PIETRO (TREBBIANO TOSCANO/MALVASIA; EMILIA ROMAGNA)

The Conte Barattieri di San Pietro estate is capably run by Massimiliana Barattieri and her brother Alberico, who make one of Italy's four or five best sweet wines, albeit in dishearteningly small quantities. This wine is so thick it's almost opaque, with heady aromas of ripe figs, dates, caramel, peach, and white chocolate, and it has an almost oily, rich texture that fills your mouth with sweet maple syrup, vanilla, ripe peach, and caramel flavors you aren't likely to forget anytime soon, even after just one taste.

4. MOSCATO GIALLO PASSITO "BARONESSE" CANTINA NALLES MAGRÉ (MOSCATO GIALLO/RIESLING; ALTO ADIGE)

Made from a rare blend of 95% yellow muscat and 5% riesling, this wine is a jewel that reaches a zenith of quality, thanks mainly to the very old, perfectly situated yellow muscat vines. The Riesling adds a little freshness and minerality, but this is one of the world's rare wines in which riesling actually has to take a backseat to another variety: the yellow muscat here is absolutely first-rate, and you'll marvel at the pure, extremely intense sweet peach, papaya, mango, and honeyed crushed stone aromas and flavors that seem to last forever.

5. ALBANA DI ROMAGNA PASSITO "SCACCO MATTO" (ALBANA; EMILIA ROMAGNA)

The owner, Cristina Geminiani, with some help from the talented winemaker Vittorio Fiore in the 1990s, has turned her grandfather's estate, purchased in the 1960s, into the undisputed quality leader in Emilia Romagna, at least with regard to sweet wines. In all honesty, this is not an easy task when you are working with albana: in my view it is a second-rate grape, but she has managed to turn it into a star, at least in Italian circles. That outcome is due mainly to this wine, which has won accolades and many awards over the years. It is very sweet, thick, and viscous, and its heady botrytis-rich nose and complex flavor make it the equal of some of the world's best dessert wines, especially in years when it has enough acidity to stand up to the high residual sugars.

6. MALVASIA PASSITA "VIGNA DEL VOLTA" LA STOPPA (MALVASIA AROMATICA DI CANDIA; EMILIA ROMAGNA)

This estate is an enchanting 30 hectares in the quiet Trebbiola valley, in the province of Piacenza. The owner, Elena Pantaleoni, is intensely dedicated to and passionate about her work, and the results show in a series of very fine wines. There's a Sherry-like feel to this wine, with a slight oxidized note that is enticing and intriguing at the same time. The wine is rich, suave, and very sweet—and yet you hardly notice the sweetness, thanks to the harmonious acids. Wine lovers may want to look for a bottle of the "Buca delle Canne," a rare wine made from semillon grapes with noble rot, which are not common in Italy.

7. VIN SANTO DEL CHIANTI CLASSICO FELSINA (MALVASIA TOSCANA/TREBBIANO TOSCANA; TUSCANY)

This is a spectacular sweet wine, an absolute gem, with layers and layers of ripe fruit, dates, aromatic herbs, white chocolate, aged Cognac, and spicy aromas and flavors. It has a lovely sweetness and a silky texture that, coupled with wonderful balance, make this wine a great success. The '97 and '98 are outstanding, especially the former (96/100), which is a bit more concentrated and complex than the latter (95/100).

8. MOSCATO PASSITO LUIGI VIOLA (MOSCATO BIANCO; CALABRIA)

Luigi Viola deserves praise for his efforts to save the Moscato di Saracena, a once famous Italian sweet wine that nearly became extinct—it was being made by local families for daily consumption only. Viola's efforts met with critical success and much praise, and now new producers of this wine are appearing on the scene, a sure sign of newfound interest. You'll marvel at the perfumed fragrances of candied orange peel, grapefruit, burned sugar, and dates, as well as at the flavors of powdered stone, apricot jam, and ripe peaches of uncommon intensity. Italy's bureaucracy has ruled that the wine cannot be called "Moscato di Saracena" at present, but it ought to be soon, when the new DOC is approved.

9. RAMANDOLO "ANNO DOMINI" ANNA BERRA (FRIULI VENEZIA GIULIA)

This wine has improved greatly over the years and recent bottles have placed it squarely among Italy's best sweet wines; it is also the best Ramandolo made today.

Ramandolo is a truly bucolic cold-climate hamlet high in the hills of northeastern Friuli, where the verduzzo grape seems to have found a nearly perfect habitat. Made from late-harvested grapes that are air-dried to further increase concentration, it ages for up to 16 months in small oak barrels. It smells of bergamot, peach, and apricot, with a hint of caramel-coated dates and figs. Rich and luscious on the palate, it has enough acidity to keep it balanced and enjoyable. The owner, Ivan Monai, is fiercely dedicated to Ramandolo, and this passion is really starting to show.

10. MALVASIA DI BOSA FRATELLI PORCU (MALVASIA DI BOSA; SARDEGNA)

One look at this wine's amber-orange color tells you it ought to be something special, and you won't be disappointed. The estate has been making high-quality wines for more than 30 years, and they deserve to be better known. This Malvasia will remind you of Marsala, but it is more refined, with pure, pretty aromas of roasted nuts, caramel, rosemary, and raisins. On the palate it seems to walk the line between sweetness and dryness, with a lovely hazelnut and burned almond quality. It finishes extremely clean and almost dry, with a lingering salty edge. Perfect on its own, or with green olives, or with almond cookies.

WINES MADE FROM INTERNATIONAL GRAPE VARIETIES

THE FOLLOWING WINES ARE THE BEST WINES made in Italy from foreign (international) grape varieties such as chardonnay, merlot, and pinot noir. A number of these wines will cost more than $100 a bottle, but I am also glad to be able to tell you about many simply fantastic wines that cost less than that. All the wines in this list are very fine and rank with Italy's best: some of them may not have been chosen for the 200 Best list only because another wine from the same estate had been chosen instead.

15 BEST RED WINES MADE FROM INTERNATIONAL GRAPES

1. "SAMMARCO" CASTELLO DEI RAMPOLLA (CABERNET SAUVIGNON/SANGIOVESE/MERLOT; TUSCANY)

There's very little sangiovese (5%) in this blend, so I can include it in this section dedicated to wines made only with international grape vaerieties. Sammarco was one of Italy's first super-Tuscans, and today it still ranks with the best and most important of them. Perhaps somewhat overshadowed by "Vigna d'Alceo" (cabernet–petit verdot), this is nonetheless one of Italy's finest wines, and it ages absolutely splendidly. The '81 is still amazingly perfumed (93/100); the 1985 is rich and luscious (96/100); and the '88 is beautifully austere and refined (95/100).

2. "GALATRONA" FATTORIA PETROLO (MERLOT; TUSCANY)

An archetypal Tuscan merlot, this highly successful wine is produced near Arezzo. The area is not famous for wine making, even though it has unlimited potential, but the Sanjust family has showed everyone just what vines planted here are capable of and has started to make many converts. This Merlot is always loaded with lots of pretty chocolate and coffee notes, and has an uncommon richness of texture that is very appealing. Rich and concentrated without veering toward jamminess or exaggeration, this wine requires a few years of bottle age to give it everthing it has, and so that it can be fully and properly enjoyed.

3. "CORTACCIO" VILLA CAFAGGIO (CABERNET SAUVIGNON; TUSCANY)

With the new ownership of the large and very capable La Vis co-op from Trentino, these wines seem to be finding their way again after a period that was less than successful. The Cortaccio is pure Cabernet Sauvignon, elegant, full-bodied, and long, with a very pleasant, long, chewy, meaty texture and a noticeable savory quality. The estate is splendidly situated in the heart of the Panzano zone, one of the best wine making *terroirs* of Italy, so you know that great wines are always possible here.

4. PINOT NERO RISERVA "MAZZON" BRUNO GOTTARDI (ALTO ADIGE)

This gorgeous estate produces a remarkable Pinot Noir, in which Gottardi reveals a truly magical touch with oak, not unlike that seen with the very best from Burgundy. There is, however, also a good deal of ripe fruit that shines through. You'll be amazed at the silkiness of the tannins and the presence of gorgeous red and black cherry flavors. Close your eyes and you couldn't be blamed for thinking this was a good *premier cru* from Gevrey-Chambertin or Nuits-Saint-Georges. The grapes grow in the Mazzon *cru*, which is unquestionably Italy's single finest site for Pinot Nero.

5. "CAMARCANDA" CA'MARCANDA (MERLOT/CABERNET SAUVIGNON/CABERNET FRANC; TUSCANY)

Gaja's top wine from his operation in Tuscany has all the usual trademarks of his wines: smooth-as-silk tannins, deep luscious fruit, and complexity. The vines are in the excellent area around Castagneto Carducci, and you'll be thrilled by the intense flavor this wine packs into a suave, strong, full-bodied frame. Aromas of tamarind, blackberry jam, and herbs and spices—such as coriander, black pepper, and bay leaf—are followed up by similar flavors. The finish is smooth and never-ending.

6. SYRAH "CASE VIA" FONTODI (TUSCANY)

Giovanni Manetti's Syrah is getting better and better as the vines age, and the recent hot vintages have actually helped: the '03 is the best ever, and the '04 isn't far behind. You'll always find plenty of blueberry, cardamom, black pepper, leather, and tobacco on both the nose and the palate, but this wine usually exhibits less of syrah's telltale smoky bacon note. A very elegant, rather refined example of syrah, it is nothing like the behemoths being produced in Australia.

7. PINOT NERO BARTHENAU VIGNA S. URBANO HOFSTÄTTER (ALTO ADIGE)

This wine undoubtedly relies a lot on new oak, but there's lots of great fruit as well; and it couldn't be otherwise, because this wine is yet another made with grapes from the Mazzon vineyard, Italy's single greatest vineyard for Pinot Nero. Cinnamon, menthol, and tobacco aromas mingle with spicy cherry notes, with more flavors of chocolate-covered cherry and spices on the rich suave finish. It usually spends 12 months in small oak barrels, and though the new oak is usually very evident when the wine is young, I have found that in due course it wears off without problems.

8. CABERNET SAUVIGNON TASCA D'ALMERITA (SICILY)

Founded in 1830, this historic estate has long produced some of southern Italy's best wines, and its Cabernet Sauvignon is a case in point: the 1990 and 1992 are two of the most famous Italian wines ever made. That being said, I find the recent efforts, though still very good, less appealing in comparison with the standout older vintages. In any case, this is a very fine wine. It spends an average of 18 months in small oak barrels, after which time you get an absolutely stunning wine with rhubarb, black currant, bitter chocolate, and blackberry aromas and flavors.

9. "COLLAZZI" I COLLAZZI (CABERNET SAUVIGNON/ CABERNET FRANC/MERLOT; TUSCANY)

This is a little-known estate but it is owned by the well-known Frescobaldi family, whose best wine carries the name of the estate. I remain surprised that, for whatever reason, this wine doesn't seem to have the popularity or the good press it deserves. It has loads of smoky plum and blackberry aromas and flavors, extremely fine tannins, and a smoky complexity and chocolaty quality on the long, suave finish.

10. "PINERO" CA' DEL BOSCO (PINOT NERO; LOMBARDY)

I still remember the time, in the summer of 1993, when I tasted this wine with the owner, Maurizio Zanella, in the Willamette Valley, alongside great wines from Burgundy and Oregon. Even though the vines were still young and the wine had only a short track record, it wasn't at all out of place in that exalted company. Today it's one of Italy's better Pinot Neros: yes, there is a very clever use of new oak here, but there are also plenty of wonderfully juicy ripe red cherry and raspberry fruit aromas and flavors to keep you going back to the glass time and time again.

11. "DETTORI ROSSO" DETTORI (SARDINIA)

Alessandro Dettori is in love with his land, and this fact transpires in all the wines he makes. He has tried hard to resurrect old grape varieties, such as pascale, that nobody was bottling for anything other than local consumption until he decided to do otherwise. The "Dettori Rosso" is a fantastic Cannonau (or Grenache) that is made from vines 60 to 120 years old, so you can imagine the concentration it has. Made with natural, local yeasts that are used to living in and working with extremely high sugar concentrations, it is the epitome of silk turned to wine. You'll love the ultra-ripe red cherries macerated in alcohol and the allspice aroma and flavor. There's a bit of residual sugar here on the long finish, so you may not find this to be a completely dry wine.

12. "LUPICAIA" CASTELLO DEL TERRICCIO (TUSCANY)

This very fine estate makes many splendid wines. The two best are this one, almost indistinguishable from a finer Bordeaux, and the Castello del Terriccio, made from a syrah–petit verdot blend that takes the name of the estate. Both wines cost more than $100 a bottle, unfortunately, but if you decide to splurge just once you can do a lot worse than these. The owner, Pucci de Medelana, has created one of Italy's cult estates, and he has a first-rate team running it.

13. "BRUNO DI ROCCA" VECCHIE TERRE DI MONTEFILI (TUSCANY)

Roccaldo Acuti is a true country gentleman, starting with his attire, and time passed in his company is always a wonderful experience. He is extremely knowledgeable about the vineyards in this bucolic corner of Tuscany, and I learn every time I listen to him. The estate—situated near Greve, very close to Panzano though on the other, cooler, side of the valley on which the famous "golden amphitheater" looks out—has long been at the top of the hierarchy of Tuscan wine producers. You will never go wrong with any wine you pick from Roccaldo's lineup. The "Bruno di Rocca" is a Cabernet Sauvignon like few others in Italy: full-bodied yet very elegant, it has plenty of cassis and cedar-box aromas and flavors, and the suave finish keeps you company for most of the evening.

14. "RUJNO" GRAVNER (FRIULI VENEZIA GIULIA)

Merlot doesn't get much better than this, and unlike Gravner's white wines, this red isn't marked by the aromas of oxidation that he obtains by using amphoras and long skin-to-must contact. There's plenty to like here: violet, blackberry, and dark chocolate aromas soar from the glass, while roasted coffee beans, cedar, and blueberry flavors mingle with fine tannins and acids. The wine is very long and smooth-textured.

15. CABERNET FRANC "ALZERO" QUINTARELLI (VENETO)

Though this wine has always been considered and labeled a Cabernet Franc, in reality the blend has almost always contained as much as 50% cabernet sauvignon. It is one of Italy's first well-made, non-vegetal Cabernets. An all too common finding in such wines is that the grapes didn't ripen properly; this one is a testament to Quintarelli's capacity to excel with just about any grape variety. A huge, concentrated wine, but with plenty of finely integrated acids that help balance the whole.

10 BEST WHITE WINES MADE FROM INTERNATIONAL GRAPES

1. "GAJA E REY" GAJA (CHARDONNAY; PIEDMONT)

Italy's best Chardonnay, named in honor of Angelo Gaja's grandmother Clotilde Rey, who was French and married into the family. She was an enlightened woman and probably ahead of her time, and Angelo acknowledges her immense contribution to improving quality at the estate. Curiously, this wine is particularly good in vintages ending in 4. The 1984 was the first truly great, modern Italian white wine, and the '94 is still the best Chardonnay made by Gaja, the amazing result of a difficult vintage. The '04 was also very good. Today Gaja is as sure a thing as there is in Italian white wines.

2. CHARDONNAY LIBRARY RELEASE CANTINA TERLANO
(CHARDONNAY; ALTO ADIGE)

Some producers, albeit very few in Italy, have always kept aside a large number of bottles so as to have stocks of older vintages to sell or present at tastings years later. When released, these wines are often called library wines. Terlano is the producer in Italy with the largest old stocks: not just Chardonnay but also Pinot Grigio and Pinot Bianco (often called Weissburgunder in Alto Adige). The Chardonnays are truly special, and very like Burgundy in texture and aromatic profile.

3. PINOT GRIS ÉLEVÉ EN BARRIQUES (PINOT
GRIGIO;VALLE D'AOSTA)

This is the oaked version of the stellar Pinot Grigio included in the 200 Best list. Though the oak is lavish, this wine is still an excellent example of what Pinot Grigio can be when treated with passion and care. It is one of the few Pinot Grigios from Italy that can compete with the ultrarich bottlings from Alsace. (But the label reads Pinot Gris, since it is made in Valle d'Aosta, a French-influenced part of Italy.)

4. SAUVIGNON "LAFOA" PRODUTTORI COLTERENZIO (ALTO ADIGE)

With more than 1.6 million bottles produced annually and more than 315 hectares of fine vineyards to use as a source of the finest grapes, this is obviously a large, important wine entity in Alto Adige. It is also a high-quality producer, with an excellent Cabernet Sauvignon to go along with this standout Sauvignon Blanc. The latter could be considered just another one of Italy's many fine Sauvignons; but as it spends about eight months in small oak barrels prior to being bottled, it has a slightly smoother texture and greater depth and complexity than other examples obtained from this grape.

5. GEWÜRZTRAMINER "SANCT VALENTIN" PRODUTTORI SAN MICHELE APPIANO (ALTO ADIGE)

The cellarmaster and winemaker Hans Terzer is a recognized genius, and he single-handedly put Alto Adige on the map of high-quality wines. He has the ability to make absolutely great wines even in huge amounts—something that is not at all easy. Today many of his wines, including this Gewürztraminer, are benchmarks in their respective categories. The "Sanct Valentin" has grapefruit, mango, and papaya aromas and flavors, and there are beautiful notes recalling varnish, green tea, and rose petals on the long, creamy, tropical fruity finish.

6. CHARDONNAY "CUVÉE FRISSONIÈRE" LES CRÊTES (VALLE D'AOSTA)

Costantino Charrère has probably done more than anyone else for Italy's native grape varietals, but he has an amazing touch with foreign grapes as well. This is the unoaked version of Chardonnay from Les Crêtes; the Cuvée Bois, by contrast, can be a little top-heavy with vanillin-buttery tones. You won't find five better Chardonnays made in Italy than this one, and it compares favorably with many of the world's best unoaked Chardonnays.

7. CURTEFRANCA CHARDONNAY CA' DEL BOSCO (LOMBARDY)

This is one of Italy's truly great, historic white wines, and a rare example of Chardonnay that isn't overoaked. I have very fond memories of the 1985 and the 1986, and though now they may be on the downward slope, other vintages from the 1990s are still just fine. This is a big fat buttery Chardonnay that has, however, enough bright acids to keep it balanced and lively on your palate. It is very fine and suave, with an elegant, mineral finish that goes on and on.

8. "CERVARO DELLA SALA" CASTELLO DELLA SALA (UMBRIA)

With the 2005 vintage, "Cervaro" seems to be less oaky than it has recently been—a very welcome change. In the 1980s the wine was very fine and the oak was somewhat in check, but the 1990s brought an increase in butterscotch and vanilla aromas and flavors that unfortunately covered up all the fruit. Today this is a solid, extremely well made Chardonnay that, though not unlike other New World wines made from the same variety, still has enough high acidity and mineral touches to set it apart.

9. CURTEFRANCA "CONVENTO DELLA SS. ANNUNCIATA" BELLAVISTA (LOMBARDY)

This wine is an extremely successful Chardonnay that sees less oak than the otherwise also very fine "Uccellanda," made by the same producer. The Convento bottling usually displays higher acids, layers of fruit, and moderately spicy tannins on a long, silky finish.

10. GEWÜRZTRAMINER "CAMPANER" PRODUTTORI CALDARO (ALTO ADIGE)

A very fine, less massive version of this grape and one that has a slew of admirers in Italy. Pretty aromas of rose petal, buttercup, and pansy intermingle nicely with grapefruit and a touch of mango. On the palate it displays a stone and tropical fruit quality that is immensely appealing. It can be drunk upon release or after a year or two of bottle age, though I like my Gewürztraminers on the young side.

10 BEST SPARKLING AND ROSÉ WINES MADE FROM INTERNATIONAL GRAPES

1. FRANCIACORTA BRUT "ANNA MARIA CLEMENTI" CA' DEL BOSCO (CHARDONNAY/OTHERS— SPARKLING WINE; LOMBARDY)

The Anna Maria Clementi, named after the mother of the owner, Maurizio Zanella, is arguably Italy's single greatest sparkling wine. It is the brainchild of the volcanic

Zanella, who back in the 1970s decided to call upon André Dubois, cellarmaster at Épernay in France, in order to show everyone that Franciacorta could make bubblies to compete with the world's best. In an effort to grow grapes of better quality, he also introduced the concept of lower yields and tighter-spaced vines, unheard of in this part of Italy at that time. The pretty hints of white chocolate along with truffle and almond notes, bright acids, and exceptional length contribute to the excellence of this wine. It is better than many famous names in Champagne, but don't take my word for it that—go out and have a try!

2. TRENTO "GIULIO FERRARI RISERVA DEL FONDATORE"
FERRARI (CHARDONNAY—SPARKLING WINE; TRENTINO)

Giulio Ferrari was born in 1879 and studied in France, where he learned the fine art of making Champagne. Correctly believing that the cool climate and high-altitude vineyards of Trentino were perfect for producing good-quality sparkling wine, he returned to the family home in 1902 to set about proving his theory, and began planting French varieties. By 1952, when he sold his winery to Bruno Lunelli, a wineshop owner in Trento, his wines had become world-famous and he couldn't keep up with demand. Today, the house of Ferrari pays homage to its founder with this fantastic sparkling wine, which ages exceptionally well (the '78, '82, and '85 are still standouts today, at 96/100, 95/100, and 94/100 points respectively). Though there are yeasty, hazelnut, and mushroom aromas and flavors, there are also plenty of the ripe fruit notes that are typical of Franciacorta and that set these wines apart from their French counterparts.

3. FRANCIACORTA RISERVA "VITTORIO MORETTI"
(CHARDONNAY/PINOT NERO; LOMBARDY)

In 1977, Vittorio Moretti, a highly successful industrialist, decided to start planting vines on his Franciacorta estate, Bellavista, thinking wine might be an interesting hobby. He soon realized that his wines held great potential and that he was on to something special. The arrival of the winemaker Mattia Vezzola was an important development, and Bellavista has never looked back. The Vittorio Moretti Riserva is a rich, heady wine of real breeding and class, uncommon length, and complexity. This is the best of the many fine sparklers made by Bellavista. The almost 50-50 blend of pinot nero and chardonnay has an extremely complex nose of chocolate hazelnut, spring flowers, honey, and citrus fruits, with a palate just as complex and a certain meatiness of texture that will allow it to stand up even to white meat dishes such as chicken and turkey.

4. TRENTO BRUT ROSÉ MASO MARTIS (PINOT NERO/ CHARDONNAY; TRENTINO)

This is perhaps Italy's single best rosé sparkling wine, but it is not yet imported into the United States. The wine-maker Antonio Stelzner has turned heads in Italy with this suave, creamy sparkler that has amazing concentration and pretty floral and small berry aromas, with hints of cherry syrup flavors. A joy to drink.

5. FRANCIACORTA BRUT MILLESIMATO BERSI SERLINI (CHARDONNAY/PINOT BIANCO; LOMBARDY)

There is no denying that these are some of the most interesting and better-made sparkling wines coming out of Italy. What separates them from the majority of otherwise competently made Franciacortas is their greater degree of complexity and depth.

6. BRUT ROSÉ METODO CLASSICO EXTRA CUVÉE FRANCESCO BELLEI (PINOT NERO; EMILIA ROMAGNA)

Owned by the Lambrusco giant Cavicchioli but still run, with regard to wine making, by the Bellei family, this is an excellent source of fine Lambruscos (the "Rifermentazione Ancestrale" bottling is one of the very best Lambruscos di Sorbara). It also produces even better sparkling wines, such as the one named here.

7. METODO CLASSICO OPERE TREVIGIANE RISERVA VILLA SANDI (PINOT NERO/CHARDONNAY; VENETO)

Villa Sandi's production has improved by leaps and bounds over the years, and it is now a very solid producer of fine wines at more than affordable prices. This pinot nero–chardonnay blend is full of nutty and floral aromas, with hints of butter and freshly baked bread. It hits the palate with plenty of zesty acidity but also a creamy texture that will remind you of mushrooms and citrus fruits. Perfect with risotto!

8. OLTREPÒ PAVESE PINOT NERO BRUT PAS DOSÉ METODO CLASSICO NATURE MONSUPPELLO (PINOT NERO; LOMBARDY)

Pierangiolo Boatti, a force of nature and a real wine enthusiast, has created a top-of-the-line sparkling wine called Cà del Tava that he hopes, not unreasonably, will be able to compete with the best from France. But its undeniably high quality comes at a steep price, and I feel that this

Nature bottling, at about half the price, offers almost as much intense flavor. Close your eyes and you won't know you aren't drinking Champagne: yeasty, toasty, and fresh, this has a gorgeous stream of fast-rising small bubbles and plenty of hazelnut flavor that will keep you and everyone around you happy the rest of the evening.

9. FRANCIACORTA BRUT COLLEZIONE CAVALLERI (CHARDONNAY; LOMBARDY)

Italy is a land of history, and so it cannot be surprising that Jacobinus de Cavaleris, ancestor of owner Giovanni Cavalleri, arrived in the area in the 1300s and that another ancestor, Giuseppe Paolo Cavalleri, was already reknowned for quality wines in the 1800s. This Collezione Brut is one of Italy's better-known Franciacortas, and always one of the best. The vineyards are located in the southwest portion of Franciacorta, in a particularly high-quality part of the Appellation. The wine is a Blanc de Blanc, meaning that it is made with 100% chardonnay grapes, and it is blessed with uncommon depth and complexity.

10. FRANCIACORTA EXTRA BRUT "COMARI DEL SALEM" UBERTI (CHARDONNAY/PINOT NERO; LOMBARDY)

This blend (80% chardonnay and 20% pinot nero) is a very dry sparkler that can stand up to the best of Champagne, though it has the typical ripe peachy fruitiness of Franciacortas. It also ages very well, as a number of vertical tastings I have done can attest. The Uberti family is very dedicated to producing top quality. Its classically structured sparkler has plenty of floral and saline nuances to add complexity to the more typical yeasty, hazelnut, and buttery aromas and flavors. Uberti has been in the wine business since 1793, and wines such as this tell you why it's been around so long.

10 BEST SWEET WINES MADE FROM INTERNATIONAL GRAPES

A number of very interesting, downright spectacular sweet wines made in Italy are from international grape varieties, but the problem is . . . finding them! Unfortunately, these wines are often made in extremely small quantities, even fewer than 1,000 bottles a year. Therefore, in the list that follows, I have placed mainly the wines most likely to be found, as well as the most reasonably priced, considering their quality. Please note that some of these wines also contain small percentages of native grapes, as these grapes, always plentiful and long associated with each region, were the logical choices for Italians to use for their sweet wines. As the international grapes arrived on Italian shores only recently, the number of sweet wines made from them is still relatively small. Nevertheless, many now being made are worth searching for, either in your wine store or on your next trip to Italy. I wish to point out the very fine "Mistigrì" by Marco Martin in Valle d'Aosta (made from pinot gris), the "Buca delle Canne," a very rare (for Italy) 100% semillon made by La Stoppa in Emilia Romagna (a 100% sauvignon), and the "Annocinque," a very successful blend of viognier, semillon, and malvasia di Candia aromatica made by Perinelli, also in Emilia Romagna.

1. GEWÜRZTRAMINER "TERMINUM" PRODUTTORI TERMENO (ALTO ADIGE)—95/100; $50

A world-class Gewürztraminer and always one of Italy's best wines, it is not made every year but only when the vintage conditions allow. It is rich, creamy, and concentrated and very typical of the grape variety. This ranks with the very best from Alsace.

2. PASSITO "COMTESS" PRODUTTORI SAN MICHELE APPIANO (ALTO ADIGE)—93/100; $50

A blend of 70% gewürztraminer, 15% riesling, and 15% sauvignon, it is always one of Italy's best sweet wines. Some of its vintages—the 2004, in particular—are truly stellar. Long, rich, and creamy, with plenty of ripe tropical fruit flavors, this wine will get all those who love sweet wines looking elsewhere than tried-and-true Alsace and Germany.

3. PASSITO "VULCAIA APRÈS" INAMA (VENETO)— 92/100; $50

One of the first-ever late-harvest Sauvignons made in Italy, where the grape variety is rarely used on its own to make sweet wines. Inama's version is beautifully smoky, redolent in date, fig, and ripe peach, and apricot aromas, and finishes long and smooth. It's the sort of wine that makes you want to grab another bowl of fruit cocktail or another fruit tart.

4. VENDEMMIA TARDIVA "TREBIANCO" CASTELLO DEI RAMPOLLA (SAUVIGNON BLANC, CHARDONNAY, GEWÜRZTRAMINER; TUSCANY)—91/100; $N/A

As is often the case with estates making some of the most important wines in a country, a wine or two of theirs does not always receive the attention or praise it deserves. Such is the destiny of Castello dei Rampolla's "Trebianco," a very serious, excellent dessert wine (60% sauvignon, 25% chardonnay, 15% gewürztraminer) that most people forget about, busy as they are in talking up, correctly, the virtues of the two famous super-Tuscans made here ("Sammarco" and Vigna d'Alceo). Lovely in its understated, refined delivery of candied apricots, ripe peaches, and honey, this accompanies perfectly blue cheeses and almond cookies, but it'll handle foie gras just as well.

5. PASSITO MOSCATO ROSA WALDGRIES
(ALTO ADIGE)—92/100; $35

The pink muscat grape, or moscato rosa, is so called not because of its color (the wine is never pink but actually a very deep red), but rather because of its perfume, which will call to mind fresh roses. A small estate owned by the Plattner family, Waldgries makes many fine wines: however, its Moscato Rosa is textbook, made in a lighter, very floral, yet deceptively concentrated style that will appeal to everyone and is the perfect accompaniment to any dessert involving fresh berries.

6. PASSITO "FREIENFELD" PRODUTTORI CORTACCIA
(ALTO ADIGE)—92/100; N/A

An amazingly successful wine made from gewürztraminer that has great balance and a smooth satin finish. All the wines of Cortaccia are suave and made for easy drinking, and this one is no exception. Lychee, grapefruit, banana, mango, and papaya are only some of the aromas and flavors you'll find in your glass.

7. PASSITO CASHMERE ELENA WALCH
(ALTO ADIGE)—91/100; $50

A blend of mainly gewürztraminer and sauvignon, this has a pretty golden color, aromas of tea leaves and chamomile, honey and ripe peaches, and is very rich and sweet on the palate, where it finishes long and smooth, with a hint of citrus for added freshness.

8. MOSCATO ROSA PASSITO "TERMINUM" PRODUTTORI
TERMENO (ALTO ADIGE)—91/100; $45

This Moscato Rosa differs from the one made by Waldgries in its richer, thicker style, but it is nonetheless spectacular, as it manages to avoid heaviness. The bright acids wonderfully delineate the cinnamon, nutmeg, raspberry, and black cherry flavors, and the finish is floral and long.

9. VENDEMMIA TARDIVA "JOSEPH" HOFSTÄTTER
(ALTO ADIGE)—91/100; $50

A late-harvest gewürztraminer that will also contain some air-dried grapes in those years when the weather turns sour, this wine has remarkably improved over the years and is now really a world-class dessert wine. The 2004 was lighter and more elegant, while the 2003 was almost too sweet and concentrated, but the basic aromas and flavors of lychee, cantaloupe, vanilla, honey, peach, and dried apricots are always there.

10. "ORO DEL CEDRO" FATTORIA LAVACCHIO
(GEWÜRZTRAMINER; TUSCANY)—87/100; $N/A

You might think the owners here are a little crazy to plant gewürztraminer in a hot region like Tuscany, but the wine will prove that they'll have the last laugh. A true late-harvest wine, possible thanks to the relatively high altitude at which the vineyard is found (roughly 1,200 feet) and a never-ending air current that will be quite evident to all those standing out on the hill. Do not expect an Alsatian-type blockbuster: this is very light and delicate, and the vines need to age some more (currently about 15 years old) so that they can deliver something a bit more complex, but it's a well-made wine and an effort that deserves encouragement. The Chianti Rufina and the Riserva by Lavacchio are very fine, too.

WINES YOU MAY NEVER HAVE HEARD OF

ITALIAN WINES CAN BE DOWNRIGHT confusing: if for no other reason, there are just too many to choose from. Here is a list of wines that are little talked about, most of them made from grapes that are mainly local varieties. Yet they are some of Italy's most delicious wines, and they deserve to be known. Even better, most of them cost very little.

15 BEST RED DISCOVERY WINES

1. FUMIN "ESPRIT FOLLET" LA CROTTA DE VEGNERON (VALLE D'AOSTA)

Not too distant a relative of syrah, fumin also has a telltale black peppery and smoky personality. A bunch of good Fumins are being made now, and this is the best.

2. "SUM" TORRE GUACETO (PUGLIA)

The very talented folks at the Accademia dei Racemi oversee production of this wine and deserve credit for having been the first to really study the ancient, forgotten susumaniello variety. Others have spoken a lot about it, but all the initial legwork and studies were done by the people here. This is lovely, soft, herbal-smoky, and wonderfully inexpensive.

3. BARBERA D'ASTI CASCINA TAVJIN (PIEDMONT)

Lovely Nadia Verrua has single-handedly turned her parents' estate into a fine wine destination: the Grignolino and the Ruché are admirable, but it's her Barbera that is usually the best wine here. Still, you won't go wrong picking any of them.

4. MAYOLET CAVE DES ONZES COMMUNES (MAYOLET; VALLE D'AOSTA)

Mayolet is a native grape variety that was always added as part of Valle d'Aosta red blends, but about five years ago Costantino Charrère, the region's most famous winemaker, tried his hand at a 100% pure mayolet bottling. It was promising enough, and now there are at least four other producers that also bottle it as such. This one is probably the best of the lot, with a very pretty spicy, floral, and blackberry set of aromas. A real rarity, but no longer an "endangered species," which is good news for all wine lovers out there.

5. PETIT ROUGE RENATO ANSELMET (PETIT ROUGE; VALLE D'AOSTA)

Make no mistake about it, this is one of Italy's absolutely best, most enjoyable and mouthwatering light reds you'll ever find. In fact, it is so good I almost inserted it directly into the 200 Best. A little-known grape, petit rouge is not the easiest to work with, and if care isn't taken in the cellar, it can deliver unpleasant aromas of wet animal fur. When well made, as is the case with Anselmet, it's pure joy, an explosion of little red berries and red cherries with a quinine, inky note on the finish to add complexity. Chill this and enjoy it all summer long. For something more complex and bigger bodied, try the Torrette, a petit rouge (with a small percentage of other local grapes included as well) that is grown in and around Torrette, the best site for this variety. Anselmet is one of Italy's least-known yet absolutely finest producers.

6. CESANESE DI OLEVANO ROMANO "VELOBRA" GIOVANNI TERENZI (LAZIO)

Slightly late-harvested cesanese grapes give a lusciously soft red that's silky on the palate. It's also unbelievably inexpensive.

7. RUCHÉ DI CASTAGNOLE MONFERRATO LUCA FERRARIS VINEYARDS (PIEDMONT)

Bright young Luca makes a slew of very fine wines, all in a fairly smooth high-alcohol style that's hard not to enjoy. And he has an absolutely phenomenal grappa, from his Ruché pomace.

8. SIREN ISABELLA MOTTURA (LAZIO)

Isabella Mottura is a determined young woman who is making truly fine wines in a beautiful part of Lazio with the help of the star winemaker Riccardo Cotarella. The Siren is a delectable, easy-drinking, inexpensive cabernet-sangiovese blend.

9. ORMEASCO DI PORNASSIO LUPI (LIGURIA)

This light red wine will do well lightly chilled on a hot summer day. Lovely herbal, even earthy nuances on the nose with plenty of small red berry aromas and a touch of orange zest. It finishes clean with slightly evident tannins that make it fine with cold cuts, fried foods, sandwiches, and barbecues. Ormeasco is a dolcetto that has adopted over time to the Ligurian *terroir*.

10. AGLIANICO DEL VULTURE "ARCÀ" GIANNATTASIO (BASILICATA)

A gorgeously situated vineyard, in a gorge but still receiving plenty of sunlight and wind, this is the source of one of the richer, smokier Aglianicos to come out of Italy in recent years. I am keeping an eye out on this producer's progress, and so far the wine holds extreme promise.

11. CASAVECCHIA VESTINI CAMPAGNANO (CAMPANIA)

This estate resurrected two ancient varieties: pallagrello, both white and black, and casavecchia, a grape that gives a wine with a lovely, delicate aromatic character. Both this wine and the Pallagrello Nero wine are interesting, fairly full-bodied, and satisfying. You owe it to yourself to try them both. My guess is that you won't be disappointed with the hints of bay leaf, ink, rhubarb, and sweet spices.

12. DONNAS CAVE COOPERATIVE DE DONNAS (VALLE D'AOSTA)

Nebbiolo by any other name is still nebbiolo. What you get in this wine, made from picoutener, the name given to nebbiolo in Valle d'Aosta, is an extremely refined infusion of rose petal and sour red cherry with a delicate spiciness, fine tannins, high acids, and a very long finish.

13. SFORZATO RONCO DEL PICCHIO FAY (LOMBARDY)

A great wine made in the manner of Amarone, from slightly dehydrated grapes, Fay is especially adept at packing in more flavor than most wines have. This small, high-quality family-run winery, with beautiful vineyards situated at about 1,600 feet above sea level, makes a number of very good wines. The velvety texture and red cherry fruitiness of this example are impossible to beat.

14. LACRIMA DI MORRO D'ALBA STEFANO MANCINELLI (MARCHE)

An unknown variety even in Italy, lacrima is wonderful: it gives amazingly perfumed wines that remind you of incense, lavender, starwberries, and quinine. It is a truly unique drinking experience and one I urge you to try:

Mancinelli is probably the most accomplished producer of all when it comes to this wine.

15. NERETTO CANAVESE CIECK (PIEDMONT)

A little-known grape variety from Piedmont has in Cieck its best producer by far. The wine smells of black pepper, ripe raspberries, and cedar. It's long and lively on your palate.

10 BEST WHITE DISCOVERY WINES

1. VERMENTINO U MUNTE COLLI DEI BARDELLINI (VERMENTINO; LIGURIA)

Made in the Riviera Ligure di Ponente, one of the best spots for Vermentino in all of Liguria, this is a very good example of what Vermentino from Liguria can deliver. Fresh and floral, with a salty, mineral finish, it is a relatively light white wine that is heavenly with shellfish and simply prepared fish dishes. The U Munte vineyard is one of the best sites for Vermentino, and it shows; this estate, founded in 1970, has improved by leaps and bounds in the last ten years, and their Pigato, another white, is also very enjoyable.

2. DRY MUSCAT "TERRE DI ORAZIO" CANTINA DI VENOSA (BASILICATA)

Dry white muscat doesn't get any more enjoyable than this one: bright, fresh, very true to type, and amazingly inexpensive.

3. FRASCATI "VIGNETO FILONARDI" VILLA SIMONE—PIERO COSTANTINI (LAZIO)

This wine shows just how much fun Frascati can be, delivering a surprising amount of creamy fruit and body that will really surprise you. It has uncommon intensity of aromas and depth of flavor buffered by excellent acidity. A wine you won't soon forget.

4. BIANCOLELLA "FRASSITELLI" CASA D'AMBRA (BIANCOLELLA; CAMPANIA)

The island of Ischia has long been associated with fine wines, and even the Emperor Tiberius enjoyed them centuries ago. D'Ambra is the best producer on the island, but there are many other producers, with wine production still a very important part of the island's economy, unlike what has happened in other island tourist destinations, such as Capri. Biancolella has a delicate citrusy and herbal aroma, and ages extremely well, over time picking up even riesling-like kerosene notes.

5. BELLONE CANTINA CINCINNATO (LAZIO)

Another standout wine from Lazio, this one costs so little you'll be laughing all the way to the bank, and the dinner table. It has lovely, ripe citrus fruit aromas and flavors and a yummy, resiny quality on the palate. It's made from the very high-quality bellone variety, which was shamelessly neglected by most producers looking to cash in on the high yields of lousy varieties such as trebbiano toscano and malvasia di Candia.

6. PETITE ARVINE CAVE DES ONZES COMMUNES (PETITE ARVINE; VALLE D'AOSTA)

There are many wonderful Petite Arvines to choose from in the Valle d'Aosta, the only region in Italy where they produce this wine. The one by this social co-op is one of the very best, and is amazingly inexpensive. Fresh, floral, and lemony, it's the sort of wine that goes marvelously well with just about any simply prepared light fish and vegetable dish. Bright and light in alcohol, it's full of easygoing charm: one glass and I'm confident you'll be hooked.

7. MÜLLER THURGAU "PALAI" POJER E SANDRI (ALTO ADIGE)

It is quite a hike up to the beautiful Palai vineyard, but once you get there you are rewarded with a postcard picture of the town of Faedo below and beautiful mountain views all around. This is one of Italy's best Müllers, and a pure, unadulterated version at that: you won't find any aromas mounting from the glass that would be more appropriate to white and yellow muscat or gewürztraminer. Rather, you'll appreciate the lovely thyme, mint, and green apple notes that, coupled with bracing acidity, will make you wish the bottle were bottomless. This wine is an absolute joy with pasta and clam sauce or smoked trout.

8. CARJCANTI GULFI (CARRICANTE; SICILY)

Carricante is a potentially great grape whose exact potential is not yet known. Certainly, it has immense up-front appeal, thanks to an intense mineral and lemony aroma that is complicated with mountain herbs and a touch of petrol, especially in older bottlings. In fact, its olfactory profile will remind you of a dry Riesling. Gulfi makes an absolutely splendid example, though its high acidity and strong mineral tones may come as a jolt to those who prefer buttery, soft, effusively fruity whites.

9. "BARBAZZALE BIANCO" COTTANERA (SICILY)

From the inzolia native variety grown high up on the slopes of the Etna volcano, this remarkably successful wine never fails, year in and year out. The most recent vintage was a little disappointing in that it lacked the usual bright freshness. But the saline quality so typical of Inzolia, its ripe apple and pear flavors, and a slight tannic bite were there, making this instantly recognizable as Inzolia, and a very successful one at that.

10. PIGNOLETTO VALLONA (EMILIA ROMAGNA)

Pignoletto doesn't ever get better than this one—a sleek, refreshing, mineral-driven wine that is thirst-quenching, light, and lively. The zippy acidity frames the green apple and citrus flavors well, and there is an enticing floral note that lasts and lasts on the long lively finish. Founded in 1986, this estate is led with talent and flair by Maurizio Vallona, who undoubtedly makes the best Pignolettos around.

10 BEST SPARKLING AND ROSÉ DISCOVERY WINES

1. "OTELLO" EXTRA DRY CANTINE CECI (EMILIA ROMAGNA)

A rare blend of lambrusco and pinot nero, this is an intelligent mix and one that goes remarkably well with many foods. Ceci is a solid producer with many fine wines for you to choose from.

2. PIGNOLETTO FRIZZANTE TENUTA BONZARA (EMILIA ROMAGNA)

Pignoletto is a high-acid variety that is perfect for making sparkling wines, and a producer such as Bonzara is able to achieve a great deal more flavor than most. Very lemony and floral, this is a light, acidic wine that will go marvelously with all fried foods.

3. "BARIGLIOTT" PATERNOSTER (BSILICATA)

A fantastic fizzy red wine, and therefore unusual. This Aglianico has such a wonderful creamy texture and such loads of fruitiness that I have no doubt you'll thank me for having turned you on to it.

4. BRUT D'ARAPRY (PUGLIA)

This is made from bombino bainco, and to my knowledge it is the only good example of sparkling wine made from this grape in Italy. That is a bit surprising, since bombino's high acidity ought to guarantee at least some measure of success. In any case, the pretty lemony and floral aromas and flavors will make you understand what d'Arapry is able to offer.

5. LUGANA SPUMANTE "SEBASTIAN" PROVENZA (LOMBARDY)

Not unlike a good Prosecco, this is a simple sparkler. It is made from a different grape altogether, but the green apple and apricot aromas and flavors are similar to those of Prosecco. A very good estate with many fine wines to pick from.

6. BARBERA "LA MONELLA" BRAIDA (PIEDMONT)

This lovely fizzy Barbera is perfect for grilled sausage or a prosciutto sandwich. Its bright berry aromas and flavors and surprising structure make it ideal with hearty soups as well. Better still, pour some into your soup—an old Italian tradition—and the soup will taste even better.

7. PROSECCO DI VALDOBBIADENE EXTRA DRY "COL DELL' ORSO" FROZZA (PROSECCO; VENETO)

An artisanally made Prosecco, quite different from many of the ones made in larger numbers. This one has a slightly rustic charm, but also greater intensity and creaminess on the palate. For all those who didn't think Prosecco could really get interesting, this is a surprisingly complex effort.

8. VELENOSI BRUT (CHARDONNAY, PINOT NERO; MARCHE)

Among the many fine wines made by Angela Velenosi, such as the Rosso Piceno "Brecciarolo," the Rosso Piceno "Roggio del Filare," and the Falerio dei Colli Ascolani Vigna Solaria, there is this little-known gem, a mainly Chardonnay sparkler (70%) that will remind you of citrus fruits and butter cookies. Perhaps not as complex as some of the best in Franciacorta, but highly enjoyable and very well made for something altogether different from the Marche.

9. BONARDA VIVACE "VAIOLET" MONSUPPELLO (LOMBARDY)

This workhorse grape gives hearty wines that are tavern staples. The version by Monsuppello has a bit more breeding and class than most, with a creamier texture and much more fruit in the mouth. There are very pretty strawberry and orange peel flavors on the long peppery finish.

10. FRANCIACORTA BRUT MILLESIMATO VILLA (LOMBARDY)

Villa is not one of the more famous Franciacorta estates, yet this is a very fine wine that is part of a solid lineup that will make it difficult for you to choose just one. Peachy-apricot aromas and a lovely concentrated set of similar flavors endear this bubbly to just about anyone who tries it. It also has a long finish and real complexity.

10 BEST SWEET DISCOVERY WINES

1. MOSCADELLO DI MONTALCINO LA PODERINA (MOSCATO BIANCO; TUSCANY)

If you have always thought of Montalcino as big red wine country, think again. In fact, in the nineteenth century, Montalcino was much more famous for the sweet white wine called Moscadello than it was for the red Brunello. La Poderina makes the single best Moscadello of today, a wine that would undoubtedly make its ancestors proud, so to speak. Rich yet lively due to fairly high acids, this has pretty tangerine and orange jam aromas with hints of rose petals and jasmine. It is quite sweet and luscious on the long finish and will be a welcome change from Sauternes or Alsatian late harvests you may be more familiar with.

2. MARSALA SUPERIORE VIGNA LA MICCIA MARCO DE BARTOLI (GRILLO; SICILY)

Marco De Bartoli is Italy's star Marsala producer: more proof, if any was needed, is given by the first sip of this wine, wholly enjoyable and very refined. It actually makes for a wonderful aperitif as well, as the hint of sweetness is buffered by almondy-herbal nuances and plenty of fresh acidity. This allows for many very creative and daring wine and food matches, and will go well with dishes as different as shellfish, spaghetti with bottarga (tuna or mullet dried roe), capers and cherry tomatoes, olives, and almond cookies.

3. TRENTINO VINO SANTO GINO PEDROTTI (TRENTINO)

Made from the native nosiola grapes, the Vino Santos of Trentino are some of the very best sweet wines of

Italy. (The "o" at the end of the word Vino is meant to differentiate them from Tuscan and other Vin Santos.) Unfortunately, they are made in very small quantities and are therefore hard to find. This one is excellent: lusciously sweet and creamy. Should you find it, don't hesitate to try it!

4. PICOLIT VALENTINO BUTUSSI (FRIULI VENEZIA GIULIA)

Butussi is a solid producer, makes many very fine wines, and has a very good hand with Picolit. Some of his older vintages are still beautifully drinkable and are always marked by elegance and a lithe yet flavor-packed frame.

5. MOSCATO GIALLO PASSITO GRAF VON MERAN "SISSI" PRODUTTORI MERANO (ALTO ADIGE)

A big favorite in Italy, with a lovely aromatic personality loaded with grapefruit, white pepper, and canned peach aromas and flavors. Very satisfying, if at times too sweet.

6. "LUDUM" MARCO CARPINETI (LAZIO)

Another fantastic wine made from bellone, a variety that takes to noble rot like few others. This is one of Italy's 15 best sweet wines, and it ought to be available in the United States as of 2009.

7. MARSALA "TERRE ARSE" FLORIO (SICILY)

A great Marsala, and a perfect example of just how wonderful this wine can be. It has dates, figs, a touch of caramel, and Sherry in its aromas and flavors; it's velvety-smooth and very long. The perfect after-dinner drink.

8. MALVASIA DELLE LIPARI "TENUTA CAPOFARO" TASCA D'ALMERITA (SICILY)

If Malvasia delle Lipari makes a comeback, it will be thanks to wines such as these: lush, creamy, and perfectly balanced between residual sugar and acids.

9. ELBA ALEATICO ACQUABONA (TUSCANY)

One of Italy's five or six best dessert wines, with red fruit cocktail and cherry jam and kirsch aromas and flavors. Aleatico does particularly well on the tiny island of Elba, just off the coast of Tuscany, and a number of standout Aleaticos are made there. They are evidence of how matching specific grape types to specific soils and climates really does matter, and can produce something magical and unique, such as this wine.

10. ELBA ALEATICO TENUTA DELLE RIPALTE (TUSCANY)

A new producer with an extra fine aromatic Aleatico; the estate is guided by none other than Pier Mario Cavallari of Grattamacco fame, so you know it can't go wrong. It's another example of the magic that is possible with Aleatico on Elba.

OLD WINES AND NEW WINES

10 BEST OLD-STYLE RED WINES

These are wines made in a very traditional manner that harks back to the Italy of centuries ago, although some modern technology is used. The list here includes Chiantis, Barolos, and other wines whose makers avoid small oak barrels, industrial yeasts, concentrators, and other technological aids that were not available (or not generally used, in the case of the small barrels) long ago. Look at them as giving you a taste of the past with every sip.

1. BAROLO "MONFORTINO" GIACOMO CONTERNO (NEBBIOLO; PIEDMONT)

This wine can age as much as six years in barrels. It doesn't get any more old-fashioned than this! (Already described in "Cult Wines," page 244.)

2. CHIANTI CLASSICO CASTELL'IN VILLA (SANGIOVESE/ CANAIOLO; TUSCANY)

One of Italy's greatest wines and one that ages splendidly: for all those out there who do not believe Chianti can age, try to find a 1975, 1978, or 1985 from this estate and get ready to be mesmerized. Sleek and refined, light and lively, this is as great as sangiovese gets, and about as hopelessly traditional as well, athough in fairness, recent, warmer vintages seem to be a little more chunky than before. The 1985 is simply a standout wine.

3. BAROLO ROCCHETTE LORENZO ACCOMASSO (NEBBIOLO; PIEDMONT)

I am sorry to say that Accomasso's wines are no longer imported into the United States, a casualty of the '90s craze for big, soft, high-alcohol red wines. You get the exact opposite with Accomasso: Barolo the way it used to be made, with long macerations on the skins and fermentation times, leading to a Barolo that is neither particularly deep in color nor very accessible when young, maintaining a high-acid, sharply tannic soul. Yet the wine ages beautifully, and some of the older vintages have weathered the vagaries of time much better than some ultra-famous names out there. The Rocchette vineyard of La Morra is a very high-quality site, and much more so than some of the names being put on labels nowadays—sites that in the days when Barolo didn't fetch the prices it does today were used to graze farm animals, or where they were cultivated with other varieties, as they were not really suited to nebbiolo.

4. BRAMATERRA SELLA (PIEDMONT)

The northeastern reaches of Piedmont have some wonderful if little-known nebbiolo-based wines such as Lessona, Gattinara, Boca, Ghemme, and Bramaterra. Sella, an estate founded in 1671, is also the name of the family we have to thank for having believed in Bramaterra when everyone else was giving up on it. These leanish, high-acid, but extremely refined wines are fortunately coming back into fashion. Their Lessona is just as wonderful.

5. PRIMITIVO DI MANDURIA ARCHIDAMO ACCADEMIA DEI RACEMI (PUGLIA)

One of the many fine Primitivos made under the umbrella of the Accademia dei Racemi, this is a tough-as-nails old-fashioned Primitivo rich in leather, tobacco, herbs, and spices with tough tannins and no sweet oak anywhere. Very fine and ridiculously cheap for its quality.

6. BAROLO CANNUBI S. LORENZO-RAVERA GIUSEPPE RINALDI

One of the wines whose makers eschew short maceration times and small barrels, this is as fine a bottle of Barolo as you'll ever taste. It is a blend of grapes from two of the better vineyard sites in Barolo, and even this fact harks back to another time. Barolo always was a blend of grapes from different sites, as it was felt that no single site could adequately capture the elusive magic of this wine. The many single vineyard bottlings of today are a very recent development, having multiplied over the past 20 years.

7. AGLIANICO DEL VULTURE RISERVA "CASELLE" D'ANGELO (BASILICATA)

Always an excellent and fairly priced wine, this very traditionally styled Aglianico speaks of its salty, mineral *terroir*, with plenty of exuberant and slightly rough tannins that need the weathering effect of time to reach a certain degree of polish. Nevertheless, it's fully enjoyable when young and becomes even better with a little time in the bottle. The vineyard is also very pretty, and one I always enjoy walking in.

8. BAROLO "OTIN FIORIN-NEBBIOLI" CAPPELLANO (PIEDMONT)

Three hectares in this famous *cru* of Serralunga, a third of which is planted in vines on their original roots, with no American rootstock, as part of an experiment by Baldo Cappellano, who wanted to get a taste of what Barolo might have been like before phylloxea struck. This and all the other wines undergo minimal intervention. There's some bottle variation, but the ones in top form are wonderful.

9. BAROLO MONPRIVATO GIUSEPPE MASCARELLO (NEBBIOLO; PIEDMONT)

Mauro Mascarello is one of the grandfathers of Barolo, a master winemaker who still makes Barolo in the tried-and-true fashion of his elders. Even though he remains faithful to the ways of yesteryear, he offers great encouragement to many of the young winemakers now trying their hand at Barolo, youngsters who look up to him and often ask for advice. The Monprivato vineyard is a very high-quality parcel of vines in the Castiglione Falletto district of Barolo, renowned for very balanced, perfumed Barolos. Mascarello's has a rigid acid spine that gives backbone to the pretty red cherry fruit present and lots of length. Wine lovers know that a good portion of the Monprivato vineyard, now farmed by Mascarello, used to belong to Violante Sobrero, one of the really great Barolo producers of the '60s and '70s.

10. "ANFITEATRO" VECCHIE TERRE DI MONTEFILI (SANGIOVESE; TUSCANY)

Not as old-fashioned or traditional or some as the other wines in this section, but one of the truest expressions of sangiovese you shall find anywhere. A simply mesmerizing wine made by Roccaldo Acuti, a master of Chianti and super-Tuscans.

10 BEST EXPERIMENTAL WINES

"Experimental" in the heading above refers to the fact that most of these wines are made with techniques used by the ancient Romans, and are an attempt to bring back to life wines as they were once made. Hence the use of amphoras and the absence of sulfur and cultured yeasts. The end result is wines that are altogether different in their fragrance and flavor profile, and that may be an acquired taste. I honestly cannot say I am a devoted fan of these "new-old" wines, though I admire the effort that goes into making them as well as the producers' willingness to try new roads. Note that in almost all cases thus far, these experimental techniques have been tried with white grape varieties, as the center of this wine making is Friuli Venezia Giulia (here abbreviated FVG).

RED

1. ROSSO GIOVANNI CROSATO (FVG)

This merlot and cabernet blend is aged in amphoras and has a distinctly creamy, soft texture. There is a very saline finish, and little of the oxidative character that wines aged in amphoras will often show. Crosato, who is an extremely talented winemaker (he makes the wines for Toros and was the winemaker at Volpe Pasini in the 1980s, when that estate was making by far its best wines), has the amphoras coated with wax so that the terra-cotta they are made of is less porous. Hence the wines have less of an oxidized look or feel.

WHITE

2. VERNACCIA DI SAN GIMIGNANO "EVOÉ"
GIOVANNI PANIZZI

This is perhaps the best of all these experimental wines that have recently become all the rage. It is a Vernaccia made by keeping the juice in contact with the skins for almost three months. That procedure is usually associated with red wines, but it works for Vernaccia. There's a very pleasant but not excessive tannic bite to this wine, and the citrus and vanilla aromas and flavors are very pure.

3. RIBOLLA GIALLA GRAVNER

Gravner was the first to try to make wine in the manner of the ancient Romans. This Ribolla is macerated on the skins for up to eight months, and so its reddish hue is not at all surprising. Chewy tannins and citrus fruit make it enjoyable enough, but it's not an everyday drinking experience. It's a far cry from most people's idea of a white wine.

4. ISCHIA BIANCO "KYMÉ" D'AMBRA (CAMPANIA)

From very talented Andrea d'Ambra, this is one of the most interesting wines of southern Italy in recent years. Made with 80% selezione d'Ambra, a special grape variety he selected in Greece and has since replanted on Ischia, and 20% of the native biancolella, this is a very herbal fragrant wine with a long iodine and almond finish, and with peach and apricot highlights.

5. "JAKOT" RADIKON (FVG)

Jakot is Tokaj spelled backward: in fact this is a 100% to-cai wine, but made in the ancient Roman fashion of long skin contact with the juice, which gives a totally different version. Therefore, the name is apt. This is one of the better experimental wines made in Italy of late, and I think the apricot liqueur and peach syrup flavors are very pretty.

6. RIBOLLA ANFORA "EXTREME" RENATO KEBER (FVG)

The contact time of juice and skin here is limited to about a month, and so the wine is not quite as extreme as those of Gravner, and I think it is also more drinkable. Keber is a very talented winemaker and this is the only wine he makes in this fashion. For a more typical taste of his wines you can choose the Pinot Grigio or Sauvignon or Pinot Bianco. The "Grici" line of wines is usually the best.

7. VITOVSKA VODOPIVEC (FVG)

This estate is also known as Damijan, from the first name of the owner. Its wines are very much in fashion and are hard to find in Italy, but they are available in the United States. Vitovska is a little-known native that has pretty apple and pear aromas and flavors.

8. "BREG" ANFORA GRAVNER (FVG)

A blend of sauvignon, pinot grigio, and chardonnay, this wine is usually richer and fatter than the Ribolla, but I feel it has less charctaer. Still, it is one of the original amphora wines and a fascianting drink, with its honeyed-almond tones and its definite oxidized note on the finish.

9. "PRULKE" ZIDARICH (FVG)

A blend of malvasia, sauvignon, and votovska, this wine has a thick creamy texture and lots of tangerine and lavender aromas and flavors. Zidarich is a very high-quality producer, and any of the wines made by him are just fine.

10. "VIGNA MAZZÌ" ROSA DEL GOLFO (PUGLIA)

Already listed among the 15 Best Sparkling and Rosé Wines, this was the first rosé in Italy to be aged in small oak barrels. It clearly showed that a small percentage of new oak would be just fine with negro amaro grapes, and this is a wine that is now inspiring imitators.

10 Best Debut Wines

This is a list of new and exciting wines that have appeared in Italy over the past two years. It is shorter than some of the other lists and includes both red and white wines. Most of these wines are not yet available in the United States, but as the estates listed do have American importers, the wines ought to find their way into your friendly neighborhood wine store soon.

Red

1. "RESECA" GULFI (SICILY)

This is made from 135-year-old vines of nerello mascalese and nerello cappuccio grown on the north side of the Etna volcano near the town of Randazzo. The vines are on original rootstock, and the wine is something special. The winemaker Salvo Foti has made a very perfumed wine with aromas of lava, raspberry, orange peel, and fresh flowers; more minerality on the palate; and lots of fresh, crunchy fruit.

2. PUGNITELLO SAN FELICE (TUSCANY)

Made with the grape variety of the same name, Pugnitello is a result of years of studies and research conducted with the aid of the University of Florence. It is a big, bold wine full of jammy, spicy red fruit and big chewy tannins that need a few years to resolve fully. Very promising.

3. "CASA ROMANA" PALLAVICINI (LAZIO)

A true Bordeaux blend, made with cabernet sauvignon, cabernet franc, petit verdot, and merlot. Pallavicini has high hopes that this wine will become the estate's most important. Lots of fresh blackberry and plum fruit along with cedar and smoky-spicy flavors.

4. "CAVALLI SELECTION" (TUSCANY)

Does the world need another boutique winery? Of course, if it's run with talent and flair, as this one is by Alessandro Cavalli, son of the fashion magnate Roberto Cavalli. Only two wines are made here: the "Cavalli Selection" and the "Cavalli Collection." The former is the one that will be distributed to and sold in stores (the latter is limited to special numbered gift boxes) and is essentially a blend of merlot, cabernet franc, and cabernet sauvignon, with small amounts of petit verdot and alicante bouché. It's still a work in progress, but a very promising one. There are pretty violet and black currant aromas with a nice balsamic finish.

5. "NERO DI ROSSO" DIESEL FARM (TUSCANY)

Renzo Rosso is the head of the Diesel fashion empire and fashionista icon, whose superexpensive jeans grace the buttocks of movie stars and pop idols all over the world. Rosso has now ensured that they'll also have something to grace their tables: his bottles of wine made at the Diesel Farm near Marostica in Veneto. Three wines are made, with the help of the star winemaker Roberto Cipresso; this Pinot Nero blend is the most interesting, though quite expensive for a relatively new wine with no track record to speak of.

WHITE

6. FIANO "EXULTET" QUINTODECIMO (CAMPANIA)

Luigi Moio is a highly talented winemaker, so it was predictable that his own new wine estate would start making one fine wine after another. After the very successful Aglianico, two new white wines have arrived: a Falanghina and a Fiano. The latter is the better of the two, with a pretty mineral sheen and varietally accurate apple and pear aromas and flavors.

7. "CIMELE" COMPAGNIA DI ERMES (LAZIO)

A lovely ottonese and bellone blend from the southeastern tip of Lazio. Lemony fresh and bright, this wine has a softly textured personality but loads of balanced acidity to keep the palate alert. The rich mouthfeel and concentrated fruit suggest old vines, and that is in fact the case.

8. CATARATTO FEUDO MONTONI (SICILY)

Until now, Feudo Montoni has been known as a top producer of red wine, and the good news is that a white wine has been brought into the fold as of 2008. However, the grandfather of the owner, Fabio Sireci, had planted many white grapes such as chardonnay and sauvignon decades ago, grapes that the estate has always sold off. The Cataratto is of especially high quality, very lemony-mineral, sleek, and compact, and it is the first white to be bottled with the pretty Feudo Montoni label.

SWEET

9. GIACCHÉ PASSITO CASALE CENTO CORVI (LAZIO)

This was an unknown wine until last year, as the grape had been all but forgotten. There is also a good dry version of Giacché, but the sweet one made from air-dried grapes is far more interesting. It is creamy and long, with pretty black pepper and lavender aromas and flavors. You'll find it pleasant and well-balanced.

10. "PASSITO" SARTARELLI (MARCHE)

Sartarelli makes many different Verdicchios, and all are very successful, but until 2008 it did not have a sweet wine in its portfolio. That's not the case anymore, since the "Passito" has appeared on the scene. The name couldn't be any simpler: it refers to the air-drying process that the grapes undergo in order to produce a dessert wine. This has honey, apple, and pear aromas with just a hint of peach, and is lithe and lively on the palate, where it is less sweet than you might have expected.

WINE ESTATES AND PRODUCERS

25 BEST TRADITIONAL WINE ESTATES AND PRODUCERS

A conservative estimate of the number of wine estates in Italy would be about 700,000, and of those about 5,000 make good to very high-quality wines. Choosing only 25 names is no easy task, but the estates I list here are those that year in and year out produce the most memorable bottles. Even more important, these are names you can count on: with your eyes closed, you can choose just about any wine they make. This isn't always true of other estates, where one wine might be great but all the rest average at best or, worse, nondescript. Any wine you choose from the listed estates ought to be very good at least, if not downright delectable. Look at them as sources for wines when you are in a crunch—when you don't have time to shop around but need to get something that you are sure won't disappoint you. One caveat: I could have chosen other wine estates to list here, but I have given precedence to those estates that make more than just a few extremely high-quality wines.

1. BRUNO GIACOSA (PIEDMONT)
Offering the greatest Barolos and Barbarescos, a fine sparkler, and excellent Dolcetto and Barbera, Bruno Giacosa may well be Italy's single best winemaker; his ability to turn grapes into something magical is beyond description.

2. CISA ASINARI MARCHESE DI GRESY (PIEDMONT)
There isn't a single bad wine made here: this producer offers perhaps Italy's best Dolcetto, one of the most enjoyable Barberas, a lineup of Barbarescos to die for, and exceptional Chardonnay and Sauvignon. There may not be a better series of wines made by anyone in Italy.

3. FRESCOBALDI (TUSCANY)
It's not easy to bring such high quality to the table in such large amounts. The Ornellaia estate is this producer's crown jewel; and don't forget about the great wines from its Pomino estate.

4. ANTINORI (TUSCANY)

As with Frescobaldi, one can't help admiring the great quality achieved by Antinori with its very large production. Antinori also gets credit for having launched Tignanello and Solaia.

5. GAJA (PIEDMONT)

Fine Barbarescos and whites, as well as an above-average Cabernet Sauvignon. Gaja is the reference point for fine Italian wines, one name you can always trust.

6. CA' DEL BOSCO (LOMBARDY)

The lineup of fantastic wines is never-ending: the sparklers and the still wines all rank among Italy's elite, and have had this status for decades. The "Pinero" Pinot Nero and the "Ca del Bosco" Chardonnay are absolutely beautiful wines one never tires of.

7. FELSINA (TUSCANY)

This producer makes one of Italy's three best Chiantis (the Riserva Rancia), one of the three better super-Tuscans (Fontalloro), one of the five best Vin Santos, and great Cabernet and Chardonnay. Giuseppe Mazzocolin is now also making unbelievably good extra-virgin olive oil.

8. DONNAFUGATA (SICILY)

Besides the famous "Ben Ryé" and the "Mille e Una Notte," there are also many wines that cost $20 to $30 or less. For example, I never tire of the "Sedara," a nonoaked nero d'Avola that is a delight just slightly chilled on hot summer days. The new "Polena" is a really fine Viognier. It won't remind you of the Rhône, but it is so enjoyable that you will find yourself wishing the Rallo family had started producing it sooner.

9. CANTINA TERMENO (ALTO ADIGE)

Just about any wine you buy from this producer will be one of the best in its category, and Italy's best Gewürztraminer and Pinot Grigio are made here. As good as these two wines are—and they are reason enough to consider this co-op among the best sources of fine wines in all of Italy—don't forget the three sweet wines: two Gewürztraminers and one made from moscato rosa (pink muscat), also absolutely stellar. The late-harvest Gewürztraminer "Roan" and the even more concentrated Gewürztraminer "Terminum" are on a par with the best sweet wines from Germany or Alsace. The Moscato Rosa "Terminum" ("Terminum" indicates this co-op's best sweet wines) has few equals in Italy. You'll love its intense rose petal, nutmeg, rhubarb, strawberry, and cinnamon aromas and flavors.

10. ISOLE E OLENA (TUSCANY)

A great Chianti, a great super-Tuscan, fine Vin Santo, and great internationals such as the Collezione DeMarchi Syrah and Cabernet Sauvignon. The best of these is about as fine a Cabernet as you'll ever get from Italy. These wines have an amazing silkiness of texture and concentration of flavors.

11. SAN GIUSTO A RENTENNANO (TUSCANY)

Italy's second-best Vin Santo; one of the better Merlots, "La Ricolma"; one of the best super-Tuscans; and an excellent base Chianti. This estate is a sure thing in Italian wine.

12. RONCHI DI CIALLA (FVG)

Two outstanding sweet wines: the Picolit and the Verduzzo. And two great reds: Schioppettino and the Refosco. These are difficult wines in that the grapes give results that aren't full of ripe fruit aromas and flavors, but rather rely on elegance and restraint. Don't forget the Ribolla Gialla, a little jewel absolutely perfect for everyday drinking, and an inexpensive one at that.

13. CERETTO (PIEDMONT)

Fantastic Barolo, exceptional Barbaresco, great Arneis. This producer offers some of Italy's most dependable wines, and at fair prices. The "Bricco Asili" Barbaresco, "Bricco Rocche Prapò," and "Bricco Rocche Bricco Rocche" Barolos from 1982 are marvelous. The estate also earns compliments for its fine artwork in the vineyards and its Michelin-starred restaurant in Alba.

14. CANTINA TERLANO (ALTO ADIGE)

Italy's longest-lived whites, with an admirable level of purity. You won't be disappointed with any bottle, though I prefer the Sauvignon and the Gewürztraminer. Don't forget to try the Lagrein "Porphyr": it might be a little more expensive than the same wine from other producers in the area, but you will find that it is worth every penny.

15. GRATTAMACCO/COLLE MASSARI (TUSCANY)

These are actually two estates run by the same person, but they embody well all that is great about Italian wine. The Grattamacco estate is one of Italy's most glorious, where many fine super-Tuscans have been made over the years, while the Colle Massari estate, located more inland in the up-and-coming Montecucco zone, has produced a series of exceptionally impressive wines in just three or four vintages. You simply cannot go wrong with anything that these two estates make, year after year.

16. TUA RITA (TUSCANY)
One of Italy's best Syrahs; one of the world's greatest Merlots, "Redigaffi"; a fine super-Tuscan, "Giusto di Notri"; the lovely, easy-to-drink "Rosso di Notri"; and a truly enjoyable aromatic white called Lodano. Again, you could pick blindfolded here!

17. LUCIANO SANDRONE (PIEDMONT)
Two of the best Barolos, a very fine Dolcetto, and a great Barbera. This producer never gets a vintage wrong. The "Cannubi Boschis" Barolo is what great Barolo is all about, a textbook example of rose petal and tar aromas with delciate spicy-mineral nuances, magically mouth-coating tannins, and a never-ending finish.

18. LIVIO FELLUGA (FRIULI VENEZIA GIULIA)
Millions of bottles and extremely high quality do not always go hand in hand, but they do here. This producer offers one of Italy's best sweet wines, the Picolit; one of the better reds, "Sossò"; a merlot-refsco-pignolo blend; and many other well-made, easy-to-drink wines that nobody will dislike, including an excellent Friulano and a very good Pinot Grigio.

19. CASTELLO DI AMA (TUSCANY)
Italy's first cult Merlot, the L'Apparita; two great single vineyard Chiantis that rank with the best wines in the world; and a very solid base or entry-level Chianti. It's hard to argue with a lineup of wines as good as this, though these wines do tend to be more expensive than most.

20. CANTINE DEL NOTAIO (BASILICATA)
One great Aglianico after another, and a very fine sweet wine: "L'Autentica." I may not be as devoted a fan of the sparkling wine "La Stipula" or the rosé "Rogito," but the other wines in the lineup are fine. What is most impressive about the red wines is that they never seem to have a bad vintage.

21. FERRARI (TRENTINO)
The oldest high-quality producer of sparkling wines in Italy, which has succeeded admirably in creating an

extremely good range of wines across the board. The pinnacle is represented by the "Giulio Ferrari Riserva del Fondatore," but the fact is that the Perlé line of sparklers is almost as good, and certainly very underrated. Congratulations to the Lunelli family, who have never wavered from the level of quality they have always set out as their mission.

22. LE MACCHIOLE (TUSCANY)
One of the world's great Merlots; a very fine Syrah; Italy's best Cabernet Franc; and an everyday red, the Bolgheri Rosso. All that and a beautiful estate on the Tuscan seaside.

23. PLANETA (SICILY)
This family has done so much to put Sicily on the wine map that one can only express thanks and admiration. And the wines aren't very expensive.

24. MASCIARELLI (ABRUZZO)
Two iconic wines—the Montepulciano "Villa Gemma" and the Montepulciano Marina Cvetic—would be enough, but the Cerasuolo (rosé) is also delicious, as is the new Trebbiano made at Castello di Semivicoli. Gianni Masciarelli was a larger-than-life personality, full of energy and love of his land, and his team is tops. The people here have, basically, never made a bad wine.

25. LA VIS E VALLE DI CEMBRA (TRENTINO)
There's something to be said for a producers' co-op that can make so many unbelievably good wines at such ridiculously low prices. Some of the limited-number bottlings, such as the Müller Thurgau "Vigna delle Forche" and the Pinot Nero "Vigna di Saosent," are really remarkable. No superstar wines, perhaps, but one great bottle after another, and at prices we can all afford.

25 BEST UP-AND-COMING WINE ESTATES AND PRODUCERS

The wine estates listed here aren't well known to the majority of wine lovers, as they have not been featured much in U.S. magazines or newspapers. In fact, many of them have not received much attention in Italian wine publications either. Yet each of them has produced at least three vintages of extremely fine wines, and each has shown clear signs of being on the road to greatness, or, at the very least, of making dependable, consistently good wines at fair prices. Other estates may have been around longer, but the listed wineries have had so many successes in the past few years that they have catapulted into the upper echelons of Italy's winemakers. I hope they will all continue to maintain their extraordinary high level of quality, but that isn't always easy to do when success beckons. More often than not, demand for a highly ranked or much coveted wine becomes such that the producer increases the number of bottles. By so doing, he can satisfy importers all over the world who are clamoring for bigger allocations, but the risk is, of course, that when production is increased the wine may no longer be as good. For example, the easiest way to increase production is simply to plant new vines: however, young vines do not produce wine of the same quality as older vines (which have roots that dig much deeper and are able to reach more mineral parts of the subsoil). Making 5,000 bottles from 30-year-old vines and making 30,000 from eight-year-old vines are not at all the same thing. We'll have to keep our fingers crossed.

1. LO TRIOLET—MARCO MARTIN (VALLE D'AOSTA)

I was the first in Italy to name Marco Martin for a major wine award (in 2006 he won the "Rising Star" award in a guide on Italy's best wines that I write in Italy), and he remains to this day one of my best discoveries. There is no question in my mind that Martin is one of Italy's 10 or 12 most talented winemakers, as just about any wine he chooses to make is at least excellent, often the best of its category. He is very likable, down-to-earth, and a pleasure to hang around with. Come here for Italy's best Pinot Grigios (nobody makes two as good as his), a fantastic sweet wine ("Mistigri"), a late-harvest Pinot Grigio, a great red ("Coteau Barrage," a syrah-fumin blend), and more.

2. KÖFERERHOF (ALTO ADIGE)

Günther Kerschbaumer is another amazingly talented young man who excels with just about every grape variety. Like Marco Martin, he's not really an unknown anymore, at least in Italy; but the public at large still does not know enough about him or his wines. His is a name to mention in the same company as Gaja, Soldera, and Giacosa—the best of the best. Anyone who thinks Müller-Thurgau and sylvaner cannot give great wines needs to come here and taste for himself.

3. CUPANO (TUSCANY)

This is the single best up-and-coming producer of Brunello di Montalcino today. The Brunello has been outstanding for a number of vintages, and even in the disastrous, rain-plagued, cold 2002 it was head and shoulders above 99% of Montalcino's production. The organically farmed vines are bordering on the biodynamic, and this may have something to do with the success being achieved by Lionel Cousin and his wife. Their love of nature has now led them to buy two horses to do some of the work in the vineyard. The Rosso di Montalcino and the "Ombrone" super-Tuscan are also spectacular. The only unfortunate thing is the rather steep price of the Brunello, but the Cousins point out that the French have no trouble asking high prices for their wines, and they feel Brunello is not inferior to the best of France.

4. FEUDO MONTONI (SICILY)

The owner, Fabio Sireci, has turned this estate—which used to sell grapes to the big historic estates of the area—into one of Italy's most interesting wine producers. Only three wines are made, but they are stellar in their respective genres. The entry-level Nero d'Avola is a joy to drink; the richer Selezione Speciale Vrucara will repay cellaring handsomely.

5. MARCO CARPINETI (LAZIO)

The little town of Cori would hardly have attracted the attention it has of late, at least in some Italian circles, if not for the exceptionally high quality and the exceptionally low prices of the white and sweet wines made by Marco Carpineti. Carpineti works with his own organically grown grapes—mostly almost extinct varieties, such as greco giallo and greco moro; or long-forgotten ones, such as bellone, that even most Italian wine writers know nothing about. I believe that "Il Moro" (made from greco giallo and greco moro) and "Collesanti" (made from bellone) are two of Italy's best 100 white wines, and that the very sweet "Ludum" (from late-harvest bellone grapes) is one of the top 10 dessert wines.

6. TENUTA DELLE TERRE NERE (SICILY)

There isn't bad wine made here, and some of the wines are spectacular. The Etna Bianco is a steal, given its intense flavor and its low price. One red is better than the next, and all the reds are a testament to what the nerello mascalese grape can produce. The Rosato eschews residual sugar and juicy fruitiness, but is a marvel of complexity.

7. DETTORI (SARDINIA)

This is already one of the better Italian estates, doing intense work with native grape varieties such as monica and pascale. Before Alessandro Dettori's hard work, finding a 100% pure Pascale bottling was not easy; such wine was bottled only by local people for their own private consumption. The house style here is characterized by high alcohol and extra ripeness, but lately I find that Alessandro has been scaling back the power, alcohol, and residual sugar in all his wines (though his reds are all a touch sweet). A welcome step, I may add. This producer has everything to be one of Italy's true stars.

8. BASTIANICH (FRIULI VENEZIA GIULIA)

Just about any wine from this estate is just fine, and a sure bet. The estate hit the ground running with its first vintage of Vespa, a thing of beauty, and an amazing result for a first effort. The Tocai "Plus" is a mesmerizingly good wine, and the reds also have a lot of character. The "Calabrone" especially looks as if it will be something special when the vines age. Bastianich has obviously found a recipe for success.

9. MAMETE PREVOSTINI (LOMBARDY)

This venerable estate has been making fine wine for 80 years and counting, but it has been discovered only recently. A great Sfursat and many other fine wines are reason enough to visit the estate; do not forget to try the family's on-site restaurant as well, for some authentic local food.

10. ROCCOLO GRASSI (VENETO)

When the vintage is right, this is one of the best addresses in Amarone. When the vintage isn't so kind, tougher grape selection and exclusion are necessary to rise into the upper tier of Italy's wine producers.

11. CANTINA SANT'AGATA (PIEDMONT)

Franco Cavallaro is a volcano, full of energy and always on the move. He also is an adamant believer in the quality of the *terroir* at Castagnole Monferrato, where the wonderful Ruché, a wine quite unlike any other in Italy, is made. Just about any wine from this producer is well made and fairly priced.

12. GRITTI (UMBRIA)

Many different wines are produced here, but what is very interesting is that the estate does many different microvinifications in order to study each single grape variety with respect to each single terroir. When you walk through the cellar, you can try wines from two or three different Sangiovese, Merlot, Cabernet Franc, Syrah, and more. Best of all, you'll find one of Italy's better pure Petit

Verdots, and Italy's best pure Malvasia Nera. The latter grape, originally from Puglia, was once more common in central Italy than it is today, and in fact was often used as part of the Chianti blend (along with the better-known canaiolo nero, for example). It is to Gritti's credit that it has stuck with an almost forgotten grape, and this patience has been rewarded with an immensely pleasant, easy-drinking wine quite unlike most other central Italian reds. As Gritti is an estate that is still growing, many of the single barrel lots I mentioned are eventually blended and bottled as a single wine, but the Malvasia Nera is bottled on its own.

13. BRUNNENHOF MAZZON (ALTO ADIGE)

I would never have guessed that a Gewürztraminer with obvious oaky touches would have been my cup of tea, or wine, but I have to admit that this is a remarkably successful wine. The Pinot Nero "Mazzon" is always a Riserva wine, as it ages an extra year in wood prior to release, and it is excellent. This is especially true in the better vintages, as pinot nero, a notoriously difficult grape, suffers more than most from cool weather and rain. A very good estate, which I'm willing to bet will get even better.

14. LA CROTTA DI VEGNERON (VALLE D'AOSTA)

A cooperative, located in Chambave, famous for many very fine wines and especially some highly interesting sweet ones, such as the Malvoisie Fletri and the Passito Muscat. It was founded in 1980 with only 25 members but now has more than 120, a sure sign of growth and of doing things right. After trying all of its wines, make sure to stop at its simple restaurant for an inexpensive but very flavorful meal.

15. SERTOLI SALIS (LOMBARDY)

This family has been present in the area for centuries and has long dabbled in wine making. However, there has lately been a resurgence of interest in making fine wines, and the quality is improving notably. The Sforzato Canua is already among the better examples, and the Valtellina Superiore wines are possibly even better at present, given their lower prices.

16. CAVE DES ONZES COMMUNES (VALLE D'AOSTA)

A simply exhilarating lineup of great little white wines— "little" in the sense of a light frame and a low cost per bottle. Yet there is a lot of flavor and elegance in each drop: come here for well-above-average Müller Thurgau, Pinot Grigio, Petite Arvine, and even Pinot Nero. No blockbusters, but trust me: sometimes good things really do come in small packages.

17. FATTORIA DI MAGLIANO (TUSCANY)
Lovely, soft, creamy rich red wines that deserve to be better known. The "Poggio Bestiale" is a Bordeaux blend of uncommon drinkability. The Morellino di Scansano may well be the best of them all; if not, it's in the top three.

18. MAURO MOLINO (PIEDMONT)
Lovely Barolos from different, very good-quality single vineyards, among which the higher-up Gallinotto is a sure thing in these increasingly hot vintages. The grace and refinement of these wines are not very common in some modern-day Barolos, which are too much iron fist and too little velvet glove.

19. ISABELLA MOTTURA (LAZIO)
The "Amatis," a 100% montepulciano (locally called violone), is rich and creamy and benefits from the Riccardo Cottarella touch; among the wines that he helps fashion but that are not yet well known to the majority of wine lovers, this is perhaps his most successful. It's a big, strapping, burly wine that somehow—very creditably—doesn't cause palate fatigue after the first couple of sips. I also love the charm of the "Siren," a sangiovese-cabernet blend.

20. QUINTODECIMO (CAMPANIA)
There is quite a bit of talent here; the star winemaker Luigi Moio wants to create a state-of-the-art winery in his native Campania. Extremely fine wines, including Greco, Fiano, and Falanghina among the whites, and a stellar Aglianico. This may well be *the* up-and-coming estate in Italy. Next year will see the launch of brand-new, super-expensive single-vineyard Taurasi.

21. PRODUTTORI VALLE ISARCO (ALTO ADIGE)
It seems really strange, and a little unfortunate to me, that one of Italy's very best and most dependable wine producers is not imported into the United States. Moreover, the wines made here are amazingly inexpensive and therefore absolutely great restaurant buys; so it remains hard to fathom why these wines do not enjoy better distribution abroad. Perhaps the Germanic-sounding grape varieties have something to do with it, but who knows, really? The fact remains that the Sylvaner and Kerner are two of Italy's best wines, and the Riesling "Aristos" are often almost as good, depending on the vintage. Don't miss out on them during your next trip to Italy.

22. PACHERHOF (ALTO ADIGE)

The usual lineup of aromatic wines typical of Alto Adige, all done in a slightly alcoholic but immensely satisfying style. Though the Sylvaner is excellent, the Kerner is the wine to go after—but I'm being picky here: the truth is that you won't be disappointed with any of the wines of Andrea Huber.

23. FERRUCCIO CARLOTTO (ALTO ADIGE)

Anyone who can produce a high-quality Pinot Nero deserves our encouragement. Pinot nero is a finicky, difficult grape to grow and to make wine from: more often than not, one fails to capture its elusive magic in the bottle. The "Filari di Mazzon" bottling by Carlotto is one of Italy's three best Pinot Neros, made from grapes grown in the famous Mazzon vineyard—which I have already gone on record as considering Italy's best site for this variety. This wine seems to be getting better all the time. Perhaps it is a little chunky and less refined than it could be, but I have no doubt that it will gain in breeding and refinement as the vines age.

24. SUAVIA (VENETO)

This Soave producer has been around for some time, and the name is not completely unknown to many people. What is new, however, is that the wines have improved remarkably over the past few years: Suavia can now be considered as one of Soave's better producers. Besides the base Soave, you can choose between the two top *crus*: the unoaked Monte Carbonare Soave and the oaked Le Rive bottling. Both are more than just fine.

25. CANTINA SANT'ANDREA (LAZIO)

I never cease to be amazed at the extremely enjoyable wines made by this estate, located at the seaside an hour south of Rome. White or red, dry or sweet, wine does not seem to hold many secrets for the owners—the Pandolfo family—and they rarely release anything that isn't at least above average, at prices that are hard to beat.

A CAN'T-MISS LIST OF MORE VERY FINE REGIONAL WINES FROM ITALY

There are countless high-quality wine estates in Italy, and so it follows that there is an almost endless number of fine wines available for you to choose from. To give readers a larger list of fine Italian wines, I include here various "can't-miss" wines, divided into categories (red, white, sparkling, rosé, and sweet). Though not included in the previous rankings and "Best" lists, these are nonetheless super wines and are the top of the heap in their respective categories. I hope you will give them a try and enjoy them as much as I do. The names on the following list, along with those already mentioned in this guide, will allow readers to pick one of Italy's top bottles for any single wine, from Aleatico to Zibibbo.

Note that the sparkling wines are further subdivided into sparkling dry, off-dry, and sweet. This is because some regions of Italy are associated particularly with sweet sparklers (as in the case of Piedmont and Moscato d'Asti), or with off-dry sparkling wines (such as Veneto and Prosecco). All the wines in this list are common and important in Italy: therefore, it would be doing the reader a disservice not to include them. If one or more categories are missing for some regions, that is because those types of wine are not commonly made there or aren't particularly worthwhile. For example, there are sparkling wines made in Lazio, but people who do not get to try them are not missing anything.

Valle d'Aosta

WHITE: Petite Arvine Château Feuillet, Blanc de Morgex et La Salle Albert Vevey (prié blanc)

RED: Fumin Vigne la Tour les Crêtes, Cornalin Institut Agricole Régional, Petit Rouge Renato Anselmet

SWEET: Malvoisie Flétri la Crotte de Vegneron (malvoisie or pinot grigio)

SPARKLING: Extra Dry "Fripon" Cave du Vin Blanc (prié blanc)

Liguria

WHITE: Cinque Terre Bisson (albarola, bosco), "Majoa" Buranco (albarola, bosco)

RED: Ormeasco di Pornassio "Le Braje"-Lupi (dolcetto)

SWEET: Sciacchetrà de Batté (bosco, albarola)

Lombardy

WHITE: Pinot Grigio Monsuppello, Pinot Grigio Raccolta Tardiva Ca' di Frara, Riesling Albani

RED: Sforzato di Valtellina "Albareda" Mamete Prevostini (nebbiolo); Bonarda Pignolo "Possessione del Console" Fratelli Agnes

SWEET: Moscato di Scanzo "Doge" La Brugherata

SPARKLING: Franciacorta Ricci Curbastro (chardonnay, pinot nero, pinot bianco)

Piedmont

WHITE: Gavi di Gavi "Etichetta Nera" La Scolca (cortese); "Martin" Franco M. Martinetti (timorasso), Derthona "Costa del Vento" Walter Massa (timorasso); Langhe Bianco G. D.Vajra (riesling)

RED: Barolo "Rocche" Renato Ratti (nebbiolo), Barolo Mariondino Parusso (nebbiolo), Barbera d'Alba "Funtanì" Monfalletto, Barbera Bricco della Bigotta Braida, Barbaresco Vanotu Pellissero (nebbiolo)

SWEET: "Solativo" Ferrando (erbaluce), Brachetto "Pian dei Sogni" Forteto della Luja (brachetto)

SPARKLING (DRY): Riserva Extra Brut Metodo Classico Deltetto (pinot nero, chardonnay), Brut Metodo Classico Bruno Giacosa (pinot nero), Brut Riserva Vintage Contratto (pinot nero, chardonnay).

SPARKLING (SWEET): Asti "La Selvatica" Caudrina (moscato bianco), "Clarté" Elio Perrone (moscato bianco)

Trentino

WHITE: Müller Thurgau "Vigna delle Forche" Cantina La Vis e Valle di Cembra; Nosiola Cesconi; Pinot Grigio Bolognani, Manzoni Bianco Fanti (incrocio Manzoni), Müller Thurgau Graziano Fontana

RED: Rosso Fayé Pojer e Sandri (cabernet sauvignon, merlot, lagrein, others); "Granato" Foradori (teroldego), Marzemino Bossi Fredrigotti

SWEET: Trentino Vino Santo Giovanni Poli; Trentino Vino Santo Pisoni (nosiola)

SPARKLING: Trento Brut Talento "Antares" Cantina Toblino (chardonnay), Trento "Tridentum" Cesarini Sforza (chardonnay, pinot nero); Trento Brut Metodo Classico Alte Masi Riserva "Graal" (chardonnay)

Alto Adige

WHITE: Gewürztraminer "Baron Salvadori" Produttori Nalles Magré; Sylvaner Manni Nossing; Sylvaner Strasserhof; Kerner Köfererhof, Kerner Produttori Valle Isarco

RED: Lagrein "Porphyr" Produttori Terlano; "Iugum"

Dipoli (merlot, cabernet sauvignon); Cabernet "Lafoa" Produttori Colterenzio (cabernet sauvignon)

SWEET: "MerVin" Vendemmia Tardiva Produttori Burggräfler (pinot bianco, chardonnay, sauvignon); Passito "Serenade" Castel Giovannelli Produttori Caldaro (moscato giallo); Passito "Nectaris" Produttori Valle Isarco

SPARKLING: Extra Brut Riserva Aruna Vivaldi (chardonnay, pinot nero)

Friuli Venezia Giulia

WHITE: Pinot Grigio Riserva Marco Felluga, "Ronco delle Acacie" Le Vigne di Zamò (chardonnay, tocai), "Broy" Collavini (chardonnay, tocai, sauvignon), Pinot Grigio "Amplius" Paolino Comelli

RED: Schioppettino Petrussa, Schioppettino Vigna Petrussa, Pignolo Dorigo, Pignolo Moschioni

SWEET: Picolit Meroi, Picolit Ermacora, "Noans" La Tunella (sauvignon, riesling, gewürztraminer), Cratis Scubla (verduzzo), Verduzzo Valchiarò.

Veneto

WHITE: Soave "Alzari" Coffele (garganega, trebbiano di Soave); Soave Classico "Staforte" Fratelli Prà, Bianco "Amedeo" La Prendina–Cavalchina (garganega, trebbiano, others), Soave Classico "Le Rive" Suavia (garganega)

RED: Amarone della Valpolicella "Campolongo di Torbe" Masi (corvina, corvinone, others), Amarone della Valpolicella "Le Vigne Ca' del Pipa" Michele Castellani (corvina, corvinone, others), Amarone della Valpolicella "Campo dei Gigli" Tenuta Sant'Antonio (corvina, corvinone, others)

SWEET: Recioto della Valpolicella "TB" Tommaso Bussola (corvina, corvinone, others), Recioto della Valpolicella "La Roggia" Fratelli Speri (corvina, corvinone, others)

SPARKLING (DRY): Prosecco di Valdobbiadene Brut Frozza

SPARKLING (SLIGHTLY SWEET): Prosecco di Valdobbiadene Extra Dry "Rù" Fratelli Bortolin

SPARKLING (SWEET): Prosecco di Valdobbiadene Cartizze Bisol

Emilia-Romagna

WHITE: "Callas" Monte delle Vigne (malvasia di Candia aromatica), Trebbiano Romagnolo "Rio" Tre Monti, "Ageno" La Stoppa (malvasia di Candia, ortrugo, trebbiano)

RED: Sangiovese di Romagna Riserva "Thea" Tre Monti, "Moro del Moro" Paola Rinaldini (lambrusco, ancellotta)

SWEET: Albana Passito "Arrocco" Fattoria Zerbina; Vin Santo di Vigoleno Alberto Lusignani (malvasia, others), Pignoletto Passito Floriano Cinti

SPARKLING: Lambrusco Reggiano Frizzante Venturini Baldini, Extra Dry "Terre Verdiane" Ceci (pinot nero, malvasia), Brut Metodo Classico "Perlage" Cantina Valtidone (pinot nero, chardonnay)

Tuscany

WHITE: Vernaccia di San Gimignano Riserva La Lastra, Vernaccia di San Gimignano Riserva "Isabella" San Quirico, Vernaccia di San Gimignano "Hydra" Il Palagione, Grattamacco Bianco (vermentino)

RED: Chianti Rufina Colognole (sangiovese), Montescudaio Rosso La Regola (cabernet franc, merlot), Montevertine Rosso Montevertine (sangiovese, canaiolo, colorino), Chianti Rufina Grignano (sangiovese), "Perbruno" I Giusti e Zanza (syrah), "Camartina" Querciabella (sangiovese, cabernet sauvignon)

SWEET: Vin Santo Avignonesi (trebbiano toscano e malvasia bianca di toscana); Vin Santo Rocca di Montegrossi (malvasia), Vin Santo del Chianti Classico Castello di Volpaia (malvasia, others)

Marche

WHITE: Verdicchio dei Castelli di Jesi "Serra Fiorese" Garofoli, Verdicchio dei Castelli di Jesi "Utopia" Montecappone, Verdicchio dei Castelli di Jesi Riserva Vigna delle Oche Crognaleti–San Lorenzo, Verdicchio di Matelica "Mirum" La Monacesca, Falerio dei Colli Ascolani Cocci Grifoni

RED: Lacrima di Morro d'Alba Vecchie Vigne "Luigino" Giusti (lacrima), Rosso Conero "Grosso Agontano" Garofoli (montepulciano), "Cùmaro" Umani Ronchi (sangiovese, others), Vernaccia di Serrapetrona Robbione Colli di Serrapetrona (vernaccia nera), "Kurni" Oasi degli Angeli (montepulciano)

SWEET: Verdicchio dei Castelli di Jesi Passito "Tordiruta" Terre Cortesi Moncaro, "Arkezia" Muffo di San Sisto Fazi Battaglia (verdicchio), Vernaccia di Serrapetrona Dolce Alberto Quacquarini (vernaccia nera)

Umbria

WHITE: Orvieto Classico "Campo del Guardiano" Palazzone (procanico, malvasia bianca, others); Orvieto "Bellori" Custodi (procanico, malvasia bianca, others); "Conte della Vipera" Castello della Sala (sauvignon), Bianco Torgiano "Il Pino" Lungarotti (trebbiano, grechetto)

RED: Sagrantino di Montefalco "Colleallodole" Antano Milziade; Sagrantino Rocca di Fabbri

SWEET: Vendemmia Tardiva La Palazzola (sauvignon, gewürztraminer, grechetto, others), Orvieto Classico "Calcaia" Barberani (procanico, malvasia bianca, others); Sagrantino Passito Ruggeri

Lazio

WHITE: Frascati "Villa dei Preti" Villa Simone (trebbiano toscano, malvasia puntinata, others); "Collesanti" Marco Carpineti (Bellone); Montecompatri "Virtù Romane" Tenuta Le Quinte (malvasia puntinata, trebbiano giallo, others), Grechetto "Poggio della Costa" Sergio Mottura

RED: Cesanese del Piglio "Torre del Piano" Casale della Ioria; Cesanese di Olevano Romano "Silene" Ciolli

SWEET: "Muffa Nobile" Castel de Paolis (sauvignon, semillon, muscadelle); Moscato di Terracina "Capitolium" Cantina Sant'Andrea; "Aphrodisium" Casale del Giglio (petit manseng, viognier, greco, others), "Ludum" Marco Carpineti (bellone)

Abruzzo e Molise

WHITE: Trebbiano d'Abruzzo Castelo di Semivicoli Masciarelli; Trebbiano d'Abruzzo "Fonte Cupa" Camillo Montori

RED: Montepulciano d'Abruzzo Valentini; Montepulciano d'Abruzzo "Toni" Cataldi Madonna

SWEET RED: Passito "Clematis" Zaccagnini (montepulciano)

Campania

WHITE: Falanghina Cantina del Taburno; "Sogno di Rivolta" La Rivolta (falanghina, fiano, greco); Fiano di

Avellino "Radici" Mastroberardino; Furore Bianco
Marisa Cuomo (fenile, others)

RED: Taurasi "Fatica Contadina" Terredora (aglianico);
Pallagrello Nero Vestini Campagnano; "Zero" De
Conciliis (aglianico)

Basilicata

WHITE: "D'Avalos" Cantina di Venosa (malvasia di
Basilicata)

RED: Aglianico del Vulture "Roinos" Eubea; Aglianico del
Vulture "Il Sigillo" Cantine del Notaio; Aglianico del
Vulture "Basilisco" Basilisco; Aglianico del Vulture
"Macarico" Macarico

SWEET: L'Autentica Cantine del Notaio (moscato bianco/
malvasia di Basilicata)

Puglia

WHITE: Bombino Bianco "Catapanus" D'Alfonso del
Sordo; Fiano Minutolo "Rampone" I Pastini–Livio
Carparelli; "Pietrabianca" Tormaresca (chardonnay)

RED: Primitivo di Manduria Attanasio (primitivo);
"Vandalo" Tenuta Cocevola (nero di Troia); Primitivo
di Manduria "Es" Gianfranco Fino

Calabria

WHITE: Cirò Bianco Librandi (greco bianco); Greco Statti
(greco bianco)

RED: "Polpicello" Odoardi (gaglioppo, magliocco, others);
Cirò Rosso "Colli del Mancuso" Ippolito (gaglioppo,
others)

SWEET: "Locride" Stelitano (mantonico); Moscato Passito
(Feudi di Sanseverino)

Sicily

WHITE: Etna Bianco "Pietramarina" Benanti (carricante);
"Polena" Donnafugata (viognier); Caricante Calabretta

RED: "Nerobufaleffj" Gulfi (nero d'Avola); "Grammonte"
Cottanera (merlot); Nero Sanloré Gulfi (nero d'Avola);
Frappato Valle dell'Acate; "Sédara" Donnafugata (nero
d'Avola); Nero d'Avola Feudo Montoni

SWEET: Passito di Pantelleria Ferrandes (muscat of
Alexandria); Malvasia delle Lipari Fenech; "Dolce"
Passopisciaro (sauvignon, others)

Sardinia

WHITE: "Salnico" Fratelli Pala (nuragus); Capichera
Vendemmia Tardiva (Vermentino), "Ruinas" Andrea
Depperu (vermentino), "Funtanaliras" Vermentino di
Gallura Cantina del Vermentino, "Buio Buio
Barricato" Mesa (carignano)

RED: Carignano "Rocche Rubia" Riserva Cantina Santadi
(carignano), "Biddas" Feudi della Medusa (cannonau,
cagnulari, others)

SWEET/AFTER DINNER: "Latinia" Cantina Santadi
(nasco); "Dirad" Ferruccio Deiana (nasco, others);
"Assoluto" Fratelli Pala (nasco, vermentino)

The Wines of Italy

ABOUT THE WINES
OF ITALY

> ## ITALIAN WINE NUMBERS:
>
> - 679,579 hectares (roughly 1.68 million acres) under vine in Italy
> - More than 770,000 wine estates
> - Italy produces roughly 20% of the world's wine, and 33% of the wine from the European Community
> - Italy's wine production is divided into roughly 60% red wines and 40% white wines
> - 316 DOC wines, 35 DOCG wines, 188 IGT wines
> - Italian wine production is a business generating 9.5 billion euros (roughly $14 billion) and is one of the country's most important industries, along with tourism and fashion
> - The sales and exports of Italian wine are booming: a 7.8% increase in export value in 2007 for a net worth of 3.5 billion euros (roughly $5 billion)
> - 19 million hectoliters of wine produced, of which 2.5 million are exported into the United States alone (an 8% increase from 2006)
> - The export of Italian wine into the United States has a net worth of almost 830 million euros (almost $1.3 billion)

IT MAY SURPRISE YOU TO LEARN THAT high-quality wine in Italy is a relatively recent phenomenon. During the three centuries when France became one of Europe's strongest nations, building an empire and at the same time a high-quality, reputable wine industry, Italy was nowhere near such efficiency (some might say that this is still true today). In France, producers were studying and selecting not just the best grape varietals, but the best clones and subvarieties of each, and then matching them to the soils most suited to them; but wine in Italy remained typically a family affair. The only goals of Italy's mostly small producers were local markets, survival even. Unlike France, Italy became a nation only recently, in 1870. Prior to that, the country was made up, for the most part, of feudal states, more or less always at war with each other. Clearly, if the countryside was a battleground for various armies—those of Florence and Milan, or Florence and Siena, as well as those from France, Spain, and the German states—there was little hope for any good-quality agriculture. At the same time, the ease with which grapes ripen in Italy's sunny climate, and the sheer abundance of wine, led Italians to take the noble beverage for granted. Indeed, foreign travelers to Italy often remarked how little care went into viticulture and wine making. One French merchant, André Jullien, wrote in the 1800s that the Italians didn't try very hard in the vineyards; they were quite content to do the minimum necessary. The resulting wines were often faulty and traveled poorly. An important consequence of these lackluster efforts was that Italian wines had no strong foreign markets until quite recently, and the absence of foreign markets meant that there was little incentive to upgrade the overall quality of the product. A quite different situation existed in France: the French wines were sold to wealthy and knowledgeable Dutch as well as English and French customers who demanded the best, keeping the producers on their toes.

Another aspect of Italian life that contributed to this sorry enological production was the system of *mezzadria,* or sharecropping, which did not end until the 1960s. During the centuries of *mezzadria,* those who lived on and worked the land had to turn over at least half of their produce to the owner, as rent. Most often, then, the farmer was allowed to keep only a small percentage of what he grew. Furthermore, a parcel of land had to produce everything needed by those who lived on it, and so agriculture was promiscuous, with vines growing alongside wheat, olive trees, and other plants, and even livestock and other farm animals. Clearly, with regard to ripening, vines growing in the silvery shadows cast by olive trees were at a disadvantage compared with vines that grew in full sunlight. Overproduction was common in the old days: in a system such as *mezzadria*, whereby one could keep only a portion of the total produced, the more made, the better. Therefore, there was never any real interest in making high-quality wine. (A cardinal rule of wine making is that the less wine you make, the better it usually is, as it's less dilute.)

Italian wine was often a consequence not just of poor-quality grapes but also of poor wine making techniques. Few farmers could go to school, let alone wine making school. Even famous wines such as Barolo and Barbaresco were often sweet and fizzy. This sorry state of affairs puzzled the Marchesa Falletti of Barolo, a noblewoman who was used to drinking the best wines of France; she couldn't fathom why her Barolo was not more like the great wines across the border. She resolved to consult an expert French winemaker, Louis Oudart, to figure out where the trouble lay; Oudart quickly rectified problems such as poor cellar hygiene, dirty barrels, and stuck fermentations. Thus one of the great modern-day wines of Italy owes its change in fortune to the intuition and determination of a woman—and this is about as Italian a story as any, given the important role that strong women have had in shaping the country.

Prior to the 1970s, wine making was in Italy somewhat haphazard. When one tasted an Italian wine as recently as about 1970, even a wine made from a fantastic variety such as nebbiolo or aglianico, it was easy to discern an underlying potential, but in reality Italy's supposedly great wines were often much less than they ought to have been. This situation began to change in the late 1960s, thanks mainly to the energy of a new, young generation of winemakers who began traveling around the world, visiting other wine making areas, tasting different wines, and learning new techniques and viticultural practices. Attention was given to renewing old, outdated, often damaged cellar equipment (how many potentially great Italian red wines of the 1950s and 1960s were ruined by dirty old barrels is anyone's guess). Today many cellars are loaded with the latest technology, and some people might argue that in the twenty-first century, Italian producers are placing too much emphasis on new buildings designed by famous architects, and on modern machinery, rather than studying rootstocks, grape clones, and soil types. On the heels of better older producers such as Bartolo Mascarello, Beppe Colla, Giovanni

Conterno, Aldo Conterno, and Mastroberardino, the 1970s and early 1980s saw the emergence of now famous names such as Angelo Gaja, Giacomo Bologna, Livio Felluga, Mario Schiopetto, Silvio Jermann, Paolo De Marchi, Giuseppe Mazzocolin, Sergio Manetti, Giovanni Manetti (no relation), and others. These led the way in a new phase of making high-quality, even faultless wines. Thanks to them and other fine producers, Italian red wines began to improve greatly as did white wines soon thereafter.

Italian winemakers still face problems, and complicated labeling is certainly one of them. Colorful labels often show three or four different names, none of which can be clearly identified as the important one. Furthermore, there is often little information about the grape used, or what an obscure grape variety (especially one obscure to foreigners) is all about, or if any oak aging was involved. Instead, the back label might evoke the owner's grandfather's mule cart, or nighttime harvests, and give no other really useful information. Then the producers wonder why shoppers move past the rows of Carignano, Pallagrello, and Tocai and opt for more familiar Merlot and Zinfandel.

Wine: An Integral Part of la Dolce Vita and the Italian Lifestyle

There is no doubt that in Italy wine is an integral part of everyday life, to an extent that may not be readily appreciated by foreigners. Undeniably, the welcoming attitude of Italian families toward wine goes a long way in explaining the healthy rapport most Italians have with it. Consider the statistics. In Europe the average age at which people first taste alcohol is quite low: 14. But in Italy the age is lower still, the lowest in Europe: 12.2 years. Yet Italy has little of the juvenile alcoholism that many Anglo-Saxon countries have. One reason is that young people grow up regularly having wine at the table; another is that there are few social taboos in Italy worse than getting drunk in public. Although generalizations are tricky, it is true that getting drunk in public is the best way to get kicked out of any milieu that counts in Italy, even among teenagers—at least until recently.

One might argue that Italians' attachment to wine, and the importance they give it, is a little excessive. True, perhaps: but could it be otherwise in a country so steeped in vinous glory? The popularity of wine in Italy began in about the seventh century BC, and it has always colored everyday events, both big and small. As early as 200 BC, vineyards were found extensively in and all around Rome, as Cato and Strabonius, two very famous Roman men of letters (among many others), accurately inform us. Wine was so prevalent in the Roman empire that the city of Rome had two seaports, one of which, the *portus vinarius*, was entirely dedicated to wine! There was also a specific area of the city, the *forum vinarium*, where wine was sold and wine vendors, buyers, and enthusiasts could meet. Pompeii, a small and very affluent town, had at least 200 wine bars in its heyday, so you can imagine that imperial Rome must have been a wine heaven. Also, most of the best wines of antiquity came from within the boundaries of what is now Italy. The best of all was said to be Falernum, a wine made not far from Rome. Falernum's praises were sung by many famous poets, including Horace, who is known to have enjoyed 20-year-old and even 100-year-old examples of it. Livia, the wife of Emperor Augustus, was known to like Pucino and Retico, wines made in what is now Veneto. Pliny, a born cataloger if there was ever one, rated wines (along with just about anything else) in order of quality, and this was long before the famous 1855 Bordeaux classification. Later, many popes and princes were wine fanatics: in particular, Pope Paul III, of the powerful Farnese family, was the first to own an extremely well stocked cellar and the first to have his own permanent sommelier. Another pope, Gregorius XVI, enjoyed wine so much that the Roman populace nicknamed him "Drinking Gregory" and joked that when he died and went to heaven he mistakenly brought along the keys to his cellar instead of those to Saint Peter's gate! The presence and importance of wine in the everyday lives of Italians has continued into modern times. Italy's first prime minister was Bettino Ricasoli, whose main claim to fame for all wine lovers is not his political legacy but that he was the inventor of modern-day Chianti. (You realize that we have our priorities straight.) Another prime minister, Camillo Benso, conte di Cavour, was the owner of a fine Barolo-producing estate, Castello di Grinzane Cavour; and although affairs of state were undoubtedly close to his heart, he still found time to call in a French enologist to help improve his red wine. Italian youngsters study these historical figures in school and rapidly become aware of the role of wine in their society throughout history.

Until recently, it was almost unheard of in Italy to sit down at the lunch or dinner table without wine being present; and some well-meaning friends of mine have been known to go looking for a good "breakfast wine" or two. In fact, the almost constant presence of wine on the Italian dining table has enabled most young Italians to become skilled at matching food and wine fairly early in life: most Italian teenagers, though they may not be experts, already know more than the basics of "white wine with fish" and "full-bodied reds with big meat dishes." Also, because wine and food have always gone hand in hand for Italians, thin, light, high-acid wines are greatly in favor. Foreigners are always puzzled by this, but when Italians are enjoying delicately pan-roasted branzino (Mediterranean sea bass) or fried calamari, the last thing they want to drink is an overoaked, butterscotchy–passion fruit cocktail of a Chardonnay that has about 14.5 degrees of alcohol—a true recipe for a disastrous dinner.

There are many other examples of wine's traditional presence in the everyday life of Italy. The rest of the world has only recently become aware of and begun paying attention to the possible health benefits of moderate daily wine consumption; but the health benefits of wine have long been known, at least intuitively or anecdotally, in Italy and other parts of Europe. In ancient times wine was the beverage of choice, if for no other reason than that its alcohol content made it a far safer drink than the water available then. The Carthaginians, after a victorious but difficult battle against the Romans, decided to cure horses and soldiers alike with the local red wine. In modern times, in the 1930s and 1940s, it was commonplace in Friuli to give young ladies a small glass of Terrano, a local wine, to ward off anemia. Today we know that Terrano is one of the wines richest in resveratrol, an all-important antioxidant that is believed to play a role in many of wine's beneficial effects on the human body. After all, Italy is the country that coined the phrase "A glass of wine a day keeps the doctor away."

Italian Wine Law and Wine Categories

The European Union requires all wines produced in Europe to fall within one of two broad categories: "table wine" (*vino da tavola*) and "quality wine" (*vino di qualità*).

Italy's wines are now divided into four basic categories, part of a pyramidal system of quality. The base of the pyramid is made up of the lowly table wine, *vino da tavola*, for which few rules and regulations are set forth. For example, these wines do not need a vintage date, so you are on your own in this regard. The grapes themselves do not have to come from a specific place, and perhaps it's better *not* to know where some of the grapes used for these wines come from.

Next is *Indicazione Geografica Tipica* (IGT), a relatively new category. Here there are some regulations that must be followed. For example, that 80% of the grapes used to make a wine have to come from the area in which the wine is made, and the wine has to have more than a passing resemblance to wines historically made in that area (hence the adjective *tipico*, "typical"). This broad category contains many very fine wines and is one that astute, cash-conscious wine lovers ought to take a good look at. On the one hand, allowing producers more leeway in the grape varieties they can use gives more creative types greater freedom to experiment. On the other hand, it can also be a catchall category in which producers turn out many wines made up of excess grapes they didn't want or couldn't sell or use to make cheap jug wine.

The next two categories are Italy's most famous: *Denominazione di Origine Controllata* (DOC) and *Denominazione di Origine Controllata e Garantita* (DOCG). The DOC was instituted in 1963, as an equivalent of the *Appellation d'Origine Contrôllée* (AOC) in France, after which it was modeled. The DOC refers to a specific wine production zone. All the wines made within that area, in order to have DOC on the label, must be produced following a very detailed, even stringent (some say too stringent) set of requirements for origin of grapes, crop level, alcohol degree, and length of time in wood. The DOCG, although the G stands for *garantita*, "guaranteed," does not, as you might read elsewhere, guarantee anything at all; and this term does not mean that these are Italy's best wines. These wines are tasted on two different occasions (rather than once, as per the DOC wines) by a government panel of experts, but they usually limit themselves to rubber-stamping the wines presented to them. If it were otherwise, a huge number of Barolos and Brunellos scoring 95 points or more over the past 10 years would have been unceremoniously thrown out, never being able to be called Barolo or the like, if for no other reason than a ridiculous purple-black hue. (Neither the sangiovese nor the nebbiolo grape can give inky-black wines, so if a wine is inky-black, the color may have been obtained by the addition of other, darker-hued grapes, an illicit practice.) The DOC and the DOCG are meant to ensure that the wine produced in an area will be faithful to the style that was historically made there, but critics argue that these categories curtail the winemakers' and producers' freedom of expression. For example, you cannot call a nebbiolo wine made in the Barolo area "Barolo," a DOCG wine, if you decide to add even 1% of merlot to it. This is because Barolo has to be, by law, a 100% nebbiolo wine. If one chooses to do otherwise, then the wine must be called something else.

Specific Qualifications

On Italian wine labels you will also find other qualifications that are actually of little or no help in identifying the character or quality of a wine.

RISERVA

This can mean many different things to many different people, and you'll go insane trying to remember all the minutiae. *Riserva* almost always refers to a wine that is supposedly of better quality and has been aged longer in oak, usually one year more (the specific amount of time for each wine is set in the official government guidelines for the production of that wine). The reasoning is that since the wine was made from higher-quality grapes and is therefore richer and more concentrated, it can stand up to and benefit from more oak. If only it were always so!

RISERVA SPECIALE

This is a term you hardly see ever anymore, as it was used commonly only up to the 1980s. It meant an extra year of aging in oak on top of the extra year that Riserva normally received. Modern tastes veer toward fruit-forward, softly tannic wines, but too much wood aging takes wines into the opposite direction, leading to wines that are tough and astringent (when still young). Nobody really cares for these, especially since few people except passionate wine buffs and collectors store or cellar wines today. Still some

Barolo or Barbaresco Riserva Speciale bottles from the 1950s, 1960s, and 1970s are spectacular.

SUPERIORE

Theoretically, a Superiore is a better wine than a Normale; in reality, this distinction almost always boils down to a wine that has a half a degree or one degree more alcohol. The reason why this should indicate a better wine is that since alcohol is derived from the fermentation of sugar, better grapes are riper grapes—that is, grapes with more sugar, which can give wines with higher potential alcohol. So a wine that has a higher alcohol content has always been thought of as a better wine.

CLASSICO

This term refers to a particular area that has historically been the finest portion of a specific wine making region, such as Soave Classico or Chianti Classico. There are two caveats. First, modern-day legislation had greatly expanded the original Classico zones so as to make people happy (they're all potential voters, you know). Thus modern-day Classico zones often bear little if any resemblance to the original Classico areas. Second, incapable producers may have been lucky enough to inherit vineyard holdings in a Classico zone: but since they don't know what they are doing, the wines will be poor despite being produced in a good area. Hence it is usually best to try the wine from a very good producer even though the vineyards may be located in a lesser area. If it is true that the single most important thing to know when choosing any wine is the grape type (after all, there's no sense grabbing a bottle of Picolit, a sweet white wine, if you're after a hearty red), the next most important is the producer's name, as that is your single best guarantee of quality. Keep in mind, of course, that if a producer excels with one variety, this doesn't mean he or she will necessarily succeed with everything else.

THE REGIONS OF ITALY AND THEIR WINES

ITALY'S GEOGRAPHY IS ESSENTIALLY CHARAC-terized by a series of mountain ranges stretching east to west in the north (the Alps) and from north to south (the Apennines), down the middle of the country's boot-shaped contour. In fact, these two mountain ranges account for almost 35% of all Italian territory. Since another 40% of Italy consists of the hills leading up to those mountains, it follows that Italy really is a hilly-mountainous country. Such topography allows for a wide range of geological differences and consequently almost ubiquitous great vineyard sites. The extremes in altitude at which Italian vineyards are planted also allow for numerous microclimates, which when added to the many soil types go a long way toward explaining Italy's unique suitability for producing grapes and wine. Geology is important in wine production: soils on which vines are planted are the result of millennia of formation and retreat of rock and ice masses (more than 100 million years of upheaval in the case of the Alps), and geological history determines which territories will be more or less suited to viticulture. Some areas will have a volcanic instead of a sedimentary origin; others will be characterized by high limestone content; still others will be richer in clay or granite. Italy, a geologist's dream, has vineyards located in nearly all possible topographical conditions, from those almost at the water's edge in some seaside locatons to some of the highest vineyards in the world, such as the prié blanc vineyards of the Valle d'Aosta, about 3,000 feet (1,000 meters) above sea level. Indeed, a common saying among Italian farmers is that the soil changes "from palm to palm," meaning that walking even small distances within a vineyard will show you many different soil types.

The lay of the land also creates different microclimates in which the grapes will grow. Italy lies between the 47th and 45th parallels, roughly corresponding in the north to the vineyards of central France and in the south to those of southern Spain and northern Africa. (Indeed, the Italian island of Lampedusa is much closer to Africa than to mainland Italy.) The climate is generally temperate, thanks to the thermoregulating effect of the Mediterranean Sea, though all extremes exist, from almost African heat in certain areas of the south to truly cold alpine areas in the north. Italy is also blessed with lots of sunlight hours and with all-important day-night temperature excursions: high daytime and low nightime temperatures allow for the formation of more aromatic precursor molecules, which lead to more perfumed, fragrant wines. In general, mean temperatures in Italy are not so high as to overripen fruit. (Overripening is a problem because wines made with overripe grapes have an overt jamminess and cooked aromas and flavors, which are, to me, undesirable characteristics.) In fact, grapes ripen so well that Italian law prohibits chaptalization, a process whereby sugar is added to fermenting grape juice or must (its technical name) in order to increase the final alcohol content of the wine. In France, by contrast, chaptalization is not only legal but widely practiced, because the temperatures in many parts of France are such that the grapes fail to ripen properly or never fully ripen. However, Italy is also starting to feel the greenhouse effect, and some fabled vineyards are now producing unmemorable wines in extremely hot years, though you won't, understandably, find many people eager to point this out. For example, insiders know that the fantastic Barbaresco vineyard Rabajà, blessed with a fairly warm microclimate, did not perform as well as lesser sites such as Pajé in the hot vintage of 2001 or the even hotter 2003. In fact, producers are now beginning to adopt new viticultural practices in an effort to ward off the effects of too much heat (for example, they will remove fewer leaves to allow for a little more shade), so that the grapes do not bake in the heat. Differences in factors such as altitude, climate, and soil composition will lead to final wines with very different personalities, even if the grapes are grown and the wines made in almost exactly the same way. For example, pinot grigio grown on the excellent riverbed plains of the Isonzo in the region of Friuli Venezia Giulia will yield results very different from those obtained when this variety is grown high up in the mountans of Alto Adige. This geographical variability is really one of the great things about Italian wine, because even when wine making techniques are more or less the same, one can actually taste clear-cut differences in the wines.

Italy is divided into 20 regions equivalent to the states of the United States. (Valle d'Aosta and Alto Adige have special statutes, but we'll consider them regions here.) Each one of Italy's regions is very much involved in wine production. To form an idea of just how much wine Italy makes, consider that if only two of these regions, Sicily and Veneto, were one nation of their own, they alone would be the world's fourth-largest wine producer.

Each region is associated with specific wines. This is very typical of the Italian wine scene: when you are in Marche, chances are the white wine you'll drink is Verdicchio; if you are in Sardinia, the likelihood is that the wine will be Vermentino; and so forth. It is useful to know which wines are most often associated with which region, as that will go a long way in helping you make sense of Italy's confusing and seemingly never-ending litany of wine names. In the box are the names of the major wines produced in each region. Trying to learn all the names of all the wines made in Italy is a superhuman and pointless exercise—the plethora of names is such that you may find your head spinning from more than the wines' sultry fumes.

ITALY'S REGIONS, MAIN CITIES, AND THE MOST IMPORTANT WINES PRODUCED

Valle d'Aosta

Aosta

Valle d'Aosta Blanc de Morgex et La Salle, Valle d'Aosta Chambave, Valle d'Aosta Donnas, Valle d'Aosta Torrette, Valle d'Aosta (a general category referring to the region of origin, followed by the grape variety, such as chardonnay or pinot grigio). Chardonnay has actually been made only recently in Valle d'Aosta, but it falls into the broad Valle d'Aosta group of wines.

Liguria

Genoa

Cinque Terre, Cinque Terre Sciacchetrà, Riviera Ligure di Ponente (follows grape variety name such as Ormeasco).

Lombardy

Milan, Pavia, Brescia, Bergamo

Franciacorta, Oltrepò Pavese (follows grape variety name or wine type such as Bianco or Rosso), Curtefranca, Valcalepio (Rosso, Bianco, and Moscato Passito, the latter being the most interesting wines made in Valcalepio), Valtellina Sforzato.

Piedmont

Turin, Alba, Alessandria, Asti

Asti, Barbaresco, Barbera d'Asti, Barbera D'Asti Sup. Nizza, Barolo, Brachetto d'Acqui, Carema, Dolcetto d'Alba, Dolcetto di Dogliani, Dolcetto di Diano d'Alba, Erbaluce di Caluso, Freisa d'Asti, Gattinara, Gavi, Ghemme, Grignolino d'Asti, Grignolino del Monferrato Casalese, Lessona, Loazzolo, Malvasia di Casorzo d'Asti, Malvasia di Castelnuovo Don Bosco, Moscato d'Asti, Ruchè di Castagnole Monferrato.

Trentino

Trento

Lago di Caldaro (also in Alto Adige), Trentino (follows grape variety name and wine type such as Rosso), Trento, Teroldego Rotaliano, Trentino Marzemino, Trentino Vino Santo.

Alto Adige

Bolzano, Merano, Bressanone

All the wines in Alto Adige are labeled with the varietal name, except for some blends. Hence a label will read "Alto Adige" followed by a grape or wine name. In two cases further subzones are indicated, before the grape variety name: these are Alto Adige Val Venosta and Alto Adige Valle Isarco. The wines most commonly produced are: Cabernet, Chardonnay, Lagrein, Gewürztraminer, Moscato Rosa, Pinot Bianco, Pinot Grigio, Pinot Nero, Merlot, Santa Maddalena, and Sauvignon.

Friuli Venezia Giulia

Udine, Gorizia, Trieste

In Friuli Venezia Giulia wines are most often labeled by grape variety, though there are also fantasy names in the case of blends. In general, the wine name is preceded by the subzone name, such as Carso or Collio, followed by the name of the grape variety. Therefore, the most common wines are: Carso, Colli Orientali del Friuli, Collio, Isonzo, and Friuli Grave. Friuli Latisana, Friuli Annia, and Friuli Aquilea are harder to find. After these initial headings comes the variety with which the wine is made, the most common being: malvasia, ribolla gialla, tocai friulano (friulano), pinot bianco, pinot grigio, chardonnay, sauvignon, cabernet franc, cabernet sauvignon, merlot, refosco del peduncolo rosso, schioppettino, pignolo, terrano.

Veneto

Verona, Venice, Treviso

Amarone della Valpolicella, Bardolino, Prosecco di Valdobbiadene, Recioto della Valpolicella, Recioto di Soave, Soave, Valpolicella.

Emilia-Romagna

Bologna, Modena, Parma, Reggio Emilia

Albana di Romagna, Lambrusco di Sorbara, Lambrusco Grasparossa di Castelvetro, Lambrusco Salamino di Santa Croce, Pagadebit di Romagna, Reggiano Lambrusco, Sangiovese di Romagna, Trebbiano di Romagna.

Tuscany

Florence, Pisa, Siena

Ansonica della Costa dell'Argentario, Bolgheri, Brunello di Montalcino, Carmignano, Chianti, Chianti Classico, Chianti Rufina, Cortona (follows grape variety name), Morellino di Scansano, Moscadello di Montalcino, Rosso di Montalcino, Rosso di Montepulciano, Vernaccia di San Gimignano, Vin Santo (Vin Santo del Chianti Classico, di Carmignano, others), Vino Nobile di Montepulciano.

Marche

Ancona

Lacrima di Morro d'Alba, Rosso Conero, Rosso Piceno, Verdicchio dei Castelli di Jesi, Verdicchio di Matelica, Vernaccia di Serrapetrona.

Umbria

Perugia

Colli Martani (follows grape variety name), Orvieto, Sagrantino di Montefalco, Torgiano (follows grape variety name and wine type, such as Rosso and Rosso Riserva).

Lazio

Rome

Aleatico di Gradoli, Castelli Romani, Cesanese del Piglio, Cesanese di Olevano Romano, Colli Albani, Cori, Est! Est!! Est!!! di Montefiascone, Frascati, Marino, Orvieto, Velletri.

Abruzzo and Molise

Pescara

Montepulciano d'Abruzzo, Trebbiano d'Abruzzo.

Campania

Naples

Aglianico del Taburno, Costa d'Amalfi (follows grape variety name and wine type, such as Rosso), Fiano di Avellino, Greco di Tufo, Ischia (follows grape variety name and wine type, such as Rosso), Taurasi.

Basilicata

Potenza

Aglianico del Vulture.

Puglia

Bari, Lecce

Castel del Monte (follows grape variety name and wine type, such as Rosso), Moscato di Trani, Primitivo di Manduria, Salice Salentino.

Calabria

Reggio Calabria

Cirò, Greco di Bianco.

Sicily

Catania, Palermo

Cerasuolo di Vittoria, Etna Rosso, Malvasia delle Lipari, Marsala, Moscato di Noto, Moscato di Pantelleria, Passito di Pantelleria, Sicilia Bianco, Sicilia Rosso.

Sardinia

Cagliari, Sassari

Cannonau di Sardegna, Carignano del Sulcis, Malvasia di Bosa, Nuragus di Cagliari, Vermentino di Gallura, Vermentino di Sardegna, Vernaccia di Oristano.

ITALY'S NATIVE GRAPE VARIETIES

THE SINGLE GREATEST ASSET THAT ITALIAN producers share, and a feature unique to Italy, is the plethora of native grape varieties.

Grape varieties can be roughly broken down into two categories: native or autochtonous and international (foreign) or allochtonous. *Native* grape varieties are those that are born in a specific land, or have grown there for thousands of years, and are not commonly found anywhere else. *International* grape varieties are those that are found everywhere in the world, having been planted recently (within roughly 100 years) in new lands in an effort to duplicate the success of French wines. Varietals such as chardonnay, merlot, and cabernet sauvignon, native to France, are used for some of the world's most famous wines. Thus, they have become the ultimate international varieties (though Italians are quick to point out that even these are Italian varieties, as most were brought over to France by the Roman legionnaires). It would be far more accurate to add a third category: *traditional* varieties, which are international grape varieties that have been grown long enough in a specific area to become part of its own tradition. Most scientists feel that any variety grown regularly in an area for 500 years or less is traditional to that area. Therefore, varietals such as cabernet franc and merlot, which have been grown in Veneto and Friuli Venezia Giulia for at least 300 years, are traditional to those areas. If a varietal has been grown in a specific place for more than 500 years, it may then be considered "local" or native.

Italy's native grape varieties have aroused considerable interest recently because many of them appear to be capable of giving world-class wines with fragrance and flavor profiles altogether different from those already well known to the public. Italy's native grapes offer jaded consumers a welcome change. Yes, true experts realize that a Cabernet from Sicily is not the same as one from Veneto or Bordeaux, just as Napa cabernets differ from those of Sonoma, but if truth be told, such minute differences are lost on the majority of consumers. Hence, wine lovers, always willing to embrace novel offerings, are eagerly turning to Italy's "new" grapes and wines.

In reality, only some of Italy's many native grape varieties are truly native, in the sense that they descend from the domestication of wild grape varieties originally found in Italy. For these reasons, many of Italy's grape varieties would best be called local. Many so-called Italian native grapes are actually of Greek or Middle Eastern origin and were brought to Italy by seafaring Phoenician and Greek colonists thousands of years ago. However, as the grape varieties grown in Italy today no longer bear any resemblance to the original varieties of Greece or other lands, they are considered, in effect, Italian natives. For example, the xinomavros variety of Greece and the negro amaro of Italy have only a similar name in common: the Greek vine, grape, and wine are altogether different from their Italian counterparts, owing to genetic mutations over time. These mutations lead to morphologic changes in the vines and ultimately to different-tasting wines.

That said, not enough is yet known about Italy's native grapes. Matters such as the best soils for them, or the ideal rootstocks or trellis systems, are still mainly conjectural. Even the important native sangiovese, from which famous wines such as Chianti and Brunello are made, did not become a subject of university studies until the 1960s, or of in-depth analyses until the 1980s, so the magnitude of the problem is evident. Not so with the French varieties, such as merlot and chardonnay: these have been studied for centuries, and there are true wine making protocols for them, which anyone can follow. You cannot blame the many hotshot consultant winemakers who did not want to work with the Italian natives in the past, and who actually advised many producers to uproot these varieties altogether in favor of new merlot or cabernet plantings. But in a hilarious turn of events, the popularity of these grapes and their wines is such today that the same winemakers are now falling all over themselves in an attempt to be seen as keepers of the faith with regard to native grapes.

IMPORTANT NATIVE VARIETALS: WHITE

ANSONICA OR INZOLIA (TUSCANY, SICILY)

This rare tannic white variety is also an excellent table grape, and that may explain why it was once so popular (it represents about 15% of Sicilian hectares under vine). Though it tends to fare poorly in overly hot areas (indeed, Sicily is probably not the best place for it), where it gives low-acid wines, interesting herbal, fruity wines are becoming commonplace thanks to improved wine making.

ARNEIS (PIEDMONT)

Once called nebbiolo bianco, arneis is popular because of its fruit-forward fresh wines that are full-bodied enough to double as wonderful aperitifs and wines that can be drunk with the whole meal. It is a variety full of character, and the best examples are very perfumed: it does best in the white soils or *terre bianche* of the Roero, on the left banks of the Tanaro River. It fares poorly in clay-rich soils that give heavier wines prone to oxidation. Often a good buy, as Arneis is usually inexpensive.

BOMBINO BIANCO (PUGLIA)

Although this grape is also found in Lazio, Abruzzo, and Emilia Romagna, most of the best wines made with it come from Puglia, though it seems likely to me that these are not exactly the same grapes. Long considered usable only to make large quantities of low-quality wine, it has undergone a remarkable resurrection and is now responsible for interesting wines that have real texture and body and are redolent of ripe yellow, resiny fruit. Gone are the days when this grape was also known as *pagadebit* ("pay your debts") or *stracciacambiale* ("rip up the promissory note"), terms that referred to the extremely large quantities of grapes it was possible to grow. A high-acid variety, it is also used to make sparkling wines.

CARRICANTE (SICILY)

Typical of the Etna volcano area, this grape thrives at higher altitudes and yields wine with a mineral-lemony aromatic profile that veers toward hydrocarbons with age. Over time, it develops a noticeable resemblance to dry riesling. This is potentially one of Italy's greatest native varieties.

CATARATTO (SICILY)

Long a workhorse grape, cataratto no longer deserves its name of "cataract" (which indicated that it made enough wine to create a waterfall or cataract). A real chameleon: depending on where it grows, some examples are intensely mineral whereas others resemble a fat, rich chardonnay.

CORTESE (PIEDMONT)

Gavi is a famous Italian wine that is made with cortese, a variety with naturally occurring high total acidity. This guarantees that Gavi is rarely flat or dull, even in hot vintages, and that the grape can be used to make sparkling wines, such as the excellent ones from the venerable house of Soldati. Cortese does best in the subzone of Rovereto, where the reddish subsoils contain iron that greatly adds to the overall finesse and power of the wines produced.

FIANO (CAMPANIA)

One of Italy's oldest and better natives, this is fast becoming an "international" grape variety, planted increasingly in faraway places such as Australia and California. Only time will tell if fiano is to become the next chardonnay, but producers love its ability to give radically different wines depending on where it is grown. Fianos grown at high altitudes are distinctly mineral and lemony; those from hot climates are fat and full of tropical fruit and smoky aromas and flavors. In truth, after twenty-five years of walking through Italy's vineyards, I am not at all sure these two wines are in fact made from the same grape variety. True fiano is probably the former, and experts such as Antonio Mastroberardino agrees with me.

GRECO (CAMPANIA)

Italy has more than 15 greco varieties, of which some are white and others are red. In fact, most of them aren't related; they have the same name because they were all brought to Italy by ancient Greeks (*greco* is Italian for "Greek"). The most famous wine made from a greco variety is the Greco di Tufo of Campania (its variety is called simply greco), but the best of these grapes is really the greco bianco of Calabria, which gives amazing if little-known sweet wines, and fine dry ones.

GRILLO (SICILY)

An interesting and potentially high-quality variety with a definite herbaceousness to its nose, this is also the best variety for making top-quality Marsala.

MALVASIA (FRIULI VENEZIA GIULIA, SICILY, LAZIO, EMILIA-ROMAGNA, PIEDMONT)

A family of grapes, and Italy has at least 14 of them. The wines produced from them could not be any more different: reds, whites, dry, sweet, still, sparkling. Malvasia has something for everyone. Friuli Venezia Giulia's malvasia Istriana is the best of the dry versions; malvasia puntinata from Lazio is a close second. The Malvasia delle Lipari (the Lipari are lovely if touristy islands off the northern coast of Sicily), made with the grape of the same name, is potentially one of Italy's better sweet white wines. Unfortunately, much of the Malvasia delle Lipari made today is from malvasia di Candia aromatica, planted in the 1980s in an effort to meet demand for the suddenly popular wine. Producers scrambled to find the true native, but there weren't enough vines left; and unlike the original variety, the Candia variety was neither typical of nor adapted to the specific, unique island microclimate. The resulting wines are nowhere near the quality of those made with the true native: there is a lesson to be learned here.

MOSCATO (EVERYWHERE IN ITALY)

Perhaps the oldest grape variety in the world, and by far the largest family of wine grapes. The three basic moscatos, from which all others are derived, are moscato bianco (white muscat in English), moscato giallo (yellow muscat), and moscato d'Alessandria or zibibbo (muscat of Alexandria). Not surprisingly, Italy grows all three. In fact, some of the country's best-known wines are made from them. Moscato d'Asti is made from moscato bianco, and Passito di Pantelleria is made from the zibibbo variety. Though the latter variety is the best suited for warm climates (and in fact is grown all over the Mediterranean basin), not all southern Italian muscat wines are made with it. Moscato di Trani from Puglia and Moscato di Noto and Moscato di Siracusa from Sicily are made with moscato bianco.

NOSIOLA (TRENTINO)

A variety little known outside Trentino, but it deserves to be better known. Light-bodied, with a distinct, delicate hazelnut aroma (nosiola is a word derived from *nocciola*, Italian for hazelnut).

RIBOLLA GIALLA (FRIULI VENEZIA GIULIA)

A grape variety typical of Friuli Venezia Giulia and grown mostly there (but there is some in Emilia-Romagna, and much more across the border in Slovenia and Croatia). Ribolla gives lovely, lemony-fresh wines; the best examples have a white pepper nuance on the nose. Unfortunately, a recent trend or fad among some winemakers is to make Ribolla in the manner of the ancient Romans, with long contact times between juice and skins and aging in terra-cotta amphoras. The former technique gives the wine a curious (at best) reddish orangey hue; the latter, because terra-cotta is highly porous, adds an oxidized Sherry-like quality. Though many experts have praised these efforts, mainly owing to the intellectual bent behind them, the proof is in the glass—and, honestly, nobody I know really likes these wines.

TOCAI FRIULANO (FRIULI VENEZIA GIULIA)

The European Union (EU) has decreed that the name "Tocai" may be used legally only by Hungary for the wines from its Tokay region. Italians are therefore calling their wine Friulano (as it is identified with Friuli Venezia Giulia), though the EU's decision is still being fought in courts. Friulanos are not unlike a faint Sauvignon Blanc, with hints of freshly cut grass, rosemary, thyme, and almonds on both nose and palate. This is not surprising, as the friulano grape is really the sauvignonasse or sauvignon vert, a cousin of sauvignon blanc.

TREBBIANO TOSCANO (TUSCANY)

A few words are necessary about this variety, but not for the reasons you might be thinking of: simply put, it makes lousy wines. In fact, the French, who call it ugni blanc, know better than to make wine with it; they use it to make Cognac. That said, trebbiano toscano is Italy's most common white grape variety and some brave hearts succeed in obtaining potable dry wines with it. However, the real magic of trebbiano toscano lies in Vin Santo, the famous sweet wine of central Italy. The trebbiano family is a large one, and some members, such as the trebbiano giallo of Lazio and Umbria and the trebbiano di Soave of Veneto, hold more promise than others.

VERDICCHIO (MARCHE)

Many Italian wine experts consider verdicchio Italy's best native white variety. They will get no argument from me. Certainly it is one of the very few Italian whites that can age well, acquiring over time a mineral resemblance to riesling (though it is not an aromatic variety, and for that reason it does not produce great sweet wines, despite what others may tell you). The best wines from verdicchio have a delicately herbal, minerally, almond character that is unmistakable. Verdicchio dei Castelli di Jesi and Verdicchio di Matelica are different wines: the latter are made more inland, and are fuller-bodied and more alcoholic than those of Jesi. The truth is that most people cannot tell the difference, though La Monacesca makes a great example of Verdicchio di Matelica.

Important Native Varietals: Red

AGLIANICO (CAMPANIA, BASILICATA)

The original Greek grape: its name probably derives from *ellanico*, meaning Greek. It is also the single best native Italian grape after nebbiolo and sangiovese, as it can give wines loaded with extract, complexity, and elegance. Some of Italy's hottest wines right now are made from aglianico, and you'll be hearing, reading, and tasting a great deal more of aglianico in the near future. Taurasi from Campania and Basilicata's Aglianico del Vulture are best: the former are relatively lighter and have tobacco and rose aromas; the latter have richer, riper fruit and a smoky quality.

BARBERA (PIEDMONT)

Barbera is the name of both the grape and the wine. The grape is one of Italy's chameleons, capable of giving simple everyday wines and deep, full-bodied wines. Barbera is a high-acid variety that, when vinified in the traditional manner, is a joy with every cold cut sandwich you can think of. When it is aged in small oak barrels, and its malolactic fermentation is completed, it smooths out considerably and becomes surprisingly rich. The two most famous Barbera wines are the Barbera d'Alba and the Barbera d'Asti, especially those from a particularly subzone called Nizza. Barbera d'Alba is fuller-bodied and Barbera d'Asti more vinous, and both have the variety's trademark purple color.

CORVINA, CORVINONE, RONDINELLA, AND MOLINARA (VENETO)

Four for the price of one, you might say. None of these native grapes can be considered a truly great variety, yet when they are blended together each adds something to the final result, which is much more than the sum of its parts. Two of Italy's best-known wines are made with these grapes: the lighter Valpolicella and the velvety and alcoholic Amarone. Valpolicella is made by pressing the grapes as soon as they are picked, whereas the grapes for Amarone are stowed away and air-dried. The grapes are essentially turned into raisins, and their juice is very sweet and concentrated. Corvina is very fragrant and perfect for air-drying, though these qualities are more evident in grapes grown on specific volcanic, mineral-rich *toar* soils as opposed to the more common sandy-clay alluvial soils. Corvinone ("big corvina"), as the name implies, gives the tannins and power that corvina lacks. Rondinella adds a lovely herbal-spicy quality, but its detractors say it is used only because of its dependable, consistent productions rather than for any inherent quality it may have. Molinara, a very lightly hued grape, gives rosy juice believed to add drinkability, though many producers feel it dilutes the wine and are doing away with it. The varieties have been named after blackbirds that are fond of the sweet berries (*corvina* means a small raven; *corvinone* means a big raven or big corvina; and *rondinella* means a swallow). Another view is that the black color of the grapes recalls the dark plumage of these birds.

DOLCETTO (PIEDMONT)

Dolcetto is the name of the grape and of the wine—another in the long line of excellent everyday table wines that Italy offers to savvy consumers who are willing to take the plunge away from tried-and-true Merlots and Zinfandels. *Dolce* in Italian means sweet, and dolcetto is so called because this grape is an excellent, sweet table grape as well. There are many different Dolcettos: the best known are Dolcetto d'Alba and Dolcetto di Dogliani. The former are fuller-bodied; the latter are fruitier, lighter, and fresher. A richer version of the wine can be called Dogliani. Dolcetto is a joy to drink; the charms of its vinous, violet, blackberry-scented nose are often lost on those producers who insist on turning it into a big, overly alcoholic wine (and possibly with other grape varieties blended in, something that is illegal). The end result is that Dolcetto is losing part of its identity and sales are plummeting.

FREISA (PIEDMONT)

A grape that is falling out of favor—unfortunately, as good examples are perfect companions to many common foods, such as cold cut sandwiches and sausages. A light but tannic wine, Freisa can be still or bubbly. The bubbly version has more fruit than other red sparkling wines, such as Lambrusco. In fact the grape's name, freisa, derives from the Latin for "strawberry." There are at least two subvarieties of freisa—the *grossa* and the *piccola*—but the best of the lot is the now even rarer freisa di Chieri, a small berried variety that offers more color and structure.

MONTEPULCIANO (ABRUZZO)

A workhorse grape if there ever was one. Montepulciano is also the name of Abruzzo's most common wine, the much-loved Montepulciano d'Abruzzo, one of the ultimate trattoria wines. The simpler versions are wonderful with barbecue and pizza, redolent of chewy red cherry fruit and with an endearing smoky quality. There are an increasing number of small barrel aged versions that are pricey and meant to impress with their sheer size, but the fact is that most are just overoaked and way too tannic to be truly enjoyable. Don't confuse this wine with Vino Nobile di Montepulciano, a sangiovese-based wine made in Tuscany.

NEBBIOLO (PIEDMONT)

Straight and simple: nebbiolo isn't just Italy's greatest grape variety, it is also one of the five greatest red varieties of the world. It is the grape from which Barolo and Barbaresco are made, imbued with red rose petal, sour red cherry, and delicate tarry-spice aromas and flavors. A translator of soil types into the glass, nebbiolo is as site-specific as pinot noir and gives wines that are as long-lived as the best Cabernets. (A good, well-kept Barolo from 1947 is still a thing of beauty.) It is grown also in Valle d'Aosta and Lombardy (where it is called picoutener and chiavennasca, respectively, though many prefer to call it nebbiolo anyway) but it gives the best results in its native Piedmont. *Always* keep in mind that nebbiolo cannot give inky-colored wines, since its skins do not have such pigments. Therefore, any blackish Barolos or Barbarescos (100% nebbiolo wines by law) have to make you wonder, at least.

NEGRO AMARO (PUGLIA)

Amaro means "bitter" in Italian, but that has nothing to do with this grape's name (what you might have read or heard elsewhere is plain wrong). The word negro amaro derives from the Greek *mavros* and the Latin *niger*, both meaning black. It's no surprise, then, that both grape and wine are fairly dark-hued. Negroamaro can give delightfully light everyday table wines such as Salice Salentino or decadently lush full-bodied reds such as the almost Amarone-like "Patriglione" and "Graticciaia" bottlings from Taurino and Agricole Vallone, respectively. In order to soften it somewhat, producers usually blend in 10% to 20% malvasia nera, a lighter grape variety. A good negro amaro wine will always have a slight tobacco and herbal note, even a highly typical shoe-polish note, on top of lusciously ripe red fruit. Don't forget that some of Italy's very best rosés are made from this grape.

NERO D'AVOLA AND NERELLO MASCALESE (SICILY)

Nero d'Avola is the most famous and most common red grape of Sicily, grown everywhere on the island except for the northeastern tip, which is the home of nerello mascalese. Nero d'Avola is a distant relative of syrah, and can have the same spicy characteristics as that variety, though it often shows (depending on where the vineyards are located) a distinctly saline, marine quality as well as a tomato paste aroma and flavor. The different aromas and flavors derive mainly from where the grapes are grown, though with at least 100 subvarieties in existence, which subvariety you have also plays a role. Some Nero d'Avolas can be light and simple, others rich and complex. Nerello mascalese is at home at the high altitude of the Etna volcano and gives wines that are much more mineral-driven and leaner than those made from nero d'Avola. Considerable excitement is being generated by this grape variety, and its highly perfumed and effusivley fruity wines are beginning to garner critical acclaim. It also appears to be a fantastic translator of different soil types, not unlike pinot noir, a variety to which it is often compared.

PRIMITIVO (PUGLIA)

This grape is better known as zinfandel in the United States. Italian versions of it are richer in tobacco and dried herb aromas and flavors and are usually less alcoholic than some decadently rich American versions. Primitivo di Manduria is the most famous, as Manduria is considered the best area for the grape. Sava, once considered even better, does not currently produce wines of note. In case you're wondering about the name primitivo, it refers to early or "primitive" ripening: in fact, this is one of the earliest grapes to be harvested in Italy.

SANGIOVESE (TUSCANY)

Italy's most common red grape variety, found everywhere except northern Italy, which is too cold for a late-ripening variety. Indisputably, the best results are achieved in Tuscany. Wines such as Chianti (made with a minimum of 80% sangiovese), Brunello di Montalcino (100% sangiovese), and Vino Nobile di Montepulciano (made with a minimum of 70% sangiovese) are famous the world over. Brunello is Italy's longest-lived wine; bottles from 1888 and 1891 are still in fine shape in the cellars of one well-known producer, Biondi Santi. Sangiovese is a family of subvarieties and clones, and not all are equally suited to viticulture and wine making; only recently has progress been made in identifying the best among them. Therefore, the old names sangiovese grosso (believed to be the sangiovese specific of Montalcino) and prugnolo gentile (specific to Montepulciano) are neither useful nor exact, though I can see why some people might prefer them to the likes of T19, R10, and BBS11. At its best, a sangiovese wine is an explosion of violets, red currants, licorice, and tobacco. With time, truffle, leather, and underbrush aromas and flavors emerge. Late-ripening, sangiovese is very vintage-sensitive, so if you wish to cellar these wines, it pays to study vintage charts. Like nebbiolo, sangiovese lacks the pigments to give black-hued wine: 100% sangiovese wines such as Brunello should not be black-hued. Unfortunately, the addition of even small amounts of merlot, cabernet, or syrah to sangiovese, though it may result in very fine wines, often makes the more delicate sangiovese character hard to recognize. The end result is yet another blend dominated by cabernet or merlot.

SCHIOPPETTINO (FRIULI VENEZIA GIULIA)

Though little known, this is one of the big four native red grapes of Friuli (the other three being refosco del peduncolo rosso, pignolo, and terrano—also the names of the wines). Schioppettinos are wonderfully perfumed with delicate black pepper, raspberry, and blackberry aromas and flavors. Long forgotten, the grape began its comeback at the end of the 1970s, and it is a good example of what a shame it would be to lose some native varieties that offer wine lovers something completely different. Unfortunately, since schioppettino has only recently been rediscovered, producers are still experimenting, and wildly different wines are being made. Some producers air-dry the grapes, Amarone-style; others harvest late; others still pick early. As a result, the true, definitive characteristics of the wine are not yet clear, but the producers of Prepotto, Schioppettino's original home, have joined forces in an effort to create more uniform wines.

IMPORTANT INTERNATIONAL VARIETIES IN ITALY

WHITE

CHARDONNAY (EVERYWHERE IN ITALY)

Ironically, chardonnay, the world's favorite white grape, has never been very popular in Italy. Even more important for you to know is that most Italian Chardonnay really isn't very good. I can already hear the cries of rage and the wails of despair, but the fact remains that Italians make many other wines that are far better and more enjoyable than their Chardonnays. The reason is that the majority of Italian Chardonnays are hopelessly overoaked, imitating the very worst in alcoholic, caramely, tropical fruity, fumy, head-spinning wines from the New World. It is not a stretch to say that probaby fewer than 15 world-class Chardonnays are made in Italy today, and even among these, the better examples are expensive. Frankly, you're much better off buying one of the many fine examples from Australia or the cooler parts of California, or the less ripe versions from New Zealand; or, of course, Chardonnays from France.

GEWÜRZTRAMINER (ALTO ADIGE)

You read it here first: Italy makes the greatest dry Gewürztraminers in the world. Though nobody (certainly not I!) will dispute the greatness of Alsatian examples of the variety, the fact is that most of the French wines often have unacceptable levels of residual sugar for what are deemed, and sold as, "dry" wines. Therefore, if you like Gewürztraminer but have been put off by some overly sweet bottlings, look no farther than Italy's northern Alto Adige region. Italian versions come in essentially two styles: floral or tropical fruit–scented. All Gewürztraminers share those features to some extent, and both styles are excellent.

MÜLLER-THURGAU AND KERNER (ALTO ADIGE)

Müller-Thurgau is said to be the result of a crossing of chasselas and riesling by Dr. Müller (who came from

Thurgau—hence the name). However, the jury is still out, and the latest evidence would seem to hint that chasselas was not one of the two parents. In fact, in most wine books you'll still read that this is a crossing of riesling and sylvaner—a statement that is most definitely wrong and has been for years. The situation gives you a measure of the problem facing this grape and the wines made from it. The grape is generally considered by wine experts (read any book on the subject) as at best a variety that needlessly takes up good vineyard sites that could be used for riesling, and at worse a weed that should be extirpated. Kerner, also a crossing—in this case between trollinger (Italy's schiava) and riesling—fares only slightly better. But in fact the better Italian wines made from these two grapes—and yes, again, you read it first here—are absolutely charming and delightful. These wines are great at the table with many different dishes, first and foremost shellfish and the more delicate spicy dishes typical of certain ethnic cuisines that are currently all the rage. I am aware that these grape will never be the source of wines as sublime as the best achieved with riesling, but there is a place for them anyway. Kerner's delightful bubble-gum, lemony-lime, and floral aromas are a joy, and the delicate minty, gin, tequila, green apple, and very lightly spicy aromas and flavors are a welcome find for all those who like aromatic wines but find Riesling, Muscat, and Gewürztraminer too much of a good thing. Last but not least, these remarkably food-friendly wines are perfect in restaurants, because the starting price is so low that the markup won't kill your wallet.

PINOT GRIGIO AND PINOT BIANCO (ALTO ADIGE, FRIULI VENEZIA GIULIA)

Italy's most popular and best-selling wine, Pinot Grigio, is often a farce, as it is well known, to begin with, that many bottles contain very little pinot grigio. A good example is Pinot Grigio from southern Italy, where little pinot grigio is planted. A victim of its own success, Pinot Grigio (from the same grape as France's pinot gris) can be an absolutely stellar wine that is remarkably flexible with food. In fact, it is probably Italy's single best white wine (when well made, that is). Part of its success can be ascribed to its embodying the best qualities of Chardonnay and Sauvignon Blanc: fruity but never as exaggerated as the former, herbal but never quite as grassy as the latter, Pinot Grigio offers something for everyone. The best Italian examples are not oaked, though there are some exceptions; and depending on which versions you choose, Pinot Grigio can handle white meat dishes as well as all the usual foods you would more commonly associate with white wine. A good Pinot Grigio will remind you of pears, green apples, and occasionally, but only in the very best examples, strawberries. This is because pinot grigio is actually a red grape, a mutation of pinot nero; and in fact even when one is standing in a vineyard, it's very hard to tell these two grapes apart until they have reached full maturity. It is then, and only then, that pinot nero's dark blue hue sets it apart from grigio's rusty-reddish tone.

Pinot bianco is in turn a mutation of pinot grigio and is most definitely a white grape. It has aromas and flavors not unlike those of a lighter-styled, nonoaked chardonnay, and was long confused with chardonnay. In the 1960s Italian Chardonnnays were commonly labeled "Pinot Chardonnay." At its best, Pinot Bianco has lovely white flower and Golden Delicious apple aromas and flavors and proves quite versatile: excellent as a before-dinner drink, it matches well with fish and vegetable hors d'oeuvres and lightly prepared fish dishes. However, its delicate aromas and flavors are easily overwhelmed by new oak: be aware that most Italian barrel fermented or oak aged examples are nothing to write home about.

RIESLING (ALTO ADIGE, LOMBARDY)

Although a little Riesling is produced in Friuli Venezia Giulia, and an increasing amount in Piedmont, most Riesling is made in Lombardy and in Alto Adige. Italian Rieslings are always bone-dry, but they are rarely of the same exciting quality as the best from Alsace, Germany, or even Australia. Alto Adige's remarkably steely and mineral wines are the best and are worth a try as a novelty if nothing else. Examples from Lombardy are richer in style and have more alcohol, though be aware that this region still has considerable plantings of riesling italico (Italic or welshriesling), a lesser grape variety completely unrelated to the noble Rhine or white riesling. A number of wines from Piedmont have recently caught my attention and that of other experts; G. D Vajra's Langhe Bianco bottling is as good an example as any. All that aside, let me whisper—but only whisper lest too many wine snobs hear me—that there really are some lovely Riesling Italicos being made in

Lombardy, Cà del Gè and Martilde among others (but poor selections of clones in the past hamper today's wines).

SAUVIGNON BLANC (ALTO ADIGE, FRIULI VENEZIA GIULIA)

Unlike Chardonnay, Sauvignon Blanc is one of Italy's very best white wines; the better examples are right up there with famous names from New Zealand and France. Not quite as grassy as some Sancerres (especially) or Pouilly-Fumés, and not quite as infused with gooseberry and passion fruit as some of the wines from New Zealand, Italian Sauvignon Blanc falls somewhere in the middle between these two types. Better examples are unoaked, but there are some very fine oaked bottlings as well. Never shy away from an Italian Sauvignon Blanc; you won't be disappointed.

SYLVANER (ALTO ADIGE)

Sylvaner is yet another in a long line of misunderstood wines. The grape varietal sylvaner yields excellent results in Italy; at its best, Sylvaner is a dainty, light-bodied, fresh, minty, green apple, and mineraly-scented wine that goes remarkably well with food. Simple fish and vegetable preparations, especially those containing sage and coriander, are best, since these two herbs seem to turn Sylvaner into a richer, multilayered wine. Italy's Sylvaners are all made in the cool-climate Valle Isarco area of Alto Adige, where the variety has adapted incredibly well. Even better, the wines cost very little: you won't be disappointed with wines by Pacherhof, Garlider, Abbazia di Novacella, Produttori Valle Isarco, Strasserhof, and Köfererhof.

VERMENTINO (SARDINIA, LIGURIA)

Originally a Spanish variety, known as rolle or malvoisie à petit grains in southern Spain and France, this has been grown in Sardinia for about 400 years, and so it is more correctly viewed as a traditional variety (though I'm sure many a Sardinian will be offended or dismayed by my not considering it a "native"). Very common in Sardinia and Liguria, it is also produced along the Tuscan coast. Wines made from this grape are delicately herbal, with hints of rosemary and thyme and with a distinct marine sea-breeze quality. Denominations include Vermentino di Gallura and Vermentino di Sardegna (Sardinia) and Vermentino dei Colli di Luni or di Ponente (Liguria). Though there are supposedly differences between them, the truth is that only real experts can ever tell them apart, and not easily.

RED

CABERNET FRANC (VENETO, FRIULI VENEZIA GIULIA, TUSCANY)

Cabernet franc was grown in Italy long before cabernet sauvignon. However, many of northern Italy's plantings of cabernet franc were really carmenère, a similar variety that is more intensely green and herbaceous. That said, true cabernet franc seems to do very well in Italy. Though much carmenère remains, an increasing amount of true cabernet franc is being planted. The vines are relatively young, but they show considerable promise. In particular, the Bolgheri area of Tuscany has done remarkably well with the variety: "Paleo," a 100% cabernet franc from the estate of Le Macchiole, is one of Italy's very best wines, and the new Poggio al Tesoro "W" wine is another standout.

CABERNET SAUVIGNON (EVERYWHERE IN ITALY)

Although some very good, even great, Cabernet Sauvignons are made in Italy, I feel that there are too many fine wines made from this variety all over the world for it to ever become truly significant in Italy. In fact, most of the best Italian wines made with this grape are never 100% pure cabernet sauvignon; they always include varying percentages of merlot, cabernet franc, or even syrah. Good examples of supposedly pure Italian Cabernet Sauvignon might be Gaja's "Darmagi" from Piedmont or Tasca d'Almerita's from Sicily, but blends such as "Sassicaia" (70% cabernet sauvignon, 30% cabernet franc) and "Ornellaia" (60% cabernet sauvignon, 30% merlot, 10% cabernet franc) are more famous and sought-after. The trouble is that many of these wines cost well over $100 a bottle.

CANNONAU (SARDINIA)

This was brought to Sardinia by the Spanish, and is more commonly known as grenache. The name cannonau derives from the Spanish name for this variety, *canonera*. Cannonau in Sardinia gives many everyday, rustic, tobacco and dry herb–filled wines that could use a little more finesse, but examples made from very old vines such as the wines by Dettori and especially "Turriga" by Argiolas rank among Italy's best.

CARIGNANO (SARDINIA)

To some wine experts, Sardinian versions of Carignan are the world's best. Elsewhere (in southern France, for example), this variety yields mainly nondescript wines of little interest. The most interesting wines made from the variety are labeled Carignano del Sulcis (a particular subzone of Sardinia) and have a charmingly soft-textured, rich, and very ripe fruity personality, with a smoky, herbal note.

PINOT NERO (ALTO ADIGE, LOMBARDY)

Known as pinot noir everywhere else, pinot nero is perhaps the trickiest of all grapes to grow and vinify. Though wine producers all over the world try hard to capture the elusive and ethereal qualities of truly great pinot noir, few succeed, and the story is no different in Italy. Much less green and vegetal than the efforts made only 20 years ago, the better versions of Italian Pinot Nero are very promising, though they still rely too much on oak for interest. Nonetheless, this is one of the most improved Italian wines in recent years, and small, up-and-coming producers such as Ferruccio Carlotto, Brunnenhof Mazzon, Graziano Fontana and Bruno Gottardi of Alto Adige and Trentino, and Isimbarda and Monsuppello in Lombardy, are joining the ranks of more established names such as Cà del Bosco.

SYRAH OR SHIRAZ (TUSCANY, SICILY)

A newcomer among Italian varieties, syrah is the ultimate warm-weather grape. It seems to thrive in parts of Sicily and Tuscany. By contrast, it has been uprooted in most of the cooler places where it was initially planted, as it fails to ripen properly. In general, Italian Syrah is closer in style to the French Hermitage or Côte Rôtie than to Australia's high-octane, super concentrated Barossa Valley wines. Some Italian Syrahs are showing particularly well, with the promise of becoming more and more interesting as the vines age. Names such as Tuscany's Syrah Tua Rita, "Scrio" by Le Macchiole, "Il Bosco" by Podere Il Bosco, Valle d'Aosta's Les Crêtes Syrah "La Tour," and even the inexpensive bottling by Casale del Giglio in Lazio are a sign that syrah is here to stay.

GLOSSARY

ACIDITY

Grapes contain three main acids: tartaric, citric, and malic; a fourth, gluconic acid, increases when grapes are hit by the desirable fungus that is necessary to make very interesting sweet wines (see "noble rot"). In the wine making process, malic acid, a hard, sharp acid, is turned into the softer lactic acid through malolactic transformation. Acidity is absolutely vital for all wines, as it guarantees liveliness and definition of aromas and flavors, and is closely linked to a wine's ability to age. Low-acid wines do not usually age well, though wines low in overall acidity but rich in alcohol and extract (such as Gewürztraminer) age better than is commonly believed. Also, sweet wines that are low in acidity are undrinkable, for all the sugar present makes them cloying and fatiguing. Too much acidity leaves one with an unpleasant impression of tartness. Therefore, the right amount of acidity is also necessary for the wines to have enough balance to make them interesting.

APPELLATION, DOC, DOCG, PRODUCTION ZONE OR AREA

The Appellation Controlée law of France, devised in the 1930s, was the first that attempted to regulate which wines could be made in specific areas and from which grapes. It also established allowable yield amounts, vineyard practices, and wine making techniques in those specific areas. This was the model for all other such laws, including Italy's Denominazione di Origine Controllata (DOC) and the later Denominazione di Origine Controllata Garantita (DOCG), which attempted to improve on it. A recent trend, one that I am not altogether in favor of, has been to try to relax the restrictions imposed on winemakers and producers, thereby allowing greater flexibility and creativity so as to make wines that may have a broader, more international appeal. However, it should never be forgotten that these laws were created to safeguard the style, aromas, and flavors typically and historically associated with the wines made in particular areas. Allowing winemakers to add, for example, large amounts of chardonnay or merlot to a regional wine could lead to yet another wine smelling and tasting of grapes that are grown all over the world. In other words, these laws help combat the standardization of wine styles, which is a real problem, as many of the world's wines now all look, smell, and taste the same. That is not an altogether unexpected turn of events if everyone everywhere uses the same grapes and similar wine making techniques.

BARREL

Wine can be aged in any number of different vessels, but there is no doubt that the best wines in the world are usually aged in oak barrels. Oak is the wood of preference, as it allows an even maturation of the wine in contact with it, acts as a vessel through which oxygen can gradually penetrate, and imparts pleasant aromas and flavors such as vanilla. The oak used is of either French or American origin (American oak barrels, made of different species of oak from the French ones, tend to give the wine aromas of coconut and sweet spices). Oak from eastern European countries is also being increasingly used, mainly because of its lower cost. Barrels are usually large wooden casks (up to and beyond 100 hectoliters, or 10,000 liters), and can in fact be so big that a grown man can stand inside one without even having to bend down to get in. These are also usually made with French oak, though in Italy it used to be common, until the 1980s, to age wines in large barrels made of eastern European (Slavonian) oak and even chestnut wood.

BARRIQUE, TONNEAU

Barrique is a French term routinely used in Italy to refer to a small French barrel: 225 liters (a volume that will allow about three hundred 750-mL bottles of wine to be made). This size is typical in Bordeaux (the *barrique* in Burgundy is 228 liters). Bigger barrels of 500 liters are called *tonneaux*. A *barrique* can cost as much as $1,000: this figure helps explain why oak-aged wines are usually more expensive than wines aged in stainless steel or cement, the other common materials of which holding vessels for wine are made. *Barriques* were all the rage in Italy in the 1980s, but the *tonneau* is being increasingly used nowadays as producers try to reduce costs and make wines that smell and taste less of oak. Clearly, since the volume of wine in a *barrique* is smaller and the surface area of the wine in contact with the wood is larger, wines that are aged in this smaller vessel are always more characterized by oak-related aromas and flavors, such as vanilla and cloves. The intensity of these aromas and flavors also depends on how new the *barrique* is: brand-new *barriques* will mark the wine more than those previously used, and after four years of use there is virtually nothing more released from the wood to the wine. At that point in time, the net gain of oak-derived molecules affecting the smell and taste of the wine is minimal. Remember that too much wood in a wine ought to be considered a defect: since wine is made from grapes, it should always smell and taste of fruit, and those wines that reek only of vanilla, cloves, and smoke are actually poorly made, no matter how appealing they may seem. In reality, the main role of barrels of all sizes is a means by which to allow oxygenation, whose slow passage over time contributes to smoother wines.

BIODYNAMIC WINES
Wines made following the doctrine of Rudolf Steiner, an Austrian who believed the vineyard and other agricultural entities to be living, closed systems that needed to be kept in balance by the use of natural preparations administered in accordance with lunar phases, tides, and planetary cycles. The goal is to create stronger, healthier vines and better wines, since the soil and plant together are viewed as a single living organism. In Italy biodynamic viticulture is still rare, as most people feel that the elimination of sulfur, a time-tested, effective, and relatively safe product, greatly increases the risk of producing faulty wines that spoil easily.

CELLAR CONDITIONS
Italians have never really had the habit of storing bottles of wine for the long term, and in fact very few estates in Italy have old stocks of bottles to sell. Wine has always been seen as a source of calories and as something to be enjoyed with a meal, so most wine in Italy was, and still is, drunk relatively young. For the same reasons, most people in Italy do not have big cellars; nor are they very interested in owning cellars filled to the brim with important bottles, though this has been changing somewhat, albeit little, over the past few years.

CRU, GRAND CRU
These terms refer to a specific plot of land of high quality, where better-than-average wines are made. When the quality of a vineyard site is exceptional, it can be referred to as a *grand cru* rather than a *premier cru*, which is still better than average but not as high in quality as a *grand cru*. These terms were born in France, where the classification of wine and vineyard quality was studied centuries ago. Systems of classification vary from region to region and country to country, but they always take into account

either geography and soil composition or the reputation of the wines produced in specific places over the centuries. In Italy, the area that has been most closely associated with *crus* is the one where Barolo and Barbaresco are made; but many of the single vineyard names on labels often tell you little about the exact potential of a specific site, as producers in Italy tend to use different techniques with grapes coming from different vineyards. For example, if a Barbaresco producer owns parcels of vines in two different sites such as Rabajà and Ovello, but ages the wine from one in big oak casks or barrels and the other in *barriques*, it becomes very hard to discern differences between single vineyards.

I warn the reader that the lack of a time-tested *cru* classification is one of the most unfortunate aspects of Italian wine. Unlike France or Germany, where the best sites have been mapped clearly over the centuries (at least of some wine making areas), Italy never proceeded to do so, with the result that many Italian wines coming from rather non-distinct plots of land still manage to score very highly with some wine writers. For example, with French wines, it almost never happens that a wine labeled simply Puligny will score higher, or be considered better, than one from the glorious vineyard of Chevalier Montrachet, or that a red Bourgogne Villages will best a fine Musigny or Volnay. This is because vineyards such as Chevalier Montrachet or Musigny have been known over the years to give the very best wines from those specific grape varieties. Conversely, in Italy, the better zones of Montalcino or Chianti, for example, were never mapped out (Renato Ratti, one of Piedmont's more enlightened producers, did so on his own for Barolo and Barbaresco in the 1970s), and nowadays it is difficult to do so, since producers who own land in less than ideal plots are understandably strongly opposed to such an action. This is unfortunate, however, because it allows for the easy brewing of scandals and has allowed for the ever-increasing importance of flying winemakers, those experts who follow a recipe for wine making and are able to come up with an acceptable wine anywhere. This state of affairs is made all the more easy because little is known about the intrinsic quality of the grapes used. For example, it is "normal" to see many Brunellos or Barolos from very poor plots of land score very highly, vintage after vintage, in many reviews, something that defies logic. True, there are some very gifted producers that can make great wines even from lesser vineyards (and in France some poorly made Musigny or Chevalier Montrachet also are scored lower than expected), but that is not generally the rule. In the end, some producers seem to make great wines from plots of land that an old-timer would tell you could never make great wine, and the question that springs to mind (even if one allows for improved vineyard and cellar technique) is if those wines really are being made only from grapes from only those specific plots of land.

FERMENTATION
Alcoholic fermentation is the process by which yeasts turn grape sugar into alcohol and carbon dioxide. It is through this reaction—well known in ancient times and eventually attributed to yeasts by Louis Pasteur in the nineteenth century—that wine is made from grape juice (or, in theory, from any fruit). Note that some people, even wine experts, will also refer to a secondary or malolactic fermentation: this is the process by which the harder, sharper malic acid is changed to the softer lactic acid. However, to speak of malolactic fermentation is wrong: by definition, "fermentation" is a chemical reaction that implies the formation of alcohol, and in the malolactic reaction this is not the case. The more exact term, which ought to be used, is malolactic transformation, because in this reaction we have the transformation of one acid into another.

LEES
This is the residue that is left in the barrel or vessel after wine has been removed and transferred elsewhere. It consists of grape skins and pips, along with dead yeast cells. Keeping wines on their lees for an extended time results in richer, more complex wines that are also protected from oxidation. However, this dead organic matter can be a wonderful medium for bacterial growth, and can lead to the formation of unpleasant odors and flavors unless extreme care is taken during the wine making process.

MUST
The technical term for grape juice that is going to be turned into wine.

NATIVE OR AUTOCHTHONOUS GRAPES
Grapes that are typical of a specific land and are not usually found in other countries. These grapes are capable of giving wines that have fragrance and flavor profiles altogether different from most other wines, often made with the same grapes everywhere. Native grapes therefore represent a formidable asset for wine making countries; they enable the production of wines that are new and different.

Noble rot (*Botrytis cinerea*)

A fungus whose scientific name is *Botrytis cinerea*. It is associated with the production of the greatest sweet wines in the world, such as those of Sauternes in France. Hence it is called noble rot, to differentiate it from the bad, or gray, rot that ruins grapes altogether. The noble rot fungus is not found everywhere; it can flourish only in places where there is an adequate water supply (hence in vineyards located near streams, lakes, or rivers) and a climate that ensures days that are alternately cool and humid and dry and warmer. Therefore, grapes affected by noble rot are really typical only of some parts of the world such as Sauternes, Barsac, Germany's Mosel and Rhine areas, Hungary, Austria. In Italy, noble rot has been historically present in the Orvieto area of Umbria and the Castelli Romani area of Lazio. The fact that so many vines affected with noble rot are now being grown all over the world is mainly due to the artificial spraying of the fungal spores directly on the grapes.

Oak

Oak is the preferred material for barrels and other containers that hold and age wine. European species of the oak tree are different from those found in North America and have always been considered the best for wine making. Nevertheless, oak from Tennessee and Kentucky appears to be particularly well suited for fine wines. Owing to the ever-increasing cost of barrels of all sizes, oak chips (illegal in Italy until recently) or liquid wood extracts are being used more and more: note, though, that these aids make it far too easy to flavor wines accordingly. This takes wine farther away from being a natural product that speaks of its grape variety and its land.

Organic grapes and wines

In Italy certified organic grapes are those grown in soils that have been free of pesticides, chemicals, or non-organic fertilizers for at least 20 years, and organic wines (the Italian term is *biologico*) are those made from such grapes. This is altogether different from the terminology in the United States, where there are three levels of organic wines: "100% organic" (which means that 100% of the grapes used to make the wine were grown without the use of chemicals), "organic" (which means that 95% of the grapes used were produced without the use of chemicals), and "made with organic grapes" (meaning that up to 70% of the grapes were produced in compliance with the rules for organic farming). Organic wines—*vini biologici* in Italian—are definitely on the rise in Italy. However, this is not as important a movement as it is in the United States. As these wines still account for only a small percentage of the overall production of Italy's many acres under vine only about 75,000 are organic certified. One reason is that many of the organic wines just aren't as good as their non-organic counterparts.

Phylloxera / prephylloxera

An aphid that feeds on the roots of European grape varieties and kills them inexorably. It arrived in Europe from the United States at the end of the nineteenth century and proceeded to destroy practically all of the vineyards; wine production was saved by grafting vines onto American rootstocks (the rootstocks are the roots and and an initial segment of the stalk of the vine) obtained from American vines whose roots are immune to this parasite. Previously known scientifically as *Phylloxera devastatrix* and now more correctly referred to as *Viteus vitifoliae*, it causes different damages to different vines. For example, while it destroys the roots of European vines but not their foliage, it behaves exactly in the opposite manner with American vines such as those of the *Vitis rupestris* and *Vitis berlandieri* varieties, in which it damages not the roots but the foliage and stalks. Prephylloxera vines are those that have never been grafted onto American rootstocks, because the original vines were planted either at very high altitudes, where it is too cold for the parasite to survive (such as high up in the Alps), or into highly sandy soil, where the aphid cannot survive. For example, in Italy there are still prephylloxera vines on the Etna volcano or in the Alpine vineyards of Valle d'Aosta.

Residual sugar

The amount of sugar left in bottled wine, or, more specifically, the unfermented grape sugar remaining after alcoholic fermentation has taken place. This concentration is measured in grams per liter (g/L) in Europe, or in percent per weight in Anglo-Saxon countries (10 g/L is equivalent to 1%). Residual sugar alone does not explain the sweetness of a wine: perceived sweetness depends on other factors, the most important being the overall acidity in the wine. For instance, 0 to 3 g/L is considered normal for a dry wine and 6 to 9 g/L is typical of an off-dry wine, but the latter can seem bone-dry if a wine is very high in acidity. A recent tendency has been to leave a little residual sugar in red wines. Producers tend to do this because a little sweetness buffers the sharp acidic bite of young wines, and softer wines tend to be preferred by the general public (and some careless wine writing experts, I may add). Unfortunately, many red wines today are starting to seem downright sweet, and this problem is manifesting itself in Italy as well, though not with the same magnitude as in the New World.

SPARKLING WINES AND THEIR CLASSIFICATION

In the somewhat confusing sparkling wine classification, dry wines are called "brut" and "extra-dry" wines are actually off-dry, though they have only a minimal level of perceived sweetness. This is because sparkling wines have so much more acidity than still wines that they seem drier than still wines containing a similar level of residual sugar. A sparkling wine labeled "dry" is actually noticeably sweet. In Italy Prosecco is offered in "extra-dry" and "dry" versions, but remember that if you want a dry one, you need to look and ask for a "brut."

SULFUR

Sulfur is one of the oldest known antibacterial and disinfectant agents. Recently it has received much bad press as a source of headaches and other health hazards. First of all, the human body produces sulfur and products containing sulfur every day, so this element is clearly not to be seen in only a negative light. It helps stabilize wine, prevents bacterial spoilage, fixes the color, and allows for clearer and more brilliant wines, and protects wine from oxidation. Highish sulfur levels (more typical of sweet wines, in which the great quantity of sugar present makes it easier for bacteria to get involved) can cause headaches, but so can the histamines and tyramines found in many other foods besides wine, such as tea, dark beer, cold cuts, and certain cheeses. Ask yourself why you don't see "contains sulfides" warnings on these foodstuffs as well.

TANNIN

Tannins are polyphenol or antioxidant molecules that are found mainly in the skins, but also in the pulp and the pips, of grapes and are important for the conservation and the structure of wines. Highly tannic wines have a richer, bigger mouthfeel and usually age better than wines that have little tannic strength. If there is too much tannin, wines become bitter—a serious flaw. As antioxidant molecules, tannins are one reason why moderate drinking is actually part of a healthy, balanced lifestyle; they are at the core of what is called the "French paradox," the observation that people who drink wine regularly—even though they may exercise less, eat more fat, and smoke more—still have a much lower reported rate of cardiac disease.

Terroir

A French term that refers to the specific area where a wine is made but takes into account more than just geology; exposure, climate, altitude, and the human factor involved in making the wine are also important. *Terroir* used to refer only to the soil the vines were planted in, but it now has a much broader meaning. It is also a sign of how times change: in my grandfather's day, saying that a wine had a taste of *terroir* was a negative comment—it meant the wine had an earthy, rustic quality.

Vino da Tavola and super-Tuscans

Vino da Tavola is the lowest level of Italian wines, and today you would probably do best to avoid wines in this category. There was a brief moment in the 1970s, because of a legislative void, when some of these wines were actually among Italy's best, but this is no longer true, as the laws have since been changed. At that time it was illegal to plant foreign grape varieties or add those varieties to Italian wines such as Chianti, a wine that had to contain white grapes as well. Some Tuscan producers wanted to do away with the white grapes, and decided to add foreign varietals anyway, believing that their creativity was being stifled and that they could make better wines in this manner. In so doing, they were changing the proportions of grape varieties in their wines, but for DOC and DOCG wines such as Chianti those percentages are fixed by law. Therefore, these new wines containing cabernet, merlot, or international grapes, and perhaps none of the white grapes, could no longer be called Chianti, and the only wine category where they could be placed at that time was the lowly *Vino da Tavola*. However, the wines were a revelation, clearly better than most Chiantis that were then being made. The wines were so good, in fact, that when the English-speaking press got hold of them, the journalists called them "super," and thus "super-Tuscan" wines were born. Today, a super-Tuscan is any top wine made by a Tuscan estate (it's usually the most expensive wine in the estate's portfolio) and it can be made either from a single grape only (such as sangiovese, cabernet franc, or merlot) or from a blend (for example, merlot and sangiovese, or merlot-syrah-sangiovese).

THE VINTAGE TABLE

KEY TO VINTAGES

Vintage quality:

5—an outstanding, "century-type" vintage (equivalent to 95–100/100)

4—a very fine vintage (90–95)

3—above-average vintage (80–89)

2—below average to average (70–79)

1—avoid altogether (below 69)

Characteristics of the wines in the specific vintage:

P—Past: now too old, these wines are almost surely over the hill.

D—Drink: early-maturing wines that are ready to drink (in the case of tannic wines such as Barolo, these are wines that will be pleasant to drink much sooner than usual and often already on release).

H—Hold: wines that need a lot of patience, as they are characterized by high acidities and tannins

Wines & Regions	1995	1996	1997	1998	1999	2000	2001	2002	2003	2004	2005	2006	2007
Aglianico del Vulture (Basilicata)	5DH	2/3D	5DH	4/5D	3/4D	4D	5DH	1D	3D	4H			
Amarone (Veneto)	4DH	3D	4/5DH	4D	3/4D	4D	4DH	1D	3D	4DH	-	-	-
Barbaresco (Piedmont)	4D	5H	3/4D	3/4D	4H	4/5DH	5H	1/2D	2/3D	4/5D	4DH		
Barbera (Piedmont)	2/3D	4D	5D	4D	4D	5D	4D	1/2PD	5DH	4/5D	4D	-	-
Barolo (Piedmont)	4D	5H	4D	3/4D	4H	4/5DH	5H	1/2D	2/3D	4/5DH	4DH	-	-
Brunello di Montalcino (Tuscany)	4DH	3D	3/4D	3D	5DH	4D	5H	1/2D	2/3D	4/5H	-	-	-
Bolgheri Rosso (Tuscany)	4/5DH	3/4D	4DH	3D	4DH	4D	5DH	1D	2D	5H			

Wines & Regions	1995	1996	1997	1998	1999	2000	2001	2002	2003	2004	2005	2006	2007
Cannonau (Sardinia)	4D	4D	5DH	4/5D	4D	4/5D	4/5DH	1D	2D	3/4D			
Chianti Classico (Tuscany)	4/5D	3D	4D	3D	4/5D	4D	4DH	1PD	2D	4/5DH	3DH	4/5H	-
Franciacorta (Lombardy)	4/5D	4/5DH	1/2D	3D	3/4D	3D	3/4DH	4D	2D				
Gattinara (Piedmont)	4DH	5H	5DH	4DH	4/5DH	4/5DH	5H	1D	4DH	4/5DH			
Gewürztraminer (Alto Adige)	4/5D	4D	3/4D	4D	4/5D	4D	5D	4D	4D	4DH	4DH	5DH	2/3D
Montepulciano d'Abruzzo (Abruzzo)	4/5DH	2D	4/5D	4D	3D	4DH	4/5DH	1D	2D	4D			

Wines & Regions	1995	1996	1997	1998	1999	2000	2001	2002	2003	2004	2005	2006	2007
Vino Nobile di Montepulciano (Tuscany)	4/5D	3D	3/4D	3D	5DH	4D	5H	1/2D	2/3D	4/5H			
Pinot Grigio (Friuli Venezia Giulia)	4/5PD	3/4PD	3PD	3PD	4PD	4PD	4PD	1/2PD	2PD	4D	3D	5DH	4DH
Primitivo (Puglia)	2D	4/5D	5D	4D	3/4D	4D	4/5D	1D	2/3D	4D	4D		
Nero d'Avola (Sicily)	4D	3/4D	5DH	4D	4DH	5DH	5DH	4D	2/3D	4/5D	3/4D	4D	
Sagrantino (Umbria)	5DH	2/3D	5DH	3/4D	4D	4/5DH	4/5DH	1D	3D	4H			
Taurasi (Campania)	4D	4D	5DH	3/4D	4D	4/5D	5DH	1D	3D	4DH			

INDEX

RENNI the RESCUER

Also by Felix Salten

Bambi